The Model Minority Stereotype: Demystifying Asian American Success

DATE DUE

			PRINTED IN U.S.A.

Editorial Review Team Members

DEDICATION

To my dear wife and three children: I do what I must for you and others.

Understanding the society of the past is the prerequisite to the master over the society of the present.

—Edward Hallett Carr, *What is History?* (1961)
Carr, E. H. (1961). *What is History?* New York, NY: Vintage

The problem with the model minority stereotype is in transforming a tremendously diverse group into a 'silent minority' that conforms to the norms and values of the majority group. The fear is that the majority group will use the model minority concept to neutralize social unrest from dissident minorities by offering the 'success' of model minorities as proof that the American dream of equal opportunity is valid for those who conform and who are willing to work hard.

—Cunanan, Guerrero, & Minamoto, 2006, p. 188

The Model Minority Stereotype: Demystifying Asian American Success

Nicholas Daniel Hartlep
Illinois State University

INFORMATION AGE PUBLISHING, INC.
Charlotte, NC • www.infoagepub.com

Library of Congress Cataloging-in-Publication Data

The CIP data for this book can be found on the Library of Congress website (loc.gov).
Paperback: 978-1-62396-358-3; Hardcover: 978-1-62396-359-0; eBook: 978-1-62396-360-6

CONTENTS

FOREWORD

Yoon Pak, PhD

As a university professor, I have taught a course on Asian Americans and education for the past twelve years to a range of students: undergraduates, graduate students, and pre-service and in-service teachers. It fulfills a general education requirement on multiple levels for undergraduates and also a foundations requirement for master's level students. The content of the course, while changing to meet the needs of a more digitally-tuned generation, typically remains the same. The course engages students to think through the contours of American race relations through the intersecting histories of education among disenfranchised groups, including Asian Americans, from the conceptions of the Common School era to the present. The historical context of knowing how and where our educational system started becomes the critical ground for seeing the place of educational "progress" in the 21st century.

We also work to conceptually dispel the homogenous definition of what it means to be an "American." I ask students to imagine who or what a prototypical American looks like and invariably they point to the ideal imagery of the blond, blue-eyed celebrity. Once in a while they will name an African American basketball star but by and large the meaning and representation of an "American" is in itself one who represents a Western European heritage. The idea that Asian Americans have existed in the United States for centuries runs counter to the knowledge base of what they learned in their K–12 experiences. To know that Filipinos were in the United States since

The Model Minority Stereotype: Demystifying Asian American Success, pages vii–xiii.
Copyright © 2013 by Information Age Publishing

the 1700s and that their descendants have deep roots in Louisiana disrupts their normative frame of reality.

In discussing who or what constitutes an "Asian American," we undertake a similar exercise, thinking about what that means. Much to the students' surprise, they are unaware that at least 40 different ethnicities comprise Asian America (Pang, Kiang, & Pak, 2003). Beyond the more common Chinese, Korean, Indian, and Japanese, most students had not heard of the diverse groups within Southeast Asia and the Pacific Islands. I try to provide an overview of the distinct histories and trajectories for the groups' arrival to the United States and the differences in immigration and refugee status that framed so much of the national discourse on immigration since 1965, but also to connect it to the earlier restrictions on citizenship (1790 Naturalization Act) as well as the violent acts resulting from exclusion laws (1882 Chinese Exclusion Act). Students then begin to see the historical patterns that begin to emerge.

For better or worse, however, I also spend an inordinate amount of time working to dispel the oft-accepted and rarely questioned model minority stereotype. In class we read the primary texts of the 1960s that fueled the mid-twentieth century stereotype. The now infamous *U.S. News and World Report* article extolling the virtues of Chinese Americans in virtually any Chinatown ("Success Story of One Minority Group in the U.S.," Dec. 26, 1966) as the well as sociologist William Petersen's article in *The New York Times Magazine* ("Success Story, Japanese American Style," January 6, 1966) depicting the plight of Japanese Americans during World War II, who had now pulled themselves up by the bootstraps, set in motion the publicity wheel of all Asians as successful immigrants who did not need governmental support nor civil rights legislation to get ahead. That ubiquitous reference to Horatio Alger, Jr.'s theme of individual triumph toward social mobility in his novels is one that resonates all too well. Rather than seek government support, one must stretch the limits of one's capabilities to rise to the top. If one fails, it is due to lack of effort; the system is not to blame. Not surprisingly, the popularization of Chinese and Japanese Americans' success came at the very time when the government passed the Civil Rights Act of 1964 (and many historians would also note that the fight for civil rights among African Americans was not a 20th-century struggle, but one that occurred even during slavery). The denigration of African American families, as well as Latin@ groups, as living in a culture of poverty existing under the auspices of governmental welfare support is a familiar trope that has guided a great deal of social and educational policies—that is, deriving perspectives from the view that these groups in particular are culturally deprived and depraved (and let us not forget the often displaced conversations related to American Indians in terms of their minority status in education being "statistically insignificant").

Even among a handful of Asian American students, the model minority stereotype leaves such an indelible mark on their psyches that to question what is deemed so "normal" runs anathema to the very essence of their being. Still more striking is how even at the end of the term, and despite all the evidentiary basis of the falsity of the stereotype, a few students do not let go of the idea of Asians, in conflation with Asian Americans as the model minority. Popular culture has made it too "real" for them to disavow those falsehoods. From the super Asian (typically nerdy) whiz-kid who excels in math and science to the almost neurotic Asian "Tiger Mom," (Chua, 2011) popular media's depiction of Asian Americans still provides a portrayal that deems Asians as hyperbole to the "norm," or how legal scholar Angelo Ancheta has aptly noted, as racialized outsiders (Ancheta, 2006).

While not to lament too much on the stasis of intellectual growth of what teaching such a course can do, as there are many more success stories of students who wake up to the "Aha!" moment, I am constantly fascinated by people's blind adherence to such ideologies in light of factual evidence that points to the contrary. Perhaps I am being too naïve in that light, but there is a core question that I keep referring back to: what is it about the model minority, or any racial stereotypes for that matter, that makes it so threatening to unlearn? In other words, why do we hold such pernicious ideas so close to our hearts? The space of this foreword is certainly too limited to delve into the psycho-philosophical nature of the question, but I raise it since particularly in the realm of education (K–12 and higher education) the stereotype continues to drive classroom practice and educational policy decisions. From assumptions about the achievement gap and affirmative action, how Asian Americans have configured in these various educational discourses have been predicated by misleading information or incomplete information. As critical scholars have revealed, there remain huge gaps within Asian American subgroups in academic achievement levels (Lee, 2009; Lew, 2003; Teranishi, 2010). And even among the more academically able students, there remain hidden costs for their seeming success (Cress & Ikeda, 2003).

What is continually undermined in this whole process is the intersectional ramifications of what all this means. To assume one group's success (i.e., Asians) requires that there be failures (i.e., African Americans and Latin@s). While much of the literature does not explicitly point to these comparisons, there are enough to indicate that an undercurrent of hostile feelings among racialized groups takes place when stereotypes are internalized. The relatively recent slate of anti-Asian violence and the government's report of increased bullying against Asian American students are no accidents (Tandon, 2011). They have been building up for decades.

In the realm of higher education, the Supreme Court's decision over the efficacy of a race-conscious admissions policy has placed Asian Americans in a precarious position. Increasingly (and inaccurately) referred to as the "New Jews" (www.80-20EF.org) in terms of the historical parallels in admissions controversies at elite institutions, the threat of an Asian invasion on college campuses creates fears that their presence leads to further eradication of African Americans and Latina@ groups, as well as the decline of White enrollment. The question of whether or not Asians constitute a racial minority (or a selective minority, depending on an institution's attempt to advance "diversity") is predicated on the assumption that all Asian Americans are academically successful, and that an increase in their numbers works to the detriment of all (Lee, 2008). Advancing diversity is good insofar as it places a ceiling on Asian American access to certain resources on college campuses where competition for funds and admissions are had. Scholars Don Nakanishi (1995) and Dana Takagi (1993) have carefully documented the early admissions debates, especially in the University of California system, and came to the conclusion that Asian Americans occupy a precarious place in higher education. They foresaw the ongoing admissions challenges that lay ahead in pitting Asian American college students against other racial minority groups for competitive slots on college campuses.

As noted previously (Ng, Lee, & Pak, 2007), the threat of success by virtue of being a model minority lies along the historical continuum that castigates Asians as the perpetual foreigner. The yellow peril and the model minority coexist on a plane that forms boundaries outside the bounds of normalcy. Since the time of Asian immigration on the west coast, popular culture (Lee, 1999) as well as politicians (Okihiro, 1994) drove home the inexplicable state of Asians as inassimilable to mainstream "American" life. These characterizations resulted in not only questioning their citizenship status, or even the possibility of becoming a fit citizen, but exclusionary laws to bar them citizenship status well into the 1950s. The well known incidences of Chinese expulsion on the heels of exclusion laws and the incarceration of Japanese Americans during World War II all point to our moments in history where the sense of Asians as the perpetual foreigner abound.

In light of these historical realities, we cannot forget the history of activism that Asian immigrant parents fought on behalf of their children to receive equal access to education. The early 20th century Supreme Court rulings in *Tape v. Hurley,* which preceded the landmark *Plessy v. Ferguson,* and *Aoki v. Deane* provide proof of institutional racism against Asian American students (as well as other racial groups) in our educational system. Furthermore, the 1974 *Lau v. Nichols* case provided for the first time recognition of services needed for students whose home language was not English. This landmark case distinguishes between what is considered "equal" to what is actually fair and equitable. As Justice William O. Douglas stated in his opinion, "there is no equality of treatment merely by providing students with the same facilities, textbooks, teachers, and curriculum; for students who do not understand English are effectively foreclosed from any meaningful education" (*Lau* v. *Nichols*, 1974, n.p.).

In these instances, it is imperative to remember that the fight for equal schooling in the courts was initiated, and largely won, by parents from *all* racial backgrounds. Success and access to schooling were paramount in the minds of *all* parents. The historical record on this speaks back to power.

Higher education's call for a more "culturally relevant" (Ladson-Billings, 1995) curriculum is also indebted to the activism of college students all over the country who witnessed so much of their education being divorced from their realities. To that end, Asian American students at San Francisco State University worked in multiracial coalitions to form the Third World Liberation Front. Their objectives to create ethnic studies, reform curriculum, hire minority faculty and staff, and increase the numbers of underrepresented students initiated a great deal of progressive changes within higher education (Umemoto, 1989). The fact that I, as a Korean American female tenured faculty, can be in the position that I am is owed largely to the student activists who broke open the locked doors of exclusion.

The struggle for freedom that began with African Americans during slavery up through the Civil Rights Movement is a collective struggle that has ultimately benefited all racial minorities, females, and students with disabilities. Rather than focusing on the intersectional nature of these historical moments, we (read: society writ large) have instead built hostilities between and among ourselves to see access to educational opportunities in highly individualistic ways. It further fuels the undue comparisons between Asian American academic achievement with African American and Latin@ underachievement. There is certainly more than meets the eye, and providing a more realistic picture is becoming increasingly important.

This is where Nicholas Hartlep's annotated sourcebook provides a critical intervention for educators to: (1) reassess their preconceptions about Asian American students as well as other students, (2) work towards unlearning the misconceptions rooted in the model minority stereotype, and (3) develop critical understandings of the diversity within Asian American student populations. The book is expertly layered in its breadth and depth of scope. Hartlep covers the relevant literature related to the model minority stereotype and its effects on students. To date, I know of no other singular work that captures this research in such a concise manner. It is also written in a highly accessible format for educators at all levels to comprehend. This enables the novice reader of Asian American studies and education to appreciate the historical experiences and current contexts of where Asian American students fit in the larger discourse in education. More than anything, the compilation of sources is meant to open our eyes and to question what so many people have come to regard as reality about Asian American students. This needs to be read and used by all educators and administrators who have a stake in educating our youth.

Yoon Pak, PhD
University of Illinois at Urbana-Champaign
Education Policy, Organization and Leadership
Core Faculty, Asian American Studies
Spring 2013

REFERENCES

Ancheta, A. (2006). Race, rights, and the Asian American experience (2nd ed.). New Brunswick, NJ: Rutgers University Press.

Chua, A. (2011). *Battle hymn of the tiger mother.* New York, NY: The Penguin Press.

Cress, C. M. & Ikeda, E. K. (2003). Distress under duress: The relationship between campus climate and depression in Asian American college students. *NASPA Journal, 40*(2), 75–96.

Ladson-Billings, G. (1995). But that's just good teaching! The case for culturally relevant pedagogy. *Theory Into Practice, 34*(3), 159–165.

Lau v. *Nichols.* (1974). Retrieved November 5, 2012, from http://education.uslegal.com/bilingualism/landmark-legislation/lau-v-nichols/

Lee, R. G. (1999). The model minority as gook. In R. G. Lee, *Orientals: Asian Americans in popular culture* (pp. 180–203). Philadelphia, PA: Temple University Press.

Lee, S. J. (2009). *Unraveling the "model minority" stereotype: Listening to Asian American youth* (2nd ed.). New York, NY: Teachers College Press.

Lee, S. S. (2008). The de-minoritization of Asian Americans: A historical examination of the representations of Asian Americans in affirmative action admissions policies at the University of California. *Asian American Law Journal, 15*(1), 129–152.

Lew, J. (2003). *Asian Americans in class: Charting the achievement gap Among Korean American youth.* New York, NY: Teachers College Press.

Nakanishi, D. T. (1995). A quota on excellence?: The Asian American admissions debate. In D. T. Nakanishi & T. Y. Nishida (Eds.), *The Asian American educational experience: A source book for teachers and students* (pp. 273–284). New York, NY: Routledge.

Ng, J. C., Lee, S. S., & Pak, Y. K. (2007). Contesting the model minority and perpetual foreigner stereotypes: A critical review of literature on Asian Americans. *Review of Research in Education, 31*(1), 95–130.

Okihiro, G. (1994). *Margins and mainstreams: Asians in American history and culture.* Seattle, WA: University of Washington.

Pang, V., Kiang, P., & Pak, Y. K. (2003). Asian Pacific American students: Challenging a biased educational system. In J. A. Banks & C. A. Banks (Eds.), *Handbook of research on multicultural education* (2nd ed., pp. 542–565). San Francisco, CA: Jossey-Bass.

Petersen, W. (1966, January 6). Success story: Japanese American style. *The New York Times Magazine,* 20–21, 33, 36, 38, 40.

Takagi, D. Y. (1993). *Retreat from race: Asian American admissions and racial politics.* New Brunswick, NJ: Rutgers University Press.

Tandon, S. (2011, October 28). Asian Americans most bullied in US schools: Study. *AFP.* Retrieved on November 5, 2012 from http://www.google.com/hosted-news/afp/article/ALeqM5ieIKEf6GvJAwc1iBJZ1itHHGbyA?docId=CNG.173 2b21b28ee34447047f9aa12dd08c5.b31

Teranishi, R. T. (2010). *Asians in the ivory tower: Dilemmas of racial inequality in American higher education.* New York, NY: Teachers College Press.

Umemoto, K. (1989). "On strike!" San Francisco State college strike, 1968–69: The role of Asian American students. *Amerasia Journal, 15*(1), 3–41.

U.S. News & World Report. (1966, December 26). Success story of one minority group in the U.S., 73–76.

INTRODUCTION

In 2012, the well-respected (at least up until that point) ESPN, a major media corporation, ran a headline on its website that read: "Chink in the Armor" (McNeal, 2012). Beneath the racist headline, ESPN prominently placed a picture of Jeremy Lin, the rookie Taiwanese American NBA player sensation who graduated from Harvard with a degree in economics. Fortunately, the headline writer was soon fired after this oversight. Notwithstanding, racialized messages like this continue to be disseminated, and history repeats itself. This is for certain. For instance, Asian Americans were rightfully upset when the MSNBC website published a headline announcing that "American beats out Kwan" after Tara Lipinsky defeated Michelle Kwan in figure skating at the 1998 Winter Olympics, since Kwan was also an American (Sorenson, 1998). Four years later, Kwan was again editorialized as being a racial "other." In 2002, the Seattle Times published a headline "American Outshines Kwan, Slutskaya in Skating Surprise" (Evans, 2002). The treatment of Kwan is not unique. Kristi Yamaguchi also has received racist commentary. As Fong (2008) rightly points out: "The fact that both Yamaguchi and Kwan are not recognized as U.S.-born citizens is evidence of the invisibility of Asian Americans because of widespread ignorance of their distinct histories and contemporary experiences" (p. 3). Cumula-

The Model Minority Stereotype: Demystifying Asian American Success, pages xv–xxiii.
Copyright © 2013 by Information Age Publishing
All rights of reproduction in any form reserved.

tively, though, these kinds of headlines and treatment serve to imply that Olympic figure skaters Michelle Kwan and Kristi Yamaguchi and also NBA player/Harvard graduate Jeremy Lin are not one of "us," but one of them. Outsiders. The "other."

YEAR 2012

In 2012 the Philadelphia Inquirer won the Pulitzer Prize for public service, the journalism profession's most coveted and prestigious prize. It received this distinction for its provocative series on school violence, especially violence perpetrated against Asians at South Philadelphia High School. I hope this book provides insight and foresight to a problem that has continued to plague Asian Americans for over five decades—the model minority stereotype. The model minority stereotype characterizes Asians in the United States as achieving the American Dream through hard work, perseverance, and extreme levels of individual effort and sacrifice. The violence directed at the Asian students in Philadelphia is linked in several ways to this stereotype. Whether perpetuated because "they all look the same," or due to their perceived success (envy), the reason for anti-Asian bias is rooted in racism. This book, I believe, is a means to an end, not an end in itself. That end is providing access to research on the model minority stereotype. A major barrier to model minority demystification lies in not fully understanding the stereotype and not having access to well-written literature that can be used to refute the myth; this was one reality that prompted me to undertake the present research.

PREVAILING STRATEGIES USED TO REFUTE THE STEREOTYPE

The approaches and methodologies historically used by model minority researchers have allowed their research to elucidate differences, diversity, hybridity, and heterogeneity among the Asian American population. This is incredibly important and helpful in combating mendacious model minority commentary. One limitation of such praxis, however, is that most of these approaches have lent themselves to self-imposed stasis as a result of relying on the same narrow approaches—yielding identical or similar results. I hope that this book breaks these self-imposed limits through the purposeful synthesis of model minority stereotype research in order that new and fresh paradigms may be generated. By having a central location, a book, in which to locate research on the model minority stereotype, I believe that lay persons, scholars, practitioners, and policymakers will have an opportunity to learn more about this myth.

I feel that future research should actively combat what I consider to be a scholastic stasis by creating avant-garde paradigms, strategies, and methodologies to uncover and understand what the model minority stereotype is—

in order to dismantle it (its form, function, and purpose). These new(er) paradigms need to recognize Whiteness, to consider rhetorical, legal, and social tropes, and to actively work against the model minority stereotype in all of its permutations. Consequently, the trope of the triumphant Asian American student—the model minority—needs to be critically analyzed.

An additional obstacle to demystifying the model minority stereotype, besides the over-reliance on current methodologies and approaches, lies in the reality that Asians in America who are suffering the most are the least likely to assert their inferiority, since these individuals are only faintly visible. Meanwhile, readers of this book should understand that at the heart of the stereotype lies a dormant belief, hidden in the interests of an institutionally racist and inhumane sincerity, that the *status quo* must be preserved. This demonstrates, yet again, why work also needs to be done at the political level. Anti-Asian racism is undeniable, and the notion that the model minority accelerates racism is unavoidable. As a result, future research must also tackle policy-level issues related to, but not limited to, Asian Americans and affirmative action, educational access, community college partnerships with four-year colleges and universities, as well as social and mental health concerns.

I am so happy that Yoon Pak and Robert Teranishi agreed to provide foreword and afterword thoughts on the model minority stereotype. Both scholars have a vast understanding of the implications of the model minority stereotype on the lives and experiences of Asian American people.

THE GENESIS OF THE BOOK

I hope to be known as a critical Asian American academic who embodies the qualities of someone who rejects "the passive Oriental stereotype and symbolizes the birth of a new Asian—one who will recognize and deal with injustices" (Hsu, 1996, p. 43). Many publications have been written from a critical Asian American perspective (e.g., Gindra, Bridge, Amerasia Journal, Counterpoint), and it is my intention to continue such a tradition. As a Korean American, I know the model minority stereotype to be inherently deceptive, especially in an era of colorblindness where racism flourishes. Asian American academic achievement spawns attention, which is used to further marginalize other minorities. Simply put: The model minority stereotype is false, hegemonic, and self-empowering for Whites.

The true story of Asian Americans is more struggle than success, more pariah than paragon, more failure than fame and fortune, and certainly, more trial than triumph. Interestingly, though, the existence of the model minority stereotype is neither geographically bound to North America (e.g., see Chung & Walkey, 1988; Dechamma, 2012; Fang, 2008, 2009a, 2009b, 2009c, 2010a, 2010b; Ha, 2011; Hannis, 2009; Ip & Pang, 2005; Jen, 2009), nor Asian Americans. Indeed, Germans (Kamphoefner, 1996), Jewish (Horsburgh, 1999; Prashad, 2006), Senegalese (Diouf-Kamara, 1997), Black Mormons (Hartlep, in press a), Black Methodists (Fuller, 2012), Black American women (Kaba, 2008), Black women in Congress (Tanenbaum, 1997), and Mormons in general (Chen, 2004; Chen & Yorgason, 1999) have been likened to being model minorities. Also, despite the fact that the stereotype appeared during the 1960s in the United States, it originated almost ten years earlier in China. According to Fang (2010b), in her provocative book *Becoming a Model Minority: Schooling Experiences of Ethnic Koreans in China*: "The official discourse that chronicled the success of ethnic Koreans as a *model minority* in China began to appear as early as in 1951" (p. 3, italics added).

The Model Minority Stereotype: Demystifying Asian American Success does not examine the myth in contexts that lie outside of North America (U.S. and Canada), or that are presented in languages other than English, such as Korean (e.g., see Choi, 2002[1]). This book strictly examines the stereotype of the model minority. There has not been an effective educational elixir to debunk this characterization. The reason is due in part to the fact that stereotypes are "pictures in our heads" (Lippman, 1922), and the pictures we see and make in our minds are largely conditioned by the entertainment and news media. The media reinforces what youth learn in children's literature (Salvador-Burris, 1978), making the myth nearly impossible to escape. As reported on a California State University Northridge website (n.d.), the average American watches more than four hours of television each day (or 28 hours/week, or two months per year). That means that in a 65-year lifespan, a person will spend nine years watching television. Moreover, research conducted by Ramasubramanian (2011) found empirical evidence that television reinforces the model minority stereotype. This means that advertisements and subliminal messaging reinforce popular ideologies, commitments, and beliefs toward Asian Americans (Dalisay & Tan, 2009). In his book *Manufacturing Consent*, well-known scholar Noam Chomsky (Herman & Chomsky, 2008) describes how the U.S. mass media, television included, fails to provide the kind of information that citizens need to understand the world. The model minority stereotype harangues minorities (especially Blacks) to emulate Asian Americans. If they just worked harder Blacks could be less dependent on social welfare and more like Asian Americans. But these beliefs and attitudes are socially created, and the media plays a role in their reinforcement and reification. Television shows such as *Grey's Anatomy* and *Law & Order* cast Asian actors in roles as successful doctors and researchers, thereby subjecting viewers to the idea that Asian Americans are

---

[1] This article is from the Korean journal, *Kukche, Chiyok Yon'gu*. (The English words for this title are *Review of International and Area Studies*). Unfortunately, this article was never published in English: full articles are published in Korean with only article titles and abstracts published in English.

scholars who, though highly erudite, lack personal skills that other (White) characters possess. This is something the Media Action Network for Asian Americans (MANAA) is dedicated to combating. MANAA has released a written memo to Hollywood, "Restrictive Portrayals of Asians in the Media and How to Balance Them," indicating how to better portray Asian Americans in media.

I wanted to write a book that would be as useful as it was "new." While annotated bibliographies have been written on Asian Americans in both book (e.g., see Fujimoto, Swift, & Zucker, 1971; Kim, 1989; Kitano, Jung, Tanaka, & Wong, 1971) and article form (Liu, 2007), no annotated bibliographic book has specifically targeted the model minority stereotype. For instance, Kim's (1989) 504-page volume dedicates limited space to the model minority stereotype; three entries are annotated. Consequently, it is my intention that *The Model Minority Stereotype* will serve as the first choice for scholars, teachers, activists, and policymakers interested in equity for Asian American people, particularly when faced with the model minority stereotype.

MATERIALS INCLUDED IN THE BOOK

Journalistic as well as scholastic and academic articles are included (newspaper stories, books, articles, book chapters, monographs, reports, published conference proceedings, and theses and dissertations). A review of the research contained in this book indicates that the model minority moniker for Asians accomplishes the following:

- Racializes success,
- Casts Asians as threats (educational and economic),
- Divides and conquers non-White minority groups,
- Supports meritocratic reasoning,
- Over-individualizes race,
- Reinforces misperceptions that Asian Americans are problem free,
- Conceals disparities within the Asian American community,
- Serves as an instrument of White supremacy,
- Reinforces Orientalism,
- Perpetuates and pigeonholes Asian Americans as perpetual foreigners through propagandistic and gross generalizations,
- Attends to Asian Americans' alleged achievement and attainment, and
- Reinforces a racial hierarchy.

The Congressional Asian Pacific American Caucus's infograph below, "Breaking the Model Minority Myth" summarizes this work nicely.

Moreover, Asian Americans are still given marginal attention by the educational enterprise, and this marginalization is exacerbated by the model

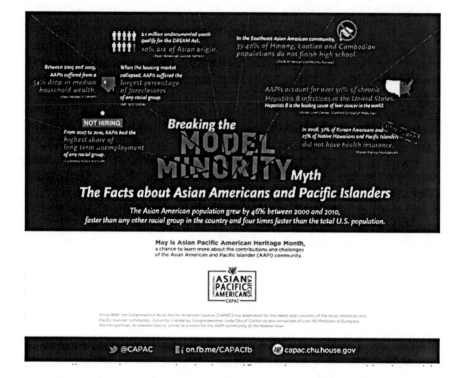

FIGURE I.1. Breaking the model minority myth: The facts about Asian Americans and Pacific Islanders. Image Credit: Gene Kim, Congressional Asian Pacific American Caucus. "Breaking the Model Minority Myth." May 2012. http://capac-chu. house.gov/media-center/model-minority-myth.

minority stereotype. Some studies have indicated that the lowest common denominator in the model minority is economic, not ethnic (Hartlep, 2012). In other words, an Asian American student may be a high achiever, but it is not being Asian that accounts for his/her high levels of achievement; rather, it may be that his/her parents are economically well off and/ or highly educated themselves. Indeed, the myth is predicated on many assumptions, one being that culture explains Asian American success. A culturally oriented accounting of Asian American student success, in practice, misrepresents the multitude and diversity of Asian American students' cultures and practices. Consequently, the myth has both *de jure* and *de facto* elements. *De jure* elements would be policies and language that serve to reinforce the idea that Asian Americans are all universally successful. *De facto* elements would be the tradition of believing that Asian Americans are highly successful, given the transformation of Asian American stereotypes.

For instance, the shift from a "yellow peril" to "model minority" stereotype illustrates that the tradition is ever changing.

With very few exceptions, Asian Americans are relegated to the margins of society. Perceived to be paragons of prosperity due to industry, Asian Americans in actuality are suffering quite a lot. The Asian American Center on Disparities Research at the University of California-Davis has conducted a good deal of research that falsifies the notion that Asian Americans are experiencing great success in a meritocratic society. Headquartered at UC-Davis and directed by Dr. Nolan Zane, the center seeks to support and co-ordinate the research efforts of researchers who study the mental health issues most important to Asian Americans. Researchers who are interested in model minority research pertaining to the social and psychological welfare of Asian Americans should be encouraged to visit the center's website. The website contains many useful resources, including a repository (http://psychology.ucdavis.edu/aacdr/publications.html) whereby interested scholars can access papers and publications written by the center's staff. Moreover, the National Research Center on Asian American Mental Health at UCLA is an important place to begin when engaging in meaningful model minority stereotype research. Lastly, the University of California at Los Angeles (UCLA) has the only law school that offers a critical race studies program. Thus, Asian critical race theorists (AsianCrits) are encouraged to check out their website (www.law.ucla.edu:80/academic-programs-and-courses/specializations/critical-race-studies/Pages/default.aspx).

The Model Minority Stereotype: Demystifying Asian American Success presents a distinctive and engaging way to read and research the model minority stereotype—one that seeks to broaden understanding of the stereotype's merits beyond the confines of what existing research has done into newer arenas of interdisciplinary and methodological research. My intent is that this book allows readers to weigh the evidence that disagrees with the validity of the model minority myth. This book also addresses many topics that most scholarship and studies have avoided—that ecologically fallacious conclusions and assertions are problematic for Asian Americans, that alternative methodologies exist that can destabilize the model minority stereotype, and that counter-storytelling (Poon & Hune, 2009) as an approach to dismantling the model minority myth is as effective as it is evocative. Therefore, it is my hope that this volume be a path breaker for discussions related to the model minority stereotype and larger discourses pertaining to Asian success. Asians' meteoric rise and their anointment as model minorities should cause both researchers and wider policymaking communities to pause. In what seems to be mounting evidence that Asian students outperform their peers, many, if not most, books on the model minority fail to address topics like homogenization, ecologically fallacious generalizations, and a bimodal distributed population.

Given that the model minority is completely compatible with the idea of a meritocracy, it is very difficult to dispel. Research indicates, however, that the rhetoric of a meritocracy is racist (e.g., see Chan & Wang, 1991). In many ways the model minority remains a fixture within discourse on achievement; thus demystification of the harmful stereotype remains unsolved and largely unaddressed. It is clear that the model minority stereotype and its attending beliefs are controversial. It is also a subject about which difficult and contested discourses are the norm. Educational researchers have approached dismantling the myth through a variety of methods that cannot necessarily be captured by one theoretical perspective or in one book alone. Nonetheless, this book attempts to collect and review research that draws on empirical and theoretical research to examine and dismantle the model minority stereotype.

The model minority stereotype reduces Asian Americans to one group, reifying success to cultural causes. Rather than acknowledge their heterogeneity, the model minority stereotype perspective originates from sociopolitical racism intended to maintain and perpetuate the *status quo* of power relations. This implies Asian Americans are successful due to their merit, absolving racism and other minorities' failures. Equally troubling is the fact that statistical aggregation obscures important inter- and intra-ethnic differences. Aggregate statistics tend to reproduce, rather than alleviate the model minority myth. The moral of the model minority story is that in order to prevent premature judgment of Asian American success, we ought to recognize and validate the Asian American population's heterogeneity. The literature that is contained in this book's chapters are based on North America (mainland and contiguous United States and Canada); although most articles are on Asian Americans, some do cover Asian Canadians.

In the 1960s Asian students were anointed with the title of model minorities. Today, Asian Americans are overrepresented in gifted and talented education and under-represented in special education classes (Hartlep, 2010; U.S. Department of Education, 2010; Yoon & Gentry, 2009). This book hopes to map the course by which we got here and to suggest a new course by which we might find our way to a better path. Chapter 1, "Testing and Asian Academic Achievement and Attainment," explores literature on the topics of testing, achievement, and attainment. Chapter 2, "Who Are Asian Americans?," covers a variety of topics, all pointing to the identity and heterogeneity of the Asian American population. Chapter 3, "Asian American Socioeconomic Standing," looks at literature that documents the economic hardships that Asian Americans face. Chapter 4, "Asian American Health and Social Welfare," shares relevant information on the overall psycho-social as well as mental health of the Asian American population. Chapter 5, "Interdisciplinary and Methodologically Approached Research on the Model Minority Stereotype," shares innovative and methodologically novel research conducted on Asian Americans that attempts to dismantle the model minority stereotype. Chapter 6, "Encyclopedic and Bibliographic Research on the Model Minority Stereotype," reports various model minority citations from annotated bibliographies and encyclopedias. Chapter 7, "Model Minority Movies and Media," is self-referential, but extremely necessary provided that many citizens watch media and movies, which in turn shapes their ideologies and perceptions of Asian Americans. Chapter 8, "Model Minority Newspaper Articles," fixates on newspaper reporting of Asian Americans as model minorities. Chapter 9, "Classical Model Minority Articles," shares journalistic and academic writings that perpetuate the misunderstanding that Asian Americans are model minorities. Chapter 10, "Dissertations and Theses on the Model Minority Stereotype," is self-referential, but importantly, it charts the history of academic research, documented and catalogued in the form of theses and dissertations. Lastly, Chapter 11, "Methodology," shares the method of finding the literature in this volume.

REFERENCE

Hartlep, N. D. (2012). *A segmented assimilation theoretical study of the 2002 Asian American student population.* Doctoral thesis, University of Wisconsin-Milwaukee, Milwaukee, WI.

CHAPTER 1

TESTING AND ASIAN AMERICAN ACADEMIC ACHIEVEMENT AND ATTAINMENT

The "model minority" stereotype presupposes Asian American deference to family, dedication and devotion to academic studies, and outright parental discipline (Abboud & Kim, 2006; Chua, 2011). The academic achievement and attainment of Asian American youth is thus believed to be extraordinary (Sue & Okazaki, 1990, 2009). Semi-autobiographical books such as Jean Kwok's (2010) novel *Girl in Translation* feed the myth that Asian Americans (in her case, Chinese Americans) can, through dogged determination, achieve the American Dream and attend an Ivy League college. Kwok (2010) writes about Kimberly Chang, a Chinese girl who must work in a sweatshop in New York City in order to help her mother, Ma, pay the bills—the largest of which was a repayment to her Aunt Paula for getting Kimberly and Ma to the United States from Hong Kong. This sub-genre of Asian-American success book is reminiscent of the Horatio Alger novels of the late nineteenth century. There seem to be some parallels at least in theme. For instance, his novels for young adults were formulaic stories of impoverished White boys attaining the American Dream through hard work and

---

rugged individualism (a boy starts out shoveling coal on the train's coal tender and ends up owning the railroad).

In her semi-autobiographical story, we read that Kimberly attends a poorly-run inner city public school, but not for long. She is quickly awarded a scholarship to attend Harrison Prep, a well-regarded preparatory high school for highly aspiring students. Kimberly does well academically, despite being suspected of cheating by Harrison teachers and administrators—well enough that she garners a full-ride scholarship to Yale. Furthering the model minority narrative and making it even more salient, Kimberly learns that she is pregnant shortly after receiving word of her Yale scholarship. *Girl in Translation* readers learn that Kimberly decides against terminating the pregnancy and keeps her son. Kimberly ends up deferring her full-ride scholarship to Yale for one year. Writes Kwok (2010): "I worked four jobs at a time while I was a student [at Yale], but I still graduated with honors and then moved on to Harvard Medical School. In those debt-ridden years before I finished medical school, I called upon any and every talent I had to become the best surgeon I could" (p. 302). The rags-to-riches story is a narrative that resonates well with the American mainstream, and I predict it is one reason that Kwok's (2010) debut novel quickly became a national bestseller.

Do labeled (model minority) Asian students become their label (successful)? The model minority stereotype believes that test scores are results of the learner's ethnicity, despite the fact that they mostly reflect factors of personal and familial socioeconomics (Hartlep, 2012). Not surprisingly, poorer Asian Americans, on average, have less ideal outcomes when compared to wealthier Asian Americans (Lew, 2006). This chapter contains literature on Asian Americans and testing, including writings on the academic achievement and attainment of Asian Americans that fight the rags-to-riches narrative Kwok (2010) and others tell. Collectively, the readings in this chapter erase any doubt that the model minority stereotype is patently false.

Administrator. (2011, December 13). 20 amazing stats about Asian-American achievement. [Onlinecollege.org Web Site]. Retrieved on December 14, 2011 from http://www.onlinecollege.org/2011/12/13/20-amazing-stats-about-asian-american-achievement/

***This on-line article attempts to set the record straight regarding Asian American achievement. The model minority stereotype contends many things, and the twenty statistics concerning Asian American achievement presented in this article are of value to model minority stereotype researchers, given that these statistics are semi-detailed—some are not entirely correct, while some are. The statistics that are not accurate must be challenged by model minority researchers, while the statistics that are accurate must be used for arguing against the existence of the model minority stereotype. The twenty amazing statistics that are taken verbatim from this article are as follows: (1) Asian Americans are not making it to the Fortune 500; (2) Asian-Americans are reaching higher levels of employment; (3) nearly all Asian Americans have at least a high school diploma; (4) Asian kids just spend more time studying; (5) Asian American kids aren't more stressed than their peers; (6) Asian American families simply earn more; (7) Asian Americans take up a disproportionate share of the nation's most prestigious universities; (8) Asians with a bachelor's degree will earn $400K less over their lifetime than Caucasians; (9) Asian Americans and Pacific Islander students struggle with high school and college completion; (10) overall, Asian Americans achieve more college degrees; (11) not every Asian group is doing so well; (12) some Asian American students face severe disadvantages; (13) the achievement gap is getting even wider; (14) Asian Americans perform well on math SAT sections, but not as well in reading and writing; (15) Southeast Asian students are sometimes misdiagnosed as learning disabled; (16) often, Asian students are not prepared for college-level coursework; (17) Asian Americans have a higher per capita income; (18) Western moms have much different ideas about education than Chinese immigrant moms do; (19) Chinese kids spend more time studying than playing sports; and (20) Asian American students are achieving at high poverty schools.

Agbayani, A., & Takeuchi, D. T. (1989). Limited access to public higher education for native Hawaiian and Filipino students in Hawaii. In G. Yun (Ed.), *A look beyond the model minority image: Critical issues in Asian America* (pp. 126–134). New York, NY: Minority Rights Group Inc.

***This book chapter examines the noticeable under-representation of Filipino and native Hawaiian students in postsecondary education within the state of Hawaii. The chapter identifies obstacles that block these students gaining admission into the University of Hawaii at Manoa, the main campus in the University of Hawaii system. These impediments were (1) Filipino and Native Hawaiian students' low SAT scores compared to other students (Whites, Japanese, and Chinese), (2) their high school academic underpreparation, (3) financial difficulties, (4) the tracking or channeling of Filipino and/or Native Hawaiian students to two-year colleges as opposed to four-year college/universities, (5) Filipino and/or Native Hawaiians' dropping out of high school, (6) the university's inaccurate measures of academic potential (using the SAT score for admission purposes), (7) the use of culturally inappropriate teaching practices within university classrooms, and (8) the lack of Filipino and native Hawaiian faculty at the University of Hawaii at Manoa. Agbayani and Takeuchi (1989) discuss the disproportionate impact that admission standards based on SAT scores have on native Hawaiian students at the University of Hawaii at Manoa, making this chapter incredibly invaluable, especially given the educational establishment's love affair with high stakes admission testing. Agbayani and Takeuchi (1989) state that "raising SAT cut-off scores by twenty points would not improve the quality of the student body, but would reduce its size including a disproportionate decrease in Native Hawaiian students at Manoa" (p. 130). This chapter really makes the reader consider what the *quid pro quo* for the use of SAT scores is, and clearly points out that not all Asian Americans are extremely successful or concentrated in four-year colleges/universities. This could be a solid contribution to a syllabus in a higher education graduate program class.

Allred, N. C. (2007). Asian Americans and affirmative action: From yellow peril to model minority and back again. *Asian American Law Journal, 14*(1), 57–84.

***Allred's (2007) law article addresses Asian Americans' distinct history with affirmative action and the unique position they occupy in its debate. Asian American relationships to affirmative action are influenced by the perception that they are model minorities. Allred (2007) writes: "For years, Asian Americans have struggled with the image of being a 'model minority'—a seemingly complimentary designation, but one that has come to be a double-edged sword" (p. 58). Asian Americans have been used as "mascots" for the abolishment of affirmative action. Consequentially, Allred (2007) points out that mascotting reinforces the model minority myth, keeping White privilege invisible. The strength of Allred's (2007) article is found in sections IV (where she addresses the mascotting of Asian Americans by conservative groups) and V (where she explicates the ways in which Asian Americans are cast as "yellow peril" nowadays). "Mascotting" refers to a White figure and/or constituency taking under its wing a minority group or individual person of color to deflect claims of being racist. Allred (2007) contends that "depicting Asian Americans as the victims of affirmative action seemingly lends its attackers more credibility by questioning the effectiveness of a system that supposedly works against a historically disadvantaged minority group" (p. 70). She also mentions that "conservative groups often portray Asian Americans as brilliant success stories, thus using Asian Americans as mascots in their arguments against race-conscious policies" (Allred, 2007, p. 72). Lastly, Allred (2007) observes that the "'yellow peril' was originally a xenophobic response to the mass immigration of nineteenth century Chinese and Japanese workers; nonetheless, it may soon represent the perceived influx of competitive Asian Americans in higher education" (p. 78). This article will be helpful for those scholars and teachers who wish to address the model minority stereotype in the context of educational affirmative action. Literature reviews ought to cite this article.

Baker, B. D., Keller-Wolff, C., & Wolf-Wendel, L. (2000). Two steps forward, one step back: Race/ethnicity and student achievement in education policy research. *Educational Policy, 14*(4), 511–529.

***This educational policy article underscores the necessity of disaggregating racial/ethnic variables when examining academic achievement. The authors analyzed data from the National Educational Longitudinal Study of 1988 in order to test the differences between using aggregate racial/ethnic variables and disaggregate racial/ethnic variables. The findings of this study indicate the problematic nature of using aggregate data, when disaggregation is possible: heterogeneity is lost and findings are inconclusive and inadequate. While this article extends the field of knowledge, advocating for disaggregation, it does not address the common problem of including Pacific Islanders under the rubric of Asian American.

Beckett, G. H. (2007). What contributes to Asian model minority academic success? An ecological perspective. *New Waves: Educational Research and Development, 11*(3), 7–10.

***Beckett states in this article that it is a condensed version of a book chapter forthcoming in Guofang Li and Lihshing Wang's edited volume *Model Minority Myth Revisited: An Interdisciplinary Approach to Demystifying Asian American Education Experiences* published by Information Age Publishing. However, Beckett's (2007) chapter did not appear in that volume. Her article shares the results of an ethnographic study of five secondary school Asian Canadian immigrant students that she conducted in Vancouver, Canada: "one Taiwanese boy (Taotao), one Taiwanese girl (Tiantian), one Chinese boy from China (Chenjian), and two girls from Hong Kong (Hongmei and Honglian, sisters)" (Beckett, 2007, p. 8). According to Beckett (2007), "Asian academic success is a complex phenomenon that should be attributed to multiple factors and examined from an ecological perspective" (p. 9). Beckett (2007) contends that an ecological approach "can account for the complexity of relevant issues" (p. 9). Beckett's article can be used in literature reviews, but it can also be cited by students and scholars who are doing model minority research that calls upon ecological perspectives and paradigms when examining Asian academic achievement.

Bell, M. P., Harrison, D. A., & McLaughlin, M. E. (1997). Asian American attitudes toward affirmative action in employment: Implications for the model minority myth. *Journal of Applied Behavioral Science, 33*(3), 356–377.

***Bell, Harrison, and McLaughlin's (1997) article examined Asian Americans' attitudes toward Affirmative Action Programs (AAP). Their article shares two interrelated studies. Study 1 participants consisted of 124 students from an introductory organizational behavior course at a large Southwestern university and 202 managers. These participants completed the Job Opinion Survey, and student and managerial survey responses were statistically analyzed. Findings indicated that attitudes toward AAP were "more favorable from Whites to Hispanics to Asians to Blacks" (p. 365). Bell, Harrison, and McLaughlin (1997) write that "the beliefs and attitudes of Asians about AAPs [in Study 1], although not identical, more closely resemble those of Hispanics and Blacks than those of Whites" (p. 367). Study 2 participants consisted of 367 students and 367 field managers. Survey data was statistically analyzed. Bell, Harrison, and McLaughlin (1997) write that "the assertions that Asian Americans are more similar to Whites than to other minorities were once again refuted by these Study 2 data on AAPs and experience with discrimination in employment" (p. 373). Both studies, especially when taken together, indicate that Asian Americans share more attitudinal similarity with Hispanics and Blacks than with Whites, invalidating the model minority stereotype. This article should be consulted when conducting future scholarly research on Asian Americans' attitudes toward affirmative action since there continues to be a dearth of research on this topic. One exception is Hartlep, Ecker, Miller, & Whitmore (2013), which analyzed Asian Pacific American college freshmen students' attitudes toward affirmative action, finding a relationship between whether or not they supported affirmative action plans in college admission processes and their political ideologies.

Coalition for Asian American Children and Families (CACF). (2011). *"We're not even allowed to ask for help": Debunking the myth of the model minority.* New York, NY: Pumphouse Projects.

***The Coalition for Asian American Children and Families (CACF), with funding from the Ford Foundation, Carnegie Corporation, Beautiful Foundation, and New York Community Trust, authored this spectacularly revealing (2011) report, "'We're Not Even Allowed to Ask for Help': Debunking the Myth of the Model Minority," which documents how Asian Americans are faring in the New York City public school system. The report underscores how the model minority myth is a burden for students and conceals Asian Pacific American heterogeneity. Using mainly 2007–2008 data provided to them by the New York City Department of Education (DOE) and the New York State Education Department (NYSED) for over 1,500 schools, much of the report's findings are disaggregated and presented in quantitative and qualitative ways. This comprehensive 51-page report not only debunks the model minority myth but also provides policy recommendations that are actionable and can assist the Asian Pacific American (APA) student population educationally as well as socially. Some of the report's most startling and illustrative findings that call into question the model minority characterization of APA students are provided below:

- "Half of New York City's APA children are in families with incomes below the 200 percent of poverty threshold" (p. 21).
- "Half of APA enrollment is concentrated in Queens. Queens is home to many of the largest and most overcrowded schools in the city" (p. 21).
- "More than one in three 2009 APA Regents diploma graduates passed Regents exams with scores that predicted they would need remedial classes before tackling college coursework" (p. 35).
- "Asian home language schools have significantly lower average percentages of teachers without appropriate credentials and of classes being taught by them" (p. 37).

The following quotation from the report effectively captures the essence and purpose of "We're Not Even Allowed to Ask for Help" (2011):

> The *Model Minority Myth is a stereotype* that ignores the histories, capacities, cultures, and personalities of an incredibly diverse group of APA children and youth that is larger than the entire enrollment of many other urban [school] systems across the United States. *The [Model Minority] Myth imposes unrealistic expectations on young people and justifies official and unofficial policies and practices that fail to meet their educational and developmental needs. This report challenges that [model minority mythic]* framework directly and urges policy-makers and community members to promote and engage in a more nuanced dialogue about APA students' reality that includes those students and their parents. (CACF, 2011, p. 45, italics added).

This report is probably too long to use effectively in its entirety for a reading in a high school or college classroom; however, it could be used by scholars looking for specific quotable ideas and/or as a reference to cite in their review of the literature. "We're Not Even Allowed to Ask for Help" (2011) is less polemical and political, and much more problem-solution(s) oriented; thus, it is bound to be better received than reports that are more critical or envelope-pushing.

Caplan, N., Choy, M. H., & Whitmore, J. K. (1992). Indochinese refugee families and academic achievement. *Scientific American, 266*(2), 36–42.

***This short article describes refugee Indochinese who are successful academically, supporting the notion of supporters of segmented assimilation that maintenance of tradition is a positive characteristic that can lead to academic success. According to the authors, "Rather than adopting American ways and assimilating into the melting pot, the most successful Indochinese families appear to retain their own traditions and values" (1992, p. 41). Further, the authors discuss the cultural values that played an important role in the educational achievement of the Indochinese refugees studied, revealing how "supposed" disadvantage was reversed or neutralized, only to turn into eventual academic advantage.

Chae, H. S. (2004). Talking back to the Asian model minority discourse: Korean-origin youth experiences in high school. *Journal of Intercultural Studies, 25*(1), 59–73.

***This article examines the educational and social experiences of Korean-origin, working class youth in New York City public high schools. Readers quickly learn that Chae's origins are Korean and that his life experiences gave him an interest in the topic of the present study, which was a pilot study for his dissertation. Data were collected from interviews with five Korean-origin high school students. The article shares examples of student counter-narratives that distilled the mendacity of the model minority myth. For example, one student (pseudonym Tae Joon) noted the following:

> I am not sure where that stereotype came from but I think it is because people don't know that many Asians. Say there is a school and there are only 50 Asians. If some of those students are really smart and do well, of course people are going to think all Asians are smart. But if they go to school where there are a lot of Asians, they will see that there are Asians who aren't doing good. (Chae, 2004, p. 66)

Another student (pseudonym Annie) said the following:

> The model minority [myth] causes teachers to see us all the same...But we aren't. It might be a shock to some people but there are real problems among Asian [youth]. But people don't care...We aren't all into math and science. Those are my worst subjects...We don't all want to be doctors when we grow up. We have other interests too. (pp. 67–68)

According to Chae (2004), "The model minority discourse, like most discourses about race, multiculturalism and diversity, reinforces uni-dimensional and static notions of identity and culture" (p. 70), which is the highest form of essentialism. It is this essentialist discourse that needs to be disrupted and replaced with more realistic ways to understand the experiences of Asian Americans (in this case Koreans) in high school. This article is one example of scholarship that shares the intimate feelings of Asian American high school students who must grapple with the model minority stereotype while in school. In conclusion, the model minority stereotype is a burden for Asian American (Korean) students. As one student (pseudonym Yun Jeong) notes: "It's harder for Asians because if you're not a genius, they [teachers] act like something is wrong with you...People think 'All the other Asians are smart, why aren't you? What is wrong with her?'" (p. 67).

Chae, Y. (2008). Cultural economies of model minority creation. In Y. Chae, *Politicizing Asian American literature: Towards a critical multiculturalism* (pp. 19–30). New York, NY: Routledge.

***Chae's (2008) chapter is the first in *Politicizing Asian American Literature: Towards a Critical Multiculturalism,* which is published in Franklin Ng's Routledge Series: "Studies in Asian Americans: Reconceptualizing Culture, History, and Politics." Chae (2008) describes ways in which Asians (read: the Chinese) have been exploited in the United States historically, as well contemporarily. Chae (2008) notes that one primary way that Asians have been exploited has been by their importation as strikebreakers in an effort to dissolve unions. These political and economic motivations led to Chinese exclusion becoming a national issue as opposed to a regional one. Capitalists use Asians as a racial "wedge" in order to divide and conquer other non-White and non-Asian minorities. The strategies that capitalists use have been extremely successful, especially since Chae (2008) states that the Chinese were unsuccessful in their unionization efforts. In the 1960s Asians (initially the Japanese) were cast as a model minority. Chae (2008) writes that "the image of Asians as a 'model minority' has helped American society justify its structural inequality and reaffirm the underlying structure by shifting the minority problem to individuals and communities rather than allowing for an examination of the unequal power structure of the society" (p. 26). Chae's (2008) chapter assists readers in understanding that the model minority was an economic creation that supported capitalism and maximized the profits of the White establishment. Chae (2008) is worth being quoted at length:

> Although Asian immigrants were '*yellow* proletariat' in the nineteenth century and are now called a 'middle-class *model minority,*' the *middlemen* status of Asian immigrants as a force for breaking labor unionism or as a '*model*' for other minorities has been continuously used to serve the needs of U.S. capitalism and political as well as ideological purposes. (Chae, 2008, pp. 24–25, italics added)

The divide and conquer function of the stereotype is dangerous: Chae (2008) asserts,

> White 'American' society has labeled Asian Americans as a 'model' compared to African Americans and Chicanos/Latino Americans and touted Asians' economic 'success' and achievement without any help from government, while contrasting African Americans and Chicanos/Latino Americans as 'aid-depending' racial minorities. (p. 25)

This is a book chapter that should be cited when scholars want to establish the divisiveness of the model minority stereotype, and to link the stereotype's creation to socio-political and economic interests.

Chan, S. & Wang, L. (1991). Racism and the model minority: Asian-Americans in higher education. In P. G. Altbach & K. Lomotey (Eds.), *The racial crisis in American higher education* (pp. 43–67). New York, NY: State University of New York Press.

***Chan and Wang's (1991) chapter focuses on the "emergent forms of racism in American higher education" (p. 43) directed toward Asian Americans. Chan and Wang (1991) begin their chapter by documenting racist and violent incidents that serve to contradict the notion that Asians are model minorities. They go on to address invidious forms of invisible and institutionalized racism that impact the lives of Asian Americans. Chan and Wang (1991) "argue that because Asian-Americans are relatively powerless in academia, their glittering scholarly achievements notwithstanding, they have had to *struggle* every step of the way—alongside other people of color—for educational equality" (p. 45, italics added). For most of the chapter Chan and Wang (1991) discuss the struggle of Asian Americans in establishing Asian American studies programs in higher education. Toward the end of the chapter, they indicate that the Asian American population is heterogeneous and that the model minority stereotype is a pragmatic and political "divide-and-conquer" tactic deployed by White supremacy in order to reduce "the chances of [Asian Americans] forming a coalition to challenge the existing structure of power in society in general and in higher education in particular" (p. 64). The chapter is unique in that not only does it lobby for Asian Americans to assert themselves by consolidating the limited power that they currently possess, it also introduces the notion of "new racism" in higher education. Chan and Wang (1991) describe this in detail accordingly:

> One of the basic principles of *new racism* is that when nonwhites or women manage to "win" on the basis of existing rules, then the rules must be changed. Though unarticulated, this is precisely the logic behind the efforts of the elite universities to limit Asian-American enrollment. (p. 63, italics added)

Chan and Wang's (1991) chapter should be read not only by students in Asian American studies programs, but also by academic affairs personnel in higher education settings. Due to the chapter's substantive research and documentation, it can be used by practitioners as well as philosophers who wish to engage with the model minority stereotype within a higher education context.

Chang, J. C. (2005). A gesture life: Reviewing the model minority complex in a global context. *Journal of American Studies* [미국학논집,], *37*(1), 131–152.

***Chang's (2005) article discusses why "the celebration of Asian achievements can be harmful to the Asians themselves" (p. 135). According to Chang (2005), the model minority complex results when Asians internalize the myth in shaping their self-identities. Chang's (2005) article examines Changrae Lee's *A Gesture Life*, developing a theorization of "gestures." According to Chang (2005), gestures are actions and decisions (symbolic and/or concrete) that Asians make while seeking approval from the dominant culture. The gestural action to gain the approval of others in order to maintain a model minority reputation is superficial—more symbolic than substantive. Thus, Asians suffering from the model minority complex act and behave as expected by others, rather than themselves. Chang's (2005) article laments the possibility that "gesturing" may occur in global contexts, making Asians likely to develop the model minority complex if they do not already suffer from it. This article can be used in courses that focus on language arts given that it reviews several of Changrae Lee's writings. As Chang (2005) notes, Changrae Lee is "considered one of the top twenty U.S. writers under the age of forty by *The New Yorker*" (p. 137).

Chang, B. & Au, W. (2007). You're Asian, how could you fail math? Unmasking the myth of the model minority. *Rethinking Schools, 22*(2), 15–19.

***Chang and Au (2007) present compelling reasons why it is racist to assume that Asian Americans are automatically stellar mathematicians, and they provide five suggestions for practicing teachers. In order to unmask the model minority, Chang and Au assert that teachers should consider the following: (1) "Don't automatically assume that your Asian-American students are 'good' students (or 'bad,' for that matter), and get to know them (Chang & Au, 2007, p. 18); (2) "Rethink how you interpret and act upon the silence of Asian-American students in your classroom" (p. 18); (3) "Teach about unsung Asian-American heroes" (p. 18); (4) "Illustrate historical, political, and cultural intersections between Asian Americans and other groups" (p. 18); and (5) "Weave the historical struggles, culture, and art of Asian-American communities into your classroom" (p. 19). The authors contend that the model minority myth masks issues such as the following: (1) student population diversity, (2) socioeconomic diversity, (3) ethnic inequalities, (4) anti-Asian racism and discrimination, and (5) unequal education outcomes. The article is written for K–12 teachers and provides several select resources on Asian Americans, which can be helpful for teachers who are looking for ways to incorporate Asian American history and culture into their classroom instruction and practices. This article can be used as a required reading for college of education students and/or in a foundations of education course for students to understand the sociological underpinnings associated with the supposed trappings of being an Asian American (and a model minority). This particular *Rethinking Schools* article also appears in Wayne Au's (2009) edited volume *Rethinking Multicultural Education: Teaching for Racial and Cultural Justice* published by Rethinking Schools.

Chen, C. & Stevenson, H. W. (1995). Motivation and mathematics achievement: A comparative study of Asian-American, Caucasian-American, and East Asian high school students. *Child Development, 66*(4), 1215–1234.

***Chen and Stevenson (1995) studied Asian American, East Asian, and Caucasian American 11th graders. They found that Asian Americans' math test scores were higher than Caucasian Americans'; also, Asian American students' parents held high educational expectations for their children. Asian American students were found to exhibit high motivation, to study math more hours, to be enrolled in more difficult math courses, and to be absent less in school when compared to Caucasian American students. The authors also found that males tended to outperform females. They conclude that culture and high levels of motivation lead to Asian American students' overall high level of achievement.

Cheryan, S. & Bodenhausen, G. V. (2000). When positive stereotypes threaten intellectual performance: The psychological hazards of "model minority" status. *Psychological Science, 11*(5), 399–402.

***Cheryan and Bodenhausen (2000) conducted an experiment in which they "tested the idea that positive stereotypes can also threaten performance by creating concern about failure to meet the high expectations held for one's [ethnic, racial, and gender] group" (p. 399). The researchers gave 49 Asian American undergraduate women a challenging mathematics test after making their ethnic or gender identity salient. Students were "randomly assigned to one of three identity-salience conditions (ethnic identity, gender identity, or a personal identity control condition)" (p. 400). Prior to taking a mathematics test, participants' identity-salience was manipulated by completing a ten-item survey. Math performance was measured by computing the ratio of the number of questions answered correctly to the number of questions attempted. Results of the math test indicated that when ethnic identity was made salient, participants' math performance was statistically significantly lower than the control condition. The possibility that "concerns about living up to the high expectations held for Asians [model minority stereotype] impeded performance by interfering with participants' mental focus during the math test" (p. 400) was found to be legitimate. Regression analyses revealed that ethnic identity salience statistically significantly reduced participants' ability to concentrate. As a result, one's ability to concentrate was found to be positively related to math performance. As Cheryan and Bodenhausen (2000) remark, this study's "findings show that even a positively stereotyped social identity [such as the case of the model minority stereotype] can constitute a threat to academic performance" (p. 401). This article is a valuable resource for future stereotype threat and model minority stereotype research. Since the present study did not specify who "Asian Americans" were, future research might consider conducting similar studies on disaggregated subgroups of Asian Americans and by gender.

Chinn, P. (2002). Asian and Pacific Islander women scientists and engineers: A narrative exploration of model minority, gender, and racial stereotypes. *Journal of Research in Science Teaching, 39*(4), 302–323.

***This "qualitative study uses narrative methodology to understand what becoming a scientist or engineer entails for women stereotyped as 'model minorities'" (p. 302). More specifically, Chinn (2002), using narrative analysis, interviewed four Asian American women (Bianca, a fourth-generation Japanese-Chinese American senior majoring in chemistry; Charlotte, a second-generation Chinese American doctoral student studying high-energy physics; Janine, a Japanese American civil engineering student; and Noriko, a Japanese American doctoral student studying in a high-energy physics program). Interview questions centered on the following: "(a) family; (b) childhood memories; (c) school experiences; (d) social factors related to peers, teachers, family, and community; (e) gender and ethnicity; (f) professional identity; and (g) expectations for the future" (p. 306). Findings suggest that these Asian American female scientists and engineers adopted practices that allowed them to better negotiate the gendered and hierarchical spaces they occupied. For instance, "all four commented on masculine practices of joking, competitiveness, drinking, and acting strong and smart or in control by not asking questions" (p. 316). The implications culled from this qualitative study for more effective instruction are many. For instance, Chinn says the following:

> The narratives of minority women…indicate that the competitive, masculine, racist social contexts of science and engineering may be invisible or appear natural and unproblematic to male students and science instructors from dominant groups, but present significant barriers to all [Asian American] females. (p. 318)

Chinn's (2002) study can be used in work done on Asian Americans in STEM (science, technology, engineering, and mathematics) and also in the over-representation/under-representation work conducted on Asian Americans in relation to gifted and talented education and special education, respectively.

Choi, D. H. (1992, Spring). The other side of the model minority myth. *Yisei Magazine, 5*(2), 20–23, 25, 26. A digitized copy is available here: http://www.hcs. harvard.edu/~yisei/ issues/spring_92/ys92_20.html

***Choi's (1992) article contends that Asians Americans' positioning as "model minorities" stems from their willingness to acquiesce with White supremacy. In part, this is due to a form of identity crisis that Asian Americans are experiencing. Choi (1992) indicates that "Asian Americans, arguably, have succeeded not only because they work hard, but also because they follow the rules, stay inconspicuous, and *never question authority*" (p. 22, italics added). Choi (1992) contradistinctively notes, "Blacks on the other hand, have always been threatening to white America with their outspokenness, their assertion of difference and readiness to testify to their oppression" (p. 22). Choi's (1992) article addresses how the model minority stereotype distorts the truth and conspires to keep Asian Americans in subordinated positions within society. Moreover, Choi (1992) argues that Asian American success and failure—the other side of the "model minority" myth—both "are largely the products of white discrimination" (p. 26). This article can be used in a variety of educational settings: as a course reading, as a source of information for academic writing, and/or as a text to drive classroom teaching and learning.

Choi, Y. & Lahey, B. B. (2006). Testing the model minority stereotype: Youth behaviors across racial and ethnic groups. *Social Service Review, 80*(3), 419–452.

***Choi and Lahey's (2006) article used data from the National Longitudinal Study of Adolescent Health, a large and nationally representative survey, to assess the validity of the model minority stereotype for Asian Pacific American (APA) youth (grades 7–12 in 1995). They focused on APA youth behaviors, such as aggressive and non-aggressive delinquent offenses, underage substance use, and sexual behavior. *Aggressive delinquent offenses* consisted of serious fighting, seriously injuring someone, threatening someone with a weapon, taking part in a group fight, pulling a knife or a gun on someone, and/or shooting or stabbing someone. *Non-aggressive delinquent offenses* consisted of painting graffiti, damaging property, stealing something worth more/less than $50, shoplifting, stealing a car, burglarizing a building, and/or running away from home. *Underage substance use* consisted of smoking, consumption of alcohol, use of marijuana, cocaine, inhalants, and/or use of other illegal drugs. *Sexual behavior* consisted of whether or not APA youth had ever had sex, been pregnant, and/or contracted a sexually transmitted disease. The results suggest that, except for substance use, APA youth do not report fewer delinquent behaviors than White youth. Moreover, APA youth report slightly higher numbers of aggressive offenses than White youth, and APA females report greater numbers of nonaggressive offenses than White females. Lastly, it was found that APA youth reported higher rates of nonaggressive offenses and substance use than Black youth. This article is highly consequential and should be cited in scholarship and advocacy work in order to dispel the notion that Asian Pacific Americans constitute a model minority group. This article also could be useful to educational psychology for dealing with guidance counseling.

Chu, L. T. (1991). Who are the model minorities among the junior college Asian-American subgroups? ERIC Document ID: ED363362.

***Chu's (1991) report looks at subgroups of the Asian American population. Using 1989 data on students attending the nine colleges in the Los Angeles Community College District (LACCD), Chu (1991) analyzed academic achievement by the following measures: ethnicity (including Chinese-, Japanese-, Korean-, Filipino-, and Vietnamese-American subgroups), marital status, age, gender, residence history, pre-college academic preparation, social class, employment status, scholarships, student aspirations, educational plans, academic involvement, and student major. Chu's (1991) findings can be summarized in the following: (1) marital status, age, academic involvement, and change in major field of study affected academic achievement across all ethnic groups; (2) the mean grade point average (GPA) for White LACCD students was 1.86, while the Asian-American aggregate was 1.76; (3) Korean-Americans had the highest GPA among all Asian-American subgroups (2.02), followed by Chinese-Americans (1.83) and Vietnamese-Americans (1.73); (4) native-English speaking Whites and Japanese-Americans had the largest proportion of respondents with GPA's of 2.99 or below; (5) Filipino- and Korean-Americans had the largest percentage of students eligible to enter the University of California or California State University systems after high school graduation, while Japanese-Americans had the least; and (6) the level of acculturation may have an impact on student performance. This paper is important since it illustrates that Asian Americans are a heterogeneous population and that, contrary to the model minority stereotype, Asian American subgroup differences in outcomes do in fact exist.

Conchas, G. Q. & Pérez, C. C. (2003). Surfing the "model minority" wave of success: How the school context shapes distinct experiences among Vietnamese youth. *New Directions for Youth Development: Understanding the Social Worlds of Immigrant Youth, 100,* 41–56.

***Conchas and Pérez (2003) studied 27 first- and second-generation Vietnamese immigrant students in a California high school. They found that there were two groups, the *dedicators,* and the *team players.* Both groups of Vietnamese students benefited from the model minority stereotype on ideological terms and structural terms. The contribution that this study makes is that "the model minority stereotype lumps all Asians into one category, ignoring within-group differences" (pp. 54–55), but as the authors of this study found, "differences even within high achieving Vietnamese high school students" (p. 55) exist, further delegitimizing the homogenization of Asian American students. This article should be cited in literature reviews as well as read by scholar practitioners. This article can be used in education courses that study diversity and in courses that address Asian American education.

DeGuzman, G. R. (1998). The impact of the model minority myth in higher education. *Journal of Student Affairs, 7*(1), 85–91.

***DeGuzman's (1998) article addresses how opponents of affirmative action use the model minority stereotype—the belief that all Asian Americans are doing well—to advocate for its abolishment. According to DeGuzman (1998), "A better understanding of the model minority myth [stereotype] will allow society to see what effects it has on Asian Pacific Americans and the implications it has in the affirmative action debate" (p. 90). DeGuzman's (1998) article is a necessary reference for work on Asian Americans and affirmative action. When states become "colorblind," affirmative action is the first program to be assaulted. Worth mentioning, this article introduces the concept that Asian Americans have gone from being "sub-humans" during times of yellow peril to now "super-minorities" during times of model minority status and colorblind racism/meritocracy.

Divoky, D. (1988, November). The model minority goes to school. *Phi Delta Kappan, 70*(3), 219–222.

***This brief article highlights the perils of the positive stereotype (model minority) for Asian American students in school. The article's messages pertain to the inaccurate assessment of Asian American students who do not speak English as a first language, as well the numerous problems that accompany the myth, such as teachers' assumptions, non-Asian students' resentment of "model minorities," and Asian American students' high risk for dropping out of school, among others. This article is a beneficial read for pre- and in-service teachers given that it illustrates how the model minority stereotype impacts teaching.

Empleo, A. C. (2006). Disassembling the model minority: Asian Pacific Islander identities and their schooling experiences. *Multicultural Perspectives, 8*(3), 46–50.

***This article points to how the model minority stereotype has implications for the under-representation of Asian Pacific American students in special education and for the overrepresentation of Asian Pacific American students in gifted and talented education. This focus is useful given the limited number of studies that examine the model minority and special education. Empleo (2006) writes the following:

> The academic problems of Asian Pacific Islanders have been neglected and ignored due to the negative effects of the model minority stereotype. Asian Pacific Islanders experience academic problems that are similar to those of

other students, which also contradict the notion of the model minority. (p. 48)

Examining the link between model minority status and special education is important for model minority research because "teachers often do not acknowledge the academic problems of Asian Pacific Islander students because of their *acceptance of the model minority stereotype*" (Empleo, 2006, p. 48, italics added).

Eng, P. & Layne, P. (2002). Asian American engineers: A model minority? *SWE, 2,* 96–100.

***Eng and Layne's (2002) article published in *SWE*, the magazine of the Society of Women Engineers, reports on the experiences of Asian American engineers based on survey data. Say Eng and Layne (2002), "In fact, although Asians constituted only 3.6 percent of the population of the United States in the 2000 census, they are almost 11 percent of engineers" (p. 96). Eng and Layne (2002) analyzed data from a 1992 Society of Women Engineers survey of men and women engineers in the United States. Their analysis revealed that Asian American engineers, both men and women, experienced "glass ceilings" in terms of pay and promotion. Eng and Layne (2002) write that "the data suggest widespread prevalence of *glass ceilings*— a phrase used by Asian men as well as women—which form serious barriers to advancement into the management positions that are the culmination of engineering careers" (p. 98, italics added). Eng and Layne (2002) discuss why "the stereotypic view of Asian women as quiet and subservient may seriously affect the career of a young Asian woman" (p. 100), as well as why Asian American women engineers are a dissatisfied group. Eng and Layne's (2002) article is good fodder for building upon the work of other model minority and Asian American "glass ceiling" scholarship (e.g., see Woo, 2000). Those in women's studies may also find use in this article.

Fong, T. (1987, June/July). Undocumented Asians shadowed by spotlight on 'model minority.' *Mediafile, 8*(3), 1, 9.

***Fong's (1987) article addresses how the model minority stereotype overshadows Asians in the United States who may be undocumented. Says Fong (1987), "Popular news reporting has failed to take note that a combination of factors have often tended to push undocumented Asians even deeper into society's shadows than their Hispanic counterparts" (p. 1). Fong's (1987) article is found in a special issue of *Mediafile* dedicated to immigration. Much of Fong's (1987) reporting addresses the consequences of the Immigration Reform and Control Act (IRCA) on the Asian American population. IRCA was signed into law by President Ronald Reagan on November 6, 1986. Fong (1987) notes the following insidious parallel: "Many Asian immigration experts draw parallels between the new Immigration Reform and Control Act and the Chinese Confession Program of the 1950s and early 1960s. The program promised legal resident status to Chinese who would confess to coming to this country with false identification papers" (p. 9). Another noteworthy observation Fong makes is that few media have reported on the problems that face the Asian American population as a result of IRCA. This article is of worth to teachers at all levels: students should be exposed to the difficulty that undocumented Asians face in America. Whether it is due to visiting workers overstaying a visa or refugees seeking a better future, there are significant numbers of Asians in American who are overshadowed by the model minority stereotype. And as Fong (1987) reminds his readers, "no one has precise figures" (p. 1) on how many there are in the United States.

Galindo, C. & Pong, S. (2011). Tenth grade math achievement of Asian students: Are Asian students still the "model minority"?—A comparison of two educational cohorts. In X. L. Rong & R. Endo (Eds.), *Asian American education—Identities, racial issues, and languages* (pp. 1–29). Charlotte, NC: Information Age Publishing.

***This book chapter uses data from the National Educational Longitudinal Study (NELS:88) and the Educational Longitudinal Study (ELS:02) in order to test whether Asian American tenth-grade students performed as well in 2002 as they did in 1990. The researchers found significant changes when examining both cohorts of students. They found (1) that Asian American students should not be considered model minorities in terms of math test achievement scores, (2) that "Asian [American] students were more likely to attend higher SES schools in 1990 than in 2002" (Galindo & Pong, 2011, p. 17), (3) that there is a decline in "Asian [American] parents' expectations for their children's education, relative to White parents' expectations" (Galindo & Pong, 2011, p. 25), and (4) that "Asian [American] student's academic achievement decreased between 1990 and 2002" (Galindo & Pong, 2011, p. 24). Overall, this chapter provides evidence that problematizes the model minority characterization that Asian American students are overachieving math students.

Gym, H. (2011, Summer). Tiger moms and the model minority myth. *Rethinking Schools, 25*(4), 34–35.

***According to the article, Gym is a parent activist and board member of the Asian Americans United, where she works on education and immigration issues. "Tiger Moms and the Model Minority Myth" addresses Amy Chua's mendaciously calculated op-ed that ran in the *Wall Street Journal*. According to Gym (2011), Chua is unrepresentative of the Asian immigrants in the United States, considering that she is a "second-generation Yale law professor with wealth and privilege" (p. 35). Gym points out that Chua's op-ed "says more about a hypercompetitive, wealthy, elitist mom seeking to one-up everyone else than it does about raising children to live in a complicated world" (p. 35). Unfortunately, the idea that tiger moms exist reinforces the model minority stereotype and is harmful for the Asian American community and other non-White minority populations. Those connected to education (e.g., students, teachers, parents) will benefit from reading this short and straightforwardly written article.

Hanson, S. L. & Meng, Y. (2008). Science majors and degrees among Asian-American students: Influences of race and sex in "model minority" experiences. *Journal of Women and Minorities in Science and Engineering, 14*(3), 225–252.

***Using National Educational Longitudinal Study of 1988 (NELS:88) data, Hanson and Meng (2008) "examine the *'model minority'* effect in science by focusing on the way race and sex work together to affect two science education outcomes (science major and science degree) in a sample of Asian-American and white students" (p. 225, italics added). Although Hanson and Meng (2008) write that "it is *not* appropriate to regard Asian-Americans as a *homogenous group*" (p. 227, italics added), their article unintentionally supports Asian American homogenization since the NELS:88 data that Hanson and Meng use does not disaggregate subgroups of Asians, and even worse, lumps Pacific Islanders into its sample. One of Hanson and Meng's (2008) key findings was "that Asian-American male and female students are equally likely to major in science, but Asian-American males are more likely to acquire elite science degrees" (p. 245). This article can be used to illustrate why Asian American females should be supported when pursuing science education and/or a science degree. It could also be used in science education classes for teacher education students.

Harris, A. L., Jamison, K. M., & Trujillo, M. H. (2008). Disparities in the educational success of immigrants: An assessment of the immigrant effect for Asians and Latinos. *The ANNALS of the American Academy of Political and Social Sciences, 620*(90), 90–114.

***The authors of this sociology article, using data from the National Education Longitudinal Study of 1988 (NELS:88), establish why comparative studies that use Whites as a reference group may be inappropriate when studying immigrant advantage. Harris, Jamison, and Trujillo (2008) found that socioeconomic background and immigrant characteristics explain most, if not all, racial/ethnic differences in academic outcomes. The authors disaggregate Asian students, but also include Pacific Americans in their analyses. This article supports the idea that Asian American students are a heterogeneous group in terms of achievement.

Hartman, J. S. & Askounis, A. C. (1989). Asian-American students: Are they really a "model minority"? *The School Counselor, 37*(2), 109–112.

***Hartman and Askounis's (1989) article is an important read for school counselors. Hartman and Askounis (1989) contend that counselors need to understand how the model minority stereotype can mask Asian American individuality and conceal real problems. Indeed, Hartman and Askounis (1989) state that "effective counseling of Asian-American students includes a knowledge and recognition of their unique cultural background" (p. 111). At three pages in length, this is the shortest article published on the model minority stereotype. This article can be used by counseling scholars and practitioners in order to meet the unique counseling needs of Asian American students.

Healey, J. F. (2009). Asian Americans: "model minorities"? In J. F. Healey, *Race. ethnicity, gender, and class: The sociology of group conflict and change* (pp. 405–452). Thousand Oaks, CA: Pine Forge Press.

***Healey's (2009) chapter is quite long, running to 47 pages, much of it devoted to spelling out Chinese and Japanese history in the United States. The chapter is filled with photographs, as well as infographics that enrich the writing. As the title implies, the question that the chapter broaches is whether or not Asian Americans are model minorities. In other words, are they "successful?" Healey (2009) repeatedly states that the Asian American population is heterogeneous and bipolar in its distribution, meaning that there are successful and not-so-successful Asians in America. Healey (2009) does a nice job at comparing and contrasting structural and cultural explanations of Asian American "success." Last, the chapter ends by providing readers with eight bullet points that summarize the chapter's main points as well as eight questions for review and study. This chapter can be used in the high school and/or college classroom as a teaching and learning resource.

Hurh, W. M. & Kim, K. C. (1989). The 'success' image of Asian Americans: Its validity, and its practical and theoretical implications. *Ethnic and Racial Studies, 12*(4), 512–538.

***This journal article demonstrates that the model minority myth is a supporter of the *status quo*. The article's authors (Hurh & Kim, 1989) also describe various methodological considerations that should be present in order to prevent erroneous conclusions when studying Asian Americans. For instance, "for the household income to be a usable index for purposes of group comparison, one has to make adjustments for the number of wage earners and the number of hours worked" (Hurh & Kim, 1989, p. 520). The authors find that the model minority myth is invalid, and that Asian Americans are in fact, disadvantaged. According to Hurh and Kim (1989), "Asian Americans still earn less than whites despite an additional year of schooling" (p. 526). Moreover, implications from this article should be taken into consideration by graduate students and by researchers engaging in empirical research on Asian Americans.

Kagawa-Singer, M. (2008). The other side of the model minority coin. *AAPI Nexus,* 6(1), 1–3.

***Kagawa-Singer's (2008) article serves as the introduction to an issue of *Nexus.* The author writes that the model minority stereotype is dangerous insofar as it hides problems faced by the Asian Pacific American (APA) population. These problems plaguing APAs are what this issue of *Nexus* examines—"the other side of the *Model Minority* coin" (p. 1, italics added).

Karkhanis, S. & Tsai, B. L. (Eds.). (1989). *Educational excellence of Asian Americans: Myth or reality.* New York, NY: The Asian/Pacific American Librarians Association.

***Nine years after the founding of the Asian/Pacific American Librarians Association (APALA) in 1980, *Educational Excellence of Asian Americans: Myth or Reality* (1989) was published. Presenting four papers of the 1988 Annual APALA convention, which was held in July of 1988 in New Orleans, Louisiana, *Educational Excellence* illustrates the diversity of perspectives on the model minority stereotype, a stereotype that hyperbolically highlights the educational excellence of Asian Americans. The collected papers contained in *Educational Excellence* were edited by Sharad Karkhanis and Betty Tsai (President of APALA at that time). Although short in length (32 pages), this book is important due to the diversity of perspectives that the representative authors hold. The first paper, written by Linus Wright, then Under Secretary of the U.S. Department of Education, provides a national perspective to the educational excellence of Asian Americans. According to Wright, generalizations of Asian American overachievement can be hazardous. Nevertheless, Wright contradicts his statements frequently by claiming that Asian Americans' success is no myth and that there are many lessons that other non-White minorities can learn from Asian Americans. It is clear that Wright subscribes to the trope of meritocratic effort and the model minority stereotype. The second paper, written by Tobin Barrozo, then provost and Vice President for Academic Affairs at Metropolitan State College in Denver, Colorado, provides a more jaundiced assessment of Asian American educational excellence from the perspective of an Asian American educator. In contrast to Wright's interpretation, Barrozo concludes that the model minority stereotype overlooks Asian American diversity. Barrozo writes that "if educational excellence is an attribute of all Asians, than [*sic*] the differences among them is [*sic*] conveniently displaced and forgotten" (p. 15, underlining in original). The third paper, authored by Chizuko Izawa, then professor of psychology at Tulane University, provides the perspective of an Asian American academician to Asian Americans' educational excellence. Izawa writes the following: "excellence or success in education or otherwise attributing to any racial group is likely to be nothing but myth" (p. 23). It is clear that Izawa believes the model minority to be too essentialist to be Asian American educational reality; Izawa therefore opposes the model minority myth's veracity. The fourth paper in *Educational Excellence* is an annotated bibliography, written by Augurio Collantes, then professor at Hostos Community College in New York. Collantes' annotated bibliography is a welcome source of information, replete with sources taken from books, newspaper stories, news media, and scholarly and popular press articles. Researchers looking for mainstream articles in the 1980s that supported the rhetoric of the model minority stereotype would benefit from reading *Educational Excellence*—in particular, Collantes' annotated bibliography.

Kato, N. R. (1999). Asian Americans defy "model minority" myth. In Y. Alaniz & N. Wong (Eds.), *Voices of color* (pp. 150–153). Seattle, WA: Red Letter Press.

***Kato's (1999) short chapter discusses how the model minority or "racist love" masks exploitation. Kato (1999) writes, "The reality of racist oppression against Asian Pacific Americans is once again being rewritten into its opposite: the myth of the model minority" (p. 150). Most importantly, though, this chapter points out the double-edged sword that comes with being considered a model minority. Kato (1999) writes, "And while the model minority mystique encourages whites to love us [Asians] for our reputed docility, it also teaches them to fear us, because we may supposedly cost them a job or a school placement" (p. 151). Written in accessible language, this chapter focuses on Asian Americans and the affirmative action debate. Readers are also introduced to the University of California Santa Barbara's Asian Sisters for Ideas in Action Now! (ASIAN!). This chapter could be useful in a freshman orientation course on college campuses where Asians are supposedly "taking over the campus" (e.g., MIT [Made In Taiwan], UCLA [University of Caucasians Lost among Asians], Harvard, etc.). It can also be useful in a higher education graduate program class on diversity in higher education.

Kim, H. & Valadez, J. R. (1995). *Reexamination of the model minority stereotype: An analysis of factors affecting higher education aspirations of Asian American students*. Paper presented at the Annual Meeting of the Association for the Study of Higher Education in Orlando, Florida. ERIC Document ID: ED391417.

***This paper was presented at the 1995 Annual Meeting of the Association for the Study of Higher Education in Orlando, Florida, and is accessible online http://www.eric.ed.gov/PDFS/ED391417.pdf. As abstracted in ERIC, this study explored the model minority stereotype by examining the differences between Asian American students and other racial groups in terms of higher education aspirations, academic achievement, and socioeconomic characteristics. It is based on subset of data from the 1988 National Education Longitudinal Study, namely 973 Asian American, 939 African American, 934 Latino, and 974 White 10th graders. The study compared student socioeconomic influences and numerous variables affecting academic aspiration and achievement. It concluded that unlike the generally-held perception, the achievement of some Asian American students is not shared by all Asian American students as a group. Although Asian Americans as a group excelled over White, African American, and Latino students, higher educational level does not appear to lead to higher occupational status for Asian Americans, as it does for White Americans. The study also found that South Asians tended to have the highest academic achievement of all Asian American groups, followed by Chinese, Southeast Asians, Koreans, Filipinos, and Japanese. Parental expectations, self-concept, and vision appeared to be the most important factors affecting higher education aspiration, regardless of the racial background of the students. An appendix provides frequency distributions, regression models, and other statistical data.

Kobayashi, F. (1999). Model minority stereotype reconsidered. ERIC Document ID: ED434167.

***This paper is accessible on-line at http://www.eric.ed.gov/PDFS/ED434167.pdf. Kobayashi's paper shares counterevidence that helps refute the foremost commonly used claims to support the idea that Asian Americans are model minorities: (1) Asian Americans exhibit lower incidence of criminal activity and almost no juvenile delinquency, (2) Asian Americans are physically and mentally healthier than other Americans, (3) Asian Americans earn higher incomes than other Americans, and (4) Asian American students are higher scholastic achievers than other American students. The paper contains many useful references, and many of the citations can be used whenever challenging the model minority stereotype. Although the paper was published by ERIC in the late 1990s, much more has been written since Kobayashi (1999) did his research. This paper can certainly be used as an important earlier work in reviews of literature.

Kobayashi, F. (2010). From middleman to model minority: Japanese Americans facing barriers. 茨城大学人文学部紀要. 人文コミュニケーション学科論集, 9, 47–54.

***Kobayashi's (2010) article examines the changing stereotypes of Asian (Japanese and Chinese) Americans, from a "middleman minority" to one of a "model minority" status. According to Kobayashi (2010), "In the case of the U.S., the middleman minority status has been applied to Chinese and Japanese Americans as intermediaries between Whites and Blacks" (p. 48). Kobayashi (2010) goes on to write that "Chinese and Japanese Americans, as the middleman minority, have been considered petit bourgeoisie, who monopolize economic sectors and gain wealth. They have played a role in bridging Whites and Blacks as go-betweens in the economic sector by contacting both parts, which do not dare to interface, with each other" (p. 48). According to this article, however, this change from middleman to a model minority left Japanese and Chinese Americans' experiences unchanged. In other words, despite the stereotype shifting from a negative view to a positive view, nothing changed structurally; Asian Americans continue to be marginalized and disenfranchised. Kobayashi (2010) indicates that the supposedly positive model minority stereotype obscures anti-Asian prejudice, which is rendered invisible through institutionalized occupational "glass ceilings" and de facto college "admission ceilings." Anti-Asian biases are also at play, and evidenced in the under-representation of Asian Americans in higher educational leadership and governmental positions. Kobayashi's (2010) article "examined how the model minority theory disguises racism against Japanese Americans by making certain barriers invisible" (p. 52). Thus, this article can be used to teach about college "admission ceilings" and employment "glass ceilings" that Asian Americans experience, especially given that some students may believe Asian Americans are overrepresented and not in need of affirmative action.

Koh, H. H. (1987). Looking beyond achievement: After "the model minority" then what? *Korean and Korean-American Studies Bulletin, 3*(1&2), 15–19.

***Koh's (1987) article is actually a speech that was delivered at the Seventeenth Annual Conference on Koreans and Korean-Americans at Central Connecticut State University on March 21, 1987. Memorably, Yale Professor of Law Koh asks his audience, "If we, as Asians and Asian-Americans are considered to be the '*model minority*,' should we view that label as a compliment or an insult?" (1987, p. 15, italics added). Koh (1987) follows that question up with another important one: "Have we, as Korean-Americans and Asian-Americans *really* made it?" (p. 15, italics in original). His speech is wonderfully written and deeply personalized. According to Koh (1987), the model minority stereotype is negative in that it causes Asian (Korean) Americans to be resented by other minorities. It also narrowly reduces Asian identity to one of being an impersonal bookworm. Koh (1987) ends his speech poetically:

> If we as Korean-Americans, are, in fact, becoming a model minority in this country, we have three choices. We can congratulate ourselves. We can say, "so what?" Or we can ask "now what?" In my opinion, it will always be too early to congratulate ourselves, for if we strive to "make it," so that we can comfortably rest on our laurels, then we will have accomplished nothing. To say "so what?" is to reject everything that our parents' generation and our own generation have actually accomplished and will go on to accomplish. But to ask "now what?" is to look critically at ourselves and our future, to recognize ways in which we have not been as broad or adventurous as we might have been, and to define what we now want to add and contribute to this society. (p. 19)

This article can be used in Asian American studies courses, as well as for teaching/learning related to Asian American identity.

Koo, D. K. (2003). Testing assumptions: IQ, Japanese Americans, and the model minority myth in the 1920s and 1930s. In S. Chan (Ed.), *Remapping Asian American history* (pp. 69–85). Walnut Creek, CA: AltaMira Press.

***Koo's (2003) book chapter is very thoughtful in that it undertakes a thesis rarely made in model minority research: the notion that IQ testing played an evolutionary role in the creation and maintenance of the model minority stereotype. As Koo (2003) writes, "Although it is difficult to trace an exact line from *testing studies* to the *model minority myth,* the resonances are evident indeed" (p. 81, italics added). In his chapter Koo (2003) examines the unique ways in which IQ test results were interpreted for Japanese Americans in the 1920s and 1930s by researchers. Koo's (2003) chapter is important because "in 1923, over 500,000 children underwent [intelligence] examination" (p. 74). Interestingly, according to Koo (2003), "In their quest to map human intelligence, researchers qualified their findings in the language of culture (nurture) but nevertheless contributed to a racialized (nature) understanding of [Japanese American] intelligence" (p. 71). For this reason Koo (2003) contends that IQ tests served to establish a racial hierarchy of intelligence, which allowed for the stereotyping of Asian (Japanese) Americans. The cultural (nurture) explanations of hard work, good study habits, and rote memorization preserved the "possessive investment in whiteness," while the genetic (nature) explanations of innate intelligence reified European American dominance and power. Koo (2003) indicates that the established racial hierarchy of intelligence was European Americans on top, Asian Americans in the middle, and African and Latino Americans on the bottom. This well written chapter can be used in educational psychology courses in the university setting, as well as cited in literature reviews.

Lee, R. G. (1999). The model minority as gook. In R. G. Lee, *Orientals: Asian Americans in popular culture* (pp. 180–203). Philadelphia, PA: Temple University Press.

***Lee's (1999) chapter maintains that the model minority myth makes invidious comparisons between Asians and Blacks. These comparisons rest on a-factual arguments, such as Asian families are stable and intact, and that Asian culture causes Asian success and superiority. Lee (1999) writes, "What distinguishes the model minority myth as a hegemonic mode of racial representation is not primarily its distance from reality but rather its power to dominate or displace other social facts" (p. 186). This chapter indicates that the model minority myth ignores much, while mythologizing even more. Lee (1999) posits that the model minority "myth presents Asian Americans as silent and disciplined; this is their secret to success. At the same time, this silence and discipline is used in constructing the Asian American as a new yellow peril" (p. 190). Again, the model minority myth is really the yellow peril problem in disguise. In reference to the chapter's title, "The Model Minority as Gook," Lee (1999) discusses the term "gook," which is one of the most common racial epithets used to disparage Asians. Although this chapter is dense and difficult to understand for those individuals with limited knowledge of Asian American history, it is nevertheless very important. Lee's (1999) chapter makes it abundantly clear that the model minority is not something that should be celebrated; nor should it be ignored by social scientists. This chapter can easily be used as an assigned reading for graduate-level sociology of education courses, as well as a citation for academicians to use in their own academic writing. Moreover, the chapter contains several references to seminal—albeit conservative—pieces of model minority literature. These "classical" references could easily be cross-referenced by those individuals interested in reading classical and conservative ("pro" model minority stereotype) literature. Reading both sides of the model minority myth debate is extremely important because deconstructing the model minority stereotype requires scholars to understand not only their position, but the position of their opponents (in this case model minority proponents). This is an important skill for graduate students to develop; therefore, this reading could be useful in education graduate classes.

Lee, S. J. (1994). Behind the model-minority stereotype: Voices of high- and low-achieving Asian American students. *Anthropology & Education Quarterly, 25*(4), 413–429.

****Lee's (1994) article is an ethnographic study based on qualitative interview data collected at a high school in Philadelphia that she calls "Academic High." Lee (1994) found that Asian American students identified themselves in distinct groups. There were the "Korean" students who had an attitude of, "we are better than the other Asian students." There were also the "Asians," the "Asian New Wavers," and the "Asian Americans." The students who identified as Asians worked hard and were motivated to do so. Asians were further subdivided into high achieving Asians and low achieving Asians. Those who identified as being Asian New Wavers resisted assimilating and/or "any behavior that encouraged academic achievement" (Lee, 1994, p. 427). The main contribution that this article makes is that it problematizes the assumption that Asian American students follow predictable and linear trajectories in terms of assimilation and acculturation. Furthermore, Lee (1994) argues that it might be best to look at intra-group differences as opposed to inter-group differences. This is an insightful thought: there may be greater diversity within one subgroup than between subgroups of Asian American students. This article can be used as a foundational source of literature for scholars and students who are building a literature review for model minority stereotype work.

Lee, S. J. (2001). More than "model minorities" or "delinquents": A look at Hmong American high school students. *Harvard Educational Review, 71*(3), 505–528.

*** Lee (2001), a third-generation Chinese American, writes, "The academic literature and the popular press convey a perception that Hmong American youth fall into two opposite groups: high achieving model minorities, and delinquents, truants, and gang members" (p. 506). In contrast, this article explores the way *structure*—such as economic forces, relationships with the dominant society, perceptions of opportunities, family relationships, culture, and educational experiences—affect Hmong American high school students' attitudes toward school. In her ethnographic research at a high school in Wisconsin, Lee (2001) found that the Hmong high school students were classified into two opposing groups. The first group was considered to be the "good" Hmong students. These students were 1.5-generation, and were in English as a Second Language (ESL) classes. The "good" students were also referred to as "newcomers" and thought to embody "traditional" Hmong culture and values. The second group was considered to be the "bad" Hmong students. These 2.0-generation students were believed to be overly Americanized and delinquent. Interestingly, Lee (2001) found that the "bad" Hmong students participated in the Hmong Club, while the "good" Hmong students participated in the Asian Club.[1]

According to Lee (2001), "Contrary to the model minority stereotype, most 1.5-generation students were not high achievers. In fact, achievement among 1.5-generation students ranged from high to low, with the majority passing their classes with average grades" (p. 515). Lee (2001) also confirms in her article that Hmong students

> are often overlooked because they are quiet and teachers assume that they are working hard. Unfortunately, these students do not receive the assistance they need in order to survive academically. Thus, the emerging stereotype of the hard-working, quiet model minority works against the [Hmong] students' best interests." (p. 515).

In summary, Lee's powerful article details the politics and perils of assimilation. Dichotomized descriptions of Hmong students—good vs. bad; model minority vs. delinquent—are untenable. Furthermore, neither school suc-

---

[1] The Hmong and Mong are two distinct groups. The Mong speak, read, and write the Mong language and the Hmong speak, read, and write the Hmong language. The Asian model minority stereotype homogenizes Asian Americans into one indistinct group, and the lumping of the Hmong and Mong together is just another example. Two excellent articles that provide information on this problem, and also the educational challenges that the Mong face can be found in the following two citations: (1) [Thao, Y. J. (2003). Empowering Mong students: Home and school factors. *The Urban Review, 35*(1), 25–42], and (2) [Thao, P. & Yang, C. (2004). The Mong and the Hmong. *Mong Journal, 1,* 1–20. Accessed online here: http://www.mong.ws/publications/Mong_and_Hmong_Article.pdf].

cess nor failure rests on a single structural—internal or external—force, but rather a mélange of myriad structures and forces. The importance of Lee's article and its status as a classic in the field is further cemented by the fact that it is reprinted in Chapter 9 (pp. 181–196) of Lee D. Baker's (2004) *Life in America: Identity and Everyday Experience*. K–12 teachers and school administrators will want to read this article.

Lee, S. J. (2003). Model minorities and perpetual foreigners: The impact of stereotyping on Asian American students. In M. Sadowski (Ed.), *Adolescents at school: Perspectives on youth, identity, and education* (pp. 41–49). Cambridge, MA: Harvard Education Press.

***Lee's (2003) concise book chapter discusses how the model minority and perpetual foreigner stereotypes impact Asian American students. For Asian Americans, those two stereotypes—model minority and perpetual foreigner—have been "the two most powerful and persistent stereotypes of Asian Americans" (Lee, 2003, p. 41). This chapter discusses how Asian American students are uniquely impacted by the stereotypes individually, as well as directly by their teachers: Lee (2003) writes that teachers automatically assume that their Asian American students do not face difficulties or challenges. More insidiously, though, "the Eurocentric curriculum that pervades most schools reinforces this stereotyp[ing] through its silence around Asian American history" (Lee, 2003, p. 42). This book chapter should be read by practicing K–12 teachers because it offers hope in the battle against the stereotyping of Asian Americans. Lee (2003) asserts that "by teaching the long and complex history of Asian Americans in this country, schools can combat the stereotype of Asian Americans as perpetual foreigners" (p. 48). Moreover, she adds, "Information about the historical roots of the *foreigner* and *model minority* stereotypes and about the political uses of these stereotypes can be incorporated into discussions of American history" (p. 48, italics added). This is by far one of the most teacher-friendly pieces of writing on the topic of the model minority stereotype. Model minority scholars also might cite this chapter when writing about the consequences of the perpetual foreigner and model minority stereotypes on Asian American students, or on identity capital.

Lee, S. J. (2005). *Up against Whiteness: Race, school, and immigrant youth*. New York, NY: Teachers College Press.

***Lee's (2005) book has been reviewed by many scholars (e.g., see De-Pouw, 2007; Hardy, 2006; Park, 2006; Pu, 2007) and is an important piece of model minority scholarship. Comprised of five chapters, *Up Against Whiteness* is an ethnographic study of "a group of first- and second-generation Southeast Asian Americans, specifically Hmong American high school students, who create their identities as 'new Americans'" (Lee, 2005, p. 1) at a school she labels University Heights High School. Her provocative chapter titles give a good overview of the book's themes: Chapter 1. "Becoming Racialized Americans;" Chapter 2. "At University Heights High School: Creating Insiders and 'Others;'" Chapter 3. "'Traditional' and 'Americanized' Hmong Students;" Chapter 4. "Wimps, Gangsters, Victims, and Teen Moms: The Gendered Experiences of Hmong American Youth;" and Chapter 5. "Race and the 'Good' School." *Up Against Whiteness* is a must to cite whenever carrying out work on the model minority stereotype.

Lee, S. J. (2007). The truth and myth of the model minority: The case of Hmong Americans. In S. J. Paik & H. J. Walberg (Eds.), *Narrowing the achievement gap: Strategies for educating Latino, Black, and Asian students* (pp. 171–184). New York, NY: Springer.

***Lee's (2007) chapter, using 2000 U.S. Census data, "highlight[s] the variation in educational achievement and attainment across various Asian American ethnic groups" (p. 172). Lee's (2007) central argument is that aggregate data hides Asian American educational achievement and attainment variation; thus, disaggregation is necessary to dispel the model minority stereotype. Moreover, Lee (2007) states that Asian American levels of achievement and attainment are more a function of class than ethnicity. Lee (2007) concludes that "Asian American ethnic groups with high rates of poverty experience low rates of educational attainment, and those with high levels of educational attainment have high median incomes" (p. 172). Lee (2007) focuses considerable attention on the challenges facing Hmong Americans in her book chapter, particularly poverty and low educational attainment. This chapter's biggest contribution lies in its unique examination of two bodies of emerging research: (1) female Hmong academic advantage and (2) teachers' differential perceptions/expectations of Hmong American students (gloss: newcomers/immigrants are constructed as being "good" students, whereas overly Americanized students are constructed as being "bad" students). In order to dismantle the myth of the Asian model minority, "educational policy makers must collect and pay attention to disaggregated data" (Lee, 2007, p. 182). This book chapter should be read by everyone who is interested in the equitable education of Asian American students (e.g., educators, educational policymakers, scholars, etc.). Scholars carrying out research on the model minority stereotype will find many uses for this chapter, as will practitioners in all levels of education or educational psychology/counseling.

Lee, S. J. (2009). *Unraveling the "model minority" stereotype: Listening to Asian American youth* (2nd ed.). New York, NY: Teachers College Press.

***Lee's (2009) seminal book has been widely cited and, indeed, must be cited when conducting model minority research. Many times reviewed (e.g., see Everhart, 1998; Ford, 1996; Kwong, 1998; Lee, 1998; Nguyen, 2011; Pak, 2001; Tuan, 1998), *Unraveling* tells of the educational experiences and achievement of Asian American high school students. In her ethnography, Lee (2009) shares many lucid observations culled from in-depth research in what she calls "Academic High School" (p. 17). Scholars, teachers, and students who are interested in examining the model minority stereotype will want to consider Lee's (2009, pp. 24–25) research questions, which were the following: (1) "What do Asian American student identities tell us about the formation of ethnic/racial identity?" (2) "How does the variation in Asian American student identity contribute to our understanding of the literature on immigrant minorities?" (3) "How did the model minority stereotype influence Asian American student identity?" (4) "What identities were encouraged and discouraged by the school?" (5) "How did the model minority stereotype influence race relations?" and (6) "What influence did the school have on race relations?" This book is a necessary component for those conducting research on the model minority stereotype. It is also an important text for teaching and learning about Asian American issues.

Lee, S. J. & Kumashiro, K. (2005). *A report on the status of Asian Americans and Pacific Islanders in education: Beyond the "model minority" stereotype.* Washington, DC: National Education Association. Retrieved from http://www.capsmer.org/assets/Files/Acheiment-Gaps/Status-Asian-American.pdf

***Lee and Kumashiro's (2005) report highlights how the model minority stereotype is problematic for Asian Americans and Pacific Islanders (AAPI). Specifically, Lee and Kumashiro (2005) indicate, "This report will go behind the *model minority stereotype* in an effort to reveal the complex and diverse realities of Asian Americans and Pacific Islander students" (p. xii, italics added). The report is comprised of four chapters and is thirty-two pages in length. Chapter 1 addresses AAPI diversity and educational attainment and achievement. Chapter 2 examines racism and AAPI experience. Chapter 3 addresses policy, and Chapter 4 shares recommendations for school personnel and education advocates. The report shares resources that scholar practitioners will want to consult. Moreover, the report includes many endnote citations that model minority scholars may want to locate. This report can be used in teacher education courses. Pre-service teachers should read the report to better understand why a "positive" stereotype proves challenging for AAPIs.

Lee, P. A & Ying, Y. (2001). Asian American adolescents' academic achievement: A look behind the model minority image. *Journal of Human Behavior in the Social Environment, 3*(3/4), 35–48.

***Lee and Ying's (2001) article is on Asian-American adolescents' attitudes and behavior regarding academic achievement from the perspectives of the 153 adolescent subjects. The authors analyzed entries to an essay contest, "Growing Up Asian American" and found that fewer than half the adolescents reported a positive attitude toward academic achievement. In contrast, a great majority of them reported that they engaged in behaviors that would enhance their academic achievement. In the authors' analysis of the essays, however, they also found significant distress among the adolescents who were striving to achieve academically. Their co-authored article also appears as a chapter in *Psychosocial Aspects of the Asian-American Experience: Diversity Within Diversity* [Lee, P. A, & Ying, Y. (2001). Asian American adolescents' academic achievement: A look behind the model minority image. In N. G. Choi (Ed.), *Psychosocial aspects of the Asian-American experience: Diversity within diversity* (pp. 35–48). New York, NY: Haworth Press.].

Lew, J. (2002, May). The truth behind the model minority. *YWCA Newsletter of the City of New York Flushing Branch, 163,* 1–2.

***Lew's (2002) piece appears in a *YWCA Newsletter* (New York) and discusses how the model minority label is not always accurate for Korean Americans. According to Lew (2002), "Model minority discourse of Asian Americans undermines the structural barriers such as poverty, racism, and access to quality schooling that all students need in order to achieve academically" (p. 1). In her two-page column, Lew (2002) considers an important GED program in operation at the New York YWCA where she was interviewing Koreans and other minority high school drop-outs. According to Lew (2002), community-based efforts such as the YWCA's to address the needs of "at-risk" youth are commendable and extremely necessary. Lew's (2002) newsletter can be cited in scholarly literature reviews given that it is based on ethnographic research she was conducting in New York.

Lew, J. (2004). The "other" story of the model minorities: Korean American high school dropouts in an urban context. *Anthropology of Education Quarterly, 35*(3), 297–311.

***Lew's (2004) article analyzes the experiences of thirty 1.5 generation (immigrants who were born in Korea and moved to the U.S. by the age of nine and second generation (U.S. born) Korean youth (age 16-19) who dropped out of high school. Data for her study was collected at a community center located in Queens, New York. The center served primarily Korean youth and had various program offerings, such as an English-as-a-second-language (ESL) and a General Educational Development (GED) program. Lew's (2004) ethnographic data consisted of youth who were in the center's GED program and were collected through interviews, participant observations, a background survey, and document analysis. What makes the study's data so rich and compelling stems in large part from the fact that the center was "located in one of the most densely populated Chinese and Korean ethnic enclaves in New York" (p. 310). Lew's (2004) interpretation of the data/findings suggests, among other things:

> Although the students internalized the model minority stereotype by connecting successful Asians and Koreans to whiteness, they also resisted such a stereotype for themselves. By distinguishing themselves from wealthy and educated Koreans and Asians who symbolically represented whiteness, they identified themselves with other minorities—a collective term symbolizing downward mobility and struggles with racism and poverty. (p. 310)

Hence, this article can be used in literature reviews on the model minority stereotype, segmented assimilation, and fictive kinship—since the unsuccessful Korean Americans dissociated with Whiteness, opting to identify with other oppressed and marginalized ethnic and racial groups.

Lew, J. (2006). *Asian Americans in class: Charting the achievement gap among Korean American youth.* New York, NY: Teachers College Press.

***This powerful book has received numerous positive reviews (e.g., see Amos, 2008; An, 2007; Bushnell, 2007; Endo, 2009; Louie, 2010). Much of the material contained in *Asian Americans in Class: Charting the Achievement Gap Among Korean American Youth* is based on the ethnographic research of Lew in New York. Lew (2006) says, "Despite the changing demographics, achievement gap, and class variance among them, Asian Americans are nevertheless seen as a *homogeneous group, a model minority* that is uniformly excelling in school and achieving economic mobility" (p. 3, italics added). Readers will also definitely want to read the powerful foreword by Jean Anyon. *Asian Americans in Class* is an important book to cite whenever one is discussing the model minority stereotype.

Lew, J. (2011). Keeping the American dream alive: Model minority discourse of Asian American children. In S. Tozer (Ed.), *Handbook of research in the social foundations of education* (pp. 614–620). New York, NY: Routledge.

***Lew's chapter looks at how structure impacts the social and educational realities of Asian American students. Lew (2011) writes the following:

> The model minority stereotype upholds the ideals of the "American dream" by legitimating deeply held beliefs of individual meritocracy that *negate important structural forces* such as race, class, and gender. After all, the model minority construct was not created by Asian Americans themselves but by the dominant cultural discourse. (p. 614, italics added)

The major argument that Lew (2011) makes here is that the model minority stereotype over-relies on *cultural explanations*, which are explanatorily insufficient since they do not account for *structural forces*. In her words, "[Asian American] school success has often been reduced to simple *cultural* arguments based on individual meritocracy—the values of education, close-knit family and hard work—rather than drawing a more nuanced picture of how these *cultural forces* shift amidst changing social contexts" (p. 615, italics added). Lew (2011) goes on to describe the model minority stereotype "as a hegemonic device" (p. 618) that mythologizes, legitimizes, sustains, and reinforces White supremacy. This easy-to-read chapter draws upon Lew's previous qualitative method research, mainly her case study of two Korean American student groups (high and low achieving) in New York City (see Lew, J. [2006]. *Asian Americans in Class: Charting the Achievement Gap Among Korean American Youth*. New York, NY: Teachers College Press.). The Korean students Lew studied (2006) were either 1.5 or 2nd generation and either attended a competitive magnet high school or a community-based GED program. This chapter is cogent and can be used as a foundational reading in social foundations of education courses.

Li, G. (2005). Other people's success: Impact of the "model minority" myth on underachieving Asian students in North America. *KEDI Journal of Educational Policy, 2*(1), 69–86.

***Li's (2005) article is a case study of an academically underachieving Chinese student—Andy. Li (2005) writes that "because of Andy's behaviors and performance in school, he did not fit the 'model minority' images that the teachers had for Asian students" (p. 79). This led his two teachers to blame the victim, who was Andy. Writes Li (2005):

> Andy did not fit the teachers' assumptions on good Asian students who were often well behaved, obedient, and successful. The teachers attributed Andy's difficulties in learning to Andy himself and his family (i.e., his personality and immaturity, his withdrawal from ESL classes and his constant use of Chinese). (p. 81)

Li's (2005) study highlights an extremely important implication for educators: they "need to be aware of the threat of the 'model minority' myth, and avoid the 'blaming the victims' approach toward students' failure" (p. 83). Teachers and teacher educators should read Li's (2005) piece in order to better understand how the model minority stereotype disservices all Asian American students—high achievers and underachievers.

Liu, X. & Li, G. (2008). Diversity and equity in science education for Asians in North America: Unpacking the model minority myth. In M-W Roth & K. Tobin (Eds.), *The world of science education: Handbook of research in North America* (pp. 369–388). Rotterdam, the Netherlands: SensePublishers.

***Liu and Li's (2008) chapter "Diversity and Equity in Science Education for Asians in North America: Unpacking the Model Minority Myth" examines the uneven science achievement of Asian Americans and Asian Canadians. Liu and Li (2008) write about why it is ironic that a dearth of literature exists on Asian American science achievement considering that the model minority implies that Asians are great scientists and mathematicians. Write Liu and Li (2008), "In this chapter, we tried to dispel the Asian 'model minority' myth by examining issues related to the outcome, input, and fairness and equity in Asian American and Canadian science education" (p. 383). Their findings suggest "that there exist vast within and across-group differences in science achievements and outcomes among the Asian population in North America" (Liu & Li, 2008, p. 383). This book chapter is helpful in that it connects the model minority stereotype with science achievement, something few have done. This chapter can be used in literature reviews and also with pre-service and in-service science educators and/or science teacher educators.

Lo, M. (2010, September 6). Model minority revisited. *The Asian Reporter, 20*(23), 6.

***Lo's (2010) one-page column appeared in the opinion section of the *Asian Reporter.* This op-ed addresses her lived experiences as an Asian American child, as well as her experiences later in life as an Asian American mother. Lo (2010) first shares about her upbringing as a child. She indicates she had a "type-A" personality, which fueled her desire to do well in school, and which, by extension, also caused her naturally to study a lot. As a parent of an Asian American girl, Lo (2010) later describes a realization that she came to when she allowed her young daughter to watch YouTube videos of young children playing the violin. After viewing the violin videos and reading many of the comments left by the viewers, Lo (2010) realized that the great majority of the comments on YouTube supported the idea that Asian kids are model minorities. Lo (2010) observed that the majority of the comments were culturally-based and linked Asian talent in violin and academics with parental involvement and an Asian culture that valued success. In her column, she clarifies why and how the myth of the Asian model minority is limiting to Asian Americans. She writes the following: "These comments [made on YouTube] essentially rehearse the same stereotypes about Asians as the model minority: Asian parents are strict and humorless and place excessive pressure on their children to succeed; Asian kids are passive, docile, and nerds; Asians value academics and music above all else; Asian kids are mechanical mimics who lack creativity and imagination; [and] Asians are not independent thinkers" (Lo, 2010, p. 6). This short article can be used as a warm up exercise or as a conversation starter in college classrooms. Again, like the other citations contained in *The Model Minority Stereotype: Demystifying Asian American Success*, Lo's (2010) column can be used as a citation for literature reviews. Most importantly though, it clearly asserts that not all Asian Americans are doing well, which makes this piece of writing important for academic and lay audiences to read.

Lou, R. (1989). Model minority? Getting behind the veil. *Change, 21*(6), 16–17.

***Lou's (1989) article tackles two issues that hide behind the "veil," or statistics that indicate Asian Americans are model minorities. Lou (1989) focuses on two topics: Asian American students who are English Language Learners, and the immense amount of parental pressure Asian Americans experience. Lou (1989) states that "evidence to the contrary [of the model minority label] is seldom sought out or welcome" (p. 16). Lou (1989) goes on to write, "American higher education is familiar with the concept of 'special services for the disadvantaged.' But it can't quite comprehend its 'model minority' as fitting the label" (p. 17). Lou's (1989) short piece draws much-needed attention to Asian Americans' language needs as English Language Learners. This article will most likely be used for and cited in literature reviews.

Ma, Y. (2010). Model minority, model for whom? An investigation of Asian American students in science/engineering. *AAPI Nexus, 8*(1), 43–73.

***Ma's (2010) article, using data from the 1988 National Education Longitudinal Study (NELS:88), examines Asian Americans' attainment of bachelor's degrees in science and engineering, their expectations, and their self-perceptions. Ma (2010) asks, for whom are Asian Americans a model? In other words, do Asian Americans truly constitute a model minority? In some respects, Ma's (2010) findings support the idea that Asian Americans are successful in science, technology, engineering, and mathematics (STEM) fields, but she points out an important possibility. Although her findings indicated that Asian American students had the highest expectation for majoring in STEM, and also had the highest rate of persistence in degree completion, Ma (2010) "found that Asian American students are not in advantageous social positions—they have less cultural capital than their counterparts at comparable socioeconomic levels" (p. 67), implying "that Asian American students and their families are consciously choosing STEM fields to circumvent the limitations of their cultural capital." She concludes her well-argued and researched study with the following caveat: "Therefore, the choice and the attainment of degrees in STEM fields among Asian American youth *seem to be a success story.* But behind the façade lie many disadvantages, in the adaptations and compromises that Asian American students make" (Ma, 2010, p. 67, italics added). Ma's (2010) article can be used in teacher preparation programs in order to caution teachers from believing that Asian American students openly select classes in STEM due to interest, rather than out of necessity. It also is an important article for those who work in fields such as educational psychology, college admission, counseling, and advising. This article raises the implication that Asian American students might want to study other fields, but might self-limit themselves due to their lack of cultural capital.

Mooko, D. R. (1995). The Asian American college student as model minority: The myth, the deception and the paradox. *The Vermont Connection, 16,* 47–57.

***This article explores the influence of the model minority myth on Asian American college students. According to the model minority myth, Asian Americans are "over-represented" on the campuses of many elite universities and colleges. However, such an assumption denies that institutional racism exists for Asian Americans, which leads to the voices of Asian Americans not being heard. Many of the arguments made in this article have been made by other scholars. For instance, Mooko's thesis is reminiscent of Takagi's (1992) book *The Retreat from Race: Asian-American Admissions and Racial Politics.* This article can be used as a reading in introductory educational foundations courses, as well as in Asian American studies courses. Mooko, a fourth generation Japanese American, presents these arguments in a clear, accessible way.

Nadal, K. L., Pituc, S. T., Johnston, M. P., & Esparrago, T. (2010). Overcoming the model minority myth: Experiences of Filipino American graduate students. *Journal of College Student Development, 51*(6), 694–706.

***This research-in-brief paper explores the experiences of Filipino American graduate students utilizing consensual qualitative research (CQR) methodology. Twenty-nine Filipino Americans who were currently or recently enrolled in a U.S. graduate school program participated in this exploratory study by taking an open-ended on-line survey. This study intentionally focused on Filipino American graduate students' experiences because there is "little research focusing on the unique experiences of this group, particularly in higher education" (p. 694, Nadal et al., 2010). The results were contextualized within the following five domains: (1) deficiencies and lack of resources for Filipino American graduate students; (2) positive experiences as Filipino American graduate students; (3) experiences with support systems; (4) experiences due to race, ethnicity, and racism; and (5) recommendations for improving Filipino Americans' graduate school experiences. Nadal et al.'s (2010) findings importantly "underscore the fallacy of the model minority myth, which contends that Asian Americans uniformly experience academic success and personal well-being" (p. 702). He and his co-authors go on to declare that their "study illustrates *the hetereogeneity of Asian Americans' experiences*" (p. 702, italics added), stressing that "research must disaggregate Asian American populations in order to understand between-group and/or ethnic differences and their impact on educational experiences" (p. 695). College professors, educators, and higher education student affairs administrators will benefit from reading this article. Nadal et al. (2010) conclude with the following caveat: "Professors and educators must recognize *the fallacies of the model minority myth*, particularly with Filipino Americans, while understanding the detriments of stereotyping groups in this manner" (p. 705, italics added). The findings of this study support the notion that Filipino American graduate students lack institutional and faculty support, while experiencing isolation and racism in the form of microaggressions; therefore, these students would benefit greatly from more Filipino American professors and university administrators being recruited by university hiring personnel.

The National Commission on Asian American and Pacific Islander Research in Education (CARE). (2008). Asian Americans and Pacific Islanders. Facts, not fiction: Setting the record straight. Retrieved from http://professionals.collegeboard.com/profdownload/08-0608-AAPI.pdf

***This report sets the record straight in terms of three fallacies about Asian American and Pacific Islanders (AAPIs): (1) AAPI students are "taking over" U.S. higher education; (2) AAPIs are concentrated only in selective four-year universities; and (3) AAPIs are a homogenous racial group with uniformity in educational and financial attainment, culture, religion, and histories (p. iii).

In terms of the first fiction, the truth is: (a) The increasing presence of AAPI students parallels increases that other student populations have experienced; (b) The AAPI student population is concentrated in a small percentage of institutions, giving the false impression of high enrollment in higher education overall; and (c) AAPIs have a wide range of academic interests including the social sciences, humanities, and education as opposed to just science, technology, engineering, and math (STEM).

In terms of the second fiction, the truth is: (a) AAPI students are evenly distributed in two-year and four-year institutions, with the majority attending public institutions; (b) AAPIs have a wide range of scores on standardized tests, which afford different levels of eligibility and competitiveness in selective admissions; (c) AAPI enrollment in public two-year community colleges is increasing at a faster rate than their enrollment in four-year colleges; and (d) AAPI community college enrollment is increasing fastest in the Midwest and the South.

Lastly, in terms of the third fiction, the truth is: (a) AAPIs are an ethnically diverse population; (b) AAPI students and their families encompass many different languages and dialects; (c) Immigration histories have an effect on the needs and assets of different AAPI communities; and (d) Economic, social, and cultural capital vary greatly among AAPIs.

This report helps readers envision the true realities of the AAPI population in the United States.

The National Commission on Asian American and Pacific Islander Research in Education (CARE). (2010). *Federal higher education policy priorities and the Asian American and Pacific Islander community.* Retrieved from http://apiasf.org/CARErepor+t/2010_CARE_report.pdf

***This report indicates that the model minority stereotype promotes a false narrative: "The dominant narrative about Asian Americans *and* Pacific Islanders in higher education is that they are a model minority—a racial group with disproportionately high enrollment in highly selective, four-year institutions and such academic fields as science, technology, engineering, and mathematics (STEM)" (p. 6, italics in original). The false narrative is disempowering to Asian Pacific Americans since "the reality is the prevailing model minority myth is inaccurate, misleading, and damaging for the AAPI population" (CARE, 2010, p. 3). This CARE (2010) report addresses three policy areas of consequence for APAs: (1) higher education, workforce development, and the AAPI community; (2) APA students in the community college sector; and (3) lessons learned from Asian American and Native American Pacific Islander-Serving Institutions (AANAPISIs). Informative, descriptive, helpful, this report can be used by policy analysts as well as lawmakers.

The National Commission on Asian American and Pacific Islander Research in Education (CARE). (2011). *The relevance of Asian Americans & Pacific Islanders in the college completion agenda*. Retrieved from http://apiasf.org/CAREreport/2011_CARE_Report.pdf

***This CARE report contains information on the size and demography of the Asian Pacific American population. It deconstructs the educational attainment of the Asian Pacific American population. One major obstacle of the model minority stereotype is that it homogenizes Asian Americans, which is why this report is helpful in asserting the heterogeneity of the population. According to CARE (2011), "Disaggregated data on the AAPI population reveal a wide range of demographic characteristics that are unlike any other racial group in America with regard to their heterogeneity" (p. 6). This report can be used when examining higher education policy as well as when analyzing whether or not the educational needs of APA students are being considered.

Pang, V. O., Han, P. P., & Pang, J. M. (2011). Asian American and Pacific Islander students: Equity and the achievement gap. *Educational Researcher, 40*(8), 378–389.

*** This article's literature review points out that not only do individuals discriminate against Asian Americans, but so do institutions. This article problematizes the idea that Asian Americans rise above discrimination. Using Asian American and Pacific Islander (AAPI) seventh-grade-students in the state of California that took the California Achievement Tests Sixth Edition Survey (CAT/6) between 2003 and 2008, testing for mean reading and math test score differences the researchers (Pang, Han, & Pang, 2011) found "statistically significant differences among the academic performance levels of AAPIs and their white counterparts" (p. 380). Among these differences was the fact that in math the mean for White Americans was statistically significantly lower than the mean for the AAPI student aggregate. In reading, the White American mean was found to be statistically significantly higher than the AAPI aggregate mean. This study contributes uniquely to the literature on AAPI student achievement because it "is the first large-scale achievement study of AAPI students" (p. 384). Since the researchers examine the academic performance of 13 AAPI disaggregated ethnic groups using one-way analysis of variance (ANOVA), readers can easily decipher differences in achievement. The multiple comparisons and post hoc tests allow for readers and researchers of the model minority to see that performance varies greatly among the different ethnic subgroups. As Pang, Han, and Pang (2011) conclude, "Academic performances in reading and math differed significantly across the 13 AAPI groups" (p. 382). Moreover, they state that "the use of the large AAPI aggregate is an impediment to providing AAPI students with educational equity because statistically significant achievement differences among AAPI ethnic groups remain hidden" (p. 384), contributing to the model minority myth. Pang and her colleagues (2011) conclude the following: "This research refutes the model minority myth according to which all AAPI groups perform at high levels. Our findings indicate that the AAPI population demonstrates a spectrum of performance, showing that ethnic subgroups have diverse strengths and weaknesses" (pp. 384–385).

Park, G. C. & Lee, S. J. (2010). The model minority myth stereotype and the underachiever: Academic and social struggles of underachieving Korean immigrant high school students. In R. Saran & R. Diaz (Eds.), *Beyond stereotypes: Minority children of immigrants in urban schools* (pp. 13–27). Boston, MA: Sense Publishers.

***"According to the rhetoric of the model minority stereotype, those who are not realizing the Americans dream through success in schools have simply failed to take advantage of the opportunities open to all. Thus, the picture of Asian American success was a message to Americans that discrimination can be overcome with hard work" (Park & Lee, 2010, p. 14).

Building on the foundation of that observation, Park and Lee (2010) describe in detail how the model minority stereotype, in part, shapes the ability of Asian Americans to access academic and social capital. The data for Park and Lee's (2010) chapter came from a one and a half year ethnographic study that took place in an inner city high school in the Midwest. Park and Lee (2010) focus on the immigrant students from Korea who were identified by teachers and other Korean students as facing academic and/or social difficulties. The question that guided their investigation was, "How does the model minority stereotype affect the school experiences of underachieving Korean immigrant students?" Chief among their investigation's many important findings is the recognition that the model minority stereotype does the following five things: (1) masks obstacles faced by Korean immigrant students; (2) contributes to students' self-silencing; (3) punishes underachieving Korean students who did not conform or fit into the stereotype; (4) has social as well as academic consequences for Korean students; and (5) influences Korean immigrant students' (in)abilities to access co-ethnic social capital (read: "good" students who embraced the model minority stereotype were able to tap into capital, whereas "bad" students, those who did not fit into the stereotype's description, were summarily shut out from such access).

Park and Lee (2010) "found that the *homogenizing* effect of the [model minority] stereotype denied much needed service to the underachieving students because the teachers didn't recognize differences in the Asian students' academic needs" (p. 25, italics added). Their chapter contributes to the model minority stereotype literature because it makes known that the stereotype needs to be better understood by scholars, students, and Asian Americans. The researchers declare that "the damaging effects of the model minority stereotype on Asian Americans must be understood not only by the students themselves, but also the school staff who take part in constructing it in school" (Park & Lee, 2010, p. 26). Consequently, those in a student affairs graduate program or those already working in the field will find this an important reading for their professional practice.

Park, E. J. W. & Park, J. S. W. (2005). Engineering the model minority. In E. J. W. Park & J. S. W. Park, *Probationary Americans: Contemporary immigration policies and the shaping of Asian American communities* (pp. 97–106). New York, NY: Routledge.

***Park and Park's (2005) chapter comes from their dual-authored *Probationary Americans: Contemporary Immigration Policies and the Shaping of Asian American Communities,* which traces the recent history of U.S. immigration law and shows how it is shaping the political and economic fortunes of Asian Americans. They discuss how immigration law—the shift in awarding H-1B visas—engineers the model minority stereotype. Through permitting only selective immigrants to enter the United States, the United States effectively creams talented Asians from their home countries. Park and Park (2005) indicate that most H-1B beneficiaries are already-educated and already-talented South Asian Indians: According to Park and Park (2005), in 2001 "close to half of all H-1B recipients were South Asian Indian" (p. 98). These South Asians who work in engineering and high-technology serve to reinforce the widely held notion that Asians are "model minorities." This book chapter documents how the model minority is engineered through immigration policy. It is a helpful source of information because it provides insights on the impact immigration policy plays on engineering the model minority stereotype. Literature reviews should include this cogent chapter.

Peng, L. (2005, December). The "model minority" checklist. *Hardboiled: The Asian American newsmagazine, 9*(3), 5. Retrieved on March 16, 2012, from http://hardboiled.berkeley.edu/issues/93/93.pdf

***Peng (2005) addresses the model minority myth by tackling three items that represent what she considers to be the "model minority" checklist: (1) a college degree equals success for Asian Americans; (2) a good income equals a comfortable income for Asian Americans; and (3) Asian Americans have perfect families. Peng (2005) addresses the "glass ceiling" that Asian Americans bump up against and writes that "Southeast Asians hold the highest high school dropout rate in the nation" (p. 5). Peng (2005) also indicates that "Asian Americans, particularly new immigrants, are more likely to be concentrated in metropolitan areas such as New York, where the cost of living is much higher" (p. 5). Furthermore, Peng (2005) informs her readers that "Asian American teenage gang activity and violence has been on the rise" (p. 5). Thus, she argues against the notion that Asian Americans represent a model minority. Peng (2005) concludes with the following suggestion: "Perhaps this shows us that not all Asian Americans fit the model minority checklist" (p. 5). This article can be used in literature reviews for studies that demystify the model minority stereotype.

Rohrlick, J., Alvarado, D., & Zaruba, K. (1998, May). *From the model minority to the invisible minority: Asian & Pacific American students in higher education research.* Paper presented at the Association for Institutional Research (AIR), Minneapolis, MN. ERIC Document ID: ED422820.

***Rohrlick, Alvarado, and Zaruba's (1998) paper was presented at the thirty-eighth Annual Forum of the Association for Institutional Research (AIR) held in Minneapolis, Minnesota, May 17-20, 1998, and was selected to be included in the ERIC Collection of AIR Forum papers. Rohrlick, Alvarado, and Zaruba's (1998) paper shares the results of a survey administered to graduating seniors from the University of Michigan, Ann Arbor in 1996. Their paper begins with a nice overview of the model minority stereotype, followed by reasons why the model minority stereotype is false. Prior to sharing the results of their survey ($n = 1,300$), they provide empirical evidence found in the literature that challenges the model minority myth. Rohrlick, Alvarado, and Zaruba (1998) administered their survey to seniors who were graduating, finding that Asian Americans who responded had less than idyllic undergraduate experiences. The implications are great for how Asian American college students have been rendered invisible by failing to conduct research on this population:

> Given their excellent enrollment rates and retention rates, and the widespread media attention paid to APA educational success, it may be too easy to write them off as a *"model minority"* and assume that they mirror majority students, a group equally deserving of our attention. Higher education schol-

ars are beginning to realize that the so-called *"model" minority* has become a nearly *"invisible" minority* in research. (Rohrlick, Alvarado, & Zaruba, 1998, p. 16, italics added)

This conference paper can be readily used with other model minority counter-narrative scholarship.

Saran, R. (2007). Model minority imaging in New York: The situation with second generation Asian Indian learners in middle and secondary schools. *The Anthropologist: Special Issue, 2,* 67–79. Retrieved on January 10, 2012, from http://www.krepublishers.com/06-Special%20Volume-Journal/T-Anth-00-Special%20Volumes/Anth-00-Special%20Issues/Anth-SI-02-Indian-Diaspora-2007.htm

***The model minority myth is an enduring problem social scientists have attempted to discredit for decades. Saran's (2007) critical ethnographic study attempted to find contradiction and complexity within the model minority stereotype. Drawing on family interviews and interviews with second generation Asian Indian students from two urban elite high schools and one high performing middle school in New York , Saran first outlines the model minority in a diversity of ways, including the following about the myth: (1) its ideological connotations, (2) its discourse of stereotyping and labeling, (3) its perpetuation of ethnic rivalry and racism, and (4) its hegemonic condition. Saran (2007) found that the Asian Indian students— high school and middle school—experienced stress and tension due to the model minority status cast upon them. Some students felt that if they did not live up to the expectations of the model minority they would lose their identity. This article is beneficial to middle and high school teachers, guidance counselors, and health service providers. The undue pressure caused by the myth can create educational, mental, and relational problems for Asian American youth.

Stanley, J. C. (1988, March/April). The gifted child today: Do Asian Americans tend to reason better mathematically than White Americans. *The Gifted Children Today, 11,* 32.

***This article supports the model minority myth. Stanley's (1988) analysis can be problematized since it uses *aggregated* SAT scores and not *disaggregated* scores. Readers of Stanley (1988) might consider consulting Teranishi (2002) to better understand why aggregation of test scores is problematic. Readers will also want to read Bracey's (1999) Asian math gene article and Bracey's (2005) Asian Indian spelling gene article.

Teranishi, R. T. (2002). The myth of the super minority: Misconceptions about Asian Americans. *The College Board Review, 195,* 17–21.

***Teranishi's (2002) article grapples with common misconceptions about Asian Americans, such as that they are overrunning prestigious colleges and universities; they do not experience poverty; and they are "super minorities." In Teranishi's (2002) professional opinion, "The Asian American population has been misrepresented in educational policy and research because they have usually been categorized and treated as a single, homogenous racial group" (p. 18). As a result, aggregation of statistics inevitably leads to the masking of Asian American homogeneity and the distortion of Asian American subgroup differences. The Asian American population "is composed of multicultural, multilingual, and multiethnic people who have different socioeconomic profiles, immigrant histories, and political outlooks" (Teranishi, 2002, p. 19). Teranishi's (2002) article focuses mainly on the argument that the model minority or "super minority" stereotype homogenizes Asian Americans. The implication of the article is that researchers and data analysts must disaggregate Asian American groups in order to reveal and better understand what the statistics/figures truly indicate.

Teranishi, R. T. (2010). *Asians in the ivory tower: Dilemmas of racial inequality in American higher education.* New York, NY: Teachers College Press.

***Teranishi's (2010) *Asians in the Ivory Tower* examines quantitative data procured from the Higher Education Research Institute (HERI) at the University of California at Los Angeles (UCLA), the National Center for Education Statistics (NCES), the U.S. Census Bureau, and the Office of Immigration Statistics, in order to problematize the model minority stereotype for Asian American and Pacific Islanders (AAPIs). As a result of his analysis, *Asians in the Ivory Tower* has been positively reviewed (e.g., see Chou, 2012; Nguyen, 2012). Teranishi is the principal investigator of the National Commission on Asian American and Pacific Islander Research in Education at New York University (e.g., see CARE, 2008, 2010, 2011).

Tran, N. & Birman, D. (2010). Questioning the model minority: Studies of Asian American Academic performance. *Asian American Journal of Psychology, 1*(2), 106–118.

***The purpose of Tran and Birman's (2010) study was to "review the academic performance literature among Asian Americans to evaluate the extent to which empirical research has *debunked* the image of Asian Americans as 'model minorities'" (p. 107, italics added). Their article is based on the analysis of 45 articles published between 1990 and 2008 on Asian Americans and academic performance. Tran and Birman's (2010) research questions were the following: (1) "How do Asian American students perform relative to other groups?"; (2) "Are Asian American students achieving academic success because of cultural values in education and hard work?"; and (3) "Do Asian American students achieve high academic performance unimpeded by barriers like racial discrimination?" With regard to question number one, Tran and Birman conclude that no definitive conclusions can be drawn; however, studies do need to control for ethnic composition of samples and generational status. In response to their second research question, Tran and Birman (2010) state the following: "Research does suggest that Asian Americans work hard and have high educational expectations. While it is likely that high educational expectations are cultural, it is *not clear* if they are a product of Asian culture, American culture, or something else" (p. 111, italics added). Lastly, Tran and Birman (2010) respond that since "discrimination [a sociopolitical factor] has not been considered as a predictor in comparative studies with Whites" (p. 112), research question three is almost impossible to answer given the extant literature. Tran and Birman (2010) conclude their article by outlining why a review of the literature on academic achievement and the model minority stereotype reveals that the myth is a "deficit model perspective" and why future model minority research must offer "non-deficit-oriented explanations for the academic performance of Asian Americans" (p. 114), which, they go on to write, "may help avoid perpetuating the deficit model view of Asian Americans and yield a more balanced view" (p. 114). This article is highly beneficial due to the conceptual and methodological concerns it raises for research on Asian American academic performance, such as the following: (1) the confounding of race, ethnic origin, and generational status; (2) the need to attend to sociopolitical factors as opposed to over-relying on cultural explanations; (3) the ways in which the deficit model perpetuates the lower status of Asian Americans; (4) the potential pitfalls of small sample sizes and statistical shortcomings in current research; and (5) the need to conduct culturally complex research by accounting for ethnicity. In summary, "this review suggests that in studies of Asian American academic performance [emic and etic] perspectives are unbalanced" (p. 116), write Tran and Birman (2010), and "the field [of education research] has overwhelmingly relied on an etic approach" (p. 116). This article will be valuable for methodologists interested in combating the model minority myth. Moreover, teachers and scholars looking for a resource that synthesizes and reviews studies of Asian American academic performance will find this article noteworthy.

Victoria, N. A. (2007). A+ does not mean all Asians: The model minority myth and implications for higher education. *The Vermont Connection, 28,* 80–88.

***This article explores the model minority and its implications for higher education. Victoria (2007) reports that the model minority myth renders the oppression Asian Americans experience invisible, while it simultaneously erases the uniqueness of Asian American students. "Another error of the model minority stereotype," writes Victoria (2007), "is that it imposes a single classification on these varied and disparate communities while internally implementing a 'divide and conquer' mentality" (p. 82). Victoria

(2007) alerts his readers that there is a glass ceiling for Asian Americans and that Asian Americans "in the United States make significantly less than their Caucasian counterparts. They [Asian Americans] also receive fewer promotions" (p. 83). This article, like many before it, alludes to the *bimodal distribution* of Asian American student performance, and why median income does not correctly assess Asian American household income due to patterns of geographical settlement and larger family sizes. Victoria (2007) is most concerned with increasing the number of Asian American leaders in higher education. In order to accomplish this goal, Victoria (2007) asserts that "institutions need to support [Asian American] practitioners in their professional development" (p. 86). This article is relevant for scholars, practitioners, and those in the field of student affairs as well as for educational sociologists and those studying educational stratification. Higher education administrators need to understand that "by the field's perpetuation of the 'model minority' myth, limited number of [Asian American] administrators will remain" (p. 86).

Wallitt, R. (2008). Cambodian invisibility: Students lost between the "achievement gap" and the "model minority." *Multicultural Perspectives, 10*(1), 3–9.

***Wallitt (2008) conducted tape-recorded interviews with Cambodians (five males and nine females) between the ages of 16 and 23. At the time of data collection some participants were still in high school, while others had dropped out or gone on to college. The model minority stereotype was found to impact teachers' perceptions of Cambodian students. Wallitt (2008) writes about "teachers who did not recognize that their students were Cambodian and how that was significant [and] contributed to students' feelings of invisibility" (p. 4). The article suggests that teachers can misread Cambodian behavior in school. According to Wallitt (2008), Cambodian students are reticent to raise their hands to participate, unless called on, showing respect for their teachers. Teachers may misread Cambodian students' participation reticence as uncaring and, ironically, conflate the students' cultural expression of respect (e.g., not raising their hand even though they may know the answer) with laziness. Further complications include the cultural mismatch between Cambodian and American mainstream attitudes and perspectives toward education: "The *Cambodian perspective* that what happens in school is the responsibility of the teacher is significantly different than the *U.S. attitude* that parents are supposed to be involved in their children's education, causing confusion and criticism from both sides" (Wallitt, 2008, p. 7, italics added). This article assists readers in understanding how cultural discontinuity can impact the learning and teaching of Cambodian students. Wallitt (2008) indicates that it was a function of their "invisibility" that caused certain Cambodian students in her study to drop out of high school. Wallitt (2008) found that teachers in her study often label Cambodian students in either/or terms: "model minority" or uneducable, deviant, or dropout. This article should be read by K–12 teachers who *are*, or *want to be*, culturally relevant practitioners/ pedagogues since the "model minority" stereotype affects teachers' perceptions of Asian American (Cambodian) students. The article is written in accessible language making it quick and easy to read.

Wan, Y. (1996, November). *Bearing the image of model minority: An inside look behind the classroom door.* Paper presented at the Annual Meeting of the National Association for Multicultural Education, St. Paul, MN. ERIC ED404432

***Wan's (1996) paper sought to "challenge the stereotypical image of Asian-Pacific American students" (p. 3) as model minorities. The paper explores the diversity of the Asian-Pacific American student population and provides recommendations and strategies that promote equitable classroom participation (cultivating cross-cultural competence, developing curriculum, and connecting the home and school). Wan (1996) states, "If teachers treat APA students based on existing assumptions, it may not only perpetuate the stereotypes, but also limit the students' opportunity to fully develop their personal, social, and academic skills" (p. 18). This conference paper can certainly be included in a literature review, but it also can be used in the college classroom, especially in teacher education courses that are designed for multicultural education.

Weaver, S. (2009). Perfect in America: Implications of the model minority myth on the classroom. *Colleagues, 4*(2), 8–11.

***Weaver (2009) metes out reasons why the model minority stereotype is inaccurate and examines the implications for students and the classroom, namely why the stereotype influences teachers' perceptions of their Asian American students. Weaver (2009) writes the following: "Due to the prevalence of the model minority myth and the overrepresentation of Asian Americans in academically gifted programs, students who struggle or have genuine learning disabilities are neglected by the educational system" (p. 10). This article is a must read for teachers and school administrators. Weaver (2009) writes with accessible, non-technical language, making this an article teachers and educational clinicians will want to read, benefiting all of those in the classroom.

Wong, M. G. (1980). Model students? Teachers' perceptions and expectations of their Asian and White students. *Sociology of Education, 53*(4), 236–247.

***This article examines teacher's perceptions of their Asian and White elementary and secondary students. The San Francisco subsample used in this study was selected by the Program Research in Integrated Multi-Ethnic Education (PRIME) of the University of California, Riverside. Using a total of 852 elementary students (466 Whites and 386 Asians) and 311 secondary students (150 Whites and 161 Asians), this study found that "Asian students at both the elementary and secondary educational levels are perceived by their teachers as 'model students,' that they are seen as more academically competent and more emotionally stable than their white counterparts" (p. 245). According to Wong (1980), "Because Asian students are perceived by their teachers as 'model students,' particularly as more academically competent than their white counterparts, teachers have higher educational expectations of them, which in turn, probably influence the Asian student's later *higher educational attainment*" (p. 246, italics added).

Woo, D. (1997). Asian American success is a myth. In W. Dudley (Ed.), *Asian Americans: Opposing viewpoints* (pp. 213–222). San Diego, CA: Greenhaven Press.

***Woo's (1997) book chapter "Asian American Success Is a Myth" was reprinted from [Woo, D. (1989). The gap between striving and achieving: The case of Asian American women. In Asian Women United of California (Ed.), *Making waves: An anthology of writings by and about Asian American women* (pp. 185–194). Boston, MA: Beacon Press.]. According to Woo (1997), the model minority stereotype "programs us to ignore structural barriers and inequities and insist that any problems are simply due to cultural values or failure of individual effort" (p. 214). Her chapter focuses on Asian American women. Specifically, Woo (1997) notes that "Asian American women are more likely than Anglo women to work fulltime and year round" (p. 217). Moreover, Woo (1997) points out the unequal returns on formal education for Asian Americans, especially for females. Woo's (1997) chapter examines achievement and reward. In other words, Asian American females' inequitable incomes and restricted choice of occupations lead Woo (1997) to declare that Asian American success is a myth. Woo's (1997) chapter could easily be assigned in a women's study course as a required reading.

Yang, K. (2004). Southeast Asian American children: Not the "model minority." *Future of Children, 14*(2), 127–133.

***Yang (2004) shows how aggregated data treats Asian Americans as one large undifferentiated group, which hides many unique needs of Asian American subgroups. This article discusses why Southeast Asian Americans are not model minorities. In particular, Yang (2004) points out that Hmong Americans' history of persecution, displacement, and war, and their current limited English skills, make them a vulnerable Asian American population. Yang (2004) juxtaposes the *policy-level* with the *practitioner-level*. Policy overlooks Southeast Asian Americans' educational needs, considering this population to be constitutive of a model minority. On the other hand, *practitioners* (teachers) frequently discriminate by holding low educational expectations for their Southeast Asian American students. Southeast Asian students are therefore, alienated in schools. Curricula does not acknowledge their language, culture, or contributions, and equally troubling is that "there are not enough Southeast Asian American teachers and staff in educational institutions" (Yang, 2004, p. 130). Yang (2004) writes that "policymakers, educators, and community leaders must recognize that Southeast Asian Americans are not part of some fictional 'model minority' that succeeds easily in the United States" (p. 131). Yang's (2004) article concludes with four helpful recommendations that will assist Asian Americans (Southeast Asians): (1) the disaggregation and dissemination of data on Asian Americans; (2) the promotion of Southeast Asian studies, courses, and personnel; (3) the support of community organizations that work for and on behalf of Asian Americans; and (4) the creation of new systems for financial and technical support for Asian Americans. Because it avoids using overly technical language, this article will be extremely useful to policymakers, practitioners, grant-makers, advocates, the media, and students of public policy.

Yang, W. (2011, May 16). Paper tigers: What happens to all the Asian-American overachievers when the test-taking ends? *New York Magazine, 44*(6), 22, 24, 26, 28, 94.

***Yang's (2011) feature article in the *New York Magazine* addresses such topics as (1) the "bamboo ceiling," an invisible barrier that maintains a pyramidal racial and power structure throughout corporate America; (2) the "unconscious bias" directed at Asian Americans; (3) the practice of "White flight" whereby Whites flee from residential/educational loci where Asian Americans are perceived to be too numerous; and (4) "tiger parenting." Yang's attitude is quite revolutionary: since the "bamboo ceiling" appears not to be caused by racism, Asian Americans must become risk-taking-social-dynamic-understanding-rule-breakers. Yang references Amy Chua's *Battle Hymn of a Tiger Mom* and declares, "If the Bamboo Ceiling is ever going to break, it's probably going to have less to do with any form of behavior assimilation than with the emergence of *risk-takers* whose success obviates the need for Asians to meet someone else's behavioral standard [the model minority stereotype]" (p. 94, italics added). Yang's anti-model-minority attitude that Asian values should be prized can be seen when he writes the following:

> Let me summarize my feelings toward Asian values: *Fuck* filial piety. *Fuck* grade-grubbing. *Fuck* Ivy League mania. *Fuck* deference to authority. *Fuck* humility and hard work. *Fuck* harmonious relations. *Fuck* sacrificing for the future. *Fuck* earnest, striving middle-class servility. (p. 24, italics added)

Ying, Y., Lee, P. A., Tsai, J. L., Hung, Y., Lin, M., & Wan, C. T. (2001). Asian American college students as model minorities: An examination of their overall competence. *Cultural Diversity & Ethnic Minority Psychology, 7*(1), 59–74. Retrieved from http://www-psych.stanford.edu/~tsailab/PDF/AA%20College%20Students.pdf

***Ying et al.'s (2001) article shares the results of their study conducted on a sample of 642 undergraduate college students attending the University of California, Berkeley, who were enrolled in psychology courses in the spring of 1995. The sample included Asian (Chinese, Korean, Filipino, South Asian, Japanese, Vietnamese, and other Asian), as well as White, African American, and multiracial students. Interested in investigating and assessing the appropriateness of the model minority stereotype, Ying et al. (2001) carried out an empirical analysis of "overall competence" by administering the Sense of Coherence Questionnaire to study participants. Bivariate and multivariate statistical analyses resulted in several interesting findings that do not support the appropriateness of the model minority characterization. First, Asian students were found to have fewer cross-racial friendships. In other words, "controlling for the demographic variables gender, birthplace, age, and SES, Asian Americans had significantly fewer numbers of cross-racial groups in their friendship network than students from all other racial groups" (Ying et al., 2001, p. 67). Second, "Asian Americans reported a significantly lower sense of coherence than Whites" (Ying et al., 2001, p. 68). These two findings indicate that if the definition of success is extended beyond the academic realm, Asian Americans should not be considered to be constitutive of a model minority. Furthermore, as Ying et al. (2001) point out, "excelling in the classroom does not implicate greater competence in real-life situations" (p. 70). This article is a noteworthy contribution to the corpus of literature on the model minority stereotype given that it broadens the term "success" to areas besides academics.

Yong-Jin, W. (1994). "Model minority" strategy and Asian Americans' tactics. *Korea Journal, 34*(2), 57–66.

***Yong-Jin's (1994) article questions the model minority "strategy" or discourse through Korean Americans. Yong-Jin (1994) indicates the following:

> The "Model Minority" discourse views as an ideal the acculturation and assimilation of the dominant white culture. Thus the discourse attempts to create a replica of white, middle-class Americans from an assortment of racialized indicators. The ideology of the American status quo is the glue holding Asian-Americans together, making them cohere as model minorities. *Thus, Asian-Americans are not only an ideal to be imitated, but an imitation of an ideal.* (p. 59, italics added)

Yong-Jin (1994) effectively explains the many implications of the model minority discourse, specifically its cause and consequence for the abolishment of affirmative action and social welfare programs. Yong-Jin (1994) also discusses "tactics" that model minority critics employ in order to "exploit the contradictions inherent in the 'model minority' discourse to provide oppositional meanings" (p. 61). This article does a splendid job analyzing the model minority discourse and should be cited in reviews of literature, especially discursive ones. A unique contribution Yong-Jin's (1994) article makes to the model minority literature is its discussion of how the stereotype and discourse influence Asian American women's sense and perception of beauty (e.g., see also Hartlep, in press b).

Yu, T. (2006). Challenging the politics of the "model minority" stereotype: A case for educational equality. *Equity & Excellence in Education, 39*(4), 325–333.

***Yu (2006) makes the point that the model minority stereotype is politically motivated. Proponents of the myth use it as evidence that a meritocracy exists in the United States. This results in the engendering of further support for things such as accountability standards, zero-tolerance policies, competition, and choice. According to Yu (2006),

> There is a strong correlation between the model minority stereotype and the standards-based, test-driven, school reform movement that emphasizes individual values and efforts but trivializes social injustice and educational inequalities, characteristics that make up the core of the model minority thesis. (p. 325)

The article first highlights the progression from a historically perceived and racialized "yellow peril" toward a "model minority" in the 1960s onward. It then delves into the idea that the model minority was constructed as a deceptive device of political control. Yu points out that the characterization of the model minority came about during the civil rights movement of the 1960s and was not coincidental, but rather intentional. According to Yu (2006), "Thus, 'Model Minority" became a political instrument used to bash other minorities, African Americans in particular" (p. 327). The article concludes with practical thoughts on creating equal education for all—most of which pertain to redistribution of educational, social, and economic resources, as well as increasing the funding that our public schools receive. This article is compelling and consequential for model minority demystification because it effectively illustrates that the motivation behind the model minority is ulterior, not positive, and that the benefactors of the model minority narrative are not Asian Americans, but rather the racist elites who control its narration.

Zhang, Q. (2010). Asian Americans beyond the model minority stereotype: The nerdy and the left out. *Journal of International and Intercultural Communication, 3*(1), 20–37.

***Zhang's (2010) article indicates that mainstream media contributes to the homogenization of Asian Americans. Most media stereotypically portrays Asians negatively. This investigation was an empirical study of whether people accept media stereotypes of Asian Americans. Zhang (2010) writes that in the media, such as television programming, Hollywood movies, and advertising, "Asian Americans are characterized as holding high-status positions requiring intelligence and advanced degrees (often in the sciences) which might reinforce the model minority stereotype" (p. 23). Zhang (2010) notes that in the 1960s "the media promoted Asians from being an oppressed racial minority to being a shiny example for other racial minorities" (p. 24). Zhang (2010) problematizes this shift in stereotyping and discusses that the yellow peril and model minority theses are not opposites—one negative and one positive—but that both serve to reinforce and maintain White supremacy. Using *cultivation theory* as a framework, which theorizes that prolonged exposure to media stereotypes may result in the acceptance of stereotypes as social reality, and a sample of 169 undergraduate students recruited from an introductory communication course (28 freshmen, 57 sophomores, 45 juniors, and 39 seniors) who attended a private Northeast university, the study found that all four of its hypotheses were correct. Hypothesis 1 postulated that "Asian Americans will be perceived as more likely to achieve academic success than other racial-ethnic groups" (p. 25); Hypothesis 2 predicted that "Asian Americans will be more likely to be perceived as nerds than other racial-ethnic groups" (p. 26); Hypothesis 3 posited that "Asian Americans will be perceived as more likely to be left out than other racial-ethnic groups" (p. 27); and Hypothesis 4 stated that "Peers will be less likely to initiate friendship with Asian Americans than other racial-ethnic groups" (p. 27). Due to its comprehensive review of the literature on Asian American stereotyping, this article is a necessary read for model minority researchers interested in the stereotyping of Asian Americans. Zhang (2010) reviews (1) the model minority stereotype, (2) the poor communicator or nerd stereotype, and (3) the foreigner stereotype and does a wonderful job of explaining why it is important to understand that "people's perceptions and judgments about Asian Americans are aligned with the media representations and these stereotypes affect people's intent to interact with Asians" (p. 32). Although public endorsement does not validate the model minority stereotype, it does illustrate the stereotype's entrenched nature as a "social reality." The article ends with limitations of the study. This study makes a unique and invaluable contribution to model minority research and should be replicated in different academic, geographic, and institutional settings.

Zhao, Y. & Qiu, W. (2009). How good are the Asians? Refuting four myths about Asian-American academic achievement? *Phi Delta Kappan, 90*(5), 338–344.

***Zhao and Qiu's (2009) article asserts that it is essential to understand and refute four myths about Asian-American academic achievement. The first myth is that Asian Americans have superior academic achievement. The second myth is that Asian American students are born smart, especially in mathematics and science. The third myth is that Asian American students are trouble-free kids. The fourth myth is that Asian American students are good at everything. One of the most troubling examples that Asian American students are not problem-free is the authors' citation of the fact that since 1996, 13 of 21 student suicide victims have been Asian American. The reason that this article is must-read is that policy implications accompany every refuted myth. The recommended policies are important because Zhao and Qiu (2009) state that "education policies should not treat Asian Americans as a *homogenous* group" (p. 340, italics added). Homogenization is something that the model minority does; therefore, it should be challenged.

REFERENCE

Hartlep, N. D. (2012). *A segmented assimilation theoretical study of the 2002 Asian American student population.* Doctoral thesis, University of Wisconsin-Milwaukee, Milwaukee, WI.

CHAPTER 2

WHO ARE ASIAN AMERICANS?

The readings reviewed in this chapter ask the question, "Who are Asian Americans?" Particularly, the writings contained in this chapter address the model minority stereotype in terms of who Asian Americans are said to be. The model minority stereotype homogenizes Asian Americans; thus, all Asians are thought to be successful and doing well. The readings in this chapter complexify this *bon sens* and help illustrate what Lisa Lowe (1991) identifies as heterogeneity, hybridity, and multiplicity, which all serve to mark Asian American differences. Asian Americans may be contemporarily viewed as model minorities, but Tang (2008) reminds us that Asian Americans have also been contemporarily vilified as "gooks," as witnessed in the public statements of U.S. Senator John McCain.

Adler, S. M. (2006). Problematizing Asian American children as "model" students. In M. N.

Bloch, D. Kennedy, T. Lightfoot, & D. Weyenberg (Eds.), *The child in the world/the world in the child: Education and the configuration of a universal, modern, and globalized childhood* (pp. 63–78). New York, NY: Palgrave MacMillan. ***Adler's (2006) chapter discusses how the model minority stereotype "is still perpetuated in America society today, resulting in the need for Asian

The Model Minority Stereotype: Demystifying Asian American Success, pages 53–130.

American parents to socialize their children to deal with racism and discrimination" (p. 63). Adler argues that the myth of the "model" student (read: the model minority) "becomes a method of colonization inhibiting Asian American students from appropriating their own identities" (p. 63). Thus, the main argument that Adler (2006) makes in her chapter is that Asian American parents must actively instruct their children about the ways that they, as Asian American youth, have been marginalized and oppressed. This chapter reviews (1) the familial and cultural structure of various Asians (e.g., Filipino, Chinese, Southeast Asian, and Japanese); (2) Asian religions and Asians' collective orientations; (3) the model minority stereotype and teacher perspectives on the model minority stereotype; (4) the socialization of Asian American children; and (5) Asian American heterogeneity, hybridity, and resistance. The gist of this chapter speaks to the notion of Asians maintaining their ethno-racial and cultural identity. Segmented assimilation theorists and scholars will find this chapter enlightening and will cite it in their scholarship.

Ang, S. W. (2012). The politics of victimization and the model minority. *CR: The New Centennial Review, 11*(3), 119–140.

***Ang's (2012) article argues "that victim narratives and the myth of the model minority are different but related discourses" (p. 119). Moreover, the model minority mystifies social violence. Ang (2012) writes, "Racial violence continues to be perpetuated by the very victims who suffer under it. As an institution that can administer 'legitimate violence,' the state cannot do so without justification, and...victims of that violence sustain the state's legitimacy on the basis of their acquiescence" (p. 136). Thus, Asian Americans are racialized—they are viewed singularly as successful—and victimized through their acquiescence. As a result, Asian Americans who do not assimilate or acquiesce to the model minority often experience, and are disciplined through, social violence. Ang's (2012) article is written at a graduate-student level and could be used in graduate-level Asian American studies courses and/or in literature reviews. This *CR: The New Centennial Review* article is unique because *CR* publishes articles that have philosophical orientations, and very few model minority stereotype articles are written from such a perspective.

Appiah, O. & Liu, Y. (2009). Reaching the model minority: Ethnic differences in responding to culturally embedded targeted- and non-targeted advertisements. *Journal of Current Issues and Research in Advertising, 31*(1), 27–41.

***Appiah and Liu's (2009) experiment examined ethnic differences in responding to culturally embedded targeted- and non-targeted advertisements. Their study "examined differences in Chinese and Caucasian consumers' psychological responses to advertisements that feature[d] varying levels of ethnic-specific cultural cues" (Appiah & Liu, 2009, p. 28). 121 Chinese and 70 White subjects participated in the experiment. Experiment participants were students enrolled in the school of communication at a large midwestern university. Advertisements for two fictitious products—soymilk and a computer—were randomly shown to experiment participants. The advertisements were altered to either reflect high culturally embedded Chinese cues or low culturally embedded Chinese cues. In other words, one version of the advertisement was not targeted in that it had no Chinese cultural referents, while another advertisement did. The Chinese referents and cues were cultural or language-based in nature. Appiah and Liu's (2009) experiment contributes to the literature on ethnic minority-oriented advertising, its results indicating that "Chinese participants evaluated the high Chinese culturally embedded ads...more favorably" (Appiah & Liu, 2009, p. 37) and that "Chinese showed a greater likelihood of purchasing the products when they were featured in high Chinese culturally embedded ads" (Appiah & Liu, 2009, p. 37). The implication is that advertisements targeting Chinese people should include not only Chinese people, but also cultural markers. This article is marginally interested in the model minority stereotype; the fact that it used the term "model minority" in its title speaks to the ubiquity of the term, not only in education, but also in the greater population. It also speaks to the taken-for-granted nature of the term and concept. This could be a very useful article in an Asian American studies class.

Asher, N. (2001). Checking the box: The label "model minority." In G. M. Hudak & P. Kihn (Eds.), *Labeling: Pedagogy and politics* (pp. 75–92). New York, NY: Routledge Falmer.

***This article discusses how South Asian students' ascribed label of "model minority" reinforces *a priori* perceptions of them as academically advanced students. Asher's book chapter is based upon interviews with 10 South Asian high school students. Findings indicate that many of the South Asian students internalized their own marginalization through abiding by the model minority stereotype's racialized expectations of behavior and eventual professional aspirations. Asher (2001) points to the need for continued qualitative research as she states the following: "In order to deconstruct the label of 'model minority' and bring to light the diverse educational realities of Asian Americans, educational researchers need to continue documenting the stories of Asian American students and sharing them within the field of education—in the curriculum of the school as well as in teacher education" (p. 89). This well-written article could be a useful addition to a graduate class on qualitative research methodology as well as a class on Asians in education.

Asian American Center for Advancing Justice. (2011). *A community of contrasts: Asian Americans in the United States 2011.* New York, NY: Asian Pacific American Legal

Center. Retrieved on November 22, 2011, from http://www.advancingjustice. org/pdf/Community_of_Contrast.pdf

****A Community of Contrasts: Asian Americans in the United States 2011* is a publication of the Asian American Center for Advancing Justice. The report mostly draws upon data from the 2010 Census and American Community Survey. The goal of the report was to provide a detailed portrait of the Asian American community in the United States. This 68-page report is the second in a series, followed by regional reports on Asian American and NHPI communities in California, the West, the Midwest, the South, and the Northeast. This brief contains current data on the five largest Asian American groups: (1) Chinese Americans, (2) Filipino Americans, (3) Indian Americans, (4) Vietnamese Americans, and (5) Korean Americans. It also presents background information on the five fastest growing Asian American groups: (1) Bangladeshi Americans, (2) Pakistani Americans, (3) Sri Lankan Americans, (4) Indian Americans, and (5) Taiwanese Americans. This is an important read for those who are beginning model minority research and who would like material to increase their background knowledge and understanding of the Asian American population. Readers especially ought to look at the glossary, which is highly informative and easily accessible.

Bascara, V. (2006). *Model-minority imperialism.* Minneapolis, MN: University of Minnesota Press.

***This volume has been reviewed by numerous people (e.g., see Park, 2007; Poblete-Cross, 2009) and is unique insofar as it "argues that contemporary Asian American cultural politics [including the model minority stereotype] set the conditions for the critical return of empire as an explanatory model for understanding the American Century" (p. ix). The book contains many great references in its chapter endnotes, including a reference to Viet Nguyen's "Model Minorities and Bad Subjects" (Bascara, 2006, p. 148). Bascara (2006) is astute since he observes that *Newsweek's* publication of "Asian Americans: A Model Minority" on December 6, 1982 was associated with the centennial of the 1882 Chinese Exclusion Act.

Brydolf, C. (2009). Getting real about the "model minority": Asian Americans and Pacific Islanders fight their stereotype. *Education Digest: Essential Readings Condensed for Quick Review, 74*(5), 37–44.

***Brydolf's (2009) report is very informative even for those who are familiar with the "model minority," providing readers with myriad resources and materials, especially for those interested in serving the needs of Asian Americans and Pacific Islanders. Focused on the state of California, many of the resources and references contained in "Getting Real About the 'Model Minority'" also apply nationally to fighting the stereotype's inaccurate assessments and appraisals. Three seminal reports are referred to herein: (1) "Asian American and Pacific Islanders / Facts, Not Fiction: Setting the Record Straight", (2) "Left in the Margins: Asian American Students & the No Child Left Behind Act", and (3) "The Diverse Face of Asians and Pacific Islanders in Los Angeles." Readers also learn about "Hmong Voices," a project of the California Voices Initiative of the Center for Multicultural Cooperation (CMC), a Fresno non-profit organization. The genesis of "Hmong Voices" was catalyzed by a series of Hmong youth suicides between 1998 and 2001. Brydolf's article also acquaints readers with the unique curricular, programmatic, and pedagogical approaches of educator Larry Ferlazzo, an award-winning English and social studies teacher at Luther Burbank High School in Sacramento, California. For those unfamiliar, Luther Burbank has been successful at educating many of its Hmong students, who many times come from "linguistically isolated" households—households that don't include anyone 14 years old or older who speaks English "very well." This report will aid practicing K–12 teachers as well as literacy (ELL) educators in better understanding the needs of Asian Americans and Pacific Islanders. As Brydolf (2009) states, "Clearly, many Asian Americans have overcome tremendous obstacles in California and elsewhere to build successful lives in the United States. But these numbers don't tell the whole story…" (p. 38).

Bucholtz, M. (2004). Styles and stereotypes: The linguistic negotiation of identity among Laotian American youth. *Pragmatics, 14*(2/3), 127–147.

***The racial dichotomy of difference—Whiteness opposed to Blackness— as well as the fact that "research on contemporary cultural ideologies associated with Asian Americans *has focused primarily on the stereotype of the model minority*" (p. 128, italics added) makes Bucholtz's (2004) article that much more original and scholarly. Bucholtz (2004) "examines how two Southeast Asian American girls in a multiracial high school in California, both refugees from Laos, navigated…two contrasting racial ideologies imposed on Southeast Asian Americans by using locally available linguistic and other semiotic resources" (p. 129). Her study draws upon data from a 1995–1996 year-long ethnographic sociolinguistic study of a multiracial high school in the San Francisco Bay area. Bucholtz (2004) calls the school in which her study took place Bay City High School and writes based upon the informal interviews she conducted with two Laotian American students: Nikki and Ada. Each girl attempted to position herself uniquely within Bay City High School milieu, but the black/white binary and dichotomized depiction of Asian Americans as "nerds" or as "gangsters" inhibited their success at doing so. In fact, Bucholtz (2004) asserts that "in navigating the stereotypes directed at them as Southeast Asian Americans, both Nikki and Ada took up identity positions that in some ways reinforced the black/white racial [construction/ideology/paradigm of students]" (p. 143). Bucholtz (2004) describes the shifting racial ideological continuum present at Bay City High School as follows (from left to right): Black, "acting Black," "acting White," and White. Somewhere in between "acting Black" and "acting White" were "gangster" and "nerd." Interestingly, Nikki adopted African American Vernacular English (AAVE) patterned speech; however, as Bucholtz (2004) indicates, she could not be mistaken for a native AAVE speaker. Notwithstanding, while Nikki was ideologically blackened to be a "gangster," and Ada was ideologically whitened to be a "nerd," this study illustrates why more research must be conducted on Asian American students' linguistic negotiation of identity considering that the intersections of gender, language, and power are tied closely to social class position. Such an example is the fact that while Nikki had friends of numerous and diverse ethnicities/races/socioeconomic classes, Ada shunned Laotian Americans, and socialized primarily with middle class White Euro-Americans. Sociolinguists who study socio-linguistic and -cultural stereotypes, semiotics, and the schooling experiences of Southeast Asian Americans will find this an incredibly important study. College professors of urban education might adopt Bucholtz's (2004) article as a potential reading in seminars or courses that examine sociolinguistic stereotypes and minorities and cultural groups.

Chang, I. (2003). The bamboo curtain rises: Mainlanders and model minorities. In I. Chang, *The Chinese in America: A narrative history* (pp. 312–333). New York, NY: Viking.

***Chang's (2003) chapter is the seventeenth of twenty in her book, *The Chinese in America: A Narrative History*. According to Chang (2003), the "bamboo curtain" was the period associated with the Mao Zedong regime. Writes Chang (2003), "The Deng-Regan pact ended three decades of isolation under the Mao regime. But as diplomacy lifted the Bamboo Curtain, the initial exchanges were shocking to visitors from both sides of the Pacific" (p. 315). Chang's (2003) chapter highlights incidences whereby Chinese Americans had been murdered at the hands of anti-Asian murderers, as seen in the cases of Jim Loo (Ming-Hai Loo) and Vincent Chin. Chang's (2003) chapter provides evidence that Asian American academic and social success creates a source of anxiety for Whites. Chang (2003) cites many "classical" model minority writings, while providing contextualizing-rich examples of how the Chinese in Monterrey Park, California, for instance, experience anti-Asian attitudes, a few examples being bumper stickers that read "Will the Last American to Leave Monterey Park Please Bring the Flag?" (Chang, 2003, p. 325) and "'DWC'—Driving While Chinese" (Chang, 2003, p. 325).

Chang, M. J. (2011). Battle hymn of the model minority myth. *Amerasia Journal, 37*(2), 137–143.

***In Chang's (2011) essay, he writes that "despite the many serious flaws with grand narratives about Asian Americans, the general public is drawn to them, which makes those stories even more effective in distorting understanding of Asian Americans" (p. 137). The model minority contributes to misunderstanding and also "can be readily turned into a Yellow Peril [stereotype] that supports rather than refutes the dangerous claim that Asians are dominating the real world" (pp. 141–142). Chang's essay critiques several sample articles, and his comments about them provide necessary insights into how Asian Americans, themselves, are reinvigorating historical anti-Asian paranoia. The title is influenced by Yale Law Professor Amy Chua's (2011) book *Battle Hymn of the Tiger Mother.* This essay could be used as a foundational reading in a critical media or critical cultural class at the high school and university level since many of the essay's references are found in such on-line accessible publications as *Huffington Post, Hyphen-Magazine, Wall Street Journal, Boston Globe, New York Magazine, The Hechinger Report,* and *ABC News.*

Chao, M. M., Chiu, C., & Lee, J. S. (2010). Asians as the model minority: Implications for U.S. government's policies. *Asian Journal of Social Psychology, 13*(1), 44–52.

***According to Chao, Chiu, and Lee's (2010) article, the model minority stereotype is a socially constructed myth. The myth was created by the ruling class in order to (1) legitimize the rhetoric of the "American Dream," (2) historically disunite African Americans and Asian Americans during the civil rights movement, and (3) promote classical conceptions of morality, citizenship, and social order. Chao, Chiu, and Lee (2010) were interested in the association among the model minority image, individual's worldviews, and attitudes towards the U.S. government's redistributive policies. The participants for their study were 155 students—80 Asian American and 75 European American—from a public university in the midwest. Of the 80 Asian Americans, 50 were of Chinese descent, 14 were of Korean descent, five identified as Asian Indian, three identified as Filipino American, two indicated they were Japanese American, and six identified as "other" Asian. The 155 participants in the study were randomly assigned to read one of three newspaper articles: the first article/condition was about a successful Asian American, the second article/condition was about a successful European American, and the third article/condition was unrelated to success. It was found that "those who believed in a malleable social reality were relatively unsupportive of government policies that help the Asian American (*vs.* African American) communities" (p. 44). This finding is important for scholars and teachers to know. If students perceive the American Dream to be real and attainable, they might be more susceptible to blaming the victims. This study found that supporters of the model minority stereotype (incremental theorists) would be more likely to be unsupportive of governmental redistributive policies aimed at helping Asian *vs.* African Americans. Consequently, this article should be cited by scholars who work with the model minority stereotype within a Black-White context. Graduate statistics courses as well as those considering conducting empirical research on this topic could also use this article as a course reading.

Chiu, P. K. (1988, May 16). The myth of the model minority. *U.S. News & World Report, 104,* 7.

***Chiu's (1988) article is only one page but does a great job at forcefully arguing that the media have begun to portray Asian (Chinese) Americans as they really are. Chiu (1988) writes, "What has happened to the law-abiding, humble Chinese American we have heard so much about?" Chiu (1988) goes on to write the following, which is valuable to consider:

> A few Chinese Americans steal when hey are desperate; a few rape when nature overwhelms them; a few sell drugs when they see an easy way to make a buck; a few embezzle when instant fortunes blind them; a few murder when passions overtake them, and a few commit crimes simply because they are wicked. It is about time for the media to report on Chinese Americans the way they are. *Some are superachievers, most are average citizens, and a few are criminals. They are only human—no more and no less.* (p. 7, italics added)

Chou, C. (2008). Critique on the notion of model minority: An alternative racism to Asian American? *Asian Ethnicity, 9*(3), 219–229.

***Chou (2008) asks the question, "What kind of racism do Asian Americans currently face?" More specifically, Chou examines the racist ideology lurking below the model minority ideology. Using the work of several well-known authors/philosophers/educators, Chou's (2008) article presents underpinnings of the model minority stereotype that are necessary to understand. A few of the most important are as follows:

- The model minority stereotype isolates Asian Americans from White Americans;
- The model minority stereotype separates Asians from Americans;
- The model minority stereotype suggests *superiority* compared to non-Whites and *inferiority* compared to White supremacy;
- The model minority stereotype replaces racial differences with cultural differences; and
- The model minority stereotype creates the illusion that the larger society has reached a colorblind state.

Notes Chou (2008), "The notion of model minority exemplifies the historical shift from a biologistic conception of race to a culturalist one. In this process, cultural differences are deployed to differentiate Asia(n) from American(n), the East from the West, and are used to characterize racially defined groups. Cultural differences are by all means essentialized and race is furthermore reduced to essentialized cultural differences" (p. 227). This article cites many interesting references that will be useful for model minority researchers and teachers.

Chou, R. S. (2008, August). *The White myth of the model minority: Disguising racial oppression.* Paper presented at the American Sociological Association 103 Annual Meeting, Boston, MA.

***Chou's (2008) abstract of her ASA conference paper reads as follows:

> The dominant white group and its leaders stand in a position of such great power that they rate groups of color socially and assign them grades on a type of minority report card. Whites give Asian American groups a model minority rating, while other groups of color receive much lower marks as problem minorities. Still, the hierarchical positions that whites are willing to give any group of color are significantly below whites on the ladder. Today, many media and scholarly discussions suggest Asian Americans are treated as white or honorary white by most white Americans, yet our data from 43 field interviews with Asian Americans show that they do not in any sense hold such a status in this society.

Chou, R. S. & Feagin, J. R. (2010). *The myth of the model minority: Asian Americans facing racism.* Boulder, CO: Paradigm Publishers.

***Chou and Feagin's (2010) book focuses on the racial framing of Asian Americans. As I noted in my own review (Hartlep, 2011),

> The book is a searing and scathing indictment of how "racial framing" impacts the lives of Asian Americans and how it leaves them vulnerable in myriad ways. The book invokes a mental map, an image of how Asian Americans truly feel and experience the world. This book helps us all to move forward; if we understand the role that "racial framing" plays in perpetuating the model minority stereotype—which serves to marginalize the experiences of Asian Americans—and the maintenance of white privilege, then surely disruption of racial framing is an appropriate way to dismantle the racism that Asian Americans face. This book, through its focus on racial framing, helps readers to better understand the duality of the model minority stereotype—successful opposed to unsuccessful—and how it causes pain and social misery for Asian Americans. (p. 105)

This book can be used in courses taught in colleges of education. It is written in an accessible way so that undergraduates will not be put off by its language and style. The book has received much praise by its reviewers (e.g., see Hartlep, 2011; Lee, 2010).

D'Angelo, R. & Douglas, H. (2009). Are Asian Americans a model minority? In R. D'Angelo & H. Douglas (Eds.), *Taking sides: Clashing views on race and ethnicity* (7th ed., pp. 311–336). Boston, MA: McGraw-Hill Higher Education.

***D'Angelo and Douglas's (2009) chapter asks the question: "Are Asian Americans a model minority?" The chapter provides one article that believes Asian Americans *are* model minorities and one article that believes Asian Americans *are not* model minorities. The *pro*-model minority stereotype article is a reprint of David A. Bell's (1985) "The Triumph of Asian-Americans" published in *The New Republic*. The *anti*-model minority stereotype article is reprinted sections of Frank H. Wu's (2002) *Yellow: Race in America Beyond Black and White*. D'Angelo and Douglas's (2009) chapter can be used in high school and college classrooms in order to teach both sides of the debate.

Danico, M. Y. & Ng, F. (2004). Asian Americans: A model minority? In M. Y. Danico and F. Ng, *Asian American issues* (pp. 23–46). Westport, CT: Greenwood Press.

***Danico and Ng's (2004) chapter investigates the merits of the model minority stereotype, examining its support and opposition. The authors discuss Asian Americans' supposed high rankings on socioeconomic indicators such as income and education, as well as Asian Americans' supposed emphases on cultural values and educational attainment. Danico and Ng (2004) write that "the perception that Asian Americans have attained economic and educational success hides the existence of a 'glass ceiling,' a barrier in occupational status that Asian Americans have yet to break" (p. 34). They go on to state that "the model minority myth ignores the group differences regarding degrees of acculturation, and variations in social, political, economic, and educational backgrounds. By focusing on the successes, and generalizing it to all Asian Americans, the model minority myth does not take into consideration the large number of students and families who suffer from poverty and illiteracy" (pp. 36–37). This chapter contains many references and quotations that will prompt scholars and students to consult further resources on the model minority and related writings. This article is information-rich, and should be cross-referenced by teachers and students. Moreover, the chapter ends with five questions that can be used as a review or to begin conversation on the model minority stereotype: (1) "What is the definition of a model minority? If one accepts the idea of a model minority, are there other groups besides Asian Americans that can qualify as model minorities? Why or why not?" (2) "If one does not accept the concept of a model minority, what problems might there be with that idea? What about the assertion that while the concept of a model minority has a few flaws, nevertheless, on the whole, the idea is a useful one?" (3) "Asian Americans is a term that refers to many different ethnic groups. Are there variations among these groups so that not all of them fit into the category of a model minority? Which groups might these be? On the other hand, are there some groups that fit into the category of a model minority? Which groups would you place in that category?" (4) "What is the history behind the view that Asian Americans are a model minority? How did that idea develop through time?" and (5) "Can the case be made that there was greater validity to the idea of Asian Americans being a model minority in the past than in the present? Or is it more true today than in the past?" (Danico & Ng, 2004, p. 41).

Dhingra, P. (2007). Model Americans and minorities: Racial identities and responses to racism. In P. Dhingra, *Managing multicultural lives: Asian American professionals and the challenge of multiple identities* (pp. 84–123), Stanford, CA: Stanford University Press.

***Dhingra's (2007) chapter is the fourth in the book *Managing Multicultural Lives: Asian American Professionals and the Challenge of Multiple Identities*. Dhingra (2007) points out the ways in which Asians are racialized and categorized. Dhingra (2007) also examines how Asian Americans respond to racism. For instance, points out Dhingra (2007), some Asian Americans "take comfort in the stereotype that Asian Americans excel in education relative to other groups owing to their supportive families" (p. 92). This chapter does a great job at pointing out how certain Asians are not deemed to be such, but rather are ascribed as being more "Arab," such as in the case of South Asians. This chapter discusses how/why the term "oriental" is conjured to refer to East Asian Americans, and how Asian Indians are ascribed terrorist status in this post-September 11 era. Consequently, Dhingra (2007) observes the following:

> South Asian Americans have put patriotic bumper stickers on their taxi cabs, draped American flags on their store windows, cut their hair and stopped wearing turbans, and monitored their dress. In times of heightened threats to national security, Asian Americans must actively perform an "American" identity so as not to become the "enemy." (p. 100)

This chapter can be used for research on the politics of race as it relates to the ascription of model minority status and model American citizenship.

DiAlto, S. J. (2005). From "problem minority" to "model minority": The changing social construction of Japanese Americans. In A. L. Schneider & H. M. Ingram (Eds.), *Deserving and entitled: Social constructions and public policy* (pp. 81–103). Albany, NY: SUNY Press.

***DiAlto's (2005) chapter examines the changing social construction of Japanese Americans. The media, as a "moral entrepreneur," (and more specifically, the media discourse) sanctions dominant group stereotypes by legitimizing ideologically biased interpretations of society. The social construction of group identity is also driven by court rulings and laws and legislation. DiAlto (2005) shares three contextual factors that contributed to the social construction of Japanese as "problem minorities" in the pre-World War II era: (1) constructing Japanese as agricultural and occupational labor competition for White Californian farmers, (2) constructing Japanese as non-Whites and non-citizens, and (3) constructing the Japanese as military and national security threats. DiAlto (2005) goes on to describe and delineate in her chapter the various ways in which the Japanese were constructed as "enemy aliens" during the World War II era, noting the following: during the Second World War "Japanese immigrants and their Japanese American children came to be constructed not as a 'problem minority' but as 'enemy aliens.' This even more damaging construction would ultimately seal their fate for exclusion and then internment" (p. 93). DiAlto (2005) notifies her readers that the social construction of the Japanese changed (from seemingly negative to seemingly positive) in the post-World War II era. In her words, "While the 1950s were an important period for the rejection of Japanese-American negative construction, the 1960s were the decade when their seemingly more positive construction as the 'model minority' emerged" (DiAlto, 2005, p. 99). DiAlto's (2005) chapter cautions that "although their current construction as a 'model minority' has been firmly in place since the 1960s, Japanese Americans at times are still plagued by their former negative construction" (p. 101). This is an important point given that many consider a positive stereotype to be better than a negative one, not understanding that the model minority stereotype is cloaked in negativity and hegemonic discourse. DiAlto (2005) also duly notes, "So while the model minority construction in many ways represents an improvement over their former status—as a problem minority and then as enemy aliens—it is to without its drawbacks" (p. 102). This chapter holds several strengths for teachers, scholars, and academics. The first is that it provides many documented court cases that may be of interest for research, teaching, and learning (e.g., court cases such as *Takao Ogawa v. United States; Hidemitsu Toyota v. United States; Porterfield v. Webb; Webb v. O'Brien; Frick v. Webb; Korematsu v. United States; Oyama v. United States*). Logically organized and written, the second strength of the chapter is its explicitness in prioritizing context in order to better understand how stereotypes and group identity are fortified through a process of social construction. College professors and graduate students interested in model minority scholarship will find this an appealing read.

Ecklund, E. (2005). 'Us' and 'them': The role of religion in mediating and challenging the 'model minority' and other civic boundaries. *Ethnic and Racial Studies, 28*(1), 132–150.

***Ecklund's (2005) study examined Korean Americans construction of boundaries through their church involvement and evangelical (Christian) beliefs. Ecklund (2005) compared Korean Americans in a church congregation composed of mostly second-generation Koreans (Grace Church) and a church congregation that was highly multiethnic (Manna Fellowship Church). Through her qualitative interviews, Ecklund (2005) found that Korean Americans who attended churches that were made up of mostly second-generation congregants largely reinforced the model minority stereotype. In other words, these church members believed that they (Koreans) were harder workers than say, African Americans were. Contradistinctively, Ecklund (2005) found that Korean American churchgoers who attended multiethnic congregations were less likely to reify the model minority stereotype. These Korean Americans attributed their successes to God and not to themselves or their own hard work per se. Ecklund's (2005) study is very helpful for model minority stereotype scholarship given that the number of Asian Americans who identify as Christian/evangelical continues to grow dramatically. Indeed, in Ecklund's (2005) own words, "Using a cultural framework that takes individual agency into consideration, I have provided evidence that Korean American evangelicals in different ethnic religious contexts *created group boundaries in different ways*" (p. 145, italics added).

Ecklund, E. H. & Park, J. Z. (2005). Asian American community participation and religion: Civic "model minorities?" *Journal of Asian American Studies, 8*(1), 1–21.

***Ecklund and Park (2005) studied Asian American community participation and religion. Using data from the 2000 public-access, Social Capital Benchmark Survey (SCBS), a nationally-drawn sample of adult Asian Americans from 30 communities in the United States (n = 29,000), Ecklund and Park (2005, p. 4) asked the following two research questions: (1) "How does religion compare to ethnicity, class, and gender, in its influence on community volunteerism?" and (2) "How do various religious traditions compare in their influence on civic participation for Asian Americans?"

Ecklund and Park (2005) hypothesized the following: (H_1) "Because race overrides ethnicity, civic participation will not differ between Asian American ethnic groups" (p. 5); (H_2) "Asian Americans with higher income and education will volunteer more than those with lower levels of income and education" (p. 5); (H_3) "Asian American women will be more likely to volunteer than Asian American men" (p. 5); (H_4) "Asian Americans who participate in their places of worship will be more likely to participate in civic voluntary organizations" (p. 6); (H_5) "Asian Americans who volunteer for a religious organization will be more likely to participate in civic voluntary organizations than those who do not volunteer for a religious organization" (p. 6); (H_6) "Asian Americans who are religiously affiliated will have greater civic participation than those who are not religiously affiliated" (p. 6); and (H_7) "Because the United States is institutionally Christian, Asian American

Protestants and Catholics will be more likely to participate in non-religious volunteering than affiliates of Eastern religions and non-religious Asian Americans" (p. 6).

The researchers found no support for the idea that Asian Americans are a "civic" model minority or are highly likely to volunteer in their communities. Ecklund and Park (2005) found "little support for the argument that additional levels of education increase the likelihood of civic participation for Asian Americans" (p. 16); additionally, "gender, overall, has no differential effect on civic participation" (p. 16). This article offers a rare investigation into an original issue of "model minority" citizenship. It will be a helpful read for religious and secular community service providers (e.g. churches, schools, and organizations) since Ecklund and Park (2005) rightly point out, "As the American population continues to undergo further religious and racial diversification, understanding the increasingly complex *intersection of religion, race, and civic participation within Asian America* is a centrally important topic" (p. 18, italics added).

Eguchia, S. & Starosta, W. (2012). Negotiating the model minority image: Performative aspects of college-educated Asian American professional men. *Qualitative Research Reports in Communication, 13*(1), 88–97.

***Eguchia and Starosta's (2012) article shares the findings of their qualitative research study. Using in-depth interview data—eight interviews with nine Asian American men, both gay and hetereosexual—and an inductive thematic analysis, Eguchia and Starosta (2012) asked:

> How do college-educated Asian American professional men negotiate the model minority image to present the performative construction of their social identity to promote positive impressions on others in the context of racialized and gendered American organizations? (p. 89)

Two themes resulted: "Are we the model minority" and "Should we perform as if we were the model minority?" Say Eguchia and Starosta (2012), "All participants feel that Asian Americans live up to the model minority image to move up the social ladder" (p. 94). This study is important, not simply because it points out that the Asian American men who were interviewed embraced the stereotype, but also because of the implications:

> There is evidence from the responses that performing the model minority image may become a way for the college-educated Asian American male professional participants to obtain or maintain a privileged job position. At the same time, presenting the model minority image may create a disadvantaged status that ultimately prevents them from moving up the organizational ladder because they have to grapple with prevailing attitudes in racialized and gendered American organizations. (p. 95)

This study can be used when writing about Asian American identity negotiation under the specter of being racialized as a model minority, in particular how Asian American college-educated men negotiate such a threat.

Endo, R. (1974). Japanese Americans: The "model minority" in perspective. In R. Gomez & C. Cottingham (Eds.), *The social reality of ethnic America* (pp. 189–213). Lexington, MA: DC Heath and Company.

***Endo's (1974) book chapter first covers the history of the Japanese who came to the United States. The anti-Japanese hysteria fanned by alarmists was driven by fear of a "yellow tide" with its attendant "yellow peril" paranoia, which was perceived to place national interests at risk. After an extensive historical survey, Endo (1974) begins his discussion of the relatively new (at the time of the article's publication) model minority stereotype. Endo (1974) points out that "the existence of discrimination is one of the major bones of contention between those who accept and those who question the success stereotype" (p. 203). Consequently, Endo (1974) further explicates the activism, socio-political consciousness, and ethnic reawakening of the Sansei (third generation) Japanese in America. This article is an important piece of model minority literature due to the fact that it was published in the early 1970s. The article should be cited in academic literature reviews, but also should be used to help develop the understanding that stereotypes of Asian Americans, in this case, Japanese, emerge out of macro-social, macro-political, and macro-economic relationships (Japan and United States, and their economies). This helps scholars and students situate and contextualize their work within society. This is an important chapter for graduate students in Asian American studies or in an educational diversity class to read to gain a historical understanding of the model minority stereotype.

Endo, G. T. & Della-Piana, C. K. (1981). Japanese Americans, pluralism, and the model minority myth. *Theory Into Practice, 20*(1), 45–51.

***Endo and Della-Piana's (1981) article addresses the belief that Japanese Americans are passive, industrious, respectful, patient, and intelligent. Although one of the shorter articles included in this book, it is helpful in two primary ways. The first is that the article addresses the experiences of Japanese Americans by generation status (*Issei, Nisei, Sansei, and Yonsei*)—allowing for readers to understand the diverse struggles Japanese have, thereby helping negate the belief that the Japanese are a homogenous group of Asian Americans. The second is that the article cites "How Children's Books Distort the Asian American Image," an extremely useful article published in 1976 in *Bridge: An Asian American Perspective* for teachers and practitioners, especially those who work with early/elementary students. Endo and Della-Piana's (1981) article is an attractive and accessible read for in-service K–12 teachers due to its nontechnical and jargon-free language.

Fong, T. P. (2008). *The contemporary Asian American experience: Beyond the model minority* (3rd ed.). Upper Saddle River, NJ: Prentice Hall.

***Fong's (2008) book has received great reviews (e.g., see Yamato, 1999) and is now in its third edition. It covers such topics as the history of Asians in America, educational opportunities for Asian Americans, workplace issues (beyond glass ceilings) for Asian Americans, anti-Asian violence, and the media's portrayal of Asian Americans. The section on the model minority stereotype on pages 62–73 is especially relevant. Writes Fong (2008), "The third edition of this book provides the most up-to-date statistics on Asian Americans available" (p. 14). Thus, the book is very relevant for model minority stereotype teaching and scholarship. The book's bibliography has many references that will be useful to those studying or teaching about Asian American issues.

Ganahl, D. J., Ge, L., & Kim, K. (2003). Stereotyping the "model minority": A longitudinal analysis of U.S. primetime network commercials, comparing Asian female and male characters to themselves and others. [Conference Proceeding]. ERIC Document ID: ED481187.

***Ganahl, Ge, and Kim (2003) examined the portrayals of Asian Americans in 189 hours of primetime television commercials in 1998 (ABC, CBS, and NBC), 1999 (ABC and FOX), and 2000 (ABC, NBC, CBS, and FOX). They had three research questions: (1) How are Asians portrayed in television commercials in terms of primary and secondary acting roles, when comparing all Asians to all characters, Asian females to all females and Asian males to all males? (2) In which product categories are Asians portrayed during television commercials, when comparing all Asians to all characters, Asian females to all females and Asian males to all males? and (3) How are Asians portrayed in television commercials, when considering characters' ages and when comparing all Asians to all characters, Asian females to all females and Asian males to all males? Their findings, based on coded results, indicated that "Asians were underrepresented in commercials and Asian females were more underrepresented than Asian males. When compared to all characters, Asians were more likely to be presented in younger, secondary roles. They were [also] more likely to be in commercials for food than automobiles" (p. 2). This paper is important because it shows that Asian Americans are much marginalized, despite their "model minority" status.

Gotanda, N. (1995). Re-producing the model minority stereotype: Judge Joyce Karlin's sentencing colloquy in *People v. Soon Ja Du*. In W. L. Ng, S. Chin, J. S. Moy, & G. Y Okihiro (Eds.), *ReViewing Asian America: Locating diversity* (pp. 87–106). Pullman, WA: Washington State University.

***Gotanda's (1995) chapter is part of a volume (*ReViewing Asian America: Locating Diversity*) based upon selected papers of the 1992 Association for Asian American Studies national meeting held in San Jose, California. Gotanda's (1995) chapter critically analyzes Judge Joyce Karlin's sentencing in *People v. Soon Ja Du*, in which "Du Soon Ja, a fifty-one-year-old Korean immigrant mother and store owner, shot and killed a fifteen-year-old African American girl in a dispute over a bottle of orange juice" (Gotanda, 1995, p. 87). The major premise in Gotanda's (1995) analysis is that Du Soon Ja, an Asian American, was cast as a model minority ("innocent victim"), while Latasha Larlins, an African American, was cast as an aggressive criminal ("guilty gangster"). Gotanda (1995) notes how Judge Joyce Karlin's assessment of the case was heavily biased against Latasha Harlin: "Because Harlins 'used her fists as weapons,' Karlin declares that she was not vulnerable. Karlin does not mention the fact that Du had shot Harlins in the *back* of the head, which logically demonstrates that Harlins was 'vulnerable' to an attack by Du" (Gotanda, 1995, p. 91). Karlin's recommendation to reduce the sentencing from prison to probation is significant, especially given the fact that this shooting occurred when Los Angeles was in the throes of race relations rioting (i.e., the 1992 Los Angeles riots). Therefore, Gotanda (1995) argues that Judge Joyce Karlin's sentencing colloquy in *People v. Soon Ja Du* reproduced the model minority stereotype. This chapter can easily be used in concert with more foundational academic and journalistic articles on the model minority stereotype in order to substantiate the claim that the stereotype is used for political reasons and, thus, is a device for a-political and a-historical rhetorical *status quo* maintenance.

Hartlep, N. D. & Porfilio, B. (Eds.). (2012). *Killing the model minority stereotype: Asian American counternarratives and complicity.* Unpublished Manuscript.

***Hartlep and Porfilio's (2012) unpublished paper is a book proposal. The purpose of this edited volume is to highlight compelling counter-narratives and innovative cultural work generated by the organic intellectuals who study how this social phenomenon impacts day-to-day developments across contexts in the United States and across the globe. The chapter contributors will employ qualitative, quantitative, and mixed research methods to provide the audience fresh ideas related to debunking this stereotype. Chapters will call upon interdisciplinary, intersectional, and critical race theoretical frameworks, among other novel stances. Contributors in this anthology will also provide auto-ethnographic accounts that serve as counter-hegemonic expressions of democracy, justice, and dialogue.

Igasaki, P. (1986, May 9). Stereotypes and a "model minority." *Chicago Tribune*, p. 23.

***Igasaki (1986) shares his thoughts about the model minority stereotype. According to him, in order to make strides and progress, Asian Americans must confront the stereotype of being perceived as quiet and non-confrontational. As Igasaki (1986) notes:

> This stereotype has its flattering aspects, but it also carries dangers and inaccuracies. It can destroy perceptions about our community's diversity and real needs, causing cutbacks in services or programs. It also can set unreasonable standards for Asian Americans. And even positive stereotypes can be flip-flopped into negative images. Hard-working can be construed as overly competitive, and quiet may be interpreted as sneaky or cold. (p. 23)

Hayes, M. (1976). *Amerasia* dispels myths of the "model minority." *Public Telecommunications Review, 4*(4), 54–56.

***In this pithy article, Mimi Hayes, the then Executive Producer of *Amerasia*, shares the difficulties and successes in securing federal grant funding—in this case, based on the Emergency School Aid Act (ESAA) of 1972—in order to produce public television programming for fourth through sixth grade Asian American schoolchildren. Although this article is only three pages in length, it is helpful for teachers and teacher educators: the last page provides a culturally sound curricula outline that could be used to model future curricula for K–12 and/or higher education classrooms. For example, curricula could be themed around topics such as "How we got here," "How we work," "How we live," "How we struggle," and "How we contribute." This article's curriculum outline will expose some students and scholars to unfamiliar or even *esoteric* Asian Americans, such as 14-year old fisherman Nakahama "John" Manjir (the first Japanese American to spend any time in the U.S.), Hiram Leong Fong (the first Chinese American United States Senator), Daniel Ken "Dan" Inouye (the senior United States Senator from Hawaii, and the President pro tempore of the United States Senate, making him the highest-ranking Japanese American politician in American history), and Patsy Matsu Takemoto Mink (a third generation Japanese American United States Congresswoman).

Hewlett, S. A., Rashid, R., Forster, D., & Ho, C. (2011). *Asians in America: Unleashing the potential of the "model minority."* New York, NY: Center for Work-Life Policy.

***This study explores "the complex workplace dynamics that keep Asians from fully realizing their potential and getting to the higher rungs of the corporate ladder" (p. 1). The study was sponsored by Deloitte, Goldman Sachs, Pfizer, and Time Warner, and included focus groups, Virtual Strategy Sessions, one-on-one interviews, and a U.S. national survey conducted by Knowledge Networks under the auspices of the Center for Work-Life Policy, a nonprofit research organization. It relied on both quantitative and qualitative data—national on-line survey data and data from virtual focus groups/interviews—conducted in 2010 and 2011. In contrast to the image of the unassertive Asian, the study revealed that Asians are just as likely as other groups to directly ask a manager or supervisor for a pay raise or a promotion. Moreover, it was found that fewer than half (46%) of Asians had a mentor in their professional lives, making them 15% less likely to have a mentor than Whites. This study confirms that Asian Americans experience a "bamboo ceiling," which should be cited by policymakers. Policymakers and other stakeholders must recognize that Asian Americans are not a model minority and deserve considerable attention when it comes to corporate leadership representation. Due to their continuing population growth, it only makes sense that Asian Americans be better (proportionally) represented in the upper echelons of corporate America. Two other key findings in the report that refute the "model minority" stereotype are as follows: (1) "Asian men are more likely to feel stalled in their careers than any other group: 63 percent of Asian men feel stalled versus 46 percent of African-American men, 51 percent of Hispanic men and 48 percent of Caucasian men" (p. 4); and (2) "Twenty-five percent of Asians feel that they face workplace discrimination because of their ethnicity while only 8 percent of African-Americans, 9 percent of Hispanics and 4 percent of Caucasians believe that Asians are treated unfairly in the workplace" (p. 4).

Ho, P. (2003). Performing the "Oriental": Professionals and the Asian model minority myth. *Journal of Asian American Studies, 6*(2), 149–175.

***Ho (2003) writes, "Asian Americans are the United States' Model Minority of the late twentieth century" (p. 149). Ho (2003) also notes, "Despite its inaccuracy, the myth persists because it reifies American ideological tenets that valorize self-sufficiency, [and] persistence" (p. 149). In researching this article, Ho (2003) examined how Chinese American and Korean American professionals "performed the Oriental." In order to secure jobs, these Asian American professionals "performed the Oriental," which reified "racist stereotypes of the homogenous alien Asian 'Other' in corporate America" (p. 169). Ho (2003) shares a story about how one of the study participants actually mimicked the behaviors of his White mentor. Ho (2003) says, "Ironically, the 'Oriental' (John) relied upon the 'Occidental' (his mentor), who was more adept at 'performing the Oriental' in the world of Chinese business, to gain entry into 'the Orient'" (p. 160). This article can be used in scholarship that examines "ethnic options" (see Waters, 1990) and the ways in which socioeconomic class impacts the behaviors of Asian Americans. The article is a longer read, but well worth the time.

Hoy, R. R. (1993). A 'model minority' speaks out on cultural shyness. *Science, 262*(5136), 1117–1118.

***Hoy (1993), an American born Chinese professor of neurobiology and behavior at Cornell University, writes the following: "No matter how many generations Asian-American scientists have been in the United States, on first meeting they will invariably be perceived as *foreigners*" (p. 1117, italics added). Hoy (1993) introduces the term "cultural shyness." According to Hoy (1993) Asian American scientists are marginalized due to "cultural shyness," which allows them to be overlooked, contributing to the "glass ceiling" they bump into professionally. Hoy (1993) describes how his high school teachers' perceptions of him changed depending on the stereotype the teacher held of Asians (e.g., Chinese are good memorizers but are not logical thinkers, or Chinese are born mathematicians, etc.). Hoy (1993) writes that

> stereotypes of the 'model minority' deny or marginalize genuine problems, such as an aversion to the spotlight, and a perception that all Asians in the U.S. are *foreign*, not American. Stereotypes of the well-behaved 'model minority' create problems for the way that other minorities relate to Asians, and deny the enormous cultural and ethnic diversity subsumed under 'Asian American.'" (p. 1117, italics added)

This brief article can be used in scholarly work in order to complement literature that problematizes the stereotype that all Asians are good at math and science. K–12 science teachers and professorial teacher educators will benefit from reading and using this short *Science* article in their classroom with their students.

Iino, M. (1989). Japanese Americans in contemporary American society: A success story? *Japanese Journal of American Studies, 3,* 115–140.

***Iino's (1989) article argues that the socioeconomic status of Japanese Americans in contemporary American society may have improved; nevertheless, they should not be considered to be model minorities. Most interesting is Iino's (1989) contextual description of Japanese Issei as *bamboo* (referring to resiliency), Japanese Nisei as *bananas* (referring to being White on the inside and Asian/Yellow on the outside), and Japanese Sansei as *bees* (referring to the mixture of the Black and Yellow Power movements). Iino's (1989) explanatory application of Marcus Lee Hansen's law of third-generation return is noteworthy and is not seen in other model minority scholarship. Consequently, since this article mainly addresses Japanese American assimilation and generational mobility, it should be used by segmented assimilation theorists for theoretical and practical work, as well as by teachers to discuss patterns of ethnic/racial uplift.

Inkelas, K. K. (2006). *Racial attitudes and Asian Pacific Americans: Demystifying the model minority.* New York, NY: Routledge.

***This study examines the complex sources and implications of the racial attitudes of Asian Pacific American (APA) college students, who, as one of the fastest growing demographics in higher education enrollments, play an increasingly significant role in campus race relations. Drawing upon research on racial attitudes, racial/ethnic identity, and college impact theory, this study explores the views of APA students on such contemporary and controversial racial issues as affirmative action principles and practices, discrimination and social inequality, and racial/ethnic identification. The study was Inkelas's dissertation—"Demystifying the Model Minority: The Influences of Identity and the College Experience on Asian Pacific American Undergraduates' Racial Attitudes"—which she completed while a student at the University of Michigan, and which consequently received the NASPA Melvene Hardee Dissertation of the Year Award.

Kagawa-Singer, M. & Hune, S. (Eds.). (2011). Forging the future: The role of new research, data, and policies for Asian Americans, Native Hawaiians, and Pacific Islanders. *AAPI Nexus Journal, 9*(1&2), iii–268. Retrieved on November 15, 2011 from http://www.aasc.ucla.edu/aascpress/nexus9_1_2_full.pdf

***According to the AASC UCLA website, this special edition, special double issue, 283-page report is arguably the most comprehensive publication to date on Asian Americans, Native Hawaiians, and Pacific Islanders (AANHPI), demographic data trends, and federal policy—including policy briefs on civil rights, economic development, education, health, and Native Hawaiians and Pacific Islanders by over 50 leading AANHPI scholars, applied-researchers, and community leaders from all over the nation. Answering President Barack Obama's call to increase participation by Asian Americans and Pacific Islanders (AAPI) in federal programs, UCLA's Asian American Studies Center is spotlighting ways to improve education, healthcare, and housing for traditionally under-represented groups, like Native Hawaiians and Hmong Americans, with this pioneering new AAPI Nexus journal special issue. The release of this journal coincides with the second anniversary of the White House Initiative on Asian Americans and Pacific Islanders (WHIAAPI), established on October 14, 2009, when President Obama signed Executive Order 13515: "Increasing the Participation of Asian Americans and Pacific Islanders in Federal Programs." The special issue includes activities of the White House Initiative on Asian Americans and Pacific Islanders from 2009–2011, and research originally presented at a WHIAAPI convention on research and data collection in December, 2010. This publication was made possible through the generous support of and sponsorship by Asian and Pacific Islander American Scholarship Fund (APIASF), Association of Asian Pacific Community Health Organizations (AAPCHO), National Coalition for Asian Pacific American Community Development (National CAPACD), CUNY Asian American/Asian Research Institute, UCLA Asian American Studies Center, National Asian Pacific American Women's Forum (NAPAWF), Okura Mental Health Leadership Foundation, Asian Pacific Partners for Empowerment, Advocacy and Leadership (APPEAL), University of California, Asian American Pacific Islander Policy Multi-Campus Research Program (UC AAPI Policy MRP), Ford Foundation Building Economic Security Over a Lifetime Initiative, University of Massachusetts at Boston, Institute for Asian American Studies, National Council of Asian Pacific Americans (NCAPA), Ford Kuramoto, and Lois M. Takahashi.

Kawai, Y. (2005). Stereotyping Asian Americans: The dialectic of the model minority and yellow peril. *Howard Journal of Communications, 16*(2), 109–130.

***The author of this article argues that the model minority stereotype, a positive stereotype, is inseparable from the yellow peril, an extremely nationalistic and negative stereotype. Using theories of racial triangulation and ambivalence of stereotypes, Kawai explains how the myth of Asians as model minorities is two-faced and that it supports colorblindness. Important to mention, Kawai (2005) states that "both historical and present U.S. and Asian contexts influence the construction of Asian American stereotypes" (p. 111). The article examines historical as well as present day examples of the model minority, explaining the relationship between the stereotype of model minority and yellow peril. The focal time period, however, is the 1980s—given that this decade marks a revival in the model minority/yellow peril dialectic. In addition to a literary analysis of this dialectic, Kawai also critically examines the 1993 Hollywood movie *Rising Sun*, looking for examples of exaggeration and stereotypical portrayals. Kawai notes that "the exaggeration of foreignness is an important feature of the yellow peril stereotype" (p. 122). Moreover, according to Kawai (2005), "People of Asian descent become the model minority when they are depicted to do better than other racial minority groups, whereas they become the yellow peril when they are described to outdo White Americans" (p. 115). This article makes noteworthy contributions to the way model minority myth researchers can understand the ideological characteristics of stereotyping, but also, in the words of Kawai:

> The point of viewing the model minority and the yellow peril stereotypes as a whole—not opposite and separate entities—lies not only in understanding the characteristics of stereotypes but also in being conscious of the political implications of the model minority stereotype that seems to be "positive" and currently more "official" than the yellow peril stereotype. (p. 126)

Kibria, N. (2002). The model minority at work. In N. Kibria, *Becoming Asian American: Second-generation Chinese and Korean American identities* (pp. 131–158). Baltimore, MD: Johns Hopkins University Press.

***Kibria's (2002) chapter explores the effect of the model minority stereotype on Asian American individuals. The model minority stereotype is insidious, notes Kibria (2002): "That is, since Asian Americans are able to pull themselves up by their own cultural bootstraps, the racial disadvantage suffered by minorities is not in fact structural to American society, and therefore no active intervention is required to remedy it" (p. 134). Kibria (2002) details how the lives of the Asian Americans in her study were affected by the model minority stereotype. For instance, Duncan, a Chinese American, indicated that he was not an Asian whiz kid despite being a medical doctor. Soo Jin, a Korean American, felt as though she did not do well academically despite having earned a law degree. And finally, Ki Hong, a Korean American, asserted that he was not a "typical" Asian since he preferred athletics over academics. Kibria (2002) found that for the Asian American participants in her study, "disclaiming model minority achievement seemed to be in part about disidentifying [oneself] from the image of the 'Asian nerd'" (p. 138). Kibria (2002) found that the model minority stereotype impacted the professional and career mobility and trajectory of the Asian Americans in her study, which was manifested in barriers such as racism and a "glass ceiling." Consequently, the model minority stereotype paints Asian Americans as ineffectual leaders by labeling them as quiet and passive. Believed to be book smart—while lacking social skills and assertiveness thought to be necessary—Asians are overlooked and under promoted in positions of leadership. Kibria's (2002) chapter also documents topics of importance for scholarly work on the model minority myth. Many of the participants in this book chapter indicated that affirmative action was at odds with Asian cultural values—such as self-sufficiency, asceticism, and independence—and therefore had the possibility of being stigmatizing for Asian Americans. To summarize Kibria's (2002) chapter:

> The model minority stereotype is the ideology that undergirds what [Kibria has] described as "a part yet apart," the double-edged position of Asian Americans today in straddling both integration into and marginalization from the dominant society. (p. 157)

The effect of the model minority on Asian American individuals is at times integrative, while at other times marginalizing. This chapter moves away from the theoretical, to dive deeply into the practical life-implications of the model minority stereotype for Asian Americans. Educators, counselors, social workers, and psychologists should read this chapter in order to better grasp how the model minority stereotype is detrimental for Asian Americans.

Kim, L. S. (2008). Continuing significance of the model minority myth: The second generation. *Social Justice, 35*(2), 134–144.

***This article is highly critical, cerebral, analytical, and philosophical in orientation. According to Kim (2008), "The model minority actually reinforces established racial inequalities" (p. 136). In the vein of racial inequality reinforcement, this article addresses elements of the deleterious stereotype. One such example is the idea that Asian Americans are "good role models"—quiet, passive, well-behaved, law abiding, and hard workers. Other examples are the "rags-to-riches" narratives that this myth propagates. Since Kim was interested in the (im)migration narratives of second generation Asian Americans, she interviewed 88 Chinese and Korean American children of immigrants. The interviewees were of high school and college age and shared similar testimonies insofar as "the children knew very little about the actual experience of their parents' decision to emigrate and their experiences upon arrival" (p. 134). According to her analysis of the interview transcript data, the shift of narratives of perpetual foreigner status is maintained through model minority mythology. This mythology has moorings that are steeped in American mythology. Kim (2008) writes, "As a form of American mythology, the idea of the model minority can be traced back to American Puritanism, which promoted a sense of independence and self-reliance through individual achievement and understood success and failure as a moral distinction" (p. 36). This is highly problematic: Kim (2008) writes that "the model minority myth associates virtue with success and sin with failure" (p. 136). This article is important for model minority myth research, for it acknowledges that certain narratives reinforce racial inequality by serving as a master-script for White supremacy. Asian critical race theoreticians (AsianCrits) may consult this authoritatively-written article.

Kim, P. S. (1994). Myth and realities of the model minority. *The Public Manager, 23*(3), 31–35.

***Allegedly, Asian Americans are "model minorities" due to their scholastic and occupational achievements. Kim's (1994) easy-to-understand article tackles the model minority stereotype in a fierce but simple way: by juxtaposing the myths and realities of the model minority stereotype. One myth is that Asian Americans are perceived as exempt from poverty. Kim discusses how median household income conceals what per capita reveals. The reality is that Asian Americans experience limited economic opportunity, and they are also underrepresented in the state and local sectors. Another reality is that "the Asian American community [in] actuality differs substantially from the myth of uniform success" (p. 33), and have greater obstacles to success than many acknowledge and/or realize. Moreover, according to Kim (1994), "Being Asian has become a disadvantage for women in a way it had not been in the recent past [up to 1978]" (p. 34). Lastly, Kim's (1994) observation of where Asian Pacific are found on the occupational hierarchy is worth quoting:

> The fact that Asian Pacific are overrepresented at both the top and the bottom of the occupational hierarchy is cited as evidence that they experience discrimination in obtaining positions commensurate with their education and training and are not promoted according to their qualification. (p. 35)

This article can be used by high school teachers and college professors as a conversation starter for much more focused discussions of the model minority as a flawed fable.

Kim, R. Y. & Im, H. (2008, August). *Looking beyond the model Asian family images: The case of Korean American immigrant marriages and families*. Paper presented at the American Sociological Association Annual Meeting, Boston, MA.

***Kim and Im's (2008) conference paper is very unique insofar as it examines the various hidden sources of tensions within Korean American marriages and identifies marriage/family support needs and strategies for the community. Using data collected during the summer of 2007, Kim and Im (2008) conducted five focus groups with 37 Korean American church and community leaders. 238 surveys were also collected by Korean Churches for Community Development (KCCD) as part of its Asian Pacific American Healthy Marriage Network (APAHMN) program. Kim and Im (2008) write that "to effectively impact marriages in the Korean American community, significant investments need to be made on educating the community on the positive and practical benefits of marriage education like improved health, communication skills and relationships with children" (p. 13). The model minority stereotype interferes with the marital realities of Asian (Korean) Americans; this conference paper is a form of a counter- story that helps combat the model minority stereotype.

Kitano, H. & Sue, S. (1973). The model minorities. *Journal of Social Issues, 29*(2), 1–9.

***Kitano and Sue's (1973) nine-page article is the introduction to a *Journal of Social Issues* special edition. According to Kitano and Sue (1973), "The purpose of this collection of papers is to examine the status of two groups, the Chinese and the Japanese" (p. 1). The special edition contains 11 articles, one commentary, and one rejoinder, totaling 218 pages.

Kramer, E. M. (Ed.). (2003). *The emerging monoculture: Assimilation and the "model minority."* Westport, CT: Praeger.

***This edited volume has received good reviews (e.g., see Lizardo, 2004). Kramer (2003) states that "the point of this book is to bring together experts from a variety of 'minority' backgrounds and from around the world to give their learned and unique perspectives on the most pervasive ideology today, which is assimilation on a global scale" (p. xi). The book is comprised of 14 chapters, all focusing on the model minority myth.

Kramer, E. (2003). Introduction: Assimilation and the model minority ideology. In E. M. Kramer (Ed.), *The emerging monoculture: Assimilation and the "model minority"* (pp. xi–xxi). Westport, CT: Praeger.

***Kramer's (2003) book chapter (introduction) summarizes each of the 14 chapters (see pp. xv–xxi) contained in *The Emerging Monoculture: Assimilation and the "Model Minority."*

Kurashige, S. (2008). Toward a model minority. In S. Kurashige, *The shifting grounds of race: Black and Japanese Americans in the making of multiethnic Los Angeles: Toward A model minority* (pp. 186–204). Princeton, NJ: Princeton University Press.

***Kurashige's (2008) book chapter covers a substantial amount of history that helps readers contextualize the historical (in)action that has caused the "model minority" myth to percolate into the American mainstream reality. Kurashige helps everyone remember that Asian Americans have historically been viewed as foreign and unpatriotic. This chapter addresses the "model minority" stereotype generally, but also specifically highlights the history of Japanese Americans. Much of the Japanese American history that is reviewed in this chapter is World War II related and tied to the myriad ways that the model minority myth constructed Japanese Americans into becoming "model" citizens. Critical historians will find this chapter useful in their teaching and scholarship. Much of the material presented in this chapter pertains to the Japanese internment. The history that it presents reminded me of Drinnon's (1987) book *Keeper of Concentration Camps: Dillon S. Myer and American Racism* and Takaki's (1998) book *Strangers from a Difference Shore: A History of Asian Americans.*

Lawler, A. (2000). Silent no longer: 'Model minority' mobilizes. *Science, 290*(5494), 1072–1077.

***Lawler's (2000) article covers the systemic and oftentimes institutionalized discrimination that Asian American scientists experience. Lawler (2000), in the wake of the firing and imprisonment of Wen Ho Lee, discusses such topics as pay and promotion inequality, as well as under-representation in leadership positions, among Asian American scientists working in national laboratories in California and New Mexico. The article highlights various Asian Americans who have become outspoken about this discriminatory treatment. According to Lawler (2000), scientific laboratories, the U.S. Department of Energy (DOE) and universities must be cognizant of the ways they treat their Asian American employees, else they run the risk of creating a reverse "brain drain" whereby highly educated, experienced, and trained Asian American scientists migrate to other countries. This article can be used for teaching and writing on the model minority stereotype, especially in terms of occupational discrimination.

Lee, R. G. (2010). The Cold War origins of the model minority myth. In J. Y. -S. Wu & T. C. Chen (Eds.), *Asian American studies now: A critical reader* (pp. 256–271). New Brunswick, NJ: Rutgers University Press.

***Lee (2010) notes that "although the deployment of Asian Americans as a *model minority* was made explicit in the *mid-1960s, its origins lay in the triumph of liberalism and the racial logic of the Cold War*" (p. 256, italics added). Lee's (2010) chapter describes the Cold War origins of the model minority stereotype. "On the international front," writes Lee (2010), "the narrative of ethnic assimilation sent a message to the Third World, especially to Asia where the United States was engaged in increasingly fierce struggles with nationalist and communist insurgencies, that the United States was a liberal democratic state where people of color [Asian Americans] could enjoy equal rights and upward mobility" (p. 257). Lee's (2010) chapter points out the following two important and often overlooked points: (1) Japan's attack on Pearl Harbor (America's entry into WWII) marked the unraveling of the yellow peril myth, and (2) "the construction of the model minority was based on the political silence of Asian America" (p. 261), since the post-War international context was a foreign relations nightmare. During the 1960s, societal and state-sponsored discrimination raised serious doubts about America's devotion to the democratic faith. The model minority myth, therefore, served as a political, rhetorical, and international public relations solution: it quelled the global perception that America was *not* democratic by affirming that it in fact *was* an egalitarian democracy founded on the principle that meritocratic effort allowed everyone to be free and prosper. This book chapter assists readers of all types (beginners and experts) in understanding that the model minority stereotype is a by-product of both political and societal contexts and forces. The 1941 "How to Tell Japs from the Chinese" *Life* article, the congressional vote to repeal the Chinese Exclusion Act in 1943, and the congressionally authorized Chinese Confession Program in 1957 are but three exemplars. Lee's (2010) chapter originally appeared in Lee's (1999) *Orientals: Asian Americans in Popular Culture* (pp. 145–179). This book chapter is an important piece of literature that needs to be included in the literature reviews of scholarly work on the model minority stereotype.

Lee, S. J., Wong, N. A., & Alvarez, A. N. (2009). The model minority and the perpetual foreigner: Stereotypes of Asian Americans. In N. Tewari & A. N. Alvarez (Eds.), *Asian American psychology: Current perspectives* (pp. 69–85). New York, NY: Psychology Press.

***This book chapter traces the genesis of two stereotypes—the model minority and the perpetual foreigner—that Asian Americans experience.

Authors Lee, Wong, and Alvarez (2009) define *model minority* as follows: "stereotype of Asian Americans that promotes the image of Asian Americans as uniformly successful in terms of economic, educational, and social capital" (p. 82). Lee, Wong, and Alvarez (2009) also define *perpetual foreigner* as follows: "stereotype of Asian Americans as being unassimilable into U.S. culture and as nonresidents regardless of their years in the United States" (p. 82). The sixteen page chapter begins by outlining the origins of the model minority (in the 1960s), pointing out that twenty years later, in the 1980s, the myth barnacled itself to Asian American academic achievement. Accordingly, the authors detail three reasons the myth is harmful to Asian Americans: (1) it masks diversity, (2) it causes interracial tension, and (3) it causes Asian Americans to self-silence.

This chapter highlights *how* and *why* the model minority stereotype is so damaging; specifically, it constrains Asian American students who struggle in school settings against racism, poverty, discrimination, and anti-foreigner sentiment. Lee, Wong, and Alvarez state the following: "The *model minority stereotype* therefore enforces the *erroneous perception* that Asian Americans no longer experience racism and discrimination and thus do not need social services like bilingual education, affirmative action, health care, welfare, and so on" (p. 74, italics added). This chapter is original in that it includes supplemental items, such as the following: six chapter discussion questions, a case study of an 18-year-old Chinese American high school senior, five case study discussion questions, the definitions of seven key terms used in the chapter, and suggested readings for future learning (including movies and web sites). The chapter will be a useful read for undergraduate as well as graduate students, as well as for beginning therapists.

Leung, Y. L. (2002). The model minority myth: Asian Americans confront growing backlash. In L. J. McIntyre (Ed.), *The practical skeptic: Readings in sociology* (pp. 321–325). Boston, MA: McGraw-Hill.

***Leung's (2002) book chapter addresses the multifaceted "backlash" that Asian Americans experience as a consequence of the model minority stereotype. For instance, Asian American educational success is considered threatening to Whites, which makes anti-affirmative action protection appealing. In other words, Whites do not consider Asian American students to need affirmative action protection. Resentment and anti-Asian American sentiments can result in death, as witnessed in the Vincent Chin murder. Leung (2002) writes the following:

> Because of the disproportionate numbers of Asian Americans in the nation's universities, some colleges are denying Asians affirmative action consideration. At Princeton University, for example, where Asians make up approximately 8.5 percent of the entering class, admissions officials no longer con-

sider Asian Americans as a minority group, despite federal regulations, which define them as a protected subgroup. (p. 323)

The main idea of Leung's (2002) book chapter can be summarized as: "Repercussions [backlash] of the model minority myth on Asian Americans could be described as 'the many being punished by the success of a few'" (p. 323). This book chapter could be cited by teachers/researchers examining Asian Americans and affirmative action. Leung's (2002) chapter is a reprint of the following article: Leung, Y. L. (1987, September/October). The Model minority myth: Asian Americans confront growing backlash. *The Minority Trendsetter: A Publication from the Center for Third World Organizing,* 5–7.

Leong, F. T. L., Chao, R. K., & Hardin, E. E. (2000). Asian American adolescents: A research review to dispel the model minority myth. In R. Montemayor, G. R. Adams, & T. P. Gullotta (Eds.), *Adolescent diversity in ethnic, economic, and cultural contexts* (pp. 179–207). Thousand Oaks, CA: Sage Publications.

***Leong, Chao, and Hardin's (2000, p. 179) book chapter argues that "research on the development of Asian American adolescents is becoming especially crucial" due to demographic trends. Important for the fields of education and sociology, their cogent chapter "reviewed the literature on Asian American adolescent development in three major areas: academic achievement, ethnic development, and psychological adjustment" (Leong, Chao, & Hardin, 2000, p. 202). Leong, Chao, and Hardin (2000) write that "the literature does not entirely support the model minority perspective, namely that Asian American adolescents are highly successful" (pp. 202-203). Accordingly, Leong, Chao, and Hardin (2000) write that the model minority

myth ignores the bimodal distribution in many Asian American communities where there are successful Asian Americans as well as Asian Americans living at the poverty level and working in "sweat shops." It [the myth] also overlooks the distribution of severe mental illnesses and major adjustment difficulties among many Asian Americans. (p. 180)

The authors effectively refute the notion that the model minority stereotype could be positive for Asian Americans, writing the following: "If Asian American adolescents are excelling in school because they fear it is their only hope for success in a discriminatory society, or if they are sacrificing pursuit of their true interests because they believe their opportunities are limited, *the model minority image cannot be seen as positive*" (p. 187, italics added). The most major contribution that this chapter makes to the corpus of literature on the model minority stereotype is found in a statement it makes about future anti-model minority stereotype research:

By portraying Asian American adolescents as uniformly successful and well-adjusted, the model minority myth has discouraged researchers from investigating the challenges they face. *Emphasizing the diversity among Asian American adolescents rather than differences between them and other groups will allow us to begin to construct a more realistic understanding of the unique and complex factors affecting the development of Asian American adolescents.* (Leong, Chao, & Hardin, 2000, p. 204, italics added)

This book chapter can be cited in literature reviews and used in college/university courses as a reading that provides students with a broad overview of important and salient issues for the adolescent Asian American population.

Li, J. (2004). Exploring Asian Americans: The myth of the "model minority" and the reality of their lives. In A. Konradi & M. Schmidt (Eds.), *Reading between the lines: Toward an understanding of current social problems* (3rd ed., pp. 198–207). Boston, MA: McGraw Hill Higher Education.

***Li's (2004) chapter addresses the model minority stereotype, which is a current social problem for Asian Americans. Li addresses five model minority myths, providing ample evidence as to why the myth is incorrect and predicated on misleading data. The myths that Li (2004) outlines are as follows: (1) "Asian Americans as an ethnic group are generally faring well" (p. 199); (2) "Asian Americans have reached and even surpassed educational and earnings parities with Whites" (p. 199); (3) "Asian Americans are successful entrepreneurs who have occupied more managerial positions" (p. 202); (4) "Asian American youth are 'whiz kids'" (p. 204); and (5) "Asian Americans don't seem to have any problems" (p. 204). All five myths share at least one of the following inadequacies:

- It overlooks cultural and socioeconomic differences existent among Asian Americans;
- It relies on statistical analyses that don't account for return on education, large family sizes, and subgroups of Asian Americans;
- It overlooks struggling Asian American students in schools;
- It homogenizes Asian Americans into being perceived as not needing assistance;
- It fails to acknowledge the "glass ceiling" barrier that Asian Americans face and bump up against as professionals;
- It misunderstands that Asian Americans' entrepreneurial and managerial positions are largely the function of self-employment, not in large firms and corporations; and
- It causes society to ignore the poverty, unemployment, and illiteracy within the Asian American population.

Li's (2004) chapter is easy to read, follow, and understand. The cogent chapter concludes with four questions for discussion:

1. "Why is 'Asian' a controversial racial designation?"
2. "How does the social construction of the model minority work against the successful extension of social policies to people who need them?"
3. "Which model minority myth associated with Asian Americans is most problematic?"
4. "How does the ideology of a model minority result in structural consequences? Consider, for example, college admissions policies, affirmative action programs, and immigration policy."

K–12 teachers and college professors of many disciplines may wish to assign Li's (2004) chapter for reading, using the four discussion questions as a review or for prompts to begin lectures or lessons. Li's (2004) book chapter is held in high esteem and therefore was reprinted and can also be found in Robert McNamara's (1999) edited volume, *Perspectives in Social Problems* (pp. 134–141). Boulder, CO: Coursewise Publishing Inc.

Look, A. (1980, November). "Model minority" makes waves: Asian/Pacific American women on the move. *Ms Gazette, 9,* 33.

***Look's (1980) article talks about the establishment of the National Association for Asian and Pacific Americans. The article is helpful for educators at all levels and scholars of all types since it prompts readers to find more information about APA women organizations, such as (1) the National Asian Pacific American Women's Forum, http://napawf.org; (2) the Asian American Business Women Association, http://www.aabwa.org; (3) the Asian American Women Artists Association, http://www.aawaa.net; (4) Asian Women in Business, http://www.awib.org; (5) the South Asian Women's Network, http://www.sawnet.org; (6) the Asian Women's Resource Exchange, http://www.aworc.org; and (7) the National Asian Women's Health Organization, http://www.nawho.org/.

Mahalingam, R. & Haritatos, J. (2010). *Gender and model minority myth and psychological well-being of Asian Americans.* Unpublished Manuscript, University of Michigan.

***Mahalingam and Haritatos's (2010) unpublished paper is referenced on Professor Mahalingam's professional website, here: http://rammahalingham.weebly.com/iii-model-minority-myth-and-psychological-well-being-of-asian-americans.html. It is summarized as follows:

I proposed a dual process model to study the complex consequences of endorsing model minority myth (Mahalingam, 2006). I developed a model minority myth scale to examine the role of model minority pride and pressure in shaping the psychological well-being of Asian Americans in gender-specific ways. I identified four modes of negotiating the pride and pressure (Poised, Stressed, Balanced and Energized) associated with being a model minority (for a review, see Mahalingam in press). In addition, we are examining the consequences of endorsing model minority beliefs in shaping the psychological well-being of Asian immigrants, Asian American men, women and adolescents.

Maclear, K. (1994). The myth of the "model minority": Rethinking the education of Asian Canadians. *Our Schools/Our Selves, 5*(3), 54–76.

***Maclear's (1994, July) *Our Schools/Our Selves* article addresses the model minority stereotype in the context of Canada. According to Maclear's clear, cogent article, the model minority stereotype impacts the Asian Canadian population negatively similarly to its effect on Asian Americans. Case in point, writes Maclear (1994), "The catch-all of a 'model minority' (seen as a 'positive stereotype') has made it possible for educators, administrators and government officials to ignore the differential needs and the very real, and often systemic, barriers faced by Asians in Canada" (p. 55). Just as the journalistic media in the United States perpetuates the model minority stereotype, so does the Canadian journalistic media. Maclear (1994) pinpoints an issue that model minority stereotype research has perennially problematized:

> If we are to cut through the constellation of stereotypes that entrap a heterogeneous grouping of "Asian" students and locate the partisan values invoked through "model minority" discourse, we should be asking several questions: "Success" on whose terms? "Model" of what? [and] "Model" for whom? (p. 57)

This article is written with educational practitioners in mind: It discusses the educational implications of the model minority stereotype and its consequences. Maclear concludes with this salient observation:

> The coding of Asian students within a narrow paradigm of "success" amounts to a form of social control. Boxed in by value-ridden expectations and pre-packaged course options, many Asian students have been denied their right to be seen as complex, diverse, and communicating subjects. (p. 71)

This article can be adopted in teacher education and preparation courses at the collegiate level. Pre-service teachers in the United States, and certainly Canada, will profit from reading and reflecting on Maclear's (1994) thoughts.

Marbley, A. F. (2011). The Asian and Asian American client's story: The myth of the model minority. In A. F. Marbley, *Multicultural counseling: Perspectives from counselors as clients of color* (pp. 49–62). New York, NY: Routledge.

***Marbley's (2011) book chapter is the fourth in her *Multicultural Counseling: Perspectives from Counselors as Clients of Color.* The chapter examines the counseling of Asian American populations and the impact that historical oppression and current "model minority" status has on the lives of Asians in America. Marbley (2011) focuses on a case study of Mai Li and Wai's, documenting the experiences of two Asian American female clients' experiences with counseling. This chapter is important because "counseling is not a part of Asian culture; therefore, counselors can create ways that are compatible with the culture to encourage Asian clients to use counseling services" (Marbley, 2011, pp. 61–62). The main argument that Marbley (2011) presents is that the model minority stereotype, problematically, homogenizes Asian Americans' experiences and histories. This chapter can be used in counseling programs and courses on culturally relevant patient care.

Matthes, M. (2007). *Chinese Americans—A model minority?* Munich, Germany: GRIN Publishing.

***Matthes' (2007) downloadable seminar paper is 23 pages in length and a quick read. Although it contains many misspellings, it nevertheless has one main strength: its reference to Ronald Reagan's (in)famous speech delivered in 1984 at the chief executive's mansion in which he praised Asian Pacific Americans for their hard work and tenacity, reifying the Asian American model minority stereotypic construction (also see Takaki, 1998, pp. 474–475).

McGowan, M. H. & Lindgren, J. T. (2003). Untangling the myth of the model minority. *Northwestern University School of Law: Public Law and Legal Theory Papers,* paper 26, 1–58. Retrieved on February 6, 2012, from http://law.bepress.com/cgi/viewcontent.cgi?art icle=1071&context=nwwps

***McGowan and Lindgren's (2003) 58-page paper attempts to untangle the model minority myth. But truthfully, their article does little to demystify the stereotype. McGowan and Lindgren (2003) state, "Both those who support the model minority critique and those who reject it—as well as those of us who both support it in many respects and question it in others—need to be careful to present our generalizations, not as essences or necessities, but as conclusions that are true to the extent that they fit the world and untrue to the extent that they don't fit what they claim to capture" (p. 58). Using General Social Survey (GSS) data, McGowan and Lindgren (2003) explore the model minority stereotype quantitatively. The two researchers examine non-Hispanic Whites' responses to a series of questions around concepts of:

(1) foreignness, (2) hostility to Asians and programs for Asians, (3) failure to see discrimination against Asians, and (4) hostility to immigrants and immigration. McGowan and Lindgren's (2003) findings are conservative. They write, "We found nothing to suggest that people who hold generally positive views about Asian Americans' hard work, wealth, and intelligence are trying to conceal their actual feelings of fear, envy, and resentment toward Asian Americans" (p. 57). This paper can be problematized—as have been other papers authored by McGowan and Lindgren (e.g., see Chang & Villazor's [2007] incisive critique)—since it operates under a colorblind set of conditions. The measures used in this study were inadequate and inappropriately assume that survey respondents will sanguinely be truthful. This article can be used in concert with the Committee of 100 Survey titled "American Attitudes Toward Chinese Americans and Asian Americans" (http://www.committee100.org/publications/survey/C100survey.pdf) to show how silly and naïve it is to believe that the model minority stereotype only reflects positive feelings, and is not used as a hegemonic and White supremacist tool that promotes racism (hidden and overt) and the oppression of non-White minorities.

Mendoza, M. L. (2001). Model minority guilt. In V. Nam (Ed.), *Yell-oh girls! Emerging voices explore culture, identity, and growing up Asian American* (pp. 283–286). New York, NY: HarperCollins.

***Mendoza (2001) writes from the standpoint of her Filipina American identity, capturing her feeling of ambivalence in the college application process as an eighteen-year-old. Her short essay addresses the guilt she felt for not checking the race/ethnicity box on her college admission applications. Mendoza was eventually admitted to the University of California, Berkeley, a campus that has quite a large Asian American presence. Mendoza (2001) elected not to check the box that she is Asian American because she thought it would hurt her chances of getting admitted. She placates her ethnicity, believing that admission officers might believe that she is Mexican American, for instance. Mendoza (2001) closes her personal essay with this reflection:

> And for those who say minorities just have to "work harder" to get where whites and some Asian Americans are now, I say stop pitting everyone against us with this "model minority" shit. I refuse to be your poster person for policies that don't give support where support is needed. (p. 286)

Mendoza's (2001) chapter should be used in a freshman English or writing course. Since college writing courses frequently focus on developing the voice of their novice and neophyte students, Mendoza's (2001) chapter can be used as a course reading given that it is a wonderful example of how her voice is heard loudly in her writing.

Miller, F. P., Vandome, A. F., & McBrewster, J. (Eds.). (2009). *Model minority.* Beau Bassin, Mauritius: Alphascript Publishing.

***Miller, Vandome, and McBrewster's (2009) edited book is somewhat of an oddity. Their ninety-eight page book consists of Wikipedia entries on the model minority and stereotypes of Asian Americans. The book also addresses Asian Americans as beneficiaries of affirmative action. Many of the Wikipedia entries cite references that are useful. Thus, this book is best used to cross-reference in order to locate model minority literature.

Min, E. (2003). Demythologizing the "model minority." In E. M. Kramer (Ed.), *The emerging monoculture: Assimilation and the "model minority"* (pp. 191–202). Westport, CT: Praeger.

***Min's (2003) book chapter attempts to demythologize the model minority stereotype of Asian Americans. Usefully, this chapter indicates that "the model minority [stereotype] bolsters the much-celebrated American dream" (p. 193) while simultaneously maintaining "the social and symbolic order of a hegemonic power" (p. 196). The contribution that this chapter makes, notably, is related to how the model minority stereotype "is a socially constructed reality that is passed-off as natural" (p. 198). It is this naturalization process that makes the stereotype so deadly and destructive. The model minority stereotype is a hegemonic device used to maintain the *status quo* while making *bon sens* to the average citizen in the United States. This book chapter can be read to gain a quick overview of the model minority stereotype.

Model minority: Japanese join mainstream America. (1978, December). *Human Behavior,* 59.

***This article appears in *Human Behavior* and opens with the following sentence: "The success of the Japanese-American community has been so great, and was achieved so rapidly, that some sociologists call them a 'model minority'" (p. 59). Citing the scholarly work of a University of Maryland sociology professor, Darrel Montero, the article discusses why assimilation into the dominant American society will lead to lowered levels of achievement and success for Japanese Americans. This article can be used by segmented assimilation theoreticians (who posit that linear or straight-line assimilation patterns do not necessarily exist), in literature reviews, as well as for referencing the work of Dr. Montero.

Muse, E. A. (2005). Separateness of church: Counter-culture and the model minority. In E. A. Muse, *The evangelical church in Boston's Chinatown: A discourse of language, gender, and identity* (pp. 107–134). New York, NY: Routledge.

***Muse's (2005) chapter is found in her book *The Evangelical Church in Boston's Chinatown: A Discourse of Language, Gender, and Identity,* which shares anthropological data on the identity construction of a rapidly growing Chinese Christian population in the United States. Muse's (2005) chapter compares the model minority to countercultural Christianity. Applying discourse analysis, Muse (2005) indicates that "the model minority is a product of the mainstream ideal of the Protestant ethic and capitalist American society" (p. 111). Muse (2005) goes on to write that "the connection between the Protestant Ethic and the model minority is that of ascetic lifestyles which emphasizes frugality, hard work, success and family" (p. 112). It is this analysis that makes "Separateness of Church: Counter-Culture and the Model Minority" such a powerful, useful, and relevant chapter. Muse (2005) found that Christianity *enhances* Chinese culture; it does not *replace* it. This chapter can be used in a variety of ways: literature reviews, feminist Asian American writing, and for teaching about the model minority's relationship to Christianity.

Museus, S. D. & Kiang, P. N. (2009). Deconstructing the model minority myth and how it contributes to the invisible minority reality in higher education research. *New Directions for Institutional Research, 142,* 5–15.

***This short article draws attention to the notion that a better understanding of the model minority myth of Asian American students can help society move toward generating a more authentic understanding of these students. Museus and Kiang's (2009) article is the first in the special issue of *New Directions for Institutional Research,* "Conducting Research on Asian Americans in Higher Education." They address five misconceptions associated with the model minority myth. These myths are as follows: (1) Asian Americans are all the same; (2) Asian Americans are not really racial and ethnic minorities; (3) Asian Americans do not encounter major challenges because of their race; (4) Asian Americans do not seek or require resources and support; and (5) college degree completion is equivalent to success. Museus and Kiang (2009) provide an incredibly straightforward definition of the model minority stereotype: "The model minority stereotype is the notion that Asian Americans achieve universal and unparalleled academic and occupational success" (p. 6). Readers will want to view the reference pages for the many great references that can be used for scholar practitioner work.

Nakayama, T. K. (1988). "Model minority" and the media: Discourse on Asian America. *Journal of Communication Inquiry, 12*(1), 65–73.

***Nakayama's (1988) article looks at the model minority stereotype as a discursive construction. Part of this social construction requires "the blurring of the distinction between 'Asians' and 'Asian Americans'" (Nakayama, 1988, p. 68), as well as the emphasis on Asian culture. This social construction—the model minority stereotype—has internal contradictions and should be questioned, according to Nakayama (1988), since the model minority discourse shifts discussion away from White supremacy. Nakayama

(1988) concludes, "From this analysis, then, we can see that the 'model minority' discursive formation situates Asian Americans as serving the social function of legitimating *status quo* institutions. Consequently, minority problems with the education system reside not in the system, but with minorities" (p. 71). This article will be useful for rhetorical scholars who are interested in examining the model minority stereotype as a rhetorical, as well as socially-constructed, device for power and *status quo* maintenance.

Nance, M. (2007). Unmasking the model minority myth. *Diverse: Issues in higher education, 24*(22), 10–11.

***Nance's (2007) article highlights the Asian Pacific American Student Success (APASS) Program at City College of San Francisco (CCSF). APASS is geared to serving Asian and Pacific Islander college students. According to Nance (2007), "Asians, who make up 41 percent of the students at CCSF, make up 99 percent of the students getting help from APASS because they're on academic probation or need assistance in various subjects" (p. 10). The APASS retention program is evidence that the model minority stereotype is simply not a true reflection of the entire population of Asian American students. Nance's (2007) article is important and highlights issues in higher education that must be addressed by policies and programs, such as retention and remediation, and APASS. This article can be cited in reviews of literature for programs that are geared toward serving low-performing Asian American college students. Readers might consider viewing the APASS webpage: http://www.ccsf.edu/apass.

Nance, M. (2007). Combating the model minority stereotype. *Diverse: Issues in higher education, 24*(15), 9.

***This article discusses "the establishment of the first University of California Asian American and Pacific Islander Policy Multi-Campus Research Program, headquartered at the Asian American Studies Center at the University of California, Los Angeles" (Nance, 2007, p. 9). The primary work this research program undertakes is combating the model minority stereotype. The article also points out that given certain constraints (proximity, lack of junior faculty, etc.), there are hurdles to cross-campus, collaborative work. This article will be useful for those interested in creating program and collaborative initiatives targeted at dispelling the model minority myth. The article interviews two model minority stereotype scholars—Paul Ong and Don Nakanishi—who may be unfamiliar to some readers.

Ng, J. C., Lee, S. S., & Pak, Y. K. (2007). Contesting the model minority and perpetual foreigner stereotypes: A critical review of literature on Asian Americans in education. *Review of Research in Education, 31*(1), 95–130.

***Ng, Lee, and Pak's chapter is the fourth of seven in the *Review of Research in Education's* "Difference, Diversity, and Distinctiveness in Education and

Learning," introduced by Laurence Parker. Ng and her colleagues' literature review is critical insofar as it documents many of the issues surrounding Asian Americans in relation to the model minority stereotype and other interrelated issues, such as foreignness, citizenship, identity, and xenophobia, and racism. This is a highly comprehensive review of the literature. Topics addressed include, but are not limited to: (1) cultural explanations to Asian American success, (2) bimodal distribution of Asian American outcomes, (3) statistical and explanatory models to interpret Asian American success, (4) anti-Asian American discrimination, and (5) the glass ceiling. This review contains many references that readers could cross-reference for teaching and research purposes.

Ngo, B. & Lee, S. J. (2007). Complicating the image of model minority success: A review of Southeast Asian American education. *Review of Educational Research*, 77(4), 415–453.

***Ngo and Lee's 38-page literature review on the education of Southeast Asian American students explores the various explanations for the struggles, successes, and educational experiences of Southeast Asian students and recognizes that the "model minority stereotype is used to silence and contain Asian Americans even as it silences other racial groups" (p. 416). The review highlights the disparities of educational outcomes that exist for Southeast Asian American students by ethnic group (Vietnamese American, Cambodian American, Hmong American, and Lao American) in the United States. For each ethnic group Ngo and Lee analyzed explanations for success, evidence of struggles, and evaluated the strengths and weaknesses of the literature. The authors point out that (1) aggregate data mask differential outcomes in terms of attainment and achievement across Asian American groups; (2) the majority of Southeast Asians came to the United States as refugees, not immigrants; (3) "although there is a significant amount of literature on Vietnamese and Hmong students, there is an obvious dearth of research on the education of Cambodian and Lao students" (p. 440); and (4) the current paradigm of successful Asian American students and unsuccessful Asian American students leaves little room for research that examines the nuances in between such polarities. As Ngo and Lee (2007) state in the article's abstract,

> Similar to other Asian American students, Southeast Asian American students are often stereotyped by the popular press as hardworking and high-achieving model minorities. On the other hand, Southeast Asian American youth are also depicted as low-achieving high school dropouts involved in gangs. The realities of academic performance and persistence among Southeast Asian American students are far more complex than either image suggests. (p. 415)

This article is highly consequential to model-minority-destroying research due to its ability to convey important messages, such as the need for disaggregation. It also provides groundwork for future research to better

> understand the complexity of experiences often masked by the model minority image [that] highlight[s] *Asian American student success.* Examining the contexts of education also will allow us [the Asian American community] to uncover the circumstances in which [Asian American] students are learning or not learning. (p. 444, italics added)

Nguyen, V. T. (2002). Model minorities and bad subjects. In V. T. Nguyen, *Race & Resistance: Literature & Politics in Asian America* (pp. 143–171). New York, NY: Oxford University Press.

***" Model Minorities and Bad Subjects" is the conclusion of the book *Race & Resistance: Literature & Politics in Asian America.* Nguyen's (2002) chapter brings up many helpful concepts related to the model minority stereotype, such as the fact that Asian Americans are the recipients of "racist love," not "racist hate," since the model minority stereotype is supposedly positive not negative to Asian Americans. In other words, Asian Americans are loved by the dominant society "because they had, by the 1960s and 1970s, accepted their place as a model minority subservient to whites" (Nguyen, 2002, p. 144). The chapter fleshes out a discursive relationship, similar to the yellow peril/model minority, between Asian Americans being "model minorities" and/or "bad subjects." Nguyen (2002) observes:

> The discourse of the bad subject, like model minority discourse, is a method of creating political meaning that concerns the place of Asian Americans in American society; the creation of such meaning is both enabling and disabling, as it is for model minority discourse. While minority discourse allows for the inclusion of Asian Americans in American society at the cost of concessions to the legitimacy of American pluralism, the discourse of the bad subject allows for opposition to the hegemony of pluralism and capitalism at the cost of an inability to meaningfully recognize ideologically contradictory Asian Americans. (p. 150)

Despite citing many classical writings on the topics of Asian Americans and model minority, Nguyen's (2002) chapter is unique, making an excellent contribution to the concept of the model minority stereotype and model minority stereotypic discourse. This chapter can be used in a variety of scholastic and instructional ways.

Niiya, B. (1999). The "model minority" discourse. In G. J. Leonard (Ed.), *The Asian Pacific American heritage: A companion to literature and arts* (pp. 35–37). New York, NY: Taylor and Francis.

***Niiya's (1999) two-page chapter may be short, but it is nothing short of a very cogent and concise reflection on the model minority discourse. The short response is that the model minority stereotype blames the victims, upholding the myth of the American Dream. In Niiya's (1999) own words:

> The American system is upheld, the problems of the oppressed are blamed on the victims and a neat roadblock is erected to quell any leanings toward organization between Asian Americans and other minorities. A "model minority" is created. (p. 36)

This chapter should be cited in literature reviews given that it cites many of the classical writings that have been used to support the model minority stereotype.

Nishioka, J. (2003). The model minority? In E. Lai & D. Arguelles (Eds.), *The new face of Asian Pacific America: Numbers, diversity and change in the 21st century* (pp. 29–35). Los Angeles, CA: AsianWeek.

***Nishioka's (2003) chapter summarizes the socioeconomic status of Asian Pacific Americans (APAs) using 2000 U.S. Census data. Her chapter covers (1) population and immigration, (2) family values, (3) homeownership and housing, (4) education, (5) labor, (6) business, (7) income, and (8) poverty. To conclude her chapter, Nishioka (2003) declares, "Regardless of statistics that support the idea of the model minority, there remain a sizeable proportion of APAs whose quality of life remains dismally poor" (p. 34). This chapter is a nice resource for readers who might not be familiar with the socio-demographics and socioeconomics of APAs.

Okamura, J. Y. (2008). Filipino Americans: Model minority or dog eaters? In J. Y. Okamura, *Ethnicity and inequality in Hawai'i* (pp. 155–186). Philadelphia, PA: Temple University Press.

***This is chapter seven in the book *Ethnicity and Inequality in Hawai'i* (2008). Okamura's (2008) chapter addresses the ways in which "Filipino American ethnic identity [in Hawai'i] has been and continues to be defined by non-Filipinos through racist stereotypes and other denigrating representations that are pervasive throughout society" (p. 155). Okamura (2008) also shares historical data on the disproportionate number of Filipinos that were executed in Hawai'i between 1900 and 1957. In fact, Okamura (2008) notes the following statistic: "Between 1900, when Hawai'i formally became a U.S. territory, and 1944, of the forty-two persons executed (all by hanging), twenty-four were Filipino (predominately young males), although they were at their highest only about one-sixth of Hawaii's population in 1930" (p. 160). The stereotypes that Filipinos eat dogs and are prone to violence ("poke-knives") are two prevalent stereotypes. The chapter discusses how Filipinos are constructed as model minorities in Hawai'i. Okamura (2008) also notes the following:

> Clearly, a major feature of the *model minority stereotype of Filipino Americans* is to represent them as immigrants, although most Filipino Americans in Hawai'i were born in the United States. The reason that they are portrayed as immigrants by the news and media is because such an image of them is more consistent with their model minority representation and with certain positive stereotypes of Filipino immigrants as hardworking and willing to accept whatever jobs are available to them. (p. 173, italics added)

This chapter can easily be used in conjunction with other writings such as Cunanan, Guerrero, and Minamoto (2006) and Edles (2003).

Okihiro, G. Y. (1994). *Margins and mainstreams: Asians in American history and culture.* Seattle, WA: University of Washington Press.

***Okihiro's (1994) book is a reworking of six lectures he delivered in 1992 under the overall title "Margins and Mainstreams: Asians in American History and Culture" at Amherst College (p. ix). The chapter titles are as follows: (1) "When and Where I Enter" (pp. 3–30); (2) "Is Yellow Black or White?" (pp. 31–63); (3) "Recentering Women" (pp. 64–92); (4) "Family Album History" (pp. 93–117); (5) "Perils of the Body and Mind" (pp. 118–147); and (6) "Margin as Mainstream" (pp. 148–175). Chapter 5, "Perils of the Body and Mind" is of particular relevance for model minority scholarship given that it clearly elucidates how two Asian American stereotypes are related, those being the model minority and yellow peril. In the words of Okihiro (1994):

> It seems to me that the yellow peril and the model minority are not poles, denoting opposite representations along a single line, but in fact form a circular relationship that moves in either direction. We might see them as engendered images: the yellow peril denoting the masculine threat of military and sexual conquest, and the model minority symbolizing a feminized position of passivity and malleability. Moving in one direction along the circle, the model minority mitigates the alleged danger of the yellow peril, whereas reversing direction, the model minority, if taken too far, can become the yellow peril. In either swing along the arc, white supremacy is maintained and justified through feminization in one direction and repression in the other. (p. 142)

In summary, Okihiro (1994) writes, "The perils of the body (the yellow peril) and mind (the model minority) are rooted within a cultural politics of assimilation and exclusion, but they also arise out of economic and political contestation" (p. xiv). Figure 2.1 below is my interpretation of the relationships between White supremacy, the model minority stereotype, and the yellow peril stereotype based upon Okihiro's (1994) work.

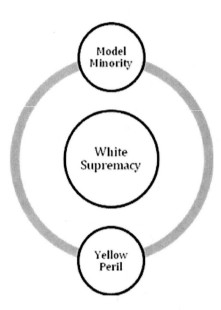

FIGURE 2.1. Model minority and yellow peril nexus

Ono, K. A. & Pham, V. N. (2009). Threatening model minorities: The Asian American Horatio Alger story. In K. A. Ono & V. N. Pham (Eds.), *Asian Americans and the media* (pp. 80–96). New York, NY: Polity Press.

***In this chapter Ono and Pham (2009) look at the media's model minority characterization that began in the 1960s. According to the authors, the "model minority discourse doubles as a yellow peril discourse" (p. 81) and "overtly masks racist policies, attitudes, and representations by alternating between admiration for and fear of Asians and Asian Americans" (p. 81). The Asian American embodiment of Horatio Alger can be seen in *Charlie Chan*, a model minority, who can be compared in contradistinction with Fu Manchu, a yellow peril. Other embodiments of Asian American Horatio Algers in the media are news anchor Connie Chung as well as the numerous TV characters cast as medical or scientific professionals. Ono and Pham (2009) argue that the model minority is a divisive discourse insofar as it doubles as a yellow peril discourse and strengthens the forever-foreigner stereotype. What makes this chapter unique is how it illustrates that the media's portrayal of Asian Americans as being over-represented in prestigious colleges and universities is a one-sided construction in that it neglects coverage of Asian Americans' under-representation in prime time television networks and other positions of leadership. The chapter also contributes new perspectives on the ways in which multiracialism is imbued within model minority construction, such as the case of model minority (Horatio Alger) Tiger Woods. According to Ono and Pham (2009), Woods, self-described as *Cablinasian*—Caucasian, Black, Indian, Asian—is a model minority because of the ways in which he represents post-racialism. According to Ono and Pham (2009), "It is important to discuss mixed-raced Asian Americans like Tiger Woods when considering the model minority stereotype" (p. 88). To summarize, this highly original chapter illustrates how the model minority stereotype serves as an exclusionary discourse. This chapter could be used as a reading in a critical media studies course or as a conversation catalyst in an Asian American studies class.

Osajima, K. (2005). Asian Americans as the model minority: An analysis of the popular press image in the 1960s and 1980s. In K. A. Ono (Ed.), *A companion to
Asian American studies* (pp. 215–225). Malden, MA: Blackwell.

***This book chapter is a quick read and does a nice job explaining how the model minority discourse evolved from the 1960s into the 1980s. Most importantly, Osajima (2005) points out that although the minority myth has been challenged in some respects, it is the maxim "the more things change, the more they stay the same" that holds sway when dealing with model minority discourse. In the 1980s the model minority stereotype began to be selectively problematized; however, during this same time the stereotype's purpose shifted from one of ideological efficacy to one of political efficacy. This ideological-political relationship is explained nicely by Osajima. Readers and researchers will find the footnotes—especially number nine—to be helpful for initial literature gathering. For those scholars and teachers who are looking for a wealth of relevant reading material, this book chapter is one-stop reading. It could be used by scholars who are writing a literature review as well as by college professors looking for an intermediate level reading for their syllabi. This book chapter is reproduced from the original chapter found in G. Y. Okihro et al. (Eds.). (1988), *Reflections on shattered windows: Promises and prospects for Asian American studies* (pp. 165–174). Pull-man, WA: Washington State University Press.

Oswald, G. (2001). Middleman, model and silent minorities? In G. Oswald, *Race and
ethnic relations in today's America* (pp. 129–147). Burlington, VT: Ash-
gate Publishing Company.

***Oswald's (2001) chapter claims that Latinos are "middleman" minori-ties, Asians are "model minorities," and Native Americans are "silent mi-norities" Oswald (2001) contends that Asians may have been a middleman minority group once, but their overall success has catapulted them into model minority status. This chapter can be used when comparing and/or contrasting Asian American model minority status with other non-Asian minority groups.

Palmer, J. D. (1999). From the "yellow peril" to the "model minority": Asian American stereotypes from the 19th century to today. *Midwest History of Education Journal, 26*(1), 33–42.

***Palmer's (1999) incisive article addresses how the model minority stereotype is harmful not only for Asian Americans, but for everyone. His article effectively captures how and why the model minority myth and the consequences of its message has left the struggles of Asian Americans hidden from mainstream society, thereby reinforcing meritocratic ideology. Thus, it is safe to say the myth has remained largely unchanged from when it originated in the 1960s. Palmer (1999) cites historical evidence that shows how Asians have been used in order to preserve White hegemony when White laborers imported Asians to serve as strike breakers. Palmer (1999) also highlights other legalized forms of power-maintaining laws used by the *status quo*: the 1882 Chinese Exclusionary Act, the 1920 Alien Land Act, and the 1924 Asiatic Exclusion Act. What makes Palmer's (1999) article appealing is that it also addresses contemporary perceptions of Asian Americans as super-bright overachievers. In these contexts—past and present—Palmer (1999) furnishes useful educational and psychosocial recommendations for policymakers. The article contains many seminal or classical (conservative) pro-model minority stereotype citations that can be used for teaching and learning. Model minority researchers will not want to go without reading and citing this article. This article would be useful in a graduate course on educational foundations, history or diversity.

Pon, G. (2000). Importing the Asian model minority discourse into Canada: Implications for social work and education. *Canadian Social Work Review, 17*(2), 277–291.

***Pon's (2000) article analyzes the model minority discourse within a Canadian context. He states that while there is a tremendous amount of literature on the model minority in the United States, there is a dearth of it in Canada. The author argues that the model minority discourse has been imported into Canada from the United States. The Canadian model minority discourse draws on the American model minority discourse, thereby reinforcing Canadian multiculturalism. As Pon (2000) notes, "The Asian 'model minority' discourse also dovetails neatly with Canadian discourses of multiculturalism" (p. 283). Similar to American journalism, Canadian journalism has reinforced the existence of a Chinese Canadian model minority (2000, p. 283). To summarize the points Pon (2000) ebulliently makes in the eruditely written article:

> By operating like two sides of the same coin, the "model minority" stereotype and multiculturalism discourse thus conveniently converge in liberalism and Orientalism. In a dialectical fashion, the "model minority" discourse, which has its roots in the United States, becomes seamlessly conjoined with

the hegemonic Canadian discourse of multiculturalism. Together the "model minority" and multiculturalism discourses can be regarded not only as hegemonic devices that maintain White domination, but as mechanism of control at the dispersal of liberal democratic governmentality. (p. 286)

Pon's (2000) article can and should be used in comparative education and educational foundation collegiate courses. This article contains many references in its bibliography that model minority scholars will want to read and review.

Puar, J. K. & Rai, A. S. (2004). The remaking of a model minority: Perverse projectiles under the specter of (counter)terrorism. *Social Text, 22*(3), 75–104.

***This article examines how South Asians are positioned in the model minority discourse post-September 11th. Puar and Rai (2004) write, "One observation might be that *the model minority myth status of South Asians* has now been tarnished for some with an association with Osama Bin Laden and other terrorist figures, leading to a shift in the racial landscape *from model minority to terrorist*" (p. 81, italics added). This article discusses how South Asians have been racialized through the symbol of "turban" being equated to terrorist/ism. Puar and Rai (2004) use examples taken from the television show *South Park* to show that South Asians are "glossed" and "homogenized" to be "Pakistani." This article argues that as a result of the United States' counter-terrorist efforts, the model minority stereotype is in turn being remade. This is an important area of study—whether or not the model minority myth is being remade—since the model minority myth plays a crucial part in the myth of U.S. "exceptionalism." The interplay between South Asians being model minorities and terrorists is a delicate balance and is worthy of further study. It is also an important article for model minority scholars to include in their cannon of knowledge since it builds on a newer aspect impacting a large group within the Asian American umbrella. Readers of this article will most likely be advanced-level undergraduates and also graduate students majoring in governmental relations, education, mass communications, and literary composition.

Ramasubramanian, S. (2011). Television exposure, model minority portrayals, and Asian-American stereotypes: An exploratory study. *Journal of Intercultural Communication, 26*(1). Retrieved from http://www.immi.se/intercultural/nr26/ramasubramanian.htm

***Ramasubramanian's (2011) article presents her exploratory study of the impact that television exposure has on viewers' attitudes toward Asian Americans. Participants from a convenience sample ($n = 323$) took an online survey instrument. Ramasubramanian (2011) hypothesized that the more television a person viewed, the more likely he/she would buy into Asian American stereotypes. Indeed, this is what she found. According to her structural equation models, television viewers who spent more time watching television were more likely to internalize model minority stereotypical media messages. The findings support cultivation theory—that television shapes our ideas about Asian Americans. This study is important for its implication that if Americans live in segregated spaces, they are likely receiving their information about Asian Americans from the media, not from actual Asian American individuals, resulting in warped attitudes and perceptions. This is an important piece to be used in communications classes as well as in undergraduate classes on popular culture.

Rangaswamy, P. (1995). Asian Indians in Chicago: Growth and change in a model minority. In M. G. Holli & P. A. Jones (Eds.), *Ethnic Chicago: A multicultural portrait* (4th ed., pp. 438–462). Grand Rapids, MI: Eerdmans.

***Rangaswamy's (1995) chapter presents research on Asian Indians in Chicago, Illinois. Rangaswamy (1995) says this about them:

> The myth of the model minority is at once true and false of the vibrant and fast-growing Asian Indian community of Chicago. On the one hand, the community is dominated by highly educated, professional elite of doctors, engineers, scientists, and college professors, who earn handsome salaries, live in comfortable suburban homes, drive luxury cars, and send their children to Ivy League schools....At the other end of the spectrum are the newly arrived, still-struggling Indian immigrants who lack language and professional skills, need basic job training, and are trapped in the clutches of a depressed economy. (p. 438)

The chapter contains helpful demographic, language, religious, political, and occupational information on Asian Indians. The chapter shares some of the struggles that come with immigrating from India and becoming overly Americanized. Particularly, it addresses many realities that segments assimilation theory attempts to figure out, such as language status, context of immigration (reception), generation status, mobility status and trajectory, and education, social, and occupational outcomes. Rangaswamy's (1995) chapter can be used in scholarly work that investigates subgroups of Asians since she writes that "Chicago's Asian Indian population has enjoyed nearly thirty years of steady and continuous growth. They are busy living up to the myth of the model minority and at the same time trying to face up to the challenges that threaten it" (p. 439). Future research questions might consider any of the following: (1) Why do some groups embrace the model minority stereotype? (2) What are the challenges for Asian Indians when it comes to being perceived as a model minority? and (3) How are Asian Indians perceived in relation to other Asian Americans?

Reyes, A. (2012). *Language, identity, and stereotype among Southeast Asian American youth: The other Asian.* New York, NY: Routledge.

Reyes's (2012) book is an ethnographic and discourse analytic study of an after-school video-making project for one-and-a-half- and second-generation Southeast Asian American teenagers. The book explores the relationships among stereotype, identity, and ethnicity that emerge in this informal educational setting. Reyes (2012) identifies how individuals can re-appropriate stereotypes of their ethnic group as a resource to position themselves and others in interactionally meaningful ways, to accomplish new social actions, and to assign new meanings to stereotypes. This is a unique book. It can be used when studying and/or teaching about the model minority stereotype.

Richards, P. M. (1996). Model minorities. *The Massachusetts Review, 37*(1), 137–147.

***In this article Phillip Richards, a Black man, shares his impressions about Asian Americans. Richards' narrative takes place in Chicago, Illinois (at the University of Chicago) and New Haven, Connecticut (at Yale University), divulging situations where Richards finds the model minority myth credible and other situations where Richards' assumptions of Asian Americans were disrupted. One situation that went against Richards' beliefs about Asian Americans being polite and self-effacing occurred at Yale. Richards (1996) recounts,

> Upon first coming to Yale, I met a slender young Asian-American physics student who wanted to know my prospective major. When I said American Studies, he smiled and congratulated me on choosing such a fine bullshit major. I was stunned and could not speak. I had encountered the ultimate Yale putdown from the least likely source that I could imagine. (p. 141)

Richards' sentiments are revelatory: Asians are supposed to be courteous and are not expected to say such hurtful comments. This article is unique for two main reasons: it is a narrative about the "model minority" myth, and its author is African American. The article and authorship demonstrate that everyone (this includes non-Whites) has preconceived beliefs about Asian Americans' achievement, behavior, and intelligence. This writing will be of interest for high school students and teachers as well as those who teach and work in the university setting.

Roshanravan, S. M. (2010). Passing-as-if: Model-minority subjectivity and women of color identification. *Meridians: Feminism, Race, Transnationalism, 10*(1), 1–31.

***Roshanravan's (2010) article brings a feminist perspective to the model minority stereotype for Asian women. According to Roshanravan's (2010) analysis, the model minority stereotype disallows Asian women from being considered a person of color. This article describes the model minority myth as a racial project that relies on historical amnesia. Moreover, as a racialized identity, the model minority stereotype is an ideological construction. Since Asian women are perceived as honorary Whites, they do not fit into the category of "women of color," causing Asian women to "pass-as-if," a term Roshanravan (2010) introduces in her chapter. The model minority stereotype effectively forces Asian women to empty themselves of their ethnicity and "pass-as-if" (adopt, mimic, participate) through assuming a depoliticized identity. This article is not for the faint of heart: It is highly technical and could be used in a feminism course or advanced gender studies course. This article could be used for a literature review for scholarly work on the model minority stereotype. It could also serve as a reference for theoretical work on the model minority stereotype. Roshanravan (2010) introduces and ties in the work of Homi Bhabha's "mimic man" and the model minority in this article. These tie-ins can be exploited in further scholarly work that problematizes the model minority stereotype, especially through a feminist lens. It also could be an important piece in a women and gender studies class because of its perspective on looking at women of color.

Saito, N. T. (1997). Model minority, yellow peril: Functions of "foreignness" in the construction of Asian American legal identity. *Asian Law Journal, 71*(4), 71–95.

***Saito (1997) discusses how the socio-legal construction of "foreignness" reinforces the racial hierarchy by recounting historical evidence that illustrates that Asians have been considered to be untrustworthy, unpatriotic, disloyal, and posing a threat to the security of the United States (e.g., such as Executive Order 9066, the Chinese Exclusion Act, and the Gentlemen's Agreement). Saito (1997) writes that foreignness is the missing piece in the model minority/yellow peril puzzle. Saito (1997) addresses the "racing" of Asian Americans as foreign through a review of "cases in which Asians attempted to obtain [U.S.] citizenship" (p. 78). Accordingly, foreignness was deeply embedded and reflected in who was considered to be a U.S. citizen and who was considered to be an alien of the state. Saito (1997) analyzes the historical record, specifically the portrayal of Asians as being the enemy. Disloyalty served as a prominent feature of the construction of foreignness, and is the reason why the Alien and Sedition Acts enforced and maintained a foreign-born criticalness. In fact, Saito (1997) writes that "during World War II, the association of foreignness with *disloyalty* was compounded by the presumption attributed to Japanese Americans 'as race'" (p. 82, italics added). Clearly, the historical record speaks to the idea that to be "Asian" has historically meant to be "excluded" due to the belief that Asians were a military threat and/or posed as economic competition. Moreover, Saito (1997) notes that "foreignness has been used to keep a large pool of labor cheap and disposable" (p. 89).

The biggest contribution that this law article makes to the demystification of the model minority stereotype is the nexus that it creates between the myth of Asians as model minorities and the construction of Asians as "foreigners." Moreover, Saito's (1997) article assists legal scholars in better understanding how the model minority myth allows society to deny the existence of racism and how the myth legitimizes the continued subordination of other people of color. It is only with the assistance of the socio-legal constructions of "foreignness" that Asian Americans have been constructed as model minorities and/or yellow perils at different times in U.S. history. This article will be useful for the field of Asian critical race theory (Asian-Crit) and for those who intend to do work on issues of Asian American legal identity. Law students would greatly benefit from reading the article, especially if they were to reflect on what contributed to the court case outcomes mentioned in the article, as well as on how these legal outcomes tie into Asian Americans' social and legal statuses in the United States.

SEARAC (Southeast Asia Resource Action Center). (2011). Southeast Asian Americans at a glance: Statistics on Southeast Asians adapted from the American Community Survey. Retrieved on November 14, 2011 from http://www.searac.org/sites/default/files/STATISTICAL%20PROFILE%202010.Final_.20111006-1_0.pdf

***This 20-page report is a must read, especially given that it uses data from the 2010 Census. It reports on the following topical areas: (1) population, immigration, and naturalization; (2) education; (3) income and employment; and (4) housing. "Southeast Asian Americans," in this report, refer to people from the following countries: Vietnam, Cambodia, and Laos. This report is an especially useful citation, especially when writing about Southeast Asian Americans.

Shankar, S. (2008). Speaking like a model minority: "FOB" styles, gender, and racial meanings among Desi teens in Silicon Valley. *Journal of Linguistic Anthropology, 18*(2), 268–289.

***Shankar's (2008) article shares the results of her research at Greene High School, a diverse school located in Silicon Valley, California. During 18 months, September 1999 through May 2001, Shankar (2008) conducted fieldwork at the high school. Shankar found that "language practices contribute[d]to how some Desis remain[ed] model minorities and continue[d] to integrate into upper middle-class white America while others share[d] more economic, academic, and professional similarities with Latinos and other local populations" (p. 283). This study highlights the ways in which South Asian students' normative language results in the perception that they are model minorities, while non-normative language users are perceived to be FOBs. The article can be used when discussing issues of language politics and the model minority stereotype.

Shih, F. H. (1988). Asian-American students: The myth of a model minority. *Journal of College Science Teaching, 17*(5), 356–359.

***Shih's (1988) article addresses how the model minority myth perpetuates the misconception that Asian American students are problem-free. According to Shih (1988), "Racial stereotypes, even those that are meant to be complementary, tend to dehumanize individuals. In the effort to meet the needs of Asian Americans, faculty as well as administrators should be aware that the current misconception of Asians as a model minority obscures some of the needs of this group while allowing other problems to be overlooked" (p. 359). Overwhelmingly, the author is concerned with the social and emotional health and wellbeing of Asian American students in college. Shih (1988) offers five suggestions for professors and college professionals who have contact with Asian American students: (1) question the students' choice of course electives, (2) encourage students to participate in social activities, (3) refer stressed students to campus counseling services, (4) encourage students to avoid taking on too many courses per semester, and (5) monitor or inquire about students' psychological health and wellbeing (e.g., study, exercise, and eating habits). Overall, this article is a valuable resource for higher education administrators and student service providers. This article also appears in the following publication: [Shih, F. H. (1989). Asian-American students: The myth of a model minority. *Chinese American Forum, 4*(3), 9–11.]

Simon, S. (2012, June 23). Behind the 'model minority,' an American struggle. *National Public Radio*. Retrieved from http://www.npr.org/2012/06/23/155622598/behind-a-wave-of-asian-immigration-stories-of-struggle

***Scott Simon (2012), a well-known National Public Radio correspondent, remarks that not all Asians in America are on scholarship at colleges and universities. Simon's (2012) thoughts are shared in text format but also can be listened to in audio format. This story aired on Weekend Edition Saturday and does a nice job at capturing lesser-known history about the Asian American population. According to Simon (2012),

> But most Asians didn't arrive in the United States as grad students or tech execs. The first Chinese immigrants built railroads and dug coal with their hands under oppressive, treacherous conditions. They were slurred as "the yellow peril," paid a pittance, abused, exploited and resented. Chinese workers were killed in riots and massacres, often organized by union miners who were immigrants themselves; the killings were more or less overlooked by local authorities. (para. 2)

This NPR model minority resource can be used in the college or high school classroom; the instructor can click on the link and broadcast it for the class to listen to.

Spring, J. (2001). Asian Americans: Exclusion and segregation. In J. Spring, *Decul-turalization and the struggle for equality: A brief history of the education of dominated cultures in the United States* (3rd ed., pp. 55–67). New York, NY: McGraw Hill.

***Spring's (2001) chapter, especially the sections "Education: From Coolie to Model Minority and Gook" (p. 62) and "Educating the 'Coolie,' 'Deviant,' and 'Yellow Peril'" (pp. 63–66), is particularly damning. A social foundationalist writing, the perspective Spring brings to the table is useful for problematizing the model minority stereotype's socio-historical and socio-cultural underpinnings.

Shrake, E. K. (2006). Unmasking the self: Struggling with the model minority stereotype and lotus blossom image. In G. Li & G. H. Beckett (Eds.), *"Strangers" of the academy: Asian women scholars in higher education* (pp. 178–194). Sterling, VA: Stylus.

***Shrake's (2006) chapter tells of her experiences as a professor, specifically in regard to her racialized and sexualized experience being an Asian American woman, and of how she reclaimed her identity, fighting against the model minority stereotype and the lotus blossom image. For instance, she writes, "I was not expected to criticize or challenge the dominant society because Asians are supposed to be apolitical, reserved, and compliant" (p. 182). Shrake (2006) states that the model minority stereotype is "a politically divisive tool" and that "the model minority image produces a specific minority position within the hegemonic racial structure in American society; one level lower than Whites and one level higher than other minorities" (p. 184). Moreover, Shrake (2006) asserts that "the model minority stereotype paints a misleading portrait of Asian Americans as a polite, docile, and nonthreatening people" (p. 184). Shrake (2006) discusses how she acquiesced in order to not "rock the boat" and to assimilate into the role that racism had for her. She also describes how she broke away from this acquiescence and reclaimed her identity as an Asian American female professor. According to Shrake (2006), her fight against the lotus blossom image and the model minority stereotype went hand in hand: "The lotus blossom image is a feminized version of the model minority stereotype and the model minority stereotype is merely an extension of the lotus blossom image" (p. 188). This chapter is beneficial to readers since it details one Asian American professor's journey and struggle with the model minority stereotype. It is also beneficial because it illustrates how the stereotype becomes gendered and sexualized. Shrake's (2006) writing can be used for scholarly research, as well as in the college classroom.

Suzuki, B. H. (1980). Education and the socialization of Asian Americans: A revisionist analysis of the "model minority" thesis. In R. Endo, S. Sue, & N. N. Wagner (Eds.), *Asian-Americans: Social and psychological perspectives, Vol. II* (pp. 155–175). Ben Lomond, CA: Science and Behavior Books

***Suzuki's (1980) book chapter provides a comprehensive critique of the model minority stereotype through a "revisionist" (alternative perspective) interpretation based on three propositions. Proposition one:

> The personality traits exhibited by Asian Americans are the result of a social-
> ization process in which the schools play a major role through their selective
> reinforcement of certain cultural behavior patterns and inculcation of others
> that are deemed "appropriate" for lower-echelon white-collar wage workers.
> (p. 166)

Proposition two:

> Although they have attained high levels of education, the upward mobility of
> Asian Americans has been limited by the effects of racism and most of them
> have been channeled into lower-echelon white-collar jobs having little or no
> decision-making authority, low mobility and low public contact. (p. 168)

Proposition three:

> The limited upward mobility of Asian Americans was achievable because of
> the demand for workers to fill lower-echelon white-collar jobs created by post
> World War II expansion in the economy (technological/bureaucratic) cou-
> pled with the type of training and socialization Asians had acquired through
> both the home and extended schooling. (p. 172)

Proposition one can be explained by the belief that Asian Americans show an inordinate amount of "obedience," "conformity," "punctuality," and "respect," while proposition two can be explained by the existence of a "glass" or "bamboo" ceiling that Asian Americans often bump up against when trying to move up the corporate or occupational ladder. Similarly, Asian American return on education is much lower than for non-Hispanic Whites, making their life earnings considerably less. Proposition three can be explained by relative functionalism, or the notion that Asian Americans fit a niche in the lower echelon of white-collar industry. While many schol-ars have written on the model minority stereotype, Suzuki (1980) makes a valiant attempt to shake-up the "inquiry" and "analysis" of model minority stereotype research. This article *can* and *should be* read by model minority stereotype scholars and students and be cited in their scholarly/academic work. The book chapter (Suzuki, 1980) is reprinted from an earlier work: [Suzuki, B. H. (1977). Education and the socialization of Asian Americans: A revisionist analysis of the "model minority" thesis. *Amerasia Journal, 4*(2), 23–51.]. Readers can also find this chapter material in the sixth book of Franklin Ng's (1998) six-volume series "Asians in America: The Peoples of East, Southeast, and South Asia in American Life and Culture": [Suzuki, B. H. (1998). Education and the socialization of Asian Americans: A revision-ist analysis of the "model minority" thesis. In F. Ng (Ed.), *Asian American interethnic relations and politics* (pp. 41–69). New York, NY: Garland Publishing, Inc.].

Suzuki, B. H. (2002). Revisiting the model minority stereotype: Implications for student affairs practice and higher education. In M. K. McEwen, C. M. Kodama, A. N. Alvarez, S. Lee, & C. T. H. Liang (Eds.), *Working with Asian American college students: New directions for student services* (vol. 97, pp. 21–32). San Francisco, CA: Jossey-Bass.

***As the title suggests, Suzuki's (2002) chapter examines the model minority stereotype in order to offer implications for student affairs practice and also for higher education. Suzuki (2002) is suspicious of the stereotype because not only is it used to discredit the existence of ethnic discrimination and racism, but it also has negative consequences for the Asian American population. Research that disaggregated its data analysis is the most effective at showing Asian American disparities. According to Suzuki (2002), perceptions of Asian American success abound at an alarming rate, even in the face of a steady stream of research that problematizes the stereotype. Suzuki (2002) writes "that as a group, Asian Americans have not yet achieved full equality and participation in American society" (p. 24). He adds that "the model minority stereotype has had the effect of *glossing over* these problems [of discrimination and racism], making them easy to ignore or neglect" (Suzuki, 2002, p. 24, italics added).

This article addresses important issues, a few of them being: (1) aggregate data conceals Asian American diversity; (2) the model minority stereotype has detrimental consequences for Asian Americans; and (3) Asian Americans are severely underrepresented in higher-level administrative positions in higher education, especially among various sub-populations. Suzuki (2002) closes his article by giving seven concrete actions that student affairs practitioners can adopt in order to help address the problems of Asian Americans in higher education. Scholars who read this article will most likely cite what Suzuki (2002) calls the "perfidious foreigner stereotype" (pp. 24–25). As Suzuki (2002) writes, "The stereotyping of Asian Americans as the model minority and as the *perfidious foreigner* has had invidious consequences for them in higher education" (p. 25, italics added). This article makes a unique contribution to the model minority scholarly discourse in that it introduces the term *perfidious foreigner*. This article can be used in graduate-level higher education and/or educational leadership and administration courses.

Suzuki, B. H. (1989). Asian Americans as the "model minority": Outdoing Whites? Or media hype? *Change, 21*(6), 13–19.

***This article addresses many of the commonly used rationales for believing Asian Americans to be a model minority while underscoring the importance of disaggregation. Examples of these rationales include high median incomes, overrepresentation at colleges and universities, and high standardized test achievement. This article's strength lies in its drawing attention to the policy implications of model minority subscription, such as the dissolution of educational affirmative action for needy Asian American students. The model minority serves purposes such as absolving society and individuals from addressing racism and inequity. The stereotype is an image or "shibboleth" (Hartlep, 2012; Suzuki, 1989, p. 13) that has evolved over time, reinforced by the media, which spins information to meet its own needs. According to Suzuki (1989), "The vast majority of Asian [American] students are not superbright, highly motivated over-achievers who come from well-to-do families" (p. 18).

Tamura, L. (1995). The Asian-American man: The model minority? In R. L. Cooper (Ed.), *We stand together: Reconciling men of different color* (pp. 61–78). Chicago, IL: Moody Press.

***Tamura (1995) argues that "the messages that an Asian male in this society receives about himself as an Asian are often negative, rigid, narrow, or stereotyped" (p. 71). The book chapter shares two representations of Asian Americans: the "hero" and the "scapegoat." The representation of an Asian "hero" can be classified as a model minority characterization, while the representation of an Asian "scapegoat" can be classified as a yellow peril. Tamura (1995) writes, "The primary problem with depicting Asians as the model minority [or as heroes] is that, like most stereotypes, it is too narrow a view. It is not accurate on either end of the success scale" (p. 63). Moreover, Tamura (1995) notes the following in regard to the yellow peril: "In the role of [the yellow peril or] scapegoat, Asians are seen as the enemy and blamed for a multitude of problems—economic, social, and political" (p. 65). Tamura (1995) traces the various ways that Asian men are characterized and castigated by the media: emasculated, vilified, and ensconced nerds who are phenotypically exaggerated. Tamura (1995) puts forth three suggestions for Asian American men (which also happen to be beneficial for all men): (1) develop a positive ethnic identity, (2) take responsibility for your own environment, and (3) seek out opportunities to engage in meaningful dialogue. The chapter concludes by asking three "take action" questions that K–12 teachers and college professors can use in their classrooms. This chapter can be used to examine the intersection of the model minority myth and Asian American males.

Takagi, D. Y. (1992). Diversity, merit, and the model minority: "Good but not exceptional

students." In D. Y. Takagi, *The retreat from race: Asian-American admissions and racial politics* (pp. 57–83). New Brunswick, NJ: Rutgers University Press. ***Takagi's (1992) chapter addresses the Asian American admission controversy. More specifically, though, Takagi (1992) examines how the model minority stereotype changed during the 1980s from being more positive to being more negative. In other words, Asian Americans were perceived as being overly competitive with Whites on the campuses of the nation's most prestigious private and public universities and colleges. As a result, Asian Americans were deemed to be overrepresented. In addition to their status as being overrepresented, Asian Americans were racialized as being not well rounded. Asian Americans were now beginning to be characterized as "overrepresented" and "good but not exceptional." This chapter can be cited whenever teaching and/or researching topics such as the model minority stereotype's influence on affirmative action policy or Asian American admission controversy.

Takaki, R. (2007). Asian Americans: The myth of the model minority. In J. H. Skolnick & E.

Currie (Eds.), *Crisis in American institutions* (pp. 148–154). Boston, MA: Pearson/Allyn and Bacon.
***Takaki's (2007) book chapter cites many of the classical journalistic writings that portray Asian Americans as model minorities. According to Takaki (2007), "Pundits and politicians have exaggerated Asian American 'success' and have created a…myth" (p. 149). The chapter references the "glass ceiling" that prevents Asian Americans from securing university administration positions, as well as anti-Asian American violence, such as the "dotbusters" ("dot" referring to the *bindi*) incident in Jersey City wherein a hate letter was published in a local newspaper threatening Asian Indians. Takaki's (2007) chapter originally appeared in his 1998 book *Strangers from a different shore: A history of Asian Americans* (pp. 474–482). It was also published as Takaki, R. (1995). The myth of the "model minority." In D. M. Newman (Ed.), *Sociology: Exploring the architecture of everyday life* (pp. 255–259). Thousand Oaks, CA: Pine Forge Press.

Takaki, R. (1998). *Strangers from a different shore: A history of Asian Americans* (Updated and Revised Edition). New York, NY: Back Bay Books.

***Takaki's (1998) history of Asian Americans is quite possibly one of the most highly recognized books on the Asian American experience. A classic, it accomplishes many noteworthy tasks that model minority stereotype researchers would be interested in. Of the book's thirteen chapters, the most notable for model minority researchers is the section titled "The Myth of the Model Minority" found on pages 474 through 484.

Takaki, R. (1995). The myth of the "model minority." In D. M. Newman & J.A. O'Brien (Eds.), *Sociology: Exploring the architecture of everyday life readings* (pp. 255–259). Thousand Oaks, CA: Pine Forge.

***Takaki's (1995) book chapter discusses issues such as income inequality for Asian men; the glass ceiling that prevents many Asian Americans from entering top management positions and the insidious ways that Asian Americans are excluded from the "old boy" network; and how Asian Americans are perceived to be inarticulate (evidenced in their supposed accents). Takaki (1995) references "groups that are not doing well, such as the unemployed Hmong, the Downtown Chinese, the elderly Japanese, the old Filipino farm laborers, and others, [who as a result] have been rendered invisible" (p. 257). Takaki (1995) goes on to note that "to be out of sight is also to be without social services" (p. 257), which is problematic. This book chapter contains references to lesser known model minority stereotype materials, such as a CBS *60 Minutes* program, "The Model Minority," which aired on February 1, 1987. This book chapter can easily be cited in reviews of literature.

Taylor, C. R., Landreth, S., & Bang, H. (2005). Asian Americans in magazine advertising: Portrayals of the "model minority." *Journal of Macromarketing, 25*(2), 163–174.

***Taylor, Landreth, and Bang's (2005) article examines portrayals of Asian Americans in magazine advertisements. Taylor, Landreth, and Bang (2005) content analyzed 1,885 ads. Based on the literature, they made seven hypotheses:

1. "The proportion of Asian American representation in magazine advertisements exceeds the overall Asian American proportion of the U.S. population" (p. 166);
2. "When Asian Americans appear in the ads, they tend to be depicted in major roles less often than other races" (p. 166);
3. "Asian Americans are frequently represented in advertisements for technology-based and business-oriented products but are less frequently represented in advertisements for non-technology-based products" (pp. 166–167);
4. "Asian Americans are more frequently portrayed in advertisements that appear in popular business press and technological publications than they are in general interest and women's magazines" (p. 167);
5. "When Asian American models appear in ads, they are depicted frequently in business settings, but they do not appear frequently in other types of settings" (p. 167);
6. "Asian American models are depicted in business relationships in advertising more frequently than they are depicted in familial or social relationships" (p. 167); and
7. "Magazines with high Asian American readership have a higher frequency of the portrayal of Asian models in their advertisements" (p. 167).

Hypotheses one, three, five, and six were *supported*. Hypotheses two and four were *partially supported*, and hypothesis seven was *not supported*. Taylor, Landreth, and Bang (2005) summarize their study's findings and importance:

> Collectively, the results of this study show that the "model minority" stereotype is reflected in mainstream magazine advertising. Although overall representation of Asian Americans has increased during the past ten years, the portrayals continue to conform to stereotypes of the group. Asian Americans are more heavily represented in ads for technology-based products, in business and science publications, and in business settings and relationships. There has been some improvement in Asian American representation in general interest magazines, but Asian models remain almost invisible in women's magazines. (p. 171)

This article is helpful because the implications of the study are serious for Asian Americans and model minority scholars.

Taylor, C. R. & Stern, B. B. (1997). Asian-Americans: Television advertising and the "model minority" stereotype. *Journal of Advertising, 26*(2), 47–61. Retrieved from http://digital.library.villanova.edu/files/VillanovaDigitalCollection/FacultyFulltext/TaylorCRaymond/3c0bcbf2-96d7-4603-a8fe-68336b696053/8bd5f835-928f-4ecc-a597-45632893b73b.pdf

***Taylor and Stern's (1997) article contributes to a lacuna in the literature: "Ironically, the positive stereotyping of Asian Americans may be one factor in the paucity of research on that minority—the portrayals do not appear problematic" (p. 48). The article addresses the following issues: (1) the extent to which Asians are visible in advertisements, (2) the types of roles in which male and female Asians appear, and (3) the types of goods and services that Asians are portrayed using and/or accessing. Taylor and Stern (1997) performed a content analysis of television advertisements from one full week of primetime programming (8PM to 11PM) on four major television networks (ABC, CBS, Fox, and NBC) during the first week of June, 1994. According to their findings, Asian females, compared to Asian males, were statistically significantly more likely to appear in a background role in an advertisement. Asians were found to be cast more frequently in advertisements for work (banks, telecommunications, retail outlets) than for home or social life (apparel, food/beverages, household supplies). By and large, the prevalent theme was that Asians' relationships were depicted as work-related or with co-workers. Accordingly, Taylor and Stern (1997) write that "advertisers may benefit by portraying Asian Americans in non-stereotypical ways" (p. 57) because it will catch consumers' attention. This article is important considering that it analyzes television advertisements, rather than print advertisements (for which more research has been done).

This article will be useful for communication courses as well as for a critical media studies course at the university level.

Tendulkar, S. A., Hamilton, R. C., Chu, C., Arsenault, L., Duffy, K., Huynh, V., Hung, M., Lee, E., Jane, S., & Friedman, E. (2011). Investigating the "model minority": A participatory community health assessment of Chinese and Vietnamese adults. *Journal of Immigrant and Minority Health, 14*(5), 850–857. doi:10.1007/s10903-011-9517-y

***According to Tendulkar et al. (2011) "this study provides important evidence to re-evaluate the 'model minority' myth" (p. 7). The authors conducted a community health assessment of Chinese and Vietnamese adults in an urban city north of Boston, Massachusetts. The findings of this three-year study do not support the model minority stereotype. In other words, the Chinese and Vietnamese adults who participated in this study reported difficulties accessing healthcare, and experienced poor overall health status. For example, the smoking rate for Vietnamese (30%) was significantly higher than for Chinese (10%), while "approximately 30% of both Chinese and Vietnamese respondents met the CES-D cutoff for concerning depressive symptoms" (p. 5). This study is useful for work that attempts to make the health needs/concerns of Asian Americans visible. Scholar practitioners dedicated to reducing public health disparities will find this an important and relevant study.

Teshima, D. S. (2006). A "hardy handshake sort of guy": The model minority and implicit bias about Asian Americans in *Chin v. Runnels. Asian Pacific American Law Journal, 11*, 122–141.

***Teshima's (2006) law article addresses implicit bias about Asian Americans. He uses the example that between 1960 and 1996 there was not a single Chinese American or Filipino American foreperson in San Francisco grand juries. The model minority stereotype created the perception that an Asian American would not make a good foreman because Asian Americans are unassertive and "mathematically and technically oriented rather than verbally skilled" (Teshima, 2006, p. 130). Teshima (2006) does a great job at walking the reader through how and why implicit bias, as seen in the model minority stereotype, impacts the experiences of Asian Americans. For instance, Teshima (2006) writes, "The statistical chance of this exclusion [there not being a single Chinese American or Filipino American foreperson selected] occurring randomly was 3 in 8.5 million, or 0.00000035%" (p. 123). The *Chin v. Runnels* case is a well-documented example of how litigating implicit bias is difficult because most in the mainstream believe that in order for discrimination to be present, there must be "intention." Teshima (2006) understandably notes that the model minority and colorblind racism, insidiously, do not "acknowledge that intentional bad actors are not the sole cause of racial discrimination. Instead, well-meaning individuals who nevertheless unconsciously stereotype also perpetuate racial inequalities" (p. 124). This article is a wonderful resource for those who use critical race theory in their own teaching, learning, and scholarship. It should be used in reviews of literature as well as in instructional materials for students of law and psychology students studying social cognition.

Toupin, E. & Son, L. (1991). Preliminary findings on Asian-Americans: The model minority in a small private east-coast college. *Journal of Cross-Cultural Psychology, 22*(3), 403–417.

***Toupin and Son's (1991) study

> examined the following research questions by matching Asian American college students with non-Asian students of comparative intellectual abilities and similar socioeconomic backgrounds: (a) Are Asian-American students more likely to major in the sciences and mathematics than non-Asians? (b) Do Asian-American students perform at a significantly higher academic level than non-Asians? and (c) Are the paths followed for acquiring a bachelor's degree different for Asian-American students than for their non-Asian peers?" (p. 405)

Participants in this study came from a small, private, and highly residential northeastern university. Ninety four matched pair *t* tests and McNemar's tests were performed for analysis on Asian Americans that were represented/comprised by collapsing all Asian ethnic subgroups into one aggregate Asian American group. Results of the study were as follows:

- Asian-Americans did less well than their non-Asian peers (p. 408).
- Asian-Americans had lower GPAs than their non-Asian peers (p. 409).
- Asian-Americans were less likely than their non-Asian peers to be on the dean's list (p. 409).
- Asian-Americans were more likely to be placed on academic probation than their non-Asian peers (p. 411).
- Asian-Americans were more likely to withdraw or be withdrawn for medical reasons than their non-Asian peers (p. 411).
- Asian-Americans were less likely than their non-Asian peers to graduate at the end of four years (p. 411).
- Asian-Americans were more likely to major in mathematics and science than their non-Asian peers (p. 412).

This study, although limited in generalizability since its analytic population was a small east coast college, is valuable for model minority research mostly because it "raises serious questions…concerning the view of Asian-Americans as the model minority [which assumes Asian-Americans are] academic[ally] success[ful] and scien[tific] wonders" (Toupin & Son, 1991, p. 416).

The myth of the model minority. (2011, Winter). *Independent School, 70*(2), 3–116.

***This special issue of *Independent School* focuses on the experiences of Asian and Asian Americans in independent schools. There are a total of eight articles, the equivalent of forty-five exclusive pages. Below are brief article summaries and annotations.

President of the National Association of Independent Schools (NAIS) Patrick F. Bassett (2011) writes the first article, "The Model Minority? The Interplay Among Myth, Stereotype, and Reality" (pp. 9, 10, 12), which discusses various elements of the model minority stereotype using the popular press as examples. Bassett references Malcolm Gladwell's *Outliers* book and Clint Eastwood's *Gran Torino* film. Bassett's arguments rely on several scholarly publications and point to the need to question the model minority stereotype, which, in and of itself, constitutes unexamined beliefs. This concise article will be interesting for those who teach critical media studies.

The second article, Vivian Wu Wong's (2011) "Getting it Right: Schools and the Asian American Experience" (pp. 24–30), makes several important proposals such as not lumping the 60+ different Asian subgroups (i.e., cultural, linguistic, philosophical, religious, and political) together as one group. According to Wu (2011), "As bad as the 'yellow peril' label is, the U.S. Commission on Civil Rights points out that, today, the most damaging stereotype for Asian Americans continues to be that of the model minority: the image that all Asian Americans had succeeded despite racism and discrimination" (p. 26). Her article provides a timeline of significant moments in Asian American history, spanning from 1790 to 1988. Wu argues that how educators teach U.S. history matters and that what history we expose students to is critically relevant. The biggest contribution of this article is in how it connects judicial declarations to the model minority stereotype and Black-White racial paradigms. *Lum v. Rice* (1927) was the decision that Martha Lum, an Asian, could not attend White schools. Inevitably, the model minority stereotype is part and parcel of the dividing of Asian and African American communities. Wu (2011) refers extensively to James Loewen's (1971) classic, *The Mississippi Chinese*. This article is important for history teachers and history professors.

The third article is John C. Lin's (2011) "Finding My Asian American Identity with Help from Ralph Ellison's *Invisible Man*" (pp. 34–38), which is Lin's personal narrative of being an American born Chinese male. His story tells of language loss, of being teased as a child, of cultural and behavioral assimilation, and of his eventual journey of self-discovery to reclaim his "hidden self." This brief article on Asian American identity will be interesting for high school and college teachers and students.

Giselle W. Chow's (2011) "The Model Minority Myth: Implications for Independent Schools" (pp. 40–46), the fourth article, speaks to the myriad ways that the stereotype of Asian brilliance impacts the education and schooling experiences of Asian American and Pacific Islander students (AAPI). According to Chow (2011), "In actuality, AAPI students represent both ends of the achievement spectrum. They are at once our nation's highest achievers and those most in need" (pp. 42–43). One implication, Chow (2011) notes, is that "in schools, the myth obscures the need for culturally relevant educational support" (p. 43). Another implication is the high suicide rates among AAPI women. Taken together, this article will be beneficial to individuals who work with AAPI youth, such as teachers, school and community counselors, and those interested in meeting the cultural, educational, and mental health needs of AAPI people.

The fifth article is Natalie J. Thoreson's (2011) "Start with Understanding: Asian Identity in a Culture of Oppression" (pp. 50–55), which addresses the multivariate ways Asian Americans are oppressed in the current educational landscape. Diversity education consultant Thoreson, a Korean American, shares theoretical and academic concepts, such as Chester Pierce's *microaggressions,* coupled with practical considerations, such as teachers prejudging their Asian students. According to Thoreson, prejudice results in less interaction and support, which is, in its worst form, discrimination. Accordingly, Thoreson (2011) writes, "Because of the way stereotypes are learned, oppression becomes difficult to differentiate from culture" (p. 54). The model minority myth is an unconscious stereotype, which is "difficult to unearth and abolish, which explains why [it is] also so persistent" (p. 54). The key to challenging the myth begins with identifying and analyzing how institutions (e.g., television, family, media, and education) perpetuate the stereotype's veracity. This article will be helpful for anti-racist educators, especially. The article contains a nice diagram showing the relationships among stereotype, oppression, discrimination, and prejudice.

The sixth article is authored by Aya Murata. "A Lasting Impact: Supporting Asian and Asian American Students" (pp. 56–64) suggests that there is a great deal we can and ought to do for the Asian and Asian American student populations. Murata notes that Asian American students confront a number of unique and complex issues, including, but not limited to the following: (1) invisibility, (2) limitations caused by the model minority stereotype, (3) issues of identity, and (4) issues of inclusion. Murata, an advisor at a boarding school, mentions that "the day-to-day experience of many Asian and Asian American students are riddled with complex issues they must address, and, yet, which are often not recognized or acknowledged by the school community" (p. 61). Murata's article ends with sound pieces of advice for educators and education: (1) create an advisor position, (2) hire more Asian American teachers and staff, (3) evaluate your school's programming to ensure it includes Asian and Asian Americans, (4) dedicate resources and time to meeting the needs of Asian and Asian American students, (5) allow students to share their Asian and Asian American history and culture within the school, and (6) get to know your Asian and Asian American students on an individual level. This article helpfully provides a list of recommended readings of interest for the Asian and Asian American communities and will be of interest for K–12 educators and administrators.

In the seventh article, "Keep Your Windows Open and Mirrors Polished: On Quality Education in Changing America" (pp. 66–72), Lucinda Lee Katz (2011) shares her personal life narrative being raised in a bilingual and bi-cultural Chinese American family. Katz's father landed at Angel Island and was soon thereafter released as a "paper son" since he passed his interrogation. This article is captivating. We learn that in 1968 Katz taught then first-grader Kinney Lau, the plaintiff in the famous *Lau v. Nichols* (1974) U.S. Supreme Court case. Using the metaphors of "window" and "mirror," Katz, a head of school, discusses her dual identity as Asian and American, as well as what school leaders and educators must aim to achieve in order to meet the unique social and educational needs of the students they claim to serve. This article will benefit practitioners who work with Asian American students given that it will build empathy for and understanding of being Asian and American in schools.

Rosetta Eun Ryong Lee's (2011) "Same and Different: Supporting Tran-sracially Adopted Asian Americans" (pp. 74–81) is the eighth and final ar-ticle in this *Independent School*. Lee's (2011) article on transracially adopted Asian Americans discusses "how schools work to support children adopted from Asian countries" (p. 76). Lee (2011) writes the following:

> Since nearly half of all foreign-born adopted children in 2009 are from Asia, and one in ten Korean American citizens entered the United States through adoption, transracial adoption is an increasingly significant Asian American issue. (p. 76)

The article discusses *micro-aggressions* that transracially adopted Asian Amer-icans experience as a result of seemingly "innocent curiosity" but which have injurious consequences. Lee (2011) advises that "all educators need to understand that transracially adopted [Asian American] students con-stantly face micro-aggressions" (p. 78). Moreover, Lee (2011) writes that these Asian Americans "are more often than not subject to unfairly high academic and social expectations stemming from the myth of the *model minority* and the quiet submissive Asian" (p. 76, italics added). This article will be useful for in-service K–12 teachers as well as school leaders and ad-ministrators.

Thrupkaew, N. (2002). The myth of the model minority. *The American Prospect, 13*(7), 38–41.

***Thrupkaew (2002) writes in "The Myth of the Model Minority" that "conservatives have exploited this racial stereotype—arguing that Asians fare well in the United States because of their strong 'family values' and work ethic. These values, they say, and not government assistance, are what all minorities need in order to get ahead" (p. 38). Thrupkaew (2002) goes on to contend that the persistence of the myth is "because political conservatives are so attached to it" (p. 38). This article addresses how Southeast Asians disprove the model minority stereotype, evidenced in their less than ideal economic (e.g., need for welfare assistance, low education, etc.) and social conditions (e.g., familial and cultural circumstances, acculturative stress, etc.). This article presents unfamiliar readers with exposure to the Southeast Asia Resource Action Center (SEARAC), which does a lot of work on behalf of the Southeast Asian population in the United States. Direct quotations are taken from Southeast Asian refugees/immigrants, which are unsettling and illustrate the severity and pervasiveness of the model minority myth. Thrupkaew (2002) merits being quoted at length:

> Wartime trauma and lack of English proficiency, acculturative stress, prejudice, discrimination, and racial hate crimes place Southeast Asians at risk for emotional and behavioral problems. (p. 40)

This article would be a good read for high school students; it will allow them to hear testimony from Southeast Asian refugees in a way that does not reinforce the model minority stereotype. K–12 teachers who teach Southeast Asian students would also benefit from reading this article.

Tran, A. (2011, Spring). Asian Americans as the model minority. *Interpolations*. Article 16 of 16, 1–10. Retrieved from http://www.english.umd.edu/interpolations/2611

***Tran's (2011) article appears in *Interpolations,* a refereed online journal showcasing superior student writing from the University of Maryland's English Department's First Year Writing Program. Tran's article is the sixteenth of sixteen and addresses the model minority stereotype. Tran (2011) blends within her review of the stereotype her own personal anecdotes and asides, which makes her article much more personal and practical. Although she only cites a few articles in her piece, its overall message is plain: The model minority stereotype is not accurate and is problematic for not only Asian Americans, but also other races, including Whites. The myth, in her words, leads to a division among and within minority groups. The myth, to use her words, is a form of "discreet discrimination" (Tran, 2011, p. 1). Tran (2011) cites a possible consequence of the model minority stereotype as undue pressure to succeed, resulting in stereotype threat. By and large, Tran (2001), only an undergraduate at the time of writing this article, appears to have a solid understanding of the form and function of the model minority stereotype. This is mostly likely self-evidentiary considering the fact that Tran is an Asian American herself. Tran (2011) writes the following:

"As part of the model minority, it is assumed that I, as well as every other Asian American student, should be hard-working with a successful future" (p. 1). This article can be used in the high school and college classroom as a required course reading.

Ueda, R. (1989). The coolie and the model minority: Reconstructing Asian-American history. *Journal of Interdisciplinary History, 20*(1), 117–124.

***Ueda's (1989) essay "The Coolie and the Model Minority: Reconstructing Asian-American History" reviews two books: (1) *Bittersweet Soil: The Chinese in California Agriculture, 1860–1910* by Sucheng Chan, and (2) *The New Chinatown* by Peter Kwong. Ueda (1989) comments:

> By dissecting two of the most pervasive images of Asian-Americans—the coolie worker and the model minority—Chan and Kwong have helped chart the course for historiography. Whereas Chan unveils the myth of coolie-ism to uncover the enterprising personality of early Chinese immigrants, Kwong replaces the complacent model-minority image with a political people building the institutions of democracy. Their interdisciplinary perspective has raised our understanding of Asian-Americans to a new plateau—one where they actively shape history through their economic and political achievements. (p. 124)

This essay can be used in interdisciplinary studies courses as well as courses on literature and historiography of the model minority stereotype.

Um, K. (2003). *A dream denied: Educational experiences of Southeast Asian American youth, issues and recommendations.* Washington, DC: Southeast Asia Resource Action Center. Retrieved on January 1, 2012, from http://www.ocf.berkeley.edu/~sasc/wp-content/uploads/2012/01/A-Dream-Denied.pdf

***Um (2003) is author of an issue paper based on findings from the first national Southeast Asian Youth Summit, University of California-Berkeley, December 9, 2000. Writes Um (2003),

> Regarded as the "model minority," Asian American families and communities are commonly assumed to be economically well-positioned to provide the essential support for their youth. Arguments have been made that Asian Americans encounter few, if any, academic challenges because support is available to them through family-financed private tutoring or community-financed after-school programs. This assumption, like many others associated with the model minority myth, fails to take into account the tremendous class disparity among Asian Americans. (p. 9)

This issue paper discusses barriers that Southeast Asian American college students face. Um (2003, p. 22) shares several recommendations as well, such as the following: (1) promoting parent, youth, and community advocacy to address educational concerns of Southeast Asian youth; (2) rethinking the existing educational curriculum to reflect more accurately the complexity of American history and society; (3) fostering collaboration among stakeholders to enhance the educational achievement of Southeast Asians in secondary and post-secondary institutions; (4) creating a scholarship program and coordinating institution; and (5) organizing activities, such as parent-student conferences, to strengthen intergenerational communication. The reporting done by Um (2003) can be used in concert with the reporting that The National Commission on Asian American and Pacific Islander Research in Education (CARE) has done in New York City (e.g., see The National Commission on Asian American and Pacific Islander Research in Education, 2008, 2010, 2011).

Vaidhyanathan, S. (2000). Inside a "model minority": The complicated identity of South Asians. *The Chronicle of Higher Education, 46*(42), B4.

***Vaidhyanathan's (2000) article addresses the costs of being a model minority for South Asian Americans, which "include a capitulation to the ideology of white superiority, trepidation about forging alliances across class, ethnic, or religious boundaries, and a willingness to be used as a silent symbol in the rollback of social-justice initiatives like welfare and affirmative action" (p. B5). This article reviews, in some ways, Vijay Prashad's (2000) *The Karma of Brown Folk*. Similar to ABC representing "American Born Chinese," Vaidhyanathan (2000) introduces the expression ABCD which represents "American Born Confused Desi." In summary, this *Chronicle of Higher Education* article shares how, in Vaidhyanathan's (2000) words, "if you want to argue that African Americans are their own worst enemy, invoke South Asians as a 'model minority'" (p. B5).

Valverde, L. A. (2003). Asian American paradox: The "model minority" still begets exclusion. In L. A. Valverde, *Leaders of color in higher education: Unrecognized triumphs in harsh institutions* (pp. 117–125). Lanham, MD: AltaMira Press.

***Valverde's (2003) chapter begins by stating that Asian Americans are referred to as model minorities "because they work to learn the language, study hard in school and want to assimilate" (p. 117). This chapter shares the testimonies of two Asian American male administrators in higher education. The first is a second-generation, born-in-the-U.S. midlevel academic leader, and the second is an Asian American immigrant, who immigrated as a young child. Both men indicate how their work was undervalued compared to that of White men and note the myriad ways in which they were used by their co-workers. Valverde (2003) writes, "White academic administrators see Asians in general as being subservient" (p. 121), adding that "while British, German, and French accents are acceptable, even prestigious in academia, Asian…accents are seen in a negative way" (p. 123). This book chapter can be used in educational administration and leadership courses in order to de-center Whiteness and Eurocentricity.

Varma, R. (2006). (Re)modeling "minority." In R. Varma, *Harbingers of global change: India's techno-immigrants in the United States* (pp. 113–130). Lanham, MD: Lexington Books.

***Varma's (2006) chapter contains many references to seminal model minority research. Varma (2006) writes that "the model minority view defies the reality of non-Asian minorities being restricted by racial discrimination. The political message hidden behind the model minority view is that the system should not be blamed for problems faced by non-Asian minorities" (p. 117). Varma (2006) also indicates that Asian Indian scientists and engineers are positioned between White and Black, but many Asian Indians have internalized the model minority stereotype. In other words, Asian Indians perceive themselves as minorities because of social and cultural differences, but they feel that they are not as marginalized as Blacks. Varma (2006) describes "Asian Indian immigrant scientists and engineers as the middle group in a three-tiered racial hierarchy, below Whites and above Blacks" (p. 114). This chapter can be used in literature reviews and in conjunction with Kim's (1999) theory of racial triangulation.

Walker, L. S. (1999, Summer). The Asian American uniform myth of success. *Heritage, 13*(2), 16–17.

***Walker's (1999) article indicates that the model minority stereotype is due to misrepresentation in statistics, which is reinforced by misrepresentation in the media. The article contains a nice bibliography that scholars and teachers can consult to gain more references to writings on the model minority stereotype. Only two pages in length, this *Heritage* article is a quick and necessary read.

Walker-Moffat, W. (1995). *The other side of the Asian American success story.* San Francisco, CA: Jossey-Bass.

***This central reading has collected numerous awards and generous reviews (e.g., see Lee, 1996). *The Other Side of the Asian American Success Story* shares the research of Walker-Moffat (1995) on the Hmong in the United States. Of the six chapters—(1) The Asian American Academic Success Myth, (2) The New Asian Americans, (3) Educating Newcomers: Lessons from Two Districts, (4) Culture and Learning, (5) The Bilingual Education Controversey, and (6) The Promise of Family-Based Multicultural Education—Chapter 1 is the most germane to the model minority stereotype. Chapter 1 cites classical model minority literature that is rarely cited in other books (e.g., see the following citations: Dillin, 1985; Roberts, 1985; and Rigdon, 1991). Despite this book's 1995 publication date, it should be considered a seminal citation for scholarship on the model minority stereotype.

Wang, L. L. (2007). Model minority, high-tech coolies, and foreign spies: Asian Americans in science and technology, with special reference to the case of Dr. Wen Ho Lee. *Amerasia Journal, 33*(1), 51–61.

***Wang's (2007) article "is a condensed version of a speech given at the Society of Professional Scientists and Engineers (SPSE) of the Lawrence Livermore National Laboratory (LLNL), operated by the University of California, under contract with the U.S. Department of Energy (DOE) on April 27, 2000" (p. 51). Wang (2007) points out that the Chinese came to the United States in two waves: the first in the second half of the nineteenth century and the second in the second half of the twentieth century. The "coolies" who immigrated during the first wave were exploited as day laborers. Wang (2007) says that there is now another form of Chinese "coolies"—high-tech "coolies" who, in the case of Dr. Wen Ho Lee, are used as scapegoats. Wang (2007) discusses how nationalist hysteria and paranoia have led to some Chinese scientists in laboratories being falsely accused of being Chinese communist spies. Wang's (2007) speech sheds light on this topic of concern and urges Asian (Chinese) Americans not to apply for jobs in national laboratories as a message of solidarity. This article/speech is important since it exposes readers/listeners to the reality of being perceived as a perpetual foreigner. For instance, Dr. Wen Ho Lee was not the first to be racially profiled. Wang (2007) shares the example of Dr. Tsien Hsue-shen (Qian Xue-sen), Goddard Professor of Jet Propulsion at Caltech, who was falsely accused of being a communist and ordered deported to China in 1950. Wang's (2007) thinking illuminates the relationship between the model minority stereotype and perpetual foreigner: "In short, Wen Ho Lee is the personification of stereotypical 'model minority.' The only problem is: why is this model minority being treated like a 'Chinaman,' with all his constitutional rights suspended?" (p. 59). This article is unique in that it addresses the historical expression, "Not a Chinaman's chance" in contemporary times.

Wei, D. (1986). The Asian American success myth. *Interracial books for children bulletin, 17*(3&4), 16–17.

***Wei's (1986) short article is written from her perspective as a teacher. Wei (1986) argues that Asian American students are not model minorities, and that "the [model minority] myth ignores the very real needs of Asian American students, including their need for bilingual education, giving an excuse to those who choose not to address the reality of Asian students' struggles" (p. 16). The main proposals Wei (1986) makes are for bilingual/bicultural education to be provided for Asian American students and for education to set "aside the success-story myth and recogni[ze] the reality of the conditions of Asian American students in our classroom[s]" (p. 17). This article can be used for furthering support for bilingual/bicultural education support services. Teachers can also use this article to lobby for educational resources for their Asian American students. Lastly, since the article is written by a teacher, it can be used as a reading in teacher preparation courses of a broad sort generally, and in literacy courses specifically.

Winnick, L. (1990). America's "model minority." *Commentary, 90*(2), 22–29.

***According to Winnick (1990), "It would be foolish and irresponsible to slight the profusion of Asian *unsuccesses* amid the profusion of *successes*" (p. 24, italics added). He also asserts in this article that "there is a growing number of Southeast Asian refugees who have been on welfare since their arrival and who may permanently remain there" (p. 24). This article highlights the Asian American population's demographic growth as well as their supposed economic successes. The article compares Asian Americans with Jewish Americans, observing a similar pattern of pariah-turned-paragon. The article discusses the historical and legal mistreatment of Asian Americans, such as the Chinese Exclusion Act of 1882, the Gentleman's Agreement of 1907, the Oriental Exclusion Act of 1924, and the Hart-Celler Immigration and Nationality Act of 1965, among other acts and legislation. Model minority researchers might consult this article when conducting scholarship that examines meritocratic rhetoric and racial affirmative action policies in the context of Asian Americans in contemporary times. As Winnick (1990) writes, "as a federally protected minority, Asian-Americans are, in principle, eligible for special preferences to compensate for underrepresentation" (p. 25).

Wong, L. (1976). The Chinese experience: From yellow peril to model minority. *Civil Rights Digest, 9*(1), 33–35.

***In this article Wong (1976) argues that the experiences of the Chinese in America are misconceived, misunderstood, and/or ignored. Wong (1976) briefly covers the history of Chinese immigration, including the practice of "paper sons" and "slots." According to Wong (1976) the Chinese were treated as *scapegoats*, representing a yellow peril. Similarly, the Chinese have now come to be *stereotyped* and "considered a 'model minority'" (Wong, 1976, p. 35). Wong (1976) writes that "this [model minority] myth developed in the wake of the urban turmoil of the late sixties. America needed a colored minority to prove that its [socio-political] system still worked" (p. 35). Wong's (1976) article can be used in literature reviews as well as for a short student reading in an Asian American studies or history course.

Wong, M. G. (2010). Model minority or perpetual foreigner?: The political experience of Asian Americans. In V. Martinez-Ebers & M. Dorraj (Eds.), *Perspectives on race, ethnicity, and religion* (pp. 153–173). New York, NY: Oxford University Press.

***Wong's (2010) book chapter describes the multifaceted nature of the Asian American political experience and is important since it contrasts the model minority stereotype and the perpetual foreigner stereotype, examining the fastest growing racial group's experiences as voters and also would-be politicians. In terms of politics, Asian Americans are not overachievers who are advantaged. Indeed, Wong (2010) points out that "Asian Americans may be advantaged relative to blacks and Hispanics, [but] they are still [politically and representationally] disadvantaged relative to whites" (p. 157). Wong (2010) also notes that "the model minority concept persists despite contradictory evidence" (p. 158). By and large, "Asian Americans lost at least three generations of political development because of federal laws that barred them from citizenship and full political participation" (Wong, 2010, p. 161), making them a less than fully developed political and constituency group within the United States' political system. Wong's (2010) chapter provides many relevant insights, namely that the model minority stereotype rests on "kernels" of truth and, more importantly, that it depends on what statistics one looks at that impacts whether or not Asian Americans can be considered "model" or "perpetual foreigner" minorities. This chapter can be used for work that centers on Asian Americans and affirmative action and/or politics.

Wong, W. (1994). Covering the invisible "model minority." *Media Studies Journal,* *8*(3), 49–59.

***Wong's (1994) article addresses the difficulty associated with accurate reporting of Asian Americans in America by the media. Journalists, when reporting on Asian Americans, need to eradicate "false notions, ignorance and insensitivity, without compromising journalistic values of fairness, balance and skepticism" (Wong, 1994, p. 59). Wong (1994) references how cute expressions and catchy phrases are often used by journalists, such as puns related to Asian food and the staple, "Asian invasion." Wong (1994) cautions the media to use reliable sources when reporting on topics related to the Asian America community. Wong (1994) cites the importance of precision: "The idea of 'foreignness' hangs over all Asian Americans, whether fifth-generation Americans or newly arrived refugees. Therefore, whenever possible, precision in identifying Asian ethnic people in America and understanding who they are, are steps toward better journalism" (p. 52). This article indicates that although Asian Americans are widely portrayed as being model minorities, they are nevertheless still invisible. This article could be used in media related college courses, including advertising. This article is also reprinted in the following citation: [Wong, W. (1997). Covering the invisible "model minority." In E. E. Dennis & E. C. Pease (Eds.), *The media in Black and White* (pp. 45–52). New Brunswick, NJ: Transaction Publishers.].

Wong, W. (2001). Crime: Bang, bang, you're dead. In W. Wong (Ed.), *Yellow journalist: Dispatches from Asian America* (pp. 206–218). Philadelphia, PA: Temple University Press.

***Wong's (2001) chapter, especially the section "The Model Minority Criminal" (pp. 208–212), is illustrative of why Asian Americans should not overreact to other Asian Americans who are criminals since doing so would buy into the idea that all Asian Americans are model minorities. In other words, the model minority stereotype of successful and law-abiding Asian Americans is just as false as the stereotype of Asian Americans as gangsters and criminals. What the alternative narrative of Asian American model minority criminals does achieve, however, is a counter-story to the master-script of Asian Americans as problem-free. Wong's (2001) chapter also includes discussion of the sexual exploitation of Southeast Asian children, including the case of Benjamin Unterreiner, a 34-year-old convicted child molester of five Southeast Asian children. This chapter is helpful for counter-narrative model minority stereotypic research.

Woo, D. (2000). The inventing and reinventing of "model minorities": The cultural veil obscuring structural sources of inequality. In T. P. Fong & L. H. Shinagawa (Eds.), *Asian Americans: Experiences and perspectives* (pp. 193–212). Upper Saddle River, NJ: Prentice Hall.

***Woo's (2000) chapter is an expanded version of Chapter 1 in her 1999 book, *Glass Ceilings and Asian Americans: The New Face of Workplace Barriers.* In her chapter, Woo (2000) points out that a cultural explanation for Asian American success selectively overlooks structural influences. Making this oversight difficult to pinpoint, Woo (2000) writes that "the model minority thesis has managed to stretch or reinvent itself *discursively,* as opposed to through new empirical research (e.g., that which shows how different subcultural tendencies achieve the same ends)" (p. 203, italics in original) due in part because the stereotype supports the belief in the American dream. Says Woo (2000), Asian "'model minorities' serve as a sign of the ongoing viability of the *American Dream*" (p. 205, italics added). Woo's (2000) chapter does not include the tables of census data that are included in her book *Glass Ceilings,* but nevertheless it is a powerful source to cite in model minority scholarship. The chapter (Woo, 2000) contains many citations that teachers and scholars can use in their practical and/or theoretical work.

Wright, D. E. & Hom, H. L. (2003). Altering frequency estimates of hindsight bias in others via stereotyping: Asians as a model minority. *Psi Chi Journal of Undergraduate Research, 8*(4), 139–143.

***Wright and Hom's (2003) article investigated the "role racial stereotypes play in influencing attributions of hindsight bias in others" (p. 139). The study was interested in testing who would be thought to show the most hindsight bias, or the "knew-it-all-along" syndrome—Blacks, Whites, or Asian Americans. Wright and Hom's (2003) study consisted of forty-seven White students sampled from an introductory undergraduate physical health and education class who were assigned to targeted racial groups: White, Black, or Asian. Participants were primed and an example was given of what "hindsight bias" was. Participants completed questionnaires, and it was found that Asians were thought to exhibit the least amount of hindsight bias. Wright and Hom (2003) assert that "White college students perceived hindsight bias frequency to be significantly lower for Asians when compared to Whites" (p. 142). They go onto conclude the following: "The belief that Asians would show less hindsight bias than the other target groups [Whites and Blacks] supports the stereotypic view that Asians are a *model minority*" (Wright & Hom, 2003, p. 142). Despite the fact that the two undergraduate authors of this *Psi Chi Journal of Undergraduate Research* article do not adequately indicate why less hindsight bias would be equated with model minority status, their study is nonetheless interesting. Future research might delve further into this topic. This article is useful in that it shows the creativity that can be captured in research investigations. It can be cited in a literature review for studies that explore the manifestations of the model minority stereotype.

Wright, L. (1988, September 1). Asians as "model minority": Myth, reality, or both? *American Libraries, 19*(8), 667.

***Wright's (1988) article alludes to what is covered in the following citation: [Karkhanis, S., & Tsai, B. L. (Eds.). (1989). *Educational excellence of Asian Americans: Myth or reality*. New York, NY: The Asian/Pacific American Librarians Association.].

Wang, T. H. & Wu, F. H. (1996, Winter). Beyond the model minority myth: Why Asian Americans support affirmative action. *Guild Practitioner, 53*, 35–47.

***Wang and Wu's (1996) article explains why the view that Asian Americans do not need affirmative action supports the model minority myth. Wang and Wu (1996) warn, "Contrary to the popular perception [that Asian Americans are model minorities], Asian Americans remain underrepresented in many areas and also continue to experience discrimination [and thus should fight for affirmative action]" (p. 35). Their article covers the origins of the model minority myth and how affirmative action has been used as a wedge issue to divide and conquer minorities, namely African and Asian Americans. According to Wang and Wu (1996), "Asian Americans should avoid allowing themselves and their communities to be used as a *wedge* by politicians whose own ideologies and ambitions explain their sudden concern for Asian Americans" (p. 36, italics added). They also go on to say that "the 'model minority' myth ensures that poor Asian Americans will be ignored" (Wang & Wu, 1996, p. 39). By and large, Wang and Wu's (1996) article supports the idea that the model minority is a rhetorical and political device that is used to maintain the *status quo*. They close their article with the following statement: "The dilemma of Asian Americans and affirmative action, however, should be recognized as a problem manufactured for political purposes" (Wang & Wu, 1996, p. 46). This article also appears as the following book chapter: [Wang, T. H. & Wu, F. H. (1996). Beyond the model minority myth. In G. E. Curry (Ed.), *The affirmative action debate* (pp. 191–207). Reading, MA: Perseus Books.]

Weaver, R. (2007, November). Every coin has two sides: Uncovering the model minority myth. *NEA Today, 26*(3), 9.

***This one-page article is written by Reg Weaver, NEA President. Weaver discusses how the model minority camouflages the unique histories of different Asian Pacific American communities. According to Weaver (2007), "The myth that all Asian Americans are high-achievers can be detrimental because it fails to address those students who need help, support, and focused resources to succeed" (p. 9). This president's viewpoint article is noteworthy since it points to the need to disaggregate data to identify the individual experiences of each ethnic subgroup. It also points out the negative consequences of such a myth for a wider educational audience; *NEA Today* is read by the K–12 teaching community.

Wexler, J. & Pyle, N. (2012). Dropout prevention and the model-minority stereotype: Reflections from an Asian American high school dropout. *Urban Review: Issues and Ideas in Public Education, 44*(5), 551–570. doi: 10.1007/s11256-012-0207-4.

***Wexler and Pyle's (2012) case-study of Andy, a 19-year-old Korean high school dropout, is notably unique. Andy was an interesting case due to the fact that as an Asian American, he was most likely racialized as a model minority, yet he dropped out of high school. As a result, the authors of this study asked Andy questions that aligned with the Institute of Education Sciences' (IES) recommendations for dropout prevention. The six recommendations (access here: http://ies.ed.gov/ncee/wwc/pdf/practice_guides/dp_pg_090308.pdf) were as follows:

1. Utilize data systems to support the identification of students at high risk of dropping out;
2. Assign adult advocates to students at risk of dropping out;
3. Provide academic support and enrichment to improve academic performance;
4. Implement programs to improve students' classroom behavior and social skills;

5. Personalize the learning environment and instructional process; and

6. Provide rigorous and relevant instruction to better engage students in learning and provide skills needed to graduate and to serve them after they leave school.

Wexler and Pyle's (2012) methodologically strong investigation revealed, among other things, that at-risk Asian Americans (in this case Andy) need advocates who can reduce the possibility of dropping out and increase the chances of staying in high school. Wexler and Pyle (2012) write the following:

> Overall, Andy agreed that at least some element of each recommendation, when implemented effectively, may provide support for at risk students which can lead to an increase in school engagement and the prevention of school dropout. Standing out as particularly important, Andy agrees with the recommendation that providing an adult advocate is a key ingredient in the prevention of dropout. (p. 15)

Wexler and Pyle's (2012) study helps add to the literature on Asian American (Korean) dropouts and the implication of the model minority stereotype (*cf.* Lew, 2004).

Whitman, D. (1987). Trouble for America's "model minority." *US News and World Report, 102*(6), 18–19.

***Whitman (1987) discusses the difficulties the Indochinese (Hmong, Laotian, Vietnamese, Cambodian) are experiencing in the United States. Whitman's article takes its framework from different quotations from Indochinese individuals and families, all of whom were refugees. The descriptions of Indochinese hardship are not atypical. Whitman's article helps expose readers to the realities behind the model minority myth, such as welfare dependency, Vietnamese violent crime, and the horror of physical and psychological traumatic memories before arriving to the United States. This short article could be passed out in a high school classroom and read aloud as a group. Students would benefit from reading the truth as opposed to stereotypical incantations that all Asian Americans, including Indochinese refugees, are successful academically and socially. As Whitman (1987) writes, "Indochinese refugees are touted as an American success story—in fact, a staggering number are poor, out of work and on relief [welfare]" (p. 18).

Wing, J. Y. (2007). Beyond Black and White: The model minority myth and the invisibility of Asian American students. *The Urban Review, 39*(4), 455–487.

Wing (2007) studied six—two 9th, two 10th, and two 12th grade—Asian American students at Berkeley High School (a racially integrated school of some 3,000 students) in relationship to the model minority myth. Wing's (2007) research question was, "What academic, social, or family problems, institutional barriers, and struggles do Asian American high school students face that may be masked by the model minority stereotype?" (p. 457). In order to carry out her investigation, Wing (2007) privately interviewed the six students, as well as analyzed quantitative data (e.g., GPA, course-taking patterns, etc.). Wing (2007) begins "Beyond Black and White: The Model Minority Myth and the Invisibility of Asian American Students" by addressing how the model minority image became embedded in U.S. culture, pointing out that "it was no accident that the model minority image emerged in the 1960s" (p. 459), referring to the stereotype's insidious use to divide and conquer other non-White minorities. Wing (2007) also directs her readers to the fact that Asians have been treated negatively (read: yellow peril, Asian horde, alien, perpetual foreigner) longer than they have been treated positively (read: model minority stereotype). Wing (2007) states, "Although the model minority myth, like the Yellow Peril before it, is a social construction serving a political purpose, it nonetheless carries serious implications and material consequences for all Asian Americans, as witnessed by the rise in hate crimes against Asians" (p. 460). This article debunks five common myths that are used to validate the model minority myth:

1. All Asian students are high academic achievers, and as a group outperform White students;
2. Asians naturally excel at math;
3. All Asian families highly value education;
4. All Asians are alike in culture language, appearance, and academic achievement; and
5. Asians do not suffer racial discrimination like other people of color.

All of these points were found to be untrue in Wing's (2007) study. Wing's (2007) article has four take-away points that readers are left to consider: (1) The model minority stereotype pits Asians against other people of color; (2) The model minority stereotype places Asian Americans in a vulnerable position in society; (3) The model minority stereotype hides from view the most in need; and (4) Asians are overlooked in the Black-White definition of race in the United States. This article would be a great read for principals, superintendents, and teacher educators who are concerned with meeting the educational and social needs of K–12 students. The biggest contribution that this article makes relates to its introduction, and how readers must understand that Asian Americans have only been recently labeled model minorities—far longer they have been labeled problems and pariahs.

Wu, F. H. (2002). *Yellow: Race in America beyond Black and White.* New York, NY: Basic Books.

***Frank H. Wu's (2002) oft-cited and oft-referenced book (e.g., see Lin, 2002; Nolan, 2003; Tseng, 2001), a 2002 Kiriyama Prize Notable book, takes a unique perspective on Asian Americans' position within America. Race relations are typically viewed using a Black-White paradigmatic lens; Wu examines where Asian Americans, Yellow, reside within this framework. Chapter two (pp. 39–77)—"The Model Minority: Asian American 'Success' as a Race Relations Failure"—will be of particular interest for scholars engaged in dismantling the model minority stereotype.

Wu, F. H. (2012). The model minority: Asian American "success" as a race relations failure. In K. E. Rosenblum & T. M. C. Travis (Eds.), *The meaning of difference: American constructions of race and gender, social class, sexual orientation, and disability* (6th ed., pp. 370–378). New York, NY: McGraw Hill.

***Wu's (2012) chapter is partially the second chapter (pp. 39–77) of the following book: [Wu, F. H. (2002). *Yellow: Race in America beyond Black and White*. New York, NY: Basic Books.]. The chapter omits sections that appear in *Yellow*, such as "Messages of the Myth." By and large, the chapter is a condensed version of Wu's (2002) *Yellow*. Scholars and researchers can cite this chapter to build their literature review, but those interested in the full chapter ought to consult the full text contained in *Yellow*.

Yee, A. H. (1992). Asians as stereotypes and students: Misperceptions that persist. *Educational Psychology Review, 4*(1), 95–132.

***Yee's (1992) article tackles how Asian Americans are perceived to be homogeneously successful, what he calls "perceptual homogeneity." Yee (1992) considers the model minority stereotype to be based on racism that dates back to when Asians in America were demonized and viewed as economic competition. Yee's (1992) article contains references to many classical model minority journalistic writings and should be cross-referenced. The article is helpful to understand that the model minority stereotype does not address the differences between attitudes and behaviors. In other words, Asian Americans may be heralded as model minorities for their success in the classroom as students, but at the same time they are viewed by society as inscrutable aliens and perpetual foreigners.

Yee, A. H. (1976). Asian Americans in educational research. *Educational Researcher, 5*(5), 5–8.

***This article points out Asian Americans' under-representation in the field of education research. The article delineates disciplines in which Asian Americans are represented and under-represented. According to Yee (1976), "The pervasive but mythical attitude has been that Asian Americans have 'made it' educationally and professionally, but…progress has been selective by field and mainly in terms of Asian-American males" (p. 7). The article concludes with four ideas or initiatives for future discussion and study that merit academic attention.

Yeh, C. (2008). Constructing a "model minority" identity: The Miss Chinatown U.S.A. beauty pageant. In C. Yeh, *Making an American festival: Chinese New Year in San Francisco's Chinatown* (pp. 56–74). Berkeley, CA: University of California Press.

***Yeh's (2008) chapter is the third in *Making An American Festival: Chinese New Year in San Francisco's Chinatown* and deals with how ethnic beauty pageants, particularly the Miss Chinatown Beauty Pageant, construct Asian Americans as a model minority. Accordingly, participants of this pageant allowed Asian (Chinese) Americans to access power of White America. The chapter describes the specific ways in which the pageant organizers judgment criteria created a model minority image of Asian American females' cultural and aesthetic beauty. Yeh (2008) writes that the pageant committee transformed the image of the Chinese coolie to that of the model minority by exotifying the contestants' bodies and also by valuing White mainstream sensibilities and ideals. One example is how "contestants often appropriated mainstream fashion...and values" (Yeh, 2008, p. 65). This book chapter makes a unique contribution to the literature on the model minority due to the fact it undertakes a highly original case of the social construction of the stereotype.

Yin, X. (2001). The two sides of America's "model minority." *Chinese American Forum, 16*(3), 27–28.

Yin's (2001) reprinted *Chinese American Forum* article originally appeared in the *Los Angeles Times* a year earlier (cf. *Los Angeles Times,* Sunday, May 7, 2000, M1 & M6). Yin's article addresses the ways in which the Asian American community has become bipolar: in many loci there are "uptown" and the "downtown" Asians. This polarization is multifaceted, and not only along lines of wealth. Yin (2001) notes that "it's important to recognize that the *economic and academic polarization that characterizes the Asian American community,*" and "understanding its impact and developing a responsible agenda to deal with it are equally important" (p. 28). According to Yin, immigration policy has accounted for one of the ways in which there are two extremes: "highly educated" and "low educated" Asians in the United States. Generally speaking (certainly not always), *Southeast* Asians (e.g., Cambodian, Hmong, Vietnamese, etc.) represent the "downtown," while *East Asians* (e.g., Chinese, Korean, Japanese, etc.) represent the "uptown" group. This is a short article and could easily be used in a high school or college classroom to begin a classroom discussion around issues of social inequality and segregation, contextualized in the model minority stereotype and the Asian American community.

Zia, H. (2000). Gangsters, gooks, geishas, and geeks. In H. Zia (Ed.), *Asian American dreams: The emergence of an American people* (pp. 109–138). New York, NY: Farrar Strauss and Giroux.

***Zia's (2000) chapter examines how Asian Americans can be considered model minorities when they are in fact racialized in other ways besides geek, such as gangster, gook, and/or geisha. Zia's (2000) chapter examines the various ways that Asian American actors have been sidelined from acting Asian-specific roles in television/movies/Broadway. This book chapter can easily be used in connection with Darrell Y. Hamamoto's (1994) *Monitored Peril: Asian Americans and the Politics of TV Representation.*

Zhou, M. & Gatewood, J. V. (Eds.). (2000). *Contemporary Asian America: A multidisciplinary reader.* New York, NY: New York University Press.

***This anthology is important and incisive. Zhou and Gatewood's (2000) goal was to "provide undergraduate and graduate students and all those interested in the Asian American community with some of the most central readings informing Asian America and Asian American Studies today" (p. xiii). The book has thirteen parts, but the eighth part (The Construction and Deconstruction of the "Model Minority") is relevant to the exploration of the model minority stereotype. Comprised of three chapters, this section focuses on the causes and consequences of the "model minority" stereotype.

Keith Osajima's chapter is titled "Asian Americans as the Model Minority: An Analysis of the Popular press Image in the 1960s and 1980s" and examines "how the image of Asian Americans as the successful minority has been able to withstand criticism and changing conditions, yet remain an important conceptual force in the popular press" (p. 449).

Lucie Cheng and Philip Yang's chapter is titled "The 'Model Minority' Deconstructed" and "focuses on the diversity of Asian Americans" (p. 461). In particular, Cheng and Yang's chapter addresses questions such as, "Do Asian experiences challenge or reinforce common stereotypes and concepts, such as the 'model minority' and 'glass ceiling'?" and "What do the changing intergroup relations mean for Asian Americans, for the formation of a pan-Asian ethnicity or coalition, and for the needs and aspirations of the reconstituted Asian ethnic groups?"

Last, Don Nakanishi's chapter "A Quota on Excellence? The Asian American Admissions Debate" addresses three questions: (1) What accounts for increased enrollment among Asian Americans at universities across the United States? (2) Does evidence exist to support the charge that there exists an admissions bias against Asian Americans? and (3) How do we explain the political support enjoyed by Asian Americans from members of both major parties?

What makes this section on the model minority so powerful is that in addition to the three chapters, the section ends with two helpful resources for students and educators. Three study questions are provided for continued discussion and thought, while sixteen further relevant readings and two films are also suggested. Nakanishi's chapter is reprinted from [Nakanishi, D. T. (1989). A quota on excellence?: The Asian American admissions debate. *Change: The magazine of higher learning, 21*(6), 39–47.].

NOTE

1. This paper is single-authored according to Professor Mahalingam's professional web site. However, according to Professor Mahalingam's (2013) chapter "Model Minority Myth: Engendering Cultural Psychology of Asian Immigrant" reference page, it is co-authored. In deference to the latter citation, I here I credit his co-author, Haritato.

CHAPTER 3

ASIAN AMERICAN SOCIOECONOMIC STANDING

This chapter contains literature on the model minority stereotype in relation to Asian Americans' socioeconomic standing. Given that the model minority stereotype implies that Asian Americans are economically stable and successful, this chapter annotates writings on critiques of such a trope. Gary Becker's (1975) neoclassical economic theorization, the notion that "the more one learns, the more one earns," is not supported when explaining the "glass ceiling" or the unequal returns on education that Asian American face (e.g., see Woo, 2000). If it were—in other words, if human capital accrued as the result of formal education—then Asian Americans would make more than White Americans since they are considered to be overeducated compared to Whites. Consequently, Asian Americans' socioeconomic standing merits attention. The following citations examine the convergence of the model minority stereotype and the socioeconomic standing of Asian Americans. The references in this chapter will be helpful for model minority stereotypic teaching and/or research.

The Model Minority Stereotype: Demystifying Asian American Success, pages 131–137.
131

Chang, C. (1998). Streets of gold: The myth of the model minority. In G. Colombo, R. Cullen, & B. Lisle (Eds.), *Rereading America: Cultural contexts for critical thinking and writing* (4th ed., pp. 366–375). Boston, MA: Bedford Books.

***This book chapter was originally published in the *Harvard Political Review* [October 1987, *14*(4), pp. 6–9]. Chang's chapter discusses why the model minority myth is wrong. The chapter focuses on how the myth impacts the following three areas: (1) Asian American affluence and homogeneity, (2) American meritocracy, and (3) Asian American educational elitism. Linking the model minority stereotype to aggregate statistics, which conceal Asian Americans' real rather than rhetorical experiences, Chang (1998) writes, "Statistics are like a bikini. What they reveal is suggestive, but what they conceal is vital" (p. 367). Model minority myth researchers will find this chapter a valuable resource to consult and cite when carrying out their scholarship for two primary reasons. The first is that Chang clearly did a considerable amount of research when writing the literature review. Only a little over seven pages in length, this relatively pithy chapter cites many seminal articles and pieces of literature that can easily be cross-referenced for further information. Second, and an even more important reason, is the fact that accompanying Chang's (1998) chapter is a companion resource guide, which summarizes and answers the questions that are presented after the actual chapter. This teaching guide is located at the end of the edited volume, after the book's index of authors and titles, and is effectively organized for its readers. The summary and answers to the questions presented in Chang's (1998) chapter are found on pages 53 and 54 of the teaching guide.

Cho, M. (1994). Overcoming our legacy as cheap labor, scabs, and model minorities. In K. Aguilar-San Juan (Ed.), *The state of Asian America: Activism and resistance in the 1990s* (pp. 253–273). Boston, MA: South End Press.

***Cho's (1994) book chapter is highly important in that it contextualizes why the model minority is such an insidious creation for people of color and for all who are oppressed. According to Cho's (1994) analysis, the model minority is a role that White supremacy wants Asian Americans to applaud and revere in order to maximize White racism and extend domination. Cho (1994), a second-generation Korean American, shares examples of how the Chinese and Koreans in New York and California are oppressed, used as "strikebreakers," and scapegoated, all in order to maintain White positions of power. The chapter is based on the interviews Cho (1994) conducted with seven Asian American activists, organizers, and community workers in November of 1992. The main premise of this chapter is that Asian Americans are used by White supremacy and that in order to regain their economic, political, and psychological freedom, Asian Americans must resist the urge of aligning themselves with Whites who don't have their best interests in mind, and also be wary of Asian "ethnics" who are pretending that they have the best intentions. Consequently, according to Cho (1994), "When we [Asian Americans] refuse to play the role of the loyal Uncle Tom or the upstanding Model Minority, we also deny [society] a valuable mouthpiece to be used to front for and exonerate a racist United States" (p. 271). Similarly, Cho (1994) notes that "Clarence Thomas personifies for black communities in this country what the *model minority myth* and its legacy does to working Asians" (p. 257, italics added). This book chapter is thoughtfully constructed and can be used as a reading in courses that seek to problematize the model minority stereotype. This chapter should also be cited in literature reviews, as it makes many worthwhile assertions, critiques, and comments that are important for the critical model minority discourse.

Chun, K. (1980, Winter/Spring). The myth of Asian American success and its educational ramifications. *IRCD Bulletin, 15*(1&2), 1–12. ERIC Document ID: ED193411

***Chun's (1980) piece appears in the double issue of *IRCD Bulletin,* a publication of the Institute for Urban and Minority Education at Teachers College, Columbia University. Chun (1980) asserts that "typical indicators of success, such as education and income [socioeconomic status], have not been properly adjusted for extraneous factors" (p. 1). Chun (1980) adds the following: "For income, for example, variables such as the number of wage earners, the education of wage earners, and the type of occupation must be considered" (p. 1). This is a fine article to cite whenever socioeconomic success is used to support the validity of the model minority stereotype.

Kim, E. H. (1975). The myth of Asian American success. *Asian American Review, 2*(1), 122–149.

***Kim's (1975) article indicates that the cultural or personality argument for Asian American success is a "hoax." In other words the myth was created for and by White Americans, and not by Asian Americans. Kim (1975) spends a great deal of time on the historically unequal social and power relations that Asians faced in America. This history is important because Kim (1975) states, "Many of the new, 'positive' stereotypes are nothing more than variations on old themes" (p. 130). Kim (1975) also posits that "the Asian American success story is a rationalization for cultural imperialism" (p. 140). Indeed, Kim (1975) draws the following conclusion from her research:

> Japanese Americans are used as "proof" of a racial equality that does not exist, and as showpieces of how docile acceptance of white supremacy is the key to success for non-white Americans. (p. 140)

Kim's (1975) article should be considered an early piece of critical anti-model minority stereotypic literature. For this reason it deserves to be cited in reviews of literature.

Diouf-Kamara, S. (1997, Summer). The Senegalese in New York: A model minority? *Black Renaissance, 1*(2), 92–115.

***This article asks the question, "Are the Senegalese in New York a model minority?" Diouf-Kamara (1997) describes the Senegalese as "steadfast workers, tireless tillers of the soil, excellent businessmen quick to grab the slightest opportunity" and points out that they are "also very unified" (p. 92). The Senegalese, who began to arrive in the early 1980s, Diouf-Kamara (1997) considers to be New York's "model immigrants." Like many Asian Americans, many Senegalese are self-employed. Diouf-Kamara (1997) also describes the Senegalese as modest model minorities. This article can be used to connect the various ways that other ethno-racial groups are likened to model minorities. Asian American studies courses can use this as a reading to show similarities with and differences between the treatment of Asians and other marginalized and diverse populations.

Junn, J. (2007). From coolie to model minority. *Du Bois Review, 4*(2), 355–373.

***This article examines a state of the art study: Asian Americans' transformation from coolie to model minority. Using 2005 U.S. Department of Homeland Security data, Junn (2007) disaggregated Asian Americans by both country of origin and class admission. Junn found that there was a high selection bias favoring high class and high education. According to her analysis, U.S. immigration policy creates a class- and education-based selection bias for immigrants. As Junn (2007) indicates, "In other words, federal policy has helped to recast the racial trope of Asian American from *coolie* to *model minority*" (p. 368, italics in original). Junn (2007) goes on to state that "in contrast, immigrants to the United States from Latin America have been disadvantaged by federal immigration policy" (p. 370). Junn's (2007) article is important for model minority stereotypical research because, as she says, the "*model minority* may be an accurate description of a selected set of Asians who successfully immigrated to the United States, but this description cannot be extended to characterize either Asian culture or Asian Americans in general; nor can it be applied in comparison to other minority groups with different trajectories of fortune" (p. 356, italics in original). Furthermore, Junn makes it clear that Asian Americans have not always been revered as successful minorities; thus, this article brings into question the historicity of the model minority stereotype, which allows critical individuals to problematize the myth's intentions and motivations.

Kao, G. (1995). Asian Americans as model minorities?: A look at their academic performance. *American Journal of Education, 103*(2), 121–159.

***Kao's (1995) article shares the results of her analysis of National Education Longitudinal Study of 1988 (NELS: 88) data. She compared White eighth graders' reading and math test scores and grades with those of Asian eighth grade students. She found that family background explained reading and math test score differences. The strength of her article, though, was that she analyzed subgroups of Asians, finding that Chinese, Korean, and Southeast Asian students scored higher math scores than their White peers, while Pacific Islanders earned lower math and reading scores than their White peers. Her article shows wide variation in achievement; thus, "the results also challenge the *model minority* image by demonstrating that Asians are *not* uniformly advantaged *educationally and economically*" (p. 151, italics added). Kao's (1995) article is a seminal piece of model minority stereotype literature.

Khator, R. (2010). Breaking the bamboo ceiling. *Presidency, 13*(2), 28–31.

***This short article on the "bamboo ceiling" is written by Renu Khator, an Asian Indian woman, who is, at the time of writing this book, president of the University of Houston and chancellor of the University of Houston system. Khator encourages her fellow Asian American colleagues to consider becoming a university president: "There are many Asian students on American campuses today, so you might consider doing it for them, if not for yourself" (p. 31). This article on the "bamboo ceiling" can be used by model minority researchers to problematize the authenticity of the myth. For example, if Asian Americans are indeed true overachievers, then meritocratic logic would concede that they should be highly qualified and represented in the ranks of university presidents. But Asian Americans are extremely scarce in terms of their representation as higher education administrators. In fact, Khator (2010) notes that statistics "indicate that Asian Americans are nearly absent from the ranks of university presidents" (p. 29).

Kim, K. C. & Hurh, W. M. (1983). Korean Americans and the "success" image: A critique. *Amerasia Journal, 10*(2), 3–21.

***Kim and Hurh (1983) were interested in examining whether or not Korean Americans were successful in terms of socioeconomics. They note that the model minority stereotype was applied originally to the Japanese and Chinese in the 1960s by the media, but that in the 1970s Koreans and the Indochinese were added to this category. For Kim and Hurh's (1983) case study of Korean immigrant adults who resided in Los Angeles, 281 males and 334 females were interviewed. Results of Kim and Hurh's (1983) interviews yielded "mixed conclusions" (p. 15). For instance, many respondents indicated that they work every Saturday or certain Sundays. The study also revealed the fact that despite being college educated, many Koreans worked in service sector jobs. A similar but abridged version of this article appears in the following: [Kim, K. C. & Hurh, W. M. (1986). Asian Americans and the "success" image: A critique. *Pacific/Asian-American Mental Health Research Center Research Review, 5*(1/2), 6–8.].

Lai, E. & Arguelles, D. (Eds.). (2003). *The new face of Asian Pacific America: Numbers, diversity & change in the 21st century.* Berkeley, CA: UCLA Asian American Studies Center Press.

***This (2003) edited volume is groundbreaking. Rich in statistics and figures, it is a resource that any researcher of the "model minority" stereotype cannot do without. This book contains infographics, tables, and contributed essays that arm its readers with information that can be used to combat the homogenization of Asian Pacific Americans. Much of the data is based upon 2000 U.S. Census data, and the reason this book is so helpful is its ability to deconstruct complex census data into meaningful and easy-to-digest figures and statistics that researchers and policymakers can use for the good of Asian Pacific Americans. The title is not indicative of the editors not doing their homework on the Asian American population. According to Lai and Arguelles (2003) the term Asian Pacific Americans is not a "term that is universally embraced. However, we hope whatever the book arguably lacks in accurate semantics it makes up for in its content and sincerity to shedding light on the diverse characteristics, experiences and issues of all Asian Americans and Pacific Islander communities" (p. 3). This book could be useful for graduate students writing a dissertation or thesis on the model minority stereotype.

McIlwain, C. D. & Johnson, L. (2003). Headache and heartbreak: The elusiveness of "model minority" status attainment for African Americans. In E. M. Kramer (Ed.), *The emerging monoculture: Assimilation and the "model minority"* (pp. 110–123). Westport, CT: Praeger.

***McIlwain and Johnson's (2003) chapter "Headache and Heartbreak: The Elusiveness of 'Model Minority' Status Attainment for African Americans" argues that model minority status for African Americans is elusive because it is a moving target. Based on the idea that model minority status is the result of successful assimilation into the White dominant society, the chapter authors contend that African Americans are no longer making the (economic, political, racial) gains that they once did during the 1980s and 1990s. Although this book chapter addresses African Americans specifically, and not Asian Americans, it still holds theoretical value, especially for examining the foundations used to cast Asian Americans as model minorities.

Wong, L. L. & Wong, C. (2006). Chinese engineers in Canada: A "model minority"? and experiences and perceptions of the glass ceiling. *Journal of Women and Minorities in Science and Engineering, 12*(4), 253–273.

***Wong and Wong's (2006) study asked: (1) Are the Chinese in Canada a model minority? (2) Does a glass ceiling exist for Chinese engineers in Canada? and (3) What are Chinese engineers' perceptions and actual experiences of the glass ceiling? Wong and Wong (2006) used two forms of data in their study: data culled from a mailed out survey to engineering graduates of the University of Calgary and secondary data procured from the 2001 Census of Canada. Their findings are best summarized in their own words:

> In Canada, the *model minority thesis* is not applicable to the Chinese. When the Chinese are assessed in terms of selected educational variables, there is a clear *bimodal distribution that is masked* when just mean years of schooling are considered. Though there is ovhghparticipation in professional occupations, there is also a large number of Chinese with low levels of education and who are in low-wage jobs. The mean income for Chinese is substantially below the mean income for all Canadians. When Chinese scientists' and engineers' incomes are examined using multiple regression analysis, there is a much lower return to their education and their experience when compared to Whites, clearly pointing to Chinese under-representation in higher paying management positions. This under-representation implicates a glass ceiling. (p. 269, italics added)

This article is important for model minority scholars given that it points out various lacunae in the literature, namely research conducted on Asians in Canada, but also the importance of multiple method studies and studies that disaggregate Asian subgroups. Future comparative research should be conducted in Canada, given that research comparing and contrasting the United States and Canada would be extraordinarily useful for the sociology of the stereotype. After all, according to Wong and Wong (2006), "It has been a *neglected* framework of scholarly investigation in Canada up to this point" (p. 255, italics added). This article can be utilized by scholar practitioners considering and formulating future scholarship centered on Asian Americans and Asian Canadians.

CHAPTER 4

ASIAN AMERICAN HEALTH AND SOCIAL WELFARE

This chapter annotates literature on Asian Americans and their health and social welfare. Since the model minority stereotype implies health and security, this chapter provides a counter narrative to such a belief. The credibility of the model minority stereotype, and the homogenization of Asian Americans into one super minority, has negative consequences and implications for Asian Americans. This is precisely why disaggregated data on Asian Americans' health is highly important. Srinivasan's (2000) article "Toward Improved Health: Disaggregating Asian American and Native Hawaiian/Pacific Islander Data" is groundbreaking for the development of this work, especially among those who are interested in issues of health and social access, equity, and justice for the Asian American population. Srinivasan (2000) writes that "when data on Asian American and Native Hawaiin/Pacific Islander ethnicities are aggregated, rates of health care use may be high overall, but the rates are higher among highly acculturated Asian Americans and Native Hawaiins/Pacific Islanders and lower for others" (p. 1732). As a result of the homogenization of the heterogeneous and diverse Asian Pacific American population in the United States, public health data

The Model Minority Stereotype: Demystifying Asian American Success, pages 139–163.
139

is skewed and public health studies are challenged. The implications for health and health care policy are enormous. The present chapter intends to help by collecting citations and references that policymakers and stakeholders can use in their respective fields of influence.

Abraham, M. (2006). Model minority and marital violence: South Asian immigrants in the United States. In R. Mahalingam (Ed.), *Cultural psychology of immigrants* (pp. 197–216). Mahwah, NJ: Lawrence Erlbaum Associates.

***Abraham's (2006) book chapter tackles the problem of the model minority as it relates to several invisible struggles found within the South Asian population. Abraham's (2006) chapter is based on an action-research study in which she interviewed South Asian immigrant women about their experiences with marital violence. Abraham (2006) shares that various South Asian Americans whom she interviewed worked diligently to uphold the model minority stereotype, resulting in rendering marital violence invisible as an issue within the South Asian American population. Consequently, Abraham (2006) found that the model minority stereotype negatively impacted South Asian women and the South Asian community. Observes Abraham (2006),

> They [South Asian immigrants] so invested in portraying the *model minority image* that they oppressed some segments of the community, and denied the prevalence of any social problems, including violence against women, within their community. (p. 200, italics added)

Abraham (2006) details the marital violence that South Asian wives experienced from their husbands, including violent—physical, mental, and sexual—abuse, intimidation, and economic deprivation. The most common ways that South Asian husbands controlled their wives was through isolation, violence, and mental/physical coercion. By threatening to send their wives back to their home country, violent husbands oftentimes made their South Asian wives beholden to them. This was especially prevalent given the fact that often these wives lacked the economic and/or familial resources necessary to terminate their unstable marriages. Of note, Abraham's (2006) chapter highlights the advocacy work that South Asian women's organizations (SAWOs) have done to circumvent Asian American marital violence in order to oppose model minority stereotypic characterizations. This book chapter is exceptionally useful for scholar practitioners and their counterparts (community-based counselors and teachers) who are dedicated to working with (South) Asian American immigrant women who may be experiencing marital violence or problems associated with the model minority stereotype.

Bodywise. (n.d.). Asian and Pacific Islander girls: Eating disorders information sheet. Retrieved on November 25, 2011, from http://www.thehormoneshop. com/BodyImage/Bodywise/uf/Asian%20American%20Girls2.pdf

***This information sheet highlights findings from studies on middle school Asian American females who have eating disorders. Eating disorders (anorexia, bulimia, purging, etc.) are a major health concern due to the fact that they often go underreported. Asian American females may be reticent seeking treatment due to cultural and social norms and mores that equate psychological problems (such as eating disorders) with individual weakness and familial shame. According to this information sheet, "Asian Americans are often perceived as the 'model minorities' and expected to be successful and high achieving. Asian American girls may attempt to seek power and identity through the pursuit of a physically ideal body" (n.p.). Moreover, studies have revealed that binge eating is more prevalent in Asian American than White females.

Chen, M. S. (2005). Cancer health disparities among Asian Americans: What we know and what we need to do. *Cancer, 104*(12), 2895–2902.

***This exhaustively-researched report documents what Chen (2005) calls the "cancer burden" affecting Asian Americans. The report begins by outlining the high prevalence of cancer among the Asian American community. It then shifts focus and shares the risks that impact Asian Americans. The article concludes by outlining specific facets that an agenda dedicated to ameliorating the "cancer burden" should contain. According to Chen (2005) Asian Americans (1) experience the highest rates of any racial/ethnic group for several forms of cancer, particularly those of infectious origins, such as cancers of the liver, uterine cervix, and stomach; (2) are the racial/ethnic group to experience cancer as the leading cause of death; (3) have an 80% higher risk for breast cancer if they are females who have resided in the United States for greater than ten years, as compared with more recent immigrants; (4) remain the lowest of any racial/ethnic group for women age forty years and older who receive mammograms; (5) are the least likely racial/ethnic group to obtain screening tests for cervical cancer (with significant variation among subgroups; and (6) are the least likely of all racial/ethnic groups to have seen a physician in the last two months. Chen (2005) also outlines the following risk factors for Asian Americans: (1) Vietnamese women have the highest incidence of cervical cancer, five times the rate of non-Hispanic White females; (2) lung cancer is the leading cause of death for Cambodians, Koreans, and Vietnamese; and (3) the incidence rate for liver cancer in the Asian American population is the highest of any racial/ethnic population. Chen concludes that any agenda dedicated to ending the "cancer burden" for the Asian American community needs to address gender and behavioral differences within and among

Asian American subpopulations. Moreover, the agenda must target preventative measures such as harm reduction and age-appropriate and gender-appropriate cancer screening.

Chen, M. S. & Hawks, B. L. (1995). A debunking of the myth of healthy Asian Americans and Pacific Islanders. *American Journal of Health Promotion, 9*(4), 261–268.

***Chen and Hawks (1995) examined "literature from the National Library of Medicine's compact disk databases (Cancerlit, CINAHL, Health, and MEDLINE), and examined pertinent federal government publications supplemented by the authors' knowledge of other published materials" (p. 261). Their review found that Asian Pacific Americans are underserved primarily for three reasons: (1) The population has grown so fast; (2) data about the health of this population is inadequate; and (3) the model minority stereotype renders this population's health needs invisible.

Cho, S. K. (1997). Converging stereotypes in racialized sexual harassment: Where the model minority meets Suzie Wong. *Journal of Gender, Race & Justice, 1*(1), 178–211.

***In her law brief, Cho (1997) identifies three key features of the model minority stereotype: (1) Asian American political subjugation, (2) comparison to African Americans, and (3) eventual success through perseverance and compatibility with the Protestant work ethic. Cho (1997) weaves together the court cases of two Asian Americans: Jane Jew, professor of anatomy at the University of Iowa in the 1970s who was denied full professorship status, and Rosalie Tung, professor of business at the University of Pennsylvania Wharton Business School in the 1980s who was denied tenure. Cho (1997) points out many ways that Asian American women are stereotyped "as politically passive, sexually exotic and compliant" (Cho, 1997, p. 208), and the venomous ways that the model minority stereotype perpetuates these racialized and gendered ascriptions of Asian women. This law brief is considered to be an Asian critical race theory (AsianCrit) classic article, and thus appears in several edited volumes, such as Richard Delgado and Jean Stefancic's (2000) *Critical Race Theory: The Cutting Edge* (2nd ed., pp. 532–542), as well as Adrien Katherine Wing's (2003) *Critical Race Feminism: A Reader* (2nd ed., pp. 349–366). This law review article is an appropriate reading for those who are interested in AsianCrit or the politics of the Asian American body. Students in law school would prosper professionally from reading it and discussing it in class.

Chun, K. & Zalokar, N. (1992). *Civil rights issues facing Asian Americans in the 1990s*. Washington, DC: Commission on Civil Rights. ERIC Document ID: ED343979.

***The U.S. Commission on Civil Rights held a series of roundtable conferences to learn about the social welfare and civil rights concerns of Asian

Americans in 1989. Chapters of this report highlight many topical areas. Some of these topical areas that the 245-page report formally addresses include (1) bigotry and violence against Asian Americans, (2) statistics on hate crimes against Asian Americans, (3) Asian Americans' access to police protection, (4) access to educational opportunity in higher education, (5) Asian Americans and the glass ceiling, (6) employment discrimination against Asian American women, (7) political representation of Asian Americans, and (8) Asian Americans' access to health care. The preceding is not even an exhaustive list, illustrating just how comprehensive this report is. In the opening lines of the report, Chun and Zalokar (1992) write, "Considering the widely held image of Asian Americans as the 'model minority,' this is hardly surprising. Yet participants at the Civil Rights Commission's Roundtable Conferences in Houston, San Francisco, and New York recounted numerous incidents of anti-Asian prejudice and discrimination" (p. 1). This comprehensively assembled report is an exceptional read for model minority scholars who are just beginning their research and for those teachers and researchers who may not know many examples of anti-Asian violence and aggression. The well-researched report will quickly rectify this, providing such examples as the notorious murders of Vincent Chin (an adopted Chinese American male), Jim (Ming Hai) Loo (a Chinese American male), Navroze Mody (an Asian Indian male), and Hung Truong (a Vietnamese male), or the tragic "Stockton Schoolyard Massacre" that happened on January 17, 1989 in Stockton, California at Cleveland Elementary School in which "a gunman dressed in military garb entered the schoolyard...and repeatedly fired an AK47 assault rifle, killing five Indochinese children and wounding 30 others" (p. 30). Such revelatory examples compiled by the report clearly demonstrate that the struggle for civil rights has not simply been an issue for African Americans, but for Asian Americans as well.

Cohen, E. (2007, May 16). Push to achieve tied to suicide in Asian-American women. *CNN.com*. Retrieved from http://www.cnn.com/2007/HEALTH/05/16/asian.suicides/index.html

***Cohen's (2007) piece highlights the fact that suicide is the second-leading cause of death for Asian American women age 15 to 24 and that experts cite the model minority stereotype and its attendant high expectations as a cause/contributor. The piece also examines the scholarship of Dr. Eliza Noh, an associate professor in the Asian American Studies Program at California State University at Fullerton. Dr. Noh's work is important and can be used when engaging in research that dispels the veracity of the minority stereotype (e.g., see Noh, 2000, 2007).

Crystal, D. (1989). Asian Americans and the myth of the model minority. *Social Casework: The Journal of Contemporary Social Work, 70*(7), 405–413.

***Crystal's (1989) article examines how the model minority stereotype serves as a barrier to better understanding the mental health needs and struggles of the Asian American population. Crystal (1989) writes that "although Asians...have a history of oppression in the United States, their increasing affluence and educational attainments seem to belie the popular image of an oppressed subgroup" (p. 405). As a result, writes Crystal (1989), "They are perceived as having few, if any, mental health problems and are thought to live in homogeneous communities composed of stable, close-knit families that 'take care of their own' with little need of outside social services" (p. 406). This fiction, coupled with their low utilization rates (use of mental health services), which is mistaken for healthy mental health, serve to marginalize Asian Americans. Crystal (1989) indicates that Asian Americans are at-risk, and thus require culturally sensitive mental health services. Crystal (1989) provides a series of recommendations: (1) the need for *culturally relevant interventions*, (2) the need to understand the *indirect/nonverbal communication style of Asian cultures*, (3) the need to understand that *the father is the patriarch in many Asian families*, and (4) the need to understand that many Asian groups rely on *informal support systems*. Taken together, Crystal's (1989, p. 412) article contributes much to our awareness of mental health needs for Asian Americans. It also contributes to an understanding of why the stereotype is a concern, rather than a compliment:

> Every myth contains a mixture of truth and falsehood, and the myth of the "model minority" is no exception. Built upon a foundation of facts, it perpetuates a dangerous fiction. Like a patronizing pat on the head, it condescends to praise while praising to condescend. Ostensibly a compliment, the badge of the "model minority" actually undermines the integrity of Asian Americans.

Educational psychology students would benefit from reading this article.

Delucchi, M. & Do, H. D. (1996). The model minority myth and perceptions of Asian-Americans as victims of racial harassment. *College Student Journal, 30*(3), 411–414.

***Delucchi and Do's (1996) short article shares their analysis of a case study of a Vietnamese American male who was assaulted/battered by a White male on a campus of the University of California in a dormitory recreation room in the early 1990s. Perceptions of Asian Americans as victims of racial harassment were found to be ambivalent on this campus. Indeed, according to Delucchi and Do (1996), "The university [of California] community's indifference may have been shaped by an implicit acceptance of the *model minority myth*" (p. 413, italics added). If the victim was African American, then perhaps the university would label the White perpetrator's action as racially motivated. Instead, Delucchi and Do (1996) share illustrative examples and contexts that demonstrate that in the eyes of the university, and many of its students, racial harassment was perceived through a predictable hierarchy. Violence directed towards African Americans would be perceived to be racially motivated, when the same animus against Asians would be considered merely hostile or discriminatory. Because Asian Americans were perceived to be part of the mainstream, as "model minorities," they could not possibly be targets of racially-motivated violence. The authors reason the following in their case study: "Consequently, unlike 'more oppressed' ethnic groups, Asian-Americans are not readily recognized as victims of racial intolerance. Therefore, the university [of California] community was less willing to infer racial motives to acts against Asians" (Delucchi & Do, 1996, p. 413). This article can be used as evidence that Asian Americans are not perceived to be persecuted or victimized due to their race/ethnicity.

Goto, S. G. & Abe-Kim, J. (1998). Asian Americans and the model minority myth. In T. M. Singelis (Ed.), *Teaching about culture, ethnicity, & diversity: Exercises and planned activities* (pp. 151–157). Thousand Oaks, CA: Sage Publications.

***Goto and Abe-Kim (1998) avoid academic jargon, making their chapter easy to read and understand. The chapter includes ideas such as Asian Americans being a bimodal distributed population and Asian Americans' mental health needs being overlooked. Goto and Abe-Kim (1998) point out that "despite common subordinate status, Asian Americans are touted as having achieved an unmatched success. An implication of the model minority myth is that institutional and psychological barriers such as prejudice are minimized and seen as 'workable'" (p. 152). They also note that "as a group, Asian Americans have not received equitable or adequate social and mental health aid" (Goto & Abe-Kim, 1998, pp. 152–153). Goto and Abe-Kim's (1998) chapter is one that teachers can immediately incorporate into their teaching instruction. The biggest contribution that their chapter makes is its inclusion of an activity for use as an instructional tool. Goto and Abe-Kim (1998) provide directions and reproducible activity cards for a model minority myth exercise. The exercise involves pre-written labels that a teacher can Xerox. The teacher assigns each student with a label. Students have their individual label taped to their back. Students move around the classroom socializing with fellow classmates. The goal of this "model minority exercise" (p. 156) is for students to infer what label is on his/her back. After this period is over, depending on the color (blue, orange, or purple) denoted on their card/label, students move into small groups. In their small "colored" groups, students then discuss how ethno-racial groups are stereotyped. It is this discussion time that is so powerful for students and their learning. By talking about the "model minority" label and stereotype in small intimate groups, students are faced with the question Goto and Abe-Kim (1998) ask their readers: "If statistics and population diversity suggest that many Asian Americans are less successful than perceived, why does the myth persist?" (p. 152).

Gupta, A., Szymanski, D., & Leong, F. (2011). The "model minority myth": Internalized racialism of positive stereotypes as correlates of psychological distress, and attitudes toward help-seeking. *Asian American Journal of Psychology, 22*(2), 101–114.

***Gupta, Szymanski, and Leong (2011) raise the question of whether internalizing the model minority stereotype impacts psychological distress and/or attitudes toward help-seeking; 291 self-identified Asian Americans participated in the study. Using a modified form of the Attitude Toward Asians (ATA) Scale, participants took a web-based survey. Statistical analysis resulted in the following finding: "higher levels of endorsement of positive Asian stereotypes were related to more somatic complaints and higher levels of psychological distress" (p. 109). Moreover, help-seeking attitude was not significantly affected by higher levels of psychological distress. Write Gupta, Szymanski, and Leong (2011), "The results of this study provide clinicians with valuable information regarding how endorsement of positive Asian stereotypes may be detrimental in a population that, despite popular belief, does have need for [social and health] services" (p. 111). Therefore, this article will be helpful for health and social service providers, including counselors and medial officials.

Hall, R. E. (2002). Myth of the "model minority": Stereotype and the reality of Asian-American gangs. *Asian Profile, 30*(6), 541–548.

***Hall (2002) indicates that racism is a risk that negatively impacts quality of life for Asian Americans. Consequently, Hall (2002) writes, "Stereotypes of Asian-Americans [as model minorities] are unrealistic and born out of racism" (p. 546). Hall's article examines the existence of Asian American gangs and Asian Organized Crime (AOC) groups and these groups' socio-historical antecedents. This article asserts, strongly, that social science is flawed methodologically unless it appropriately addresses racism. According to Hall (2002), in order to be non-hegemonic toward Asian American experience, social scientists must "accommodate an ontological effort and epistemological sensitivity to a unique population [*viz.* Asian Americans]" (p. 541). This article is a valuable resource for teachers and researchers, especially given that few people know the uglier side of Asian American violence and criminalization in the United States. Social isolation, traumatic refugee history, language difficulties, cultural and familial dissonance, and poverty are but a few contributors to why Asian American youth join gangs. Hall (2002) points out that Asian American gang members initially join for power, protection, identity, and sense of "family" or belonging. This article is incredibly important because "very little is being done to analyze or study the causes of Asian-American crime and victimization" (Hall, 2002, p. 546) and also because "Asian-American street gangs are a rapidly growing problem in America" (Hall, 2002, p. 546).

Hall, R. E. (2001). "Model minority" as Eurocentric stereotype: Southeast Asian gangs. *Loyola Journal of Social Sciences, 15*(2), 135–146.

***Hall (2001) examines the idea that Southeast Asians are a model minority by contrasting the Eurocentric stereotype with the evolution of Asian (particularly Southeast Asian) gangs. According to Hall (2001), the model minority "stereotype is a sociological demonstration of racism" (p. 135) and "the concept of a 'model minority' has caused Asians to retreat into invisible communities where their many problems are easily overlooked or ignored by governmental and social service agencies" (p. 148). Hall explains that (Southeast) Asian American youth join gangs because they find support and identity within them, social needs that they are lacking and desperately desire due to generational divisions between themselves and their families and divisions from their peers, divisions that are exacerbated by language acquisition challenges. What makes Hall's (2001) article unique is its push to rectify the methodological and Eurocentric biases latent in social scientific research, especially in the face of great demographic and racial shifts within the United States. This article will be useful for those who are interested in meeting the unique needs of Southeast Asian American students. Community workers in the field of health and human services, as well as those who work in the non-governmental or non-profit sector, will also find this article valuable. Moreover, scholars doing work on the model minority stereotype will find this an important article to bring up since, as Hall (2001) writes, "The evolution of Asian gangs throughout Western societies has been all but ignored due to the Eurocentric hegemony of Western social science literature" (p. 144).

Hayashi, M. C. (2003). *Far from home: Shattering the myth of the model minority.* Irving, TX: Tapestry Press.

***This book is about rethinking the preconceptions about health and Asian Americans. Hyashi's (2003) book addresses the unique social and health needs of Asian Americans (in particular women), drawing on her own work and the establishment of the National Asian Women's Health Organization (NAWHO). A helpful supplement at the end of the book contains many references of interest regarding issues such as: (1) Asian American women and heart disease, (2) reproductive health needs of Vietnamese American women, (3) violence among young Asian American women, (4) reproductive and sexual health of Asian American women, (5) cervical cancer and Asian American women, (6) depression among Asian American women, and (7) Asian American women and breast cancer. This book should be read by those who work with Asian Americans in the fields of social work, counseling, community education, and medicine.

Iijima, C. K. (1998). Political accommodation and the ideology of the "model minority": Building a bridge to White minority rule in the 21st century. *Southern California Interdisciplinary Law Journal, 7*(1), 1–40.

***According to Iijima (1998) the model minority stereotype was at play when the Japanese received reparations for their unjust internment. Consequently, writes Iijima (1998), the Japanese in America can be readily compared and contrasted to Africans who were cruelly enslaved in America. While the Japanese Americans (Nisei) were remunerated $20,000 from the United States in payment for their internment, no such reparations have been distributed for the inhumane enslavement that Africans in America experienced in chattel slavery times. As a result, Iijima's (1998) article fits nicely with Eric Yamamoto's (1992) *Denver Journal of International Law and Policy* article "Friend, or Foe or Something Else: Social Meanings of Redress and Reparations." For instance, "Political Accommodation and the Ideology of the 'Model Minority': Building a Bridge to White Minority Rule in the 21st Century" can be used in concert with Yamamoto's (1992) article to illustrate an example of White "interest convergence" (Bell, 1980) in relation to why the Japanese Americans (a model minority) received reparations and African Americans (an inferior minority) did not. Iijima (1998) writes that

> Asian Pacific Americans are at a crossroads in terms of where they will stand in the coming era of race relations—either to be used to solidify the control of white supremacy or to be a force standing against it. (p. 40)

Thoughtful and highly erudite, Iijima's (1998) model minority stereotype law article aids in the advancement of critical race theorization in ways that have not been fully explored.

Iijima, C. K. (1998). Reparations and the "model minority" ideology of acquiescence: The necessity to refuse the return to original humiliation. *Boston College Law Review, 40*(1), 385–427.

***According to Iijima (1998), close scrutiny of the model minority reveals that it strengthens the appearance, internationally, that the United States is a country committed to equality, justice and meritocracy. Thus, he writes, the model minority is part of conservative racial politics/policies, and its silent message is that all minorities should be able to overcome their trials and tribulations. Asian Americans' accolades of supposed achievement stand in sharp relief to accommodating White supremacist racial politics. Iijima (1998) notes the following about model minority role-playing:

The carrot of political reward for political accommodation is a particular temptation for Asian Americans, for Asian Americans find themselves in a peculiar place in the developing racial hierarchy. If Asian Americans accept their *model minority role*, it no doubt will come with the "reward" of higher racial status. (p. 410, italics added)

Iijima's (1998) law article addresses important elements contextualized within a racial acquiescence framework, namely, the ways in which the model minority stereotype (exemplified in post-World War II Japanese reparations), such as racial tiering, hegemony, structural or institutionalized racism, and demographic shifts, are problematic for Asian Americans. Iijima (1998) notes, as many others have before him, that the model minority stereotype is selectively "wielded in defense of the racial status quo" (p. 425) and more importantly that "the responsibility of [Asian Americans who are] being oppressed is first to survive and then to resist" (p. 427). Consequently, Iijima's (1998) article addresses a central issue of importance for racial middle-people when demystifying the model minority stereotype, the necessity to refuse to be a pawn for White supremacy: Asian American resistance. This article makes a significant scholarly contribution to the corpus of literature on the model minority stereotype and deserves to be read by AsianCrit scholars and theoreticians. Moreover, it is only when Asian Americans realize that they are oppressed and resist that real change can take place, for as Iijima (1998) points out, "In order to have the continued opportunity to express their 'generosity,' the oppressors [White supremacy] must perpetuate injustice as well" (p. 385). Progress for Asian Americans will only be made with active Asian American resistance. While the model minority stereotype applauds Asian Americans publicly for their supposed success, privately White supremacy is fearful that it will lose its power, and, thus, utilizes Asian American "success" to divide and conquer other oppressed and subordinated people of color.

Jang, D. & Surapruik, A. (2009). Not the model minority: How to address disparities in Asian American health care. *Asian American Policy Review, 18,* 91–106.

***This article "provides an overview of disparities in health care and health status experienced by Asian Americans, Native Hawaiians, and Pacific Islanders and highlights policies at the federal level that would help address these disparities and promote health equity" (p. 91). Although this article examines Native Hawaiians and Pacific Islanders, it is an important document since it interrogates and problematizes a 1985 Secretary of the U.S. Department of Health and Human Services report that used aggregate data that "led to the finding that Asian Americans as a group are healthier than other racial groups in the United States" (p. 91). This article indicates otherwise.

Johnson, B. D. & Betsinger, S. (2009). Punishing the "model minority": Asian-American criminal sentencing outcomes in federal district courts. *Criminology,* *47*(4), 1045–1090.

***Johnson and Betsinger (2009), using data from the United States Sentencing Commission (USSC) for FY1997 through FY2000, examined the sentencing outcomes in federal district courts. The researchers found that Asian Americans were punished more similarly to White offenders compared with Black and Hispanic offenders. Johnson and Betsinger (2009) point out that "as the fastest growing minority group in the United States, now constituting a sizable incarcerated population, research on the criminal processing of Asian offenders is timely and needed" (p. 1046). This article is highly significant and important given that Asian Americans, as model minorities, are thought to be law-abiding and therefore less impacted by the justice system. This article can be used when carrying out or conceptualizing current and future model minority stereotype research.

Jung, J. (1985, November). The model minority? [Review of S. Sue & J. K. Morishima, *The mental health of Asian-Americans.* Jossey-Bass, 1982.] *Contemporary Psychology: A Journal of Reviews, 30*(11), 895–896.

***Jung's (1985) book review examines the mental health problems of the Asian American population. Jung (1985) writes that the "stereotype that Asian Americans are a model minority that has achieved economic success and at the same time has managed to avoid suffering the major ills facing other minority groups—such as high levels of juvenile delinquency, poverty, drug abuse, and poor academic achievement" (p. 895) leads to people disbelieving that they have mental health problems.

Kelsey, M. E. (1994). Welfare policies and racial stereotypes: The structural construction of a model minority. *Exploration in Ethnic Studies, 17*(1), 63–78.

***Kelsey's (1994) article is helpful in that it addresses the shortcomings of "cultural" explanations for Asian American success. Kelsey (1994) writes that "cultural approaches to social mobility hold poor racial and ethnic communities responsible for structural conditions beyond their control. Moreover, cultural explanations for the economic successes of Indochinese refugees reinforce contemporary characterizations of Asian Americans as a 'model minority'" (p. 65). However, Kelsey (1994) also indicates that an entirely structuralist analysis fails to recognize human agency in achieving success. That being said, Kelsey's (1994) article shares her findings from an ethnographic study she conducted with twenty families who resettled in California from remote regions of Laos during 1979 to 1985. Kelsey (1994) found that welfare policies in the state of California, as well as nationally, aided Southeast Asian refugees in gaining more education and economic stability in the United States. Harkening back to the beginning of her article, Kelsey (1994) reiterates,

> State aid raised Southeast Asian refugees' level of education, enhanced their job skills and ultimately increased their employability. These state-provided assets are overlooked by cultural explanations, which reduce social mobility to a given set of attitudes of education, hard work, and family commitment. (p. 75)

This article can be used by researchers and scholars when developing empirical and theoretical studies, since it does a nice job at comparing and contrasting the influence of class, race, structural, and social policy on the model minority stereotype.

Koo, D. J., Peguero, A. A., & Shekarkhar, Z. (2012). The "model minority" victim: Immigration, gender, and Asian American vulnerabilities to violence at school. *Journal of Ethnicity in Criminal Justice, 10*(2), 129–147.

***Koo, Peguero, and Shekarkhar (2012) write "Despite the model minority stereotype, many Asian Americans experience exclusion, alienation, and marginalization in the United States" (p. 131). Using data from the Educational Longitudinal Study of 2002 (ELS:2002) and using hierarchical generalized linear modeling (HGLM), this study explored how immigration and gender are related to the victimization of Asian American youth within U.S. schools. Findings indicated that "once immigration and gender are considered, there is an increased likelihood of being victimized at school for Asian American immigrant youth" (p. 141). Using the ELS:2002 data, a nationally representative dataset, is important since it "oversampled to obtain a sufficient representation [of Asian Americans] for statistical analyses" (p. 135). Say Koo, Peguero, and Shekarkhar (2012), "Despite the *model minority stereotype*, many Asian Americans experience exclusion, alienation, and marginalization in the United States" (p. 131, italics added). This study would be interesting to replicate with disaggregated Asian American student groups. It should be consulted when conducting model minority teaching and/or research.

Kim, B. L. (1973). Asian-Americans: No model minority. *Social Work, 18*(1), 44–53.

Kim (1973) writes that "the myth that Asian-Americans comprise a homogenous model minority ignores the many difficulties these heterogeneous communities face" (p. 44). Kim's (1973) article briefly reviews Asians'—Chinese, Japanese, and Filipinos—historically-documented experiences with racism. Anti-Asian fervor commenced in the 1850s, leading to the creation of phrases like "a Chinaman's chance" (p. 47) and racially hostile legislation that prohibited, penalized, and profoundly hurt Asian Americans. This article vehemently argues against the model minority thesis, hence its title. According to Kim (1973) it is the "insensitivity, ignorance, and inadequacy of...community agencies that prefer to maintain the myth that Asian-Americans are successful and take care of themselves" (p. 51) that harms Asian Americans the most. This is the reason why Kim (1973) argues that "the social work profession [needs to] be ready to learn about and appreciate the strengths, aspirations, problems, and needs of the various Asian American groups and the differences among them" (p. 52). This article is beneficial for allied health providers to read.

Kuramoto, F. H. (1994). Drug abuse prevention research concerns in Asian and Pacific Islander populations. In A. Cázares & L. A. Beatty (Eds.), *Scientific methods for prevention research* (NIH Publication No. 94-3631, pp. 249–272). Rockville, MD: National Institute on Drug Abuse.

***Kuramoto's (1994) chapter from the National Institute on Drug Abuse Research Monograph Series report titled *Scientific Methods for Prevention Intervention Research* highlights Asian and Pacific Islanders' (1) bimodal income pattern; (2) low per capita incomes; (3) high poverty rates, which are oftentimes unrecognized and misunderstood; (4) low economic returns for their educational investment; and (5) significant alcohol, tobacco, and other drug problems. Most of the chapter is dedicated to delineating the many difficulties and concerns when conducting drug abuse prevention research in Asian and Pacific Islander populations. Some of these challenges are caused by socio-cultural and/or methodological complexities. As Kuramoto (1994) notes, "the demographic characteristics of Asians and Pacific Islanders are considerably more *complex* than the so-called myth of the *model minority* would imply" (p. 259, italics added). Moreover, Kuramoto notes that

> the myth of the model minority tends to stereotype Asians and Pacific Islanders as a group that is unaffected by drug abuse. In reality, however, there are Asian drug traffickers producing and smuggling illicit drugs from the 'Golden Triangle' in Asia to the United States, some of which then are distributed in the United States by Asians and Pacific Islanders. (p. 263)

Clearly, then, the most salient contribution that this chapter makes to deconstructing the model minority stereotype is its comprehensive coverage of the myriad challenges to conducting research on the health and social needs of Asian Americans. Failure to address these unique concerns reinforces the model minority stereotype via the faulty impression that Asian Americans have no health needs that merit attention.

Lee, S. & Rotheram-Borus, M. J. (2009). Beyond the "model minority" stereotype: Trends in health risk behaviors among Asian/Pacific Islander high school students. *Journal of School Health, 79*(8), 347–354.

***The objective of Lee and Rotheram-Borus's (2009) study was to examine the trends in health risk behaviors among Asian/Pacific Islander high school students who took the San Diego City Schools Youth Risk Behavior Survey (YRBS) between 1993 and 2005. Four areas of risk were studied and examined: (1) alcohol drinking, (2) cigarette smoking, (3) marijuana use, and (4) HIV/AIDS communication with parents. According to Lee and Rotheram-Borus (2009), from 1993 to 2005 condom use at last sexual intercourse was consistently lower among Asian/Pacific Islander students than their cross-ethnic peers. Moreover, there was a significant increasing trend in lifetime smoking, drinking, and marijuana use. Parental communication regarding human immunodeficiency virus (HIV) and/or acquired immunodeficiency syndrome (AIDS) was significantly less frequent and decreased over time. Lee and Rotheram-Borus's (2009) "findings challenge the notion of API [Asian/Pacific Islander] youth being the 'model minority'" (p. 353). Further, Lee and Rotheram-Borus (2009) warn that given "that API [Asian/Pacific Islander] youth are the 'model minority' [the myth] should be acknowledged and addressed in the design and implementation of school-based health programs and services" (p. 353). This article will be of interest to school administrators and health-care professionals.

Lee, S., Juon, H., Martinez, G., Hsu, C. E., Robinson, E. S., Bawa, J., & Ma, G. X. (2009). Model minority at risk: Expressed needs of mental health by Asian American young adults. *Journal of Community Health, 34*(2), 144–152.

***The researchers of this study, Lee et al. (2009), were interested in better understanding the potential sources of stress that affect the mental health of Asian American young adults. Lee et al.'s (2009) qualitative method study was based on 17 focus group participants (five males and 12 females) between the ages of 18 and 30. Their study makes a unique contribution to the scholarship on the model minority myth's influence on the mental health of Asian Americans since it disaggregated Asian Americans by subgroups and examined four "under-represented" subgroups that are frequently omitted or understudied (three Cambodian, six Indonesian, one Taiwanese, and one Thai). In addition to these eleven focus group participants who came from under-represented subgroups, one Asian Indian, one Chinese, three Korean, and one Vietnamese also participated in the study. Consequently, Lee et al. (2009) found two potential sources of stress affecting the mental health of Asian Americans.

The first source was *parental pressure to "succeed."* According to Lee et al. (2009), the "Asian American stereotype of being smart and accomplished—the model minority myth—sustained by non AA, may have placed additional pressure on AA youths" (p. 148). The second source of stress was *Asian American discrimination and/or isolation.* In addition to these two major sources of stress, the researchers also found five factors that inhibited the help-seeking behavior of the Asian Americans that they studied: (1) the stigma associated with mental health, (2) the lack of awareness of mental health needs, (3) the desire to avoid worrying their parents and/or families, (4) the lack of mental health professionals who could offer culturally and linguistically appropriate care, and (5) the costs associated with mental health services. Lee et al. (2009) write the following: "Asian parents consider academic success as the most important thing in their children, and thus AA youths feel pressure to meet this expectation" (p. 150). In conclusion, the "model minority" stereotype by outsiders, coupled with high parental expectations, serve as major sources of stress for Asian American young adults. These stressors may in turn affect Asian Americans' mental health status. This article uniquely illustrates the convergence of cultural, communal, and social forces when considering stressors influencing Asian American young adults' psychological/physical health and stability. Consequently, this article is important given the havoc the model minority stereotype can wreak on Asian Americans by presuming that the mental health of Asian Americans is sound. Also worth mentioning, Lee et al. (2009), in their review of the literature, write the following: "Among females 15–24 years old Asian Americans and Pacific Islanders (AAPIs) have the highest rate of suicide deaths (14.1%) compared to other racial/ethnic groups (White 9.3%, Black 3.3%, and Hispanic 7.4%)" (p. 145). Clearly, as the title of this article suggests, Asian Americans are at risk.

Leong, F., Leach, M., Yeh, C., & Chou, E. (2007). Suicide among Asian Americans: What do we know? What do we need to know? *Death Studies, 31*(5), 417–434.

*** Suicide among Asian Americans has long been understudied; this article seeks to contribute information and insight to the dearth of such studies. Some of the article's salient points that researchers might want to know and cite are as follows:

- the elderly and adolescent age groups are most likely to complete suicide among Asian Americans;
- as a group, for all women residing in the United States, East Asian women have the highest proportional rate of suicide over the age of 65;
- the model minority and its intense pressure to succeed may cause psychological stress and higher suicide rates among the Asian American population;
- most suicide research on Asian Americans has focused on Chinese, Japanese, and Filipinos; and
- the literature on religion and suicide indicates that Hindu males attempt suicide to a greater degree than females, and seemingly few studies on suicide have examined Asian American Bhuddists, Taoists, and/or Confucianists.

Leong and his co-authors point out the methodological as well as cultural barriers that make suicide research on the Asian American population daunting and difficult (e.g., small sample sizes, cultural reticence of Asian Americans to come forward with their data/stories, and lack of existing literature to draw upon).

Lester, D. (1992). Suicide among Asian Americans and social deviancy. *Perceptual and Motor Skills, 75*(3), 1134.

***This one page report indicates that suicide differs by Asian American subgroup. This article can be used when doing work on the model minority stereotype and the mental health service needs of Asian Americans.

Lin-Fu, J. S. (1988). Population characteristics and health care needs of Asian Pacific Americans. *Public Health Reports, 103*(1), 18–27.

***The health care needs of Asian Pacific Americans (APAs) have received relatively little attention by researchers. This public health report begins by reviewing the population characteristics of the APA community. According to Lin-Fu (1988), APAs are "extremely heterogeneous and bipolar in socioeconomic status and health indices" (p. 18). Accordingly, health care and social workers need to "bear in mind the extreme heterogeneity of the Asian Pacific Americans, particularly in providing health education and counseling services" (p. 20). The healthcare costs for the nation as a whole are increased when APAs health concerns and heterogeneity are neglected. Lin-Fu suggests that the health and social needs of APAs go largely unnoticed "because...they continue to be stereotyped as a uniquely successful minority without many problems or needs" (p. 19). Lin-Fu (1988) notes that, insidiously, "the general assumption about the good health status of Asian Pacific Americans as a group tends to mask the serious health problems and needs of some subgroups, such as the Southeast Asian refugees and other recent immigrants" (p. 21). This health care article is not only important because it discusses three specific health problems and needs for the APA community—(1) genetic disorders, other diseases, and mental health; (2) severe ethno-cultural barriers to health care; and (3) special anatomical and physiological characteristics—but also because it gives many concrete examples of how health educators and medical staff must better understand APA cultural and gastronomical behaviors in order to better serve their health and welfare needs. Two such examples are as follows: (1) knowing about "the common consumption of highly salted food in Asian diets and the frequent use of coconut products (which have a high saturated fat content) in many Southeast Asian cuisines" (p. 25) and (2) the need for "physicians [to] be mindful of the lighter body weight common among Asian Pacific American immigrants and refugees to avoid [medical] overdose[s]" (p. 25).

Panelo, N. D. (2010). The model minority student: Asian American students and the relationships between acculturation to Western values, family pressures, and mental health concerns. *The Vermont Connection, 31,* 147–155.

***Panelo's (2010) article addresses the reality of being an Asian American student. According to Panelo (2010), "Though the idea of being a model minority seems like a positive perception of Asian Americans and their community, this designation has negative effects" (p. 150). It is unstable mental health that this article attends to, the negative effect of unstable mental health that may arise from being perceived as a model minority. Panelo (2010) makes it clear that Asian American students are not model minorities. Rather than the problem-free caricature, many Asian American students face myriad cultural, familial, and parental pressures that can lead to mental health concerns. Asian Americans face difficulties acculturating to Western values, which, according to Panelo (2010) "student affairs professionals should learn to recognize" (p. 151). Panelo (2010) makes it clear that "student affairs professionals can help with transition and support for Asian American students on campus by being cognizant of the developmental hardships associated with the process of acculturation" (p. 153). This article can be used in the work of segmented assimilation theorists and scholars, as well as in student affairs. What makes this article compelling is that it is written by a first-generation Filipino American in a matter-of-fact way.

Qin, D. B., Way, N., & Rana, M. (2008). The "model minority" and their discontent: Examining peer discrimination and harassment of Chinese American immigrant youth. In H. Yoshikawa & N. Way (Eds.), *Beyond the family: Contexts of immigrant children's development* (pp. 27–42). Hoboken, NJ: Jossey-Bass.

***This chapter is very similar to: [Qin, D. B., Way, N., & Mukherjee, P. (2008). The other side of the model minority story: The familial and peer challenges faced by Chinese American adolescents. *Youth & Society, 39*(4), 480–506.]. Qin, Way, and Rana's (2008) chapter explores the reasons that Chinese American first- and second-generation adolescents experience peer discrimination and harassment. For instance, Qin, Way, and Rana (2008) write,

> On the one hand, the *model minority myth* may serve some Chinese American students well by encouraging the teachers to have high expectations of them; on the other hand, this myth haunted the Chinese kids as it led to other students, Black, Latino, and White, to resent and harass them for the preferential treatment they received from the teachers. (p. 35, italics added)

This chapter can be used for model minority stereotype literature reviews, as well as for locating other sources on the model minority stereotype.

Qin, D. B., Way, N., & Mukherjee, P. (2008). The other side of the model minority story: The familial and peer challenges faced by Chinese American adolescents. *Youth & Society, 39*(4), 480–506.

***This article shares qualitative research that was conducted with first- and second-generation Chinese American adolescents in New York ($n = 40$) and Boston ($n = 80$). Data was collected between 1996 and 2001 and consisted of semi-structured and structured interviews with the adolescents. Findings from these interviews substantiated that, contrary to the stereotype that Asian Americans come from stable families, many participants indicated tension and familial stress. Contributing to these stressors were language barriers that existed, parent work schedules, and high parental educational expectations. This article contains many quotations from the Chinese adolescents, which makes this article a useful source of counter-narratives to the model minority stereotype.

Rigdon, J. E. (1991, July 10). Exploding myth: Asian American youth suffer a rising toll from heavy pressures. *Wall Street Journal,* A1. Retrieved from http://www.joanrigdon.com/clips/asiansuicide.html

***Rigdon's (1991) *Wall Street Journal* article examines the consequences of the model minority stereotype for Asian American high school and college students. Rigdon (1991) writes the following:

> In school, they are saddled with the "Model-Minority" myth, which says that Asians are bound to excel at whatever they do. Thinking this way, many educators expect Asians to overcome academic and emotional difficulties without help from special programs available to members of other minority groups. Meanwhile, students of other races, goaded to do as well as those of the Model Minority, resent Asians. (p. A1)

Suicide is the foremost health issue that Rigdon (1991) addresses in this piece, and it is an issue that needs to be taken seriously by those concerned about the psychosocial and educational needs of Asian American students. This *Wall Street Journal* article cites the names and ages of a handful of Asian Americans who have taken their own lives, presumably due to pressures of being held to unrealistic educational standards.

Saphir, A. (1997). Asian Americans and cancer: Discarding the myth of the "model minority." *Journal of the National Cancer Institute, 89*(21), 1572–1574.

***Saphir's (1997) article explores cancer among Asian Americans. According to Saphir's (1997) reporting, "while some Asian Americans have better health profiles than their white counterparts, others, notably recent immigrants from Southeast Asia, do not" (p. 1572). Saphir (1997) notes, "Recognition that cancer is a problem for Asian Americans has been slow, largely because detailed data on cancer incidence and mortality in Asian subgroups has only recently become available" (p. 1572). This article does a great job at stressing the importance of disaggregating Asian American ethnic groups whenever examining health disparities and outcomes like cancer. This article can be used for scholar practitioners and/or health care providers when addressing the unique health needs of Asian Americans. As Saphir (1997) notes in her article's title, it is high time that we discard the myth of the model minority stereotype.

Suicide Prevention Resource Center (SPRC). (n.d.). Suicide among Asian Americans/Pacific Islanders. Retrieved on December 10, 2011, from http://www.sprc.org/library/asian.pi.facts.pdf

***This report was funded by the Suicide Prevention Resource Center (SPRC) and highlights a review of research on suicide among Asian Americans and Pacific Islanders. The report included the following points: (1) elderly Asian American/Pacific Islander women have higher rates of suicide than Whites or Blacks; (2) for women aged 75 and older, the suicide rate for Asian Americans/Pacific Islanders was 7.95 per 100,000, compared to the White rate of 4.18 and the Black rate of 1.18; (3) Asian Americans and Pacific Islanders are significantly less likely than Whites to mention their mental health concerns to a friend or relative (12% vs. 25%), a mental health professional (4% vs. 26%), or a physician (2% vs. 13%); and (4) in the Asian American population, suicide risk increases with age.

Sue, S., Sue, D. W., Sue, L., & Takeuchi, D. T. (1995). Psychopathology among Asian Americans: A model minority? *Cultural Diversity and Mental Health, 1*(1), 39–51.

***Sue, Sue, Sue, and Takeuchi's (1995) article looks at the psychopathology among the Asian American population compared to international studies on Asian populations. They believe "that the most fundamental problem in Asian American research is not the construction of valid measures, rather, it is the nature of the population" (p. 47). Sue et al. (1995) describe why the Asian American population is such a difficult population to study. They point out that the population is small (3% of the U.S. population is Asian American while 60% of the world's population is Asian), changing demographically, and diverse and heterogeneous (many different ethnic groups, foreign-born, native-born, etc.). According to Sue et al. (1995) this heterogeneity among the Asian American population "is playing havoc with our [researchers'] abilities to draw conclusions or make [valid] generalizations [about Asian Americans' psychological health and wellbeing]" (p. 48). What makes this article useful for practical, conceptual, philosophical, methodological, experimental, and theoretical model minority stereotype scholarship—whether one likes to admit it or not—is that Sue et al. (1995) discuss the implications of these problems when attempting to understand the psychopathology of Asian Americans. For instance, from the authors' perspective, research that aggregates Asian Americans is not harmful, so long as it is used as a beginning point for more refined and specific subgroup research. Moreover, the authors of this study maintain that the idea that "research concerning [Asian American] mental health issues should continue to be based on both the aggregate group (all Asian Americans) and particular Asian ethnicities" (p. 49). Sue et al. (1995) write the following about the mental health (psychopathology) of Asian Americans:

> In summary, the specific prevalence rates of mental disorders among Asian Americans have been difficult to determine. Sufficient evidence does exist to show that Asian Americans are not significantly less prone to mental disorders than other ethnic groups. The relatively small population, heterogeneity, and changing demographic characteristics have hindered a more precise determination of prevalence rates within the Asian American population. (p. 49)

This article can be used in statistics courses since it describes important concepts, such as aggregation, disaggregation, and the idea of a "range-restriction" (Sue et al., 1995, p. 48) limitation when conducting statistical analyses (*viz.* needing a full range of scores, not just high-scorers or low-scores to detect trends/patterns in achievement for instance). This article was reprinted in the following book chapter format: [Sue, S., Sue, D. W., Sue, L., & Takeuchi, D. T. (1998). Psychopathology among Asian Americans: A model minority? In P. B. Organista, K. M. Chun, & G. Marín (Eds.), *Readings in ethnic psychology* (pp. 270–282). New York, NY: Routledge.].

Tang, M. (2007). Psychological effects on being perceived as a "model minority" for Asian Americans. *New Waves: Educational Research and Development, 11*(3), 11–16.

***Tang's (2007) article addresses "the impacts of the model minority myth on the psychological welfare of Asian Americans through a comprehensive literature review" (p. 11). Tang (2007) suggests that the model minority stereotype is dangerous since it reinforces a misconception that obstructs a truer understanding of Asian American psychological wellbeing. Tang's (2007) article examines the following issues relate d to Asian Americans and the model minority stereotype: invisibility, identity confusion, psychological impacts, diversity, and psychosocial status. This article can be cross-referenced since it cites many important model minority stereotype writings.

Thompson, T. L. & Kiang, L. (2010). The model minority stereotype: Adolescent experiences and links with adjustment. *Asian American Journal of Psychology, 1*(2), 119–128.

***By "examining adolescents' MMS [model minority stereotype] experiences and attitudes, links with academic and psychological adjustment" Thompson and Kiang's (2010, p. 119) study contributes much to the model minority stereotype literature. A total of 165 ninth and tenth grade Asian

American adolescents, sampled from six public secondary schools in the Southeastern United States, participated in the study by completing a self-reported questionnaire. Results were that 99.4% of all students reported being stereotyped at least once, and that most students reacted to the model minority stereotype negatively, meaning they felt that the judgment was inaccurate and that that it limited their individuality. Although the adolescents in Thompson and Kiang's (2010) study disclosed negative, positive, mixed, and/or neutral feelings about these experiences, this study points to the reality that Asian American adolescents face being stereotyped. This highlights why it is important to conduct research on this student population. Scholars may cite this article when conducting research on Asian Americans and "stereotype threat" (Steele, 1997, 2011) or "stereotype promise" (Lee, 2012). This article definitely should be cited in literature reviews.

Uba, L. (1994). Psychopathology in the "model minority." In L. Uba, *Asian Americans: Personality patterns, identity, and mental health* (pp. 158–195). New York, NY: Guilford Press.

***Uba (1994) wrote a cerebral and captivating book chapter. Psychopathology in the "Model Minority"

> looks at (1) rates of mental disorders among Asian Americans and the difficulties in assessing these rates, (2) interethnic and intraethnic differences in rates of psychopathology, (3) predictors of mental disorders among Asian Americans, and (4) types of mental disorders commonly found among Asian Americans. (Uba, 1994, p. 158)

Uba (1994) writes, "Southeast Asian refugees have particularly high rates of psychopathology," (p. 172) adding that "there is evidence that foreign-born Asian Americans have more mental disorders than American-born Asian Americans" (p. 173). This chapter contests the notion that Asian Americans are model minorities who do not experience psychopathological challenges or abnormalities. More psychopathological (read: the study of mental illness) studies should be undertaken in relation to Asian Americans and the model minority stereotype.

Varma, S. C. & Siris, S. G. (1996). Alcohol abuse in Asian Americans: Epidemiological and treatment issues. *American Journal of Addictions, 5*(2), 136–143.

***Varma and Siris (1996) share their understanding of what the research on alcohol abuse in Asian Americans reveals. Varma and Sirius (1996) write, "Although Asian Americans have often been called a 'model minority,' evidence has accumulated that they are not immune to psychosocial problems, such as the development of alcoholism" (pp. 136–137). They contend that "therefore, with their increasing numbers and importance to

American society, a broader understanding of their potential for alcohol abuse has become important" (Varma & Sirius, 1996, p. 137). This article shares the results of many epidemiological studies and finds that given the current literature, an exact portrait of Asian American alcoholism is hard to come by due to immense heterogeneity and socio-cultural and linguistic diversity. This article can be used in research courses to illustrate the care that must be taken when carrying out model minority and/or Asian American health research. The article is also helpful for quantitative researchers who are attempting to identify datasets that have disaggregated Asian American data on alcoholism.

Võ, L. T. (2004). The politics of social services for a "model minority": The Union of Pan Asian Communities. In L. T. Võ, *Mobilizing an Asian American community* (pp. 34–65). Philadelphia, PA: Temple University Press.

*** Võ's (2004) chapter discusses the history of the Union of Pan Asian Communities (UPAC), which began in the 1970s, and addresses how the model minority stereotype impacts Asian Americans' (in)ability to access and receive social service support. The chapter highlights the difficulty that arises when talking about the health and social needs of various Asian American subgroups, providing many useful facts that researchers, teachers, and scholars might not know, such as the fact that "the Disadvantaged Minority Health Improvement Act of 1990 was part of a concerted effort to ensure the collection of data on Asian Pacific Americans" (p. 55). The model minority stereotype challenges Asian Pacific Americans' ability to secure social welfare support since people are skeptical that they face struggles and difficulties. This book chapter can be used to discuss the social and mental health support needs of the Asian Pacific American community.

Wong, F. & Halgin, R. (2006). The "model minority": Bane or blessing for Asian Americans? *Journal of Multicultural Counseling and Development, 34*(1), 38–49.

***Wong and Halgin's (2006) article asks a profound question: "Is the model minority a bane or blessing for Asian Americans?" After reading their article, it is apparent that the stereotype is a bane. How could the model minority stereotype be a blessing to Asian Americans? The stereotype is detrimental; as Wong and Halgin (2006) write, "Being inaccurately perceived as a *model minority* prevents Asian Americans from receiving access to important services, such as educational programs that help students with academic difficulties, governmental financial and social programs, and higher education opportunities" (p. 46, italics added). Thus, the model minority myth is a bane since it impedes rather than facilitates access to various opportunities for Asian Americans. Equally important, readers learn that "Asian Americans have negative feelings about this [model minority] label" (p. 40) and that "the model minority label is not accurate because it does not apply to all Asian Americans" (Wong & Halgin, 2006, p. 41). This is an important article for professionals, especially counselors who work with the Asian American population, because it elucidates issues of concern that the model minority stereotype conveniently glosses over: Asian/American identity struggles, Asian American heterogeneity, Asian ethnic diversity, and other issues that, if known, dismiss the derogatory stereotype. Wong and Halgin (2006) write that "there is no data to support the perception that Asian Americans do better academically [than other minorities]" (p. 44), which begs the question, how can the model minority be anything other than a bane?

Yoshihama, M. (2001). Model minority demystified: Emotional costs of multiple victimizations in the lives of women of Japanese descent. In N. G. Choi (Ed.), *Psychosocial aspects of the Asian-American experience: Diversity Within Diversity* (pp. 201–224). New York, NY: Haworth Press.

***Yoshihama's (2001) chapter is a reprint of another work [Yoshihama, M. (2001). Model minority demystified: Emotional costs of multiple victimizations in the lives of women of Japanese descent. *Journal of Human Behavior in the Social Environment, 3*(3/4), 201–224.] and also appears as [Yoshihama, M. (2001). Model minority demystified: Emotional costs of multiple victimizations in the lives of women of Japanese descent. In N. G. Choi (Ed.), *Psychosocial aspects of the Asian-American experience: Diversity within diversity* (pp. 201–224). New York, NY: Haworth Press.]. Yoshihama (2001) examined the prevalence of domestic violence and interpersonal victimization among a random sample (*n* = 211) of women of Japanese descent—both immigrants from Japan and Japanese Americans—in Los Angeles. Says Yoshihama (2001), "Women's victimization has received little attention in mental health research on Asian Pacific Americans" (p. 205). Yoshihama's (2001) chapter is a significant contribution to the literature on the status of Asian Pacific Americans' mental health insofar as "the present study expands research on Asian Pacific Americans' mental health by focusing specifically on domestic violence and other types of interpersonal victimization experienced by a community-based random sample of women" (p. 2005). Yoshihama's (2001) study included the following measures: 31 forms of physical violence, 21 forms of emotional violence, and 11 forms of sexual violence. Findings of the study indicated that psychological distress was something Japanese immigrants as well as Japanese American women experienced as a result of violence and victimization. More specifically, Yoshihama (2001) points out that "the severity of domestic violence significantly contributed to a higher degree of current psychological distress" (p. 216). Mental health workers should consult this document whenever working with those in the Asian Pacific American population, especially women, who may be experiencing violence and victimization.

Yun, G. (Ed.). (1989). *A look beyond the model minority image: Critical issues in Asian America.* New York, NY: Minority Rights Group Inc.

***The Asian and Pacific American Project of the Minority Rights Group Inc. organized a conference on Asian Americans, which took place on October 4–5, 1985 at Columbia University. *A Look Beyond The Model Minority Image: Critical Issues in Asian America,* edited by Grace Yun, is a collection of the papers presented at this "Perceptions, Policies and Practices" conference. In order that societal, educational, civil, and political problems be ameliorated, they first must be identified and be made known. Accordingly, "this volume offers information on the contemporary status of Asian Americans who are said to have already 'made it,' but also provides insights into the lives and circumstances of those whom success has yet eluded" (p. ix). 151 pages in length, this book has four sections dedicated to "critical issues" that challenge the model minority image: (1) civil rights, (2) social and cultural needs, (3) employment, and (4) higher education. *A Look Beyond* provides evidence of scholars' struggle "toward the larger effort to dispel the myth of a 'problem-free' Asian America, which the model minority image promotes, so that urgent and pressing needs in Asian American communities may be readily identified and promptly addressed" (pp. ix–x).

Sections 1–4 include discussions on such topics as: homelessness in Asian American communities, societal perceptions and attitudes toward Asians in the United States, inequitable employment conditions and job mobility in New York's Chinatown, increasing difficulty for Asian Americans finding entrance to American universities, and the persistence of corporate organizational discrimination for Asian Americans. In the twenty-plus years since the publication of its original clarion call, the Project has continued to drive research in these critical areas.

REFERENCE

Bell, D. A. (1980). *Brown v. Board of Education* and the interest-convergence dilemma. *Harvard Law Review, 93*(3), 518–534.

CHAPTER 5

INTERDISCIPLINARY AND METHODOLOGICALLY APPROACHED RESEARCH ON THE MODEL MINORITY STEREOTYPE

This chapter presents model minority research that was conducted using an interdisciplinary and/or methodologically unique approach. What this means, simply, is that the author(s) addressed the problem of the model minority stereotype in highly nuanced and calculated ways. Prashad (2000) responded to W. E. B. Du Bois's famous question "How does it feel to be a problem?" by asking a question of his own: "How does it feel to be a *solution?*" (Prashad, 2000, p. 6, italics added). Prashad was addressing how South Asians have become looked at as being representatives of model minorities. Prashad's (2000) *The Karma of Brown Folk* can be considered a foundational piece of interdisciplinary model minority criticism insofar as it documents, for the first time, the notion that not only is the model minority stereotype anti-Asian racism, but in addition to being anti-Black

The Model Minority Stereotype: Demystifying Asian American Success, pages 165–211.
Copyright © 2013 by Information Age Publishing
All rights of reproduction in any form reserved.

racism, "the *model minority* thesis is...a pillar of *inferential racism*" (Prashad, 2000, p. 170, italics added). Moreover, Prashad (2000) notes that inferential racism and "White supremacy [do] not endow all of Asia with equivalent value," adding that "the media began to differentiate between those Asians with cultural worth and those whom they saw as less worthy" (p. 160). It is because of this that interdisciplinary work is such an important facet in debunking the model minority stereotype. The citations referenced in this chapter all used interdisciplinary and/or methodologically unique approaches to falsifying the stereotype that Asian Americans are "successful" (however operationalized).

Alumkal, A. W. (2002). The scandal of the "model minority" mind? The Bible and second-generation Asian American evangelicals. *Semeia, 90*(91), 237–250.

***Alumkal's (2002) article is "an ethnographic study of two Asian American [one Chinese and one Korean] evangelical churches in the New York metropolitan area" (p. 239). Since Asian Americans are lauded for being model minorities, "one might expect Asian Americans to be immune from the *evangelical intellectual scandal*" (Alumkal, 2002, p. 238, italics added). According to this article, the "evangelical intellectual scandal" refers to anti-intellectual evangelism. This is why Alumkal interviewed second-generation Chinese and Korean evangelicals to test whether or not they interpreted the Bible in a "model minority" fashion (*viz.* in "intellectual" ways). Findings conclude that second-generation Asian American evangelicals in fact, think about the Bible in the same ways as Whites, thus invalidating the possibility that there exists a "model minority" mind. Readers of this article will include scholars looking for literature to bolster their literature reviews as well as those who are interested in assimilation and sociology of religion. This article shows how the model minority stereotype is not confined to education, but rather, extends into all parts of society: secular and religious.

Alvarez, A. N., Juang, L., & Liang, C. T. (2006). Asian Americans and racism: When bad things happen to "model minorities." *Cultural Diversity and Ethnic Minority Psychology, 12*(3), 477–492.

***The "primary purpose of the current study was to examine the scope of Asian Americans' experiences with racism" (Alvarez, Juang, & Liang, 2006, p. 478). Alvarez, Juang, and Liang (2006) used Harrell's *racism-related stress model* and Helms and Cook's *psychodiagnostic model of racial identity development* in order to examine how Asian Americans perceive and respond to racism. Particularly, the three authors were interested in "sociocultural communicators" (read: individuals and institutions) and "racial identity schemas" (read: perceptions). The authors present and test a mediational model in which racial identity mediates the relationship between racial socialization and perceptions of racism. Alvarez, Juang, and Liang (2006) sampled undergraduate students from a large west coast university who were enrolled in an introductory psychology course ($n = 254$). Students were Chinese, Filipino, Vietnamese, Bangladeshi, Lao, and Korean. All of the students completed a 50 question instrument that measured their racial identity attitude. Results indicated that the mediational model was supported by the study's findings. According to Alvarez, Juang, and Liang (2006), "Contrary to the privileged status implied by the model minority stereotype, the results of the current study suggest that racism directed at Asian Americans occurs at a scope and frequency that merit further attention" (p. 487). Moreover, this study contributes to the understanding of Asian Americans' experiences with racism. The study found that "Asian Americans' perceptions of racism are directly shaped by the conversations and discussions that one has in regards to race and racism as well as indirectly shaped by the influence of these discussions on one's racial identity and racial worldview" (Alvarez, Juang, & Liang, 2006, p. 489). This article can be used by scholars and academics interested in further understanding the relationships between the model minority stereotype and Asian Americans' experiences with racism. Moreover, quantitative researchers might use this article when considering model creation for studies that use statistical analyses.

Bhatt, A. J. (2003). Asian Indians and the model minority narrative: A neocolonial system. In E. M. Kramer (Ed.), *The emerging monoculture: Assimilation and the "model minority"* (pp. 203–220). Westport, CT: Praeger.

***Bhatt's (2003) chapter focuses on the construction of Asian Indians as model minorities. Constructing Asian Indians as model minorities creates the appearance that they have earned equal status in the United States. Bhatt (2003) writes that "[Asian] Indians are touted as a *model minority* because of their economic standing in the U.S. society" (p. 209, italics added). Bhatt's (2003) most quotable statement is the following:

> Because it is predominantly discursive in nature (lacking physical proof of the ideology) *the model minority system* is presented as apolitical. This empowers the dominant group in that they are taken at face value. Additionally, *the model minority ideology* is couched in the greater *narrative of equality* in the United States. (p. 215, italics added)

This book chapter is particularly important for research on, and teaching about, Asian American model minority stereotypes.

Bhattacharyya, S. (2001, November). *From "yellow peril" to "model minority": The transition of Asian Americans.* Paper presented at the Annual Meeting of the Mid-South Educational Research Association, Little Rock, AR. ERIC ED462462

***Bhattacharyya's (2001) paper investigates factors influencing the emergence of a new ethnic identity for Asian Americans as model minorities. For instance, while Asian Americans were once considered "unassimilable heathens," they have been transformed from "cruel, enemy aliens" to "industrious, quiet, law-abiding citizens." The conference paper, "From 'Yellow Peril' to 'Model Minority': The Transition of Asian Americans" can be used in scholarly writing and is reminiscent of the writings of Shim (1998), Hannis (2009), and Allred (2007).

Busto, R. V. (1996). The gospel according to the model minority?: Hazarding an interpretation of Asian American evangelical college students. *Amerasia Journal, 22*(1), 133–147.

***Busto's (1996) article discusses "how the model minority stereotype provides a context for understanding the relationship between Asian American students and evangelical Christianity" (p. 140). According to Busto (1996), Asian Americans' presence and membership in evangelical Christian parachurch organizations like Campus Crusade for Christ (CCC), The Navigators, InterVarsity Christian Fellowship (IVCF), and Asian American Christian Fellowship (AACF) at Stanford University continue to grow at a significant pace. Similar to the model minority stereotypical characterization of Asian Americans as academic "whiz kids," Busto (1996) introduces the notion that Asian Americans can also be viewed through a lens of being God's "whiz kids" since they are overrepresented among Christian parachurch organizations. Consequently, Busto (1996) writes that "in their portrayal of Asian Americans, evangelical Christians and organizations have embraced a religious version of the model minority by promoting Asian American evangelicals as 'spiritual giants' and aggressive evangelizers" (p. 140). This article can be used by those individuals who are looking for a non-academic nexus between Asian Americans and the model minority stereotype. This article also appears in David K. Yoo's edited volume *New Spiritual Homes: Religion and Asian Americans* (pp. 169–201) published in 1999 by the University of Hawai'i Press.

Chang, R. S. & Villazor, R. C. (2007). Testing the "model minority myth": A case of weak empiricism. *Northwestern University Law Review Colloquy, 101,* 101–107.

***Chang and Villazor's (2007) cogent, concise, and critical law review article is incredibly important to the field of critical Asian American jurisprudence and bleeds into the study of the model minority stereotype. Why? Because Chang and Villazor (2007) sharply critique Miranda Oshige McGowan and James Lindgren's (2006) law review article on affirmative action entitled "Testing the Model Minority Myth." According to Chang and Villazor (2007) there is good reason to question the model minority stereotype and problematize McGowan and Lindgren's empiricism. Chang and Villazor (2007) point out three shortcomings of McGowan and Lindgren's (2006) study. McGowan and Lindgren's study relied upon General Social Survey (GSS) data, which is, according to Chang and Villazor (2007), prone to: (1) falsification problems (respondents consciously lying to pollsters); (2) response biases (e.g., questionnaire wording, context of questions, etc.); and (3) unreliability (face-to-face interactions between respondent and pollster). Chang and Villazor (2007) conclude their critique stating the following:

> Professors McGowan and Lindgren's article is timely in light of the debate over affirmative action and the role that Asian Americans play in that process. Unfortunately, they limit the scope of their analysis to the results of surveys of non-Hispanic whites produced from *face-to-face interviews* about their racial attitudes. From this, they make claims about the *model minority stereotype* in the real world. *Their data and conclusions are likely to be used by those who seek to end affirmative action and who seek to use affirmative action as a wedge issue to create divisions among Asian Americans and other racial minorities.* (p. 107, italics added)

This article can be used by critical Asian American law scholars interested in critical jurisprudence, Asian critical race theory (AsianCrit), and individuals who are committed to demystifying the model minority stereotype through channels of methodology and measurement. As many of the articles summarized in this book point out, the model minority stereotype is damaging and damning because it is used by the power elite as a divisive wedge. Chang and Villazor's (2007) article underscores this effectively and should be cited for this reason. This article exemplifies how scholars must critique the model minority in novel and fresh ways.

Chao, M. M, Chiu, C., Chan, W., Mendoza-Denton, R., & Kwok, C. (2012). The model minority as a shared reality and its implication for interracial perceptions. *Asian American Journal of Psychology*, 1–12. doi: 10.1037/a0028769.

***Chao, Chiu, Chan, Mendoza-Denton, and Kwok's (2012) article utilized shared reality theory to explore the model minority stereotype in three separate studies. According to Chao et al. (2012), "an idea becomes a shared reality when people, independent of whether there is objective evidence for the validity of the idea, assume the idea to be widely known and shared in the community" (p. 2). In Study 1, 290 undergraduate students completed a paper-and-pencil survey. In Study 2, 188 undergraduate students read various descriptions of a minority group. Participants estimated the percent (from 0 to 100) of the U.S. adult population that would consider that description to be constitutive of Asian Americans, African Americans, and/or European Americans. In Study 3, 155 undergraduate students completed several short questionnaires, read various newspaper articles with descriptions of successful and unsuccessful Asian Americans, African Americans and European Americans, and then completed another survey.

Study 1 showed "that the stereotypic image of Asian Americans as being diligent, high achieving, and quiet is consensually shared among Americans" (Chao et al., 2012, p. 5), while Study 2 found that "exposure to the model minority image in news media can influence racial perceptions in the shared reality, exaggerating the perceived acceptance toward Asian

Americans relative to African Americans in the community" (Chao et al., 2012, p. 8). The results of Study 3 "suggest that media exposure to Asian American successes increases European Americans' acceptance of the model minority myth as a shared reality" (Chao et al., 2012, p. 9). Thus, Chao et al.'s (2012) study makes a significant contribution to the field of model minority studies in that it called upon a theoretical framework seldom employed. Its findings—particularly that many believe in the model minority stereotype—illustrate why future advocacy and academic work is necessary when it comes to the stereotype of successful Asian Americans. This study can be used in educational psychology as a course reading.

Chen, C. H. (2004). *Mormon and Asian American model minority discourses in news and popular magazines.* Lewiston, NY: Edwin Mellen Press.

***Chen's (2004) book is about Mormon and Asian American "model minority" discourses in news and popular magazines. Using critical (Foucauldian) discourse analyses, her book desires to raise critical consciousness. Chapters 2, 3, 4, and 5 will be the most interesting to readers. Chapter 2 discusses early Mormon images. Chapter 3 addresses Mormon model minority discourse. Chapter 4 is spent addressing early Asian American imagery embodied in the yellow peril. Chapter 5 examines exclusively Asian American model minority discourse. This book will interest scholars from many disciplinary fields, specifically communication, mass media, and sociology. The book includes 15 figures (images) that can be used in the classroom or lecture hall in order to illustrate how Fred R. Barnard's phrase, "a picture is worth a thousand words," is often correct.

Chen, C. H. (2004). "Outwhiting the Whites": An examination of the persistence of Asian American model minority discourse. In R. A. Lind (Ed.), *Race, gender, media: Considering diversity across audiences, content, and producers* (pp. 146–153). Boston, MA: Allyn and Bacon.

***Chen's (2004) book chapter examines the persistence of the Asian American model discourse. "The American mass media helped create and perpetuate it," writes Chen (2004, p. 146), referring to the model minority stereotype. Chen (2004) describes Asian American stereotypes (like the yellow peril and model minority) as simple pictures that make life more manageable. Chen (2004) says the problem with writings that argue against the model minority myth is that they are written "within a model minority *discourse*. Even while they claimed that the stereotype was misleading, much written within their stories continued to support the stereotype" (p. 148). In other words, despite a desire to demystify the model minority stereotype, "journalists in the 1980s and 1990s kept reproducing important aspects of the stereotype" (p. 149). This book chapter makes a bold and brave clarion call to the future study of the model minority discourse: de-center Asian American success. Chen (2004) writes that "journalists can effectively combat the stereotype [of Asian American success] only by writing from *outside* the model minority *discourse*" (p. 152, italics added). This highly important book chapter could be used in a high school or college classroom. Educators can have their students read the chapter and respond to the four questions that follow the chapter on pages 152 and 153.

Chen, C. H. & Yorgason, E. (1999). "Those amazing Mormons": The media's construction of Latter-Day Saints as a model minority. *Dialogue: A Journal of Mormon Thought, 32*(2), 107–128.

***Chen and Yorgason's (1999) article examines not only the media's construction of Latter-Day Saints as a "model minority," but specifically the *model minority discourse.* Accordingly, Chen and Yorgason (1999) write the following: "'Model minority discourse' encompasses a complex set of ways to create meaning. It glorifies certain culturally dominant values and practices. And it positions a group of people as representatives of, but not fully participants in, the social life of the majority" (p. 108). The ways that Mormons are constructed as model minorities is reminiscent of Asian Americans. Most importantly, this article addresses the problems of such a model minority discourse—pointing out how it supports the dominant groups' beliefs and values. Mormon minority status implies "that Mormons and Mormonism are rich, successful, powerful, and their influence is spreading" (Chen & Yorgason, 1999, p. 114). The model minority discourse also problematically implies themes of self-reliance, hard work, loyalty, obedience, and that "Mormons are *paragons* of American citizenship" (Chen & Yorgason, 1999, p. 114, italics added), which justifies America's supposed meritocratic system. What makes this article unique is that it examines the media's construction of the model minority moniker for Mormons through an analysis of discourse. Mormons' evolution from "satyrs" to "saints" is eerily similar to the evolution of Asian Americans from "pariahs" to "paragons." This article effectively problematizes the profuse praise both have received. This article would be a powerful read for students in mass communication courses at the university level, as well as for academics interested in creating newer paradigms for studying the "model minority" stereotype.

Chen, C. H. & Yorgason, E. (1997, August). *Use of Asian American history in the news media: The discourse of "model minority."* Paper presented at the Meeting of the Association for Education in Journalism and Mass Communication—Minorities and Communication, Chicago, Illinois.

***Chen and Yorgason's (1997) conference paper examines the model minority discourse. They conclude, "Asian Americans are seen to provide a 'model' of self-help for dealing with social ills, but their continuing 'minority' status marks them as people to be feared and closely watched" (Chen & Yorgason, 1997, p. 11). They go on to say, "White racism sees a threat in Asian Americans' 'success' and generates fear of Asian Americans. To maintain *status-quo* institutions and power relationships between dominant and minority, the media have created a model minority discourse" (Chen & Yorgason, 1997, p. 11). Chen and Yorgason (1997) describe the iterations that the discourse follows: "protagonist faces adversity à protagonist ignores the adversity and works hard à protagonist overcomes the adversity and achieves success" (p. 3). For this reason, this conference paper is assistive in understanding what model minority discursive messages effectually mean and why the discourse of successful Asian Americans is problematic for racial and power relationships. The model minority stereotype fortifies the *status quo* by actively supporting Asian American assimilation and cultural essentialism. Consequently, this paper can be used as an instructional and also a curriculum resource for teaching against the model minority stereotype.

Cheng, C. (1997). Are Asian American employees a model minority or just a minority? *Journal of Applied Behavioral Science, 33*(3), 277–290.

***Cheng's (1997) article examines whether or not Asian American employees should be considered model minorities (the model minority thesis). Cheng (1997) compares and contrasts two perspectives: the model minority phenomenon (that Asian Americans *are* model minorities) and the model minority myth (that Asian Americans *are not* model minorities). Cheng (1997) writes the following:

> Underlying this disagreement is a basic methodological difference between the two sides. Supporters of the Model Minority Phenomenon have used aggregated statistics on educational attainment, occupational distribution, household income, and so on. Critics, by contrast, have disaggregated the supportive side's arguments and find importance in selective immigration, the high numbers of hours worked, the high number of individuals per household, and so on. In short, the critics have found a bimodal distribution within Asian America—both a low-pay, low-skill group and a more educated, higher paid professional group. (p. 279)

Thus, Cheng (1997) concludes, "The Asian American Model Minority Thesis is either supported or disconfirmed, depending on whether the data are aggregated or disaggregated" (p. 283). This article clearly discusses the methodological underpinnings of the contentious model minority stereotype and points out the importance of critics to disaggregate data by Asian American subgroup.

Cheng, L. & Yang, P. Q. (1996). Asians: The "model minority" deconstructed. In R. Waldinger & M. Bozorgmehr (Eds.), *Ethnic Los Angeles* (pp. 305–344). New York, NY: Russell Sage Foundation.

***Cheng and Yang's (1996) book chapter is published in *Ethnic Los Angeles,* which is composed of four parts—I. Introduction, II. Changing Demographics, 1970–1990, III. Major Ethnic Groups, and IV. Conclusion—and is found in part III. Cheng and Yang (1996) effectively deconstruct the model minority stereotype by focusing on the diversity of Asian Americans. The chapter, specifically pages 312–324, is dedicated to debunking the model minority stereotype. The authors do a nice job of discussing how socio-political realities, including immigration legislation and the alignment of the myth's creation and the 1960s civil rights movement, create the illusion that Asian Americans are model minorities. Cheng and Yang's (1996) chapter is a must to cite in model minority teaching and research.

Chu, N. V. (1997). Re-examining the model minority myth: A look at Southeast Asian youth. *The Berkeley McNair Journal, 5,* 167–176.

***Chu's (1997) article indicates that "in as little as 100 years of American history, Asian Americans have gone from being the bucked-toothed, slant-ed-eyed, uncivilized 'yellow peril' to hardworking, musically-talented, and mathematically-brilliant 'model minority'" (p. 167). Chu's (1997) article has many quotable thoughts, especially for practitioner scholars interested in the topic of the model minority stereotype. Many of Chu's (1997) arguments address the rhetorical nature of the myth and the fact that the myth blames the victim (Blacks). Says Chu (1997):

> The myth tells us first that the American dream exists, and secondly that racial inequalities don't; that is, America is nonracist in that the racial differences that exist between different groups of Americans do not play a role in achieving the American dream. Therefore, given this assumption that America is still a land of equal opportunity, "success" comes to those who are determined and work hard, and that failure comes to those who are lazy and don't try, *regardless of race.* (p. 169, italics in original)

This article is helpful for teachers in that it clearly illustrates why and how the model minority myth (and myth-based perceptions) plays a role in discounting Asian American students' experiences, preventing them from receiving the help that they need. Chu (1997) implores readers to recognize the challenges that Asian Americans, especially Southeast Asian Americans, face, in order to improve their lives and quality of education.

Cunanan, V., Guerrero, A., & Minamoto, L. (2006). Filipinos and the myth of model minority in Hawai'i: A pilot study. *Journal of Ethnic and Cultural Diversity in Social Work, 15*(1/2), 167–192.

***Cunanan, Guerrero, and Minamoto (2006) conducted focus group interviews with seven community leaders, ten parents, four youth, and three young adult professionals during summer and fall of 2002 in O'ahu, Hawai'i. An important study because it explored the model minority stereotype in the U.S. (but in Hawai'i), the researchers found that Filipinos are not perceived as model minorities, but rather, they are stereotyped negatively as delinquents. According to Cunanan, Guerrero, and Minamoto (2006), "When asked if they thought that Filipino Americans living in Hawai'i are part of the model minority, most of the participants [in their study] disagreed" (p. 186). The present study is important since it suggests

> ...the need to consider the unique historical and social circumstances of different parts of the country [mainland U.S. versus non-mainland U.S.], rather than grouping them together under one homogenizing label that would overlook the potential needs of communities at risk. (p. 186)

This article also contains numerous bibliographical references that model minority researchers, teachers, and scholars will find useful for their individual work. "Filipinos and the Myth of Model Minority in Hawai'i: A Pilot Study" is also adaptable for use in a wide variety of college seminar courses.

Daseler, R. (2000). Asian Americans battle "model minority" stereotype. In A. Minas (Ed.), *Gender basics: Feminist perspectives on women and men* (2nd ed., pp. 45–49). Belmont, CA: Wadsworth.

***Daseler's (2000) chapter states that the model minority is problematic on the grounds that it makes invidious comparisons. The model minority stereotype, according to Daseler (2000), "den[ies] their many social, psychological, and financial difficulties and falsi[fies] the actual record of their assimilation into American culture" (p. 46). In other words, says Daseler (2000), "By holding up Asian Americans as a model for other minorities, mainstream culture could, in effect, deny that racial prejudice was to blame for unemployment and poverty among African Americans, Latinos, and others" (p. 46). This chapter is short, but important, especially since "contrary to the myth of invulnerability, Asian American students have a significantly higher rate of major depression and diagnosed schizophrenia than European Americans" (Daseler, 2000, p. 47). This chapter can be used in scholarly work on the model minority stereotype, as well as in the high school and college classroom. Three reading questions are provided at the beginning, followed by three further questions at the end of the chapter. This is an important reading that teachers and professors can use in their classes and courses respectively. Daseler's (2000) chapter is reprinted from the following publication: [Daseler, R. (1994, Summer). Debunking the myth: Asian Americans battle "model minority" stereotype. *Pomona College Today*, 20–23.].

Edles, L. D. (2003). "Race," "ethnicity," and "culture" in Hawai'i: The myth of the "model minority" state. In L. I. Winters & H. L. DeBose (Eds.), *New faces in a changing America: Multiracial identity in the 21st century* (pp. 222–246). Thousand Oaks, CA: Sage Publications, Inc.

***Edles' (2003) book chapter addresses the misclassification of Hawai'i as a model minority state. According to Edles (2003), many believe Hawai'i to be an example of multiculturalism, and a paradise given the high number of interracial marriages and multiracial people. However, Edles (2003) points out that "there are significant historical, theoretical, and empirical problems with the myth of Hawai'i as the model minority state" (p. 225). Indeed, the myth "ignores the colonial history of Hawai'i" (Edles, 2003, p. 225). Edles (2003) provides a reasonable timeline of Hawaiian history, history that refutes the popular myth that Hawai'i is a model minority state. Edles' (2003) chapter could be used in collaboration with others who have written about the notion that Hawai'i does not contain model minorities (e.g., see Cunanan, Guerrero, & Minamoto, 2006). It can also be used in literature reviews, as well as to teach the commonly untaught history of the state of Hawai'i.

Edles, L. D. (2004). Rethinking "race," "ethnicity" and "culture": Is Hawai'i the "model minority" state. *Ethnic and Racial Studies, 27*(1), 37–68.

***"Based on an open-ended survey of over one hundred [128] students at the University of Hawai'i, Manoa, as well as other documentary materials" (p. 43), Edles (2004) examined the validity of the notion that Hawai'i represents a mélange of multiracial people, constituting a "model minority" state. Edles (2004) laments that "whether in its *'individual'* or 'state' version, the 'model minority' myth infers that 'race' is an *individual* problem; and that the solution to racism is *individual* as well" (p. 42, italics added). Edles' (2004) article makes a significant contribution to the sociology of the model minority stereotype literature insofar as it introduces the theoretical/methodological idea of the "over-individualization" of race while explicating through sociological analyses how race, ethnicity, and culture works. Edles rightly points out that the same logic that holds a man cannot be sexist if he is married to a woman is just as invalid as the assertion that Hawaiians don't experience racism due to the state's increasing rates of interracial marriage and miscegenation. Edles (2004) indicates that "just as there are significant historical, theoretical, and empirical problems with the original 'model minority' myth, there are significant historical, theoretical, and empirical problems with the myth of Hawai'i as the 'model minority' state" (p. 40). History majors in college may find this article worthwhile to read. Model minority researchers and scholars may consider citing this lengthier article in their literature reviews or they might read it simply to expand their own learning.

Education Trust. (2010). *Overlooked and underserved: Debunking the Asian "model minority" myth in California schools.* [Policy Brief]. Oakland, CA: Education Trust West. Retrieved on December 18, 2011, from http://www.edtrust.org/sites/edtrust.org/files/ETW%20Policy%20Brief%20August%202010–Overlooked%20and%20Underserved.pdf

***This policy brief outlines the need for better data collection on Asian Pacific Americans in the State of California. According to the Education Trust (2010),

> When policymakers and educators fail to account for these important factors, the prevailing myth of Asians as the "model minority" becomes the governing paradigm. Although the mind-set affects all Asian and Pacific Islander students, those with additional needs—recent immigrants, low-income students, English-language learners, and low-performing students—suffer most from this myth. (p. 6)

Overlooked and Underserved: Debunking the Asian "Model Minority" Myth in California Schools makes three disaggregation recommendations. The first recommendation pertains to *enrollment data.* California needs to disaggregate enrollment data by Asian and Pacific Islander subgroup to show enrollment and demographic patterns in California schools. These data also should reveal how many students in each subgroup are from low-income families, are English language learners, and receive special education services. The second recommendation relates to *high school data.* Districts and the state should disaggregate California High School Exit Examination pass rates, dropout rates, graduation rates, and A–G graduation rates by Asian and Pacific Islander subgroup to provide a clearer picture of success in high school and access to higher education. The final recommendation regards *achievement data.* The state of California must release California Standards Test results by Asian subgroup on ELLs and low-income students so that policymakers and educational stakeholders can ensure resources are targeted toward specific areas and Asian Pacific Islander subgroups of need.

Farole, S. (2011). Social justice implications of the model minority. *McNair Scholars Journal, 10,* 69–78.

***Farole's (2011) article investigated "whether priming individuals with the model minority stereotype would cause them to look down upon Blacks and to react less favorably toward policies meant to remedy inequality" (p. 69). Farole (2011) administered an on-line questionnaire to 70 (31 male, 38 female, 1 undisclosed) University of Washington undergraduate students. "The questionnaire used in [the] study consisted of twelve items gauging support for meritocracy, four items measuring support for policies that address racial inequality, and seven items measuring the endorsement of Black stereotypes in Symbolic Racism" (Farole, 2011, p. 71). This study is important for efforts that work toward social justice and debunking the model minority stereotype because, in Farole's (2011) words, "In terms of the model minority [myth], majority groups may use the model minority status of Asians as an example to question inequality for minorities. Whites may also uphold the model minority concept as a reason for providing less support for policies directed toward racial inequality, suggesting beneficiaries of these policies should have to work hard like [Asians] the model minority in order to become successful" (p. 70). Farole (2011) concludes with the following: "Despite the facts that [statistically] significant results were not found for the effect of the model minority stereotype on support for social justice policies and attitudes toward Blacks, the model minority stereotype yields significant consequences in everyday life" (p. 76). This article can be used as a roadmap for future scholarly investigations that survey the social justice implications of the model minority stereotype. Undergraduate psychology students and university students in introductory statistics courses may find this an assistive article to read since it presents the applied research study of an undergraduate student at the University of Washington. Model minority scholars will find this study useful when building literature reviews around similar thematically- and methodologically-approached scholarly work of their own.

Freedman, J. (2005). Transgressions of a model minority. *Shofar: An Interdisciplinary Journal of Jewish Studies, 23*(4), 69–97.

***Freedman's (2005) 28 page article examines Asian Americans and Jewish Americans, exploring their contemporary (21st century) and historical (20th century) treatment as "model minorities." According to Freedman (2005), "the stereotypical Jew and the stereotypical Asian have long borne a striking resemblance to each other" (p. 72). Historically, Freedman points out examples of the *orientalization* of Jewish Americans. Freedman (2005) writes that "popular characterizations of Asians projected onto them economic abilities and appetencies [gloss: affinities] associated with the stereotypical Jew" (p. 82). Freedman names this tendency to reinforce the similarity of Jews and Asians in his analysis of history "discursive bleeding"—the "seeping, usually at a level of somewhere below full consciousness, of associations from one racial and ethnic group to another, in this case from the long-established patterns of response to Jews to newer ones being crafted to explain and understand Asian difference" (p. 87). According to Freedman's (2005) notion of "discursive bleeding," the model minority stereotype is at the intersection of the ascripted identities of Jewish and Asian Americans. Like Asian men, writes Freedman, Jewish men are rendered effeminate. Freedman (2005) goes on to state the following: "The myth of superior Asian intellectual endowment has another point of contact with constructions of the Jew: accompanying it is an understanding of the Asian man as being less than manly" (p. 93). Thus, the waves of history ebb and flow but ultimately repeat. Freedman's (2005) article assists in deconstructing model minority myth paradigmatic fiction through a challenging, yet ultimately successful, synthesis and critique of the alleged attributes of Asian American and Jewish American success. The article is not only interesting, it is informationally rich. It provides references to important seminal readings for Asian Americans, such as Edward Said's (1978) *Orientalism,* Gish Jen's (1997) *Mona in the Promised Land,* and Lan Samantha Chang's (1998) *Hunger: A Novella and Stories.* Unusually, the article includes visual images—like sculptor Jacob Epstein's "Day of Atonement" and "A Little Girl of Hester Street" and Puck's "The Difference Between Them"—which stimulate the reader's experience reading the written text. Freedman's article is an excellent resource for those who teach in a college classroom and also for those scholars who are interested in better understanding the evolution and transformation of the model minority stereotype, and who would like to use this knowledge in their own academic work.

Gee, H. (2009). Review essay: Asian Americans, critical race theory, and the end of the model minority myth. *Temple Political & Civil Rights Law Review, 19*(1), 149–186.

***In "Asian Americans, Critical Race Theory, and the End of the Model Minority Myth," Gee (2009) reviews such topics as Asian Americans, affirmative action, critical race theory, and the model minority stereotype. Gee (2009) writes that "the tendency to frame affirmative action in black and white terms diminishes the significance of Asian American under-representation and invites misconceptions colored by the model minority myth. Thus, the myth prevents institutions from placing Asian Americans in the affirmative action equation" (p. 2). It also "conceals violence against Asians" (p. 12). The article is divided into five thematic sections: (1) Asian foreignness and the racial hierarchy, (2) the model minority myth and social science research, (3) Asian Americans and Whiteness as a legally-produced reality, (4) Asian Americans and the media, and (5) the possibility of the model minority ending.

The largest contribution that this law review article makes is the sheer quantity and profundity of its resources, which researchers, scholars, and students can cross-reference. Readers will be well-served if they read the article's copious footnotes, which offer information and sources for those interested in learning more about the stereotype. While the article is most appropriate to read in a law school classroom, other extralegal educators may assign it to their students. Moreover, researchers who are looking for lesser-known examples of anti-Asian nativism in the United States (i.e., the two hunting incidents that occurred in Wisconsin involving Hmong men) and various ways to link these incidents to the model minority myth will find Gee's (2009) article assistive as well as educative. Lastly, the idea that the model minority could possibly end is a provocative idea that requires further inquiry. Much of the existing critical legal scholarship documents the fact that Asian Americans do not fit into the existing Black/White binary; however, this article goes further in that it advocates for "Asian American perspective" (p. 4).

Gilbert, G. R. (2003). Is business mistreating America's model minority? *Journal of Applied Social Psychology, 33*(8), 1571–1587.

***Gilbert's (2003) article addresses the treatment of Asian Americans by food establishments (e.g., college cafeterias, franchised fast-food restaurants, concessions at sporting events, movie theater concessions, international airport concessions, shopping mall food court concessions, diner-type restaurants, and sports-bar-type restaurants) in south Florida (Dade and Broward Counties). The Customer Satisfaction Survey Instrument was completed by 4,377 (141 [3.8%] Asian; 873 [23.3%] Black; 1,459 [39.0%] Caucasian; and 1,268 [33.9%] Hispanic) participants who ate at various food establishments. "Asians were found to rate both satisfaction with customer service...and satisfaction with the service setting...lower than non-Asians" (Gilbert, 2003, p. 1582). Moreover, "Asians rated "competence of service provider," "ease to get help needed," and "security within the establishment" lower than did Caucasians and Hispanics. Gilbert's (2003) study supports the idea that "business is mistreating" Asians in America despite the fact that they are widely believed to be model minorities.

Green, D. O. & Kim, E. (2005). Experiences of Korean female doctoral students in academe: Raising voice against gender and racial stereotypes. *Journal of College Student Development, 46*(5), 487–500.

***This article makes a contribution to model minority research in that it intentionally studies the experiences of female Korean doctoral students. Little research has examined female Asian American graduate students' experiences in U.S. colleges and universities. This study employed a qualitative method inquiry and interviewed twelve South Korean female doctoral students who attended a research institution in a midsized Midwestern city. Green and Kim (2005) found that the Korean doctoral students (1) had a burden of perpetuating the model minority stereotype, (2) were sexualized as being "cute" Asian girls as opposed to capable and strong women, (3) spoke up with a louder voice than if they were in Korea, (4) intentionally interacted with diverse individuals in order to become more comfortable and empowered, and (5) maintained supportive relationships as a coping strategy. According to this study's authors, the female Korean doctoral students, in order "to attenuate the influence of these gender and racial stereotypes, employed two major coping strategies: interacting with diverse individuals to find a comfort zone and maintaining supportive relationships" (p. 497). This study points to the need for future research to study the intersection of the model minority stereotype and gendered educational expectations.

Guillermo, E. (2011). Advancing the race conversation: Chinese man vs. model minority. *Diverse: Issues in higher education, 28*(10), 20.

*** Guillermo, a former host of NPR's "All Things Considered," has covered diversity issues for 30 years. Guillermo's (2011) one-page article compares and contrasts two well-known Asian (Chinese) Americans: Lee Mun Wah and Frank Wu. Guillermo (2011) describes Lee Mun Wah, an acclaimed filmmaker and educator, as "Chinese man," and Frank Wu, chancellor and dean of the University of California's Hastings College of the Law, as "model minority." Guillermo (2011) shares his impressions of both men after hearing them at the National Conference on Race and Ethnicity in American Higher Education. Frank Wu was an afternoon keynote, while Lee Mun Wah was a facilitator of workshops. This article illustrates the different ways in which Asian Americans are perceived professionally and personally. While Wu was dapper and dressed in a suit and tie, Wah was dressed more casually. Although both men are Chinese, they are received differently. This article can be used as a way to shake up how professionally successful Asian Americans are talked about. It is logical that Wu would be perceived as a model minority stereotype given his work in higher education. It is also logical that Wah would be classified as simply Chinese given his less prestigious work as a documentary filmmaker. What needs to be addressed by future work, though, is how the identities of Asians become crystallized and conditioned by exaggeration, rhetoric, and ethnic stereotypes. This article is also nice for readers who may not be familiar with Wah's "StirFry" Seminars, and who may wish to do some investigative work. Author's note: *The Color of Fear* (1994) is one of Wah's better known films about race relations and stereotyping that he directed.

Hartlep, N. D. (2012). Harvard to the NBA: Deconstructing Jeremy Lin as a "model minority." *Korean Quarterly, 15*(3), 18.

***Hartlep's (2012) column critiques the idea that Jeremy Lin is a model minority. Lionized as a model minority who earned a Harvard degree in economics and plays in the National Basketball Association (NBA), "Lin is only the most current embodiment of the *model minority*. Before Lin, Amy Chua garnered much press on her radical parenting styles" (Hartlep, 2012, p. 18, italics added). Hartlep (2012) points out that the exaltation of Lin must be set in the context of anti-Asian sentiment. For instance, "During the 2012 Super Bowl, a political advertisement was aired showing a stereotypical Asian American woman who was vilified as an evil 'Yellow Peril'" (Hartlep, 2012, p. 18). This column can be used in connection with Mayeda's (1999) "From Model Minority to Economic Threat: Media Portrayals of Major League Baseball Pitchers Hideo Nomo and Hideki Irabu" published in the *Journal of Sport and Social Issues*. The model minority stereotype has clear implications for race and ethnicity's salience in athletics and sports (also see Hylton, 2009); this column continues such a conversation.

Hattori, T. (1999). Model minority discourse and Asian American jouis-sense. *Differences: A Journal of Feminist Cultural Studies, 11*(2), 228–247.

***Hattori's (1999) article examines model minority discourse. Hattori (1999) writes the following:

> The stereotype of the model minority as the ideal immigrant, often ascribed to Asians in America, predicates social acceptance upon exceptional capitalist achievement. Model minority discourse is the term that describes the Asian American psychic institutions that emerge from this predication and, to the extent that model minority discourse inhabits Asian American culture and studies, describes the process of minority collaboration in dominant cultural motives within works and institutions allegedly devoted to ethnic and racial emergence, provocation, and resistance. (p. 231)

This article presents the model minority stereotype as "a creative racial (and racist) jouis-sense" (p. 237)—in other words, an Asian American, or "the model minority subject whose social inclusion is simply a function of their economic sufficiency within and utility to the dominant culture" (p. 238). Hattori's (1999) analysis is similar to that which is shared in Sakamoto, Takei, and Woo's (2012) article "The Myth of the Model Minority Myth." Hattori's (1999) chapter can be used to illustrate how the model minority stereotype perpetuates capitalistic class-stratifications within society, and it can be used in English courses or Asian American studies courses as reading material.

Hawkins, N. (2009). Becoming a model minority: The depiction of Japanese Canadians in the globe and mail, 1946–2000. *Canadian Ethnic Studies, 41*(1–2), 137–154.

***Hawkins (2009) was interested in determining whether or not the portrayal of Japanese Canadians in the media has changed over time and, if so, what accounts for this change. Using content/frame analysis, she studied 228 news/entertainment/sport/family/business/classified stories printed in the *Globe and Mail* from 1946 to 2000. The *Globe and Mail* is an authoritative news source in Canada, featuring national and international news. Given that *Globe and Mail* is Toronto-based, and also due to the fact Toronto has the largest Japanese Canadian population in Canada, it made a good deal of sense to study the newspaper, which has been published since 1844. According to Hawkins' (2009) findings, Japanese Canadians were portrayed in three distinct frames: (1) the "Unthreatening Frame" (1946–1980), (2) the "Justified Victims Frame" (1981–1990), and (3) the "Model Minority Frame" (1991–2000). Her study's findings point to the complex ways in which Japanese Canadians' experiences have changed over time. Hawkins

(2009) is worth quoting at length, when she writes the following distinction between American and Canadian model minority depictions:

> Unlike American studies of the portrayal of Asian Americans in the media, Japanese Canadians were not framed as technological experts or academic over-achievers. What is unique in this Canadian model minority imagery is that Japanese Canadians were depicted as economically and academically successful members of Canadian society in general. (pp. 148–149)

This article would be excellent to read in a critical media studies course or a journalism course, not only because of its analysis of newspaper depictions of Japanese, but also because it exposes its readers to many facts that unfamiliar literary and news-consuming readers may not know about the Japanese, such as the following: (1) Manzo Nagano was the first known Japanese migrant to Canada in 1877; (2) Issei are first generation Japanese; (3) Nisei are second generation Japanese; (4) Sansei are third generation Japanese; (5) Japanese were interned in Canada; and (6) In 1950 Justice Bird awarded approximately $1.2 million in damages to Japanese Canadians for economic losses due to internment.

Horsburgh, B. (1999). The myth of a model minority: The transformation of knowledge into power. *UCLA Women's Law Journal, 10,* 165–202.

***Horsburgh's (1999) book review is on Daniel A. Farber and Suzanna Sherry's *Beyond All Reason: The Radical Assault on Truth in American Law.* Horsburgh (1999) addresses why the thoughts of Farber and Sherry are inconvenient truths and why treating Jews as model minorities is problematic. This book review essay can be used when examining how the treatment of Asian Americans is antedated by the treatment of Jewish Americans. Horsburgh's (1999) analysis is well reasoned and erudite.

Hsu, R. Y. (1996). "Will the model minority please identify itself?" American ethnic identity and its discontents. *Diaspora: A Journal of Transnational Studies, 5*(1), 37–63.

***Hsu (1996) states that "knowledge is the key to power; and true power is held through the acquiescence of those who are ruled" (p. 37). Her article, therefore, examines the "hegemonic project" that is the "model minority" stereotype. Hsu (1996) introduces a rehabilitative concept of ethnicity. This rehabilitative concept of ethnicity is related to the trope of the American dream, which accomplishes three things: (1) functions as proof that America works and the democratic moorings of its society are well-founded; (2) encourages an immigrant to voluntarily become a member of American society, convincing him/her that certain national beliefs are natural, thereby subscribing to American mythology; and (3) engenders the idea that what benefits a segment of the community is thereby beneficial to the whole society. Importantly, Hsu (1996) points out the following: "The image of America as liberal, democratic, and welcoming has never been true for Asian Americans and other people of color, in either socio-economic or cultural terms" (p. 42). Thus, the model minority stereotype serves as a rhetorical, political, and ideological device to maintain the inequitable *status quo*. Consequently, Hsu (1996) notes that "if the colonizer is able to convince the colonized that his belief system is universal and natural, then he has in effect made transparent the very presence of his rule" (pp. 39–40). Hsu's (1996) analysis of the model minority stereotype in the context of American ethnic identity finds that the myth is merely a nationalistic master-script codified through other American myths, such as the construction of America as the "promised land," the idea of American bootstrap success, and the notion that there exists an American democracy. This comprehensively researched article will be useful for all readers, but especially for high school teachers and professors of higher education. It makes the important observation that "the creation of the 'model minority' myth in the 1960s, for example, was intimately tied to the nation's [America's] need to narrate itself as a democratic community; Asian American ethnicity was [thus] written into the national mythology" (p. 42).

Hu, A. (1989). Asian Americans: Model minority or double minority? *Amerasia, 15*(1), 243–257.

***Hu's (1989) cogent article examines whether the model minority stereotype is real or media myth. Hu (1989) writes the following:

> Asians, in my view, are the only major racial group that can be best characterized as a "double" minority. Depending on which Asians you choose, they fit both the pattern of a privileged "overminority" and a disadvantaged "underminority." (pp. 244–245)

Consequently, Hu's (1989) article is extremely important to the demystifying of Asian American success because of its careful examination of Asian Americans as a population. Hu (1989) is worth being quoted at length when he points out the following:

> Asians have what has been called a "square," or "bipolar," distribution. In fact, the normal curve is much wider for Asians than for other groups, with disproportionally far more people both above and below average, and relatively fewer people in the middle. This is the result of the history of Asian immigration, which includes substantial numbers of both professional and unskilled immigrants. Moreover, groups such as the Japanese and Chinese have assimilated over four or more generations, while other Asians are recent immigrants, many of them impoverished refugees. When persons at the extremes balance each other out, the result is an average that would lead one to believe that Asians are either just a bit better than average if judging by household income, or a bit worse on a per capita basis. But this

hides the fact that Asians have unusual amounts of both wealth and poverty. (p. 245, italics added)

Moreover, "Asian Americans: Model Minority or Double Minority?" addresses important theoretical and practical issues for the Asian American community, such as Asian female advantage, something that has received little scholarly attention, as well as the ways in which the media mythologizes Asian American test achievement.

For instance, Hu (1989) points out that "*Newsweek* and *Time* may proclaim Asian Americans to be academic whizzes because of their slightly higher math scores. But since Asians actually score lower than Whites on their combined sum of both math and verbal tests—and this is what colleges usually count—the SATs actually put Asians at a disadvantage" (p. 248, italics in original). The remainder of this article includes coverage of topics such as the following:

- ethnic disparities among rich and poor Asian Americans,
- affirmative action and Asians Americans,
- subjective bias' impact on college admissions of Asian Americans,
- discussions of diversity and where Asian Americans fit within this discourse, and
- anti-Asian racial violence.

Hu's (1989) thoroughly researched article will be well-received by researchers who are familiar with the literature on the model minority stereotype but who are looking for subtler, more nuanced judgments to demystify the model minority stereotype. Although scholars and academics will constitute the largest audience for this article, practitioners and in-service educators may also consider reading it for insights on how to better understand the diverse and bimodally distributed Asian American population.

Jew, C. G. (1995). Resemblance? How new Asian Immigrants compare with the "model minority. In C. K. Jacobson (Ed.), *American families: Issues in race and ethnicity* (pp. 157–175). New York, NY: Garland Publishing, Inc.

***Jew's (1995) book chapter explores findings from her statistical analysis of data taken from the 1980 and 1990 Public Use Microdata Sample (PUMS). Jew (1995) analyzed various Asian ethnic groups, such as Filipinos, Chinese, Vietnamese, Koreans, Japanese, and Asian Indians, "comparing variables that indicate[d] the level of [their] assimilation achieved" (p. 159). Jew's (1995) findings indicate that incomes varied widely among the Asian subgroups, and that "Asians are usually not able to translate their high education into correspondingly high incomes" (p. 162). Adds Jew (1995), "Despite our assumptions that Asian Americans fare remarkably well under their own efforts, we ignore that their success is not universally distributed among all Asian Americans" (p. 173). She asserts that it is homogenization that causes the belief that all Asian Americans experience economic success. Jew's (1995) book chapter is helpful insofar as it illustrates the necessity of disaggregating Asian Americans by ethnic subgroup. The variation that is hidden by aggregation begins to be seen when researchers disaggregate data during analysis. This chapter can be read in quantitative statistics courses, and can be used when students begin to craft research studies using publicly available data, like the PUMS.

Kaba, A. J. (2008). Race, gender and progress: Are Black American women the new model minority? *Journal of African American Studies, 12*(4), 309–335.

***Kaba (2008) argues that "Black American women are becoming America's new model minority" (p. 311). Using various social, economic, and educational indicators, Kaba (2008) indicates that "one could expand the model minority concept to include Black American females" (p. 310). While Kaba's article valiantly tries to make an original case—that Black women are becoming model minorities—many conceptual and theoretical necessities are absent in his argument. For instance, if Black women are transitioning from the stereotypical "welfare queens" to model minorities, who are the ideologically-blackened "others" to which the model minority stereotype compares itself? One of the foundational pillars, or touchstones, that the model minority myth stands for is the maintenance of White supremacy. White supremacy is maintained through the myth given that it divides and conquerors non-Whites, benefiting Whites and the racial *status quo*. By definition, then, Black women represent the other non-White racial/gender group that is compared to Asian Americans. Nevertheless, the weaknesses of this article are also its strengths. This article provides a set of fresh ideas that future research can begin using to come up with new, non-binary lenses and paradigms for the development of new theories. Asian critical race (AsianCrit) theorists may find this article inspirational for future examinations and critical analyses of the legal and extralegal ways in which the model minority myth maintains the *modus operandi* through the emphasizing of Black-White binary comparisons and judgments.

Kamphoefner, W. D. (1996). German Americans: Paradoxes of a "model minority." In S. Pedraza & R. G. Rumbaut (Eds.), *Origins and destinies: Immigration, race, and ethnicity in America* (pp. 152–160). Belmont, CA: Wadsworth Publishing Company.

*** Kamphoefner's (1996) chapter discusses how Germans are considered by some to represent a model minority immigrant group. Initially, Kamphoefner (1996) notes, Germans were invisible, but later, they "came to be looked upon as more desirable, particularly when contrasted with newer arrivals from southern and eastern Europe" (p. 153). Kamphoefner (1996) also indicates that the construction of Germans as a model minority was "based as much on prejudice as on objective criterion" (p. 153). In similar ways to Asian Americans, Germans have been stereotyped historically as "stable, hard-working, dependable, and thrifty" (Kamphoefner, 1996, p. 154). However, Kamphoefner (1996) points out that the construction of Germans as model minorities came about as a result of, not these latter dispositions, "but rather because the dominant culture came around the[m]" (p. 155). Interestingly, though, Kamphoefner's (1996) chapter never mentions what the term model minority really means or its historical origins. This chapter can be used as an example of how ethnic, racial, and religious groups other than Asians have been dubbed model minorities.

Kang, M. (2010). I just put Koreans and nails together: Nail spas and the model minority. In M. Kang, *The managed hand: Race, gender, and the body in beauty service work* (pp. 133–164). Berkeley, CA: University of California Press.

***Kang's (2010) chapter "examines how the performance of pampering body labor disciplines the bodies of Asian manicurists into docile service to other women's bodies" (p. 135). According to Kang (2010), "Rather than a single stereotype, the model minority references a constellation of factors that frame Asians not only as a laudable racial group but as proof that the United States is open and egalitarian" (p. 136). Kang's (2010) analysis of upper-class nail spas and their social construction of Korean manicurists as model minorities is insightful and cutting edge. This book chapter should be referenced in literature reviews as well as read in college courses such as Asian American studies, women studies, and sociology courses. Many of the arguments that Kang (2010) puts forth are reasonable and well-defended, making for an intellectually stimulating reading.

Lee, J. K. (2002). Where the talented tenth meets the model minority: The price of privilege in Wideman's "Philadelphia fire" and Lee's "native speaker." *NOVEL: A Forum on Fiction, 35*(2/3), 231–257.

***Lee's (2002) article compares and contrasts the Asian American model minority myth and the notion of there being an African American "talented tenth." According to Lee's (2002) analysis, Asian Americans and African Americans must retreat from notions that they constitute a model minority and/or talented tenth position in society; otherwise, they will be complicit in the oppression of their fellow contemporaries. Thus, the price for their retreat will be a loss of privilege, since, as Lee (2002) writes, "the talented tenth and the model minority reinforce one another" (p. 254). This article can be used for teaching or research purposes. Lee's (2002) connection of the Du Boisian notion of "talented tenth" with the model minority stereotype presents interdisciplinary substantive scholarship coupled with methodologically-rich thought processes that can certainly inspire future work along the lines of critical explorations of the model minority stereotype. This is a highly consequential piece of scholarship.

Lee, T. (1991). Trapped on a pedestal: Asian Americans confront model-minority stereotype. In J. A. Kromowski (Ed.), *Racial and ethnic relations* (pp. 95–98). Guildford, CT: Duskhin Publishing Group.

***Lee's (1991) chapter shares various arguments that model minority stereotype scholars can cite and use in their own scholarship. According to Lee (1991) the model minority stereotype "denies Asian Americans legal and social protection against discrimination" (p. 95). As Lee (1991) notes, "Although Asian Americans are three to five times as likely as whites to be engineers and doctors, they are also two to four times as likely to work in food services or textiles" (p. 96). This short chapter makes many important arguments that refute the validity of the model minority stereotype. For instance, Lee (1991) writes that "the stereotype of the successful minority hurts those Asian Americans who need the most help, because the success of some is used as an excuse to deny benefits to all" (p. 96), adding that "the portrayal of Asian Americans as a super-minority not only dehumanizes Asian Americans, but creates unreasonable expectations (much as the super-mom image does)" (p. 98). This chapter is clear and easy to follow. It would make an effective read in an undergraduate Asian American Studies Course. This chapter originally appeared as [Lee, T. (1990). Trapped on a pedestal: Asian Americans confront model-minority stereotype. *Dollars & Sense*, 12–15.].

Lei, J. L. (1998, April). *(Op)posing representations: Disentangling the model minority and the foreigner.* Paper presented at the Annual Meeting of the American Educational Research Association, San Diego, CA. ERIC ED421564

***Lei's (1998) twenty-four page conference paper was presented at the American Educational Research Association (AERA) Annual Meeting held in San Diego, California. The paper examines how the representations of Asian Americans as model minorities and perpetual foreigners play off one another to shape the positioning and experiences of Asian American students in U.S. schools and maintain the dominant racial order in the United States. According to Lei (1998) Asian Americans continually face assumptions of them as foreigners and as "un-American," regardless of their generation status. The model minority and the perpetual foreigner, opposing representations, place Asian American students in a peculiar and vulnerable position in the racial order—affecting not only how they are seen by non-Asians, but also how they perceive themselves and the people around them (non-Asians).

Li, G. (2009). Behind the "model minority" mask: A cultural ecological perspective on a high achieving Vietnamese youth's identity and socio-emotional struggles. In C. C. Park, R. Endo, & X. L. Rong (Eds.), *New perspectives on Asian American parents, students, and teacher recruitment* (pp. 165–192). Charlotte, NC: Information Age Publishing.

***Li's (2009) chapter shares the findings of a single case study of Hanh (pseudonym), a high-achieving Vietnamese adolescent (16-year old) female. Data—semi-structured interviews and field notes—was collected between May 2004 and June 2005. Li (2009) writes that "behind the 'model minority' mask, Hanh was experiencing multilayered school, social, and familial stresses" (p. 173). This observation captures the essence of the chapter title. Hanh's narratives indicated that she had multiple stressors placed on her, such as the need to serve as a language broker for her family members, as well as the challenges that came with the model minority stereotype, many of which caused her to internalize her concerns, frustrations, and struggles. Li (2009) indicates that teachers and professionals who work with Asian American children can learn from Hanh's narrative. For instance, Li (2009) suggests that "even students who are perceived as a *'model minority'* are not problem-free" (p. 186, italics added) and that

> teachers, administrators as well as school counselors must forgo the stereotypical image of Asian American students as a *model minority* that is presented in mass media and treat each student, high achieving or not, as an individual who comes from a particular family background and has specific academic and socio-emotional needs. (p. 187, italics added)

This chapter can be read by college of education students who will most likely teach and work with students like Hanh out in the field. By understanding the multilayered school, social, and familial stresses that Asian American students assume, teachers will be better able to teach and reach them given their own realities, rather than relying on the stereotype of Asian American students as model minorities.

Li, G., & Wang, L. (Eds.). (2008). *Model minority myth revisited: An interdisciplinary approach to demystifying Asian American educational experiences.* Charlotte, NC: Information Age Publishing.

***This edited volume is part of the *Chinese American Educational Research and Development Association Book Series.* The book has five sections. Each section considers an interdisciplinary approach and perspective in demystifying the model minority. Section one examines a sociocultural perspective, while section two grapples with a psychological perspective. Section three explores an educational perspective, and section four studies a methodological perspective. The fifth and final section uses the perspective of policy in attempting to argue against the inaccuracy of the model minority myth. This book is highly original and, in the words of Stacey Lee, author of the volume's foreword, "The interdisciplinary nature of the volume provides a holistic understanding of how the stereotype operates in the lives of Asian Americans" (p. x). *Model Minority Myth Revisited* is helpful since each chapter in the book features detailed papers on the model minority stereotype.

Lo, M. (2008). Model minorities, models of resistance: Native figures in Asian Canadian literature. *Canadian Literature, 196*(1), 96–112.

***Lo's (2008) "Model Minorities, Models of Resistance: Native Figures in Asian Canadian Literature" article primarily examines Asian Canadians' extollation of representing a model minority. Comparing and contrasting the racialization patterns of Asian Americans and Asian Canadians in Canadian literature, Lo (2008) interestingly likens the model minority to a "containment" device. In other words, the model minority serves to restrict the mobility and expression of both Asian Canadians and Asian Americans. The purpose of Lo's (2008) article was to examine "the work of prominent Asian Canadian writers, Joy Kogaw, and SKY Lee, [in order to] demonstrate how Native characters and culture are figured to *contest* the particular formations of [the] Asian Canadian [model minority stereotype]" (p. 97, italics added). This is an important article because, as Lo (2008) rightly points out, "Asian Canadians, like Asian Americans, are often perceived as either perpetual foreigners (the yellow peril, the enemy alien) or as exemplars of successful assimilation, capital accumulation, and traditional Asian family values (the *model minority*)" (p. 97, italics added). Lo's (2008) article indicates that the model minority stereotype says less about Asian Canadians and more about Native/Aboriginal/First Nation conquest. This analysis is provocative considering that many times model minority scholarship addresses what the discourse implies rather than analyzing the intentions behind those who perpetuate the discourse.

Maddux, W. M., Gallinsky, A. D., Cuddy, A. J. C., & Polifroni, M. (2008). When being a model minority is good...and bad: Realistic threat explains negativity toward Asian Americans. *Personality and Social Psychology Bulletin, 34*(1), 74–89.

***This methodologically strong and rigorously sound study examined how realistic threat explains the negativity of attitudes and emotions toward Asian Americans. Maddux and his colleagues predicted that the model minority stereotype leads to a sense of *realistic threat*, which activates negative attitudes and emotions. Findings of their study support this idea. Maddux et al.'s (2008) study was comprised of four mutually supportive studies. Study 1 participants consisted of 76 undergraduates at Northwestern University; Study 2 called upon 105 undergraduates at Ohio State University; Study 3 analyzed 40 undergraduates from Ohio State University; and the participants of Study 4 consisted of 97 undergraduate students at Northwestern University. According to Maddux and colleagues, "the perception that Asian Americans or other groups have certain model minority traits—including being hardworking, intelligent, and ambitious—leads to a sense that such groups pose a threat to other groups in terms of educational, economic, and political opportunities, and that such a sense of *realistic threat may lead to negative attitudes and emotions*" (p. 86, italics added). They go on to state that "in other words, the belief that Asian Americans or other model minorities are intelligent and ambitious may actually be considered negative when such traits are associated with negative outcomes for oneself or ones group (i.e., fewer jobs, poorer grades)" (pp. 86–87). The substantial contribution that this study makes to the study of the model minority stereotype is its introduction of *realistic threat* and its theoretical support that the causal relationship is as follows: Model Minority Stereotype à *Realistic Threat* à Negative Affect and Evaluations.

Mahalingam, R. (2013). Model minority myth: Engendering cultural psychology of Asian immigrants. In E. L. Grigorenko (Ed.), *Handbook of U.S. immigration and education* (pp. 119–136). New York, NY: Springer Publishing.

***Mahalingam's (2013) chapter discusses the cultural psychology of Asian immigrants, namely, "the psychological impact of idealized representations such as the MMM [model minority myth on Asian immigrants]" (Mahalingam, 2013, p. 119). The concepts of model minority pressure and model minority pride that Mahalingam's theoretical—dual-pathway—model tested, are extremely fascinating. Mahalingam (2013) writes the following:

> Those who feel discriminated against scored high on beliefs about being a model minority and on model minority pride and pressure. Pride positively relates to measures of resilience, such as John Henryism, and pressure negatively relates to JH." (p. 132)

This book chapter is incredibly strong theoretically (see Figure 5.1 about Asian American resiliency), as well as methodologically, and can be used in concert with the work of Jennifer Lee's (2012) "stereotype promise" that she is developing with the Russell Sage Foundation.

Mahmud, T. (2001). Genealogy of a state-engineered "model minority" "not quite/ not White" South Asian Americans. *Denver University Law, 78*(4), 657–686.

***Mahmud's (2001) book review focuses on the critical legalist's understanding that South Asians have been historically as well as contemporarily racialized as model minorities. Mahmud (2001) reviews Vijay Prashad's best-selling book, *The Karma of Brown Folk* (2000).

Mannur, A. (2005). Model minorities can cook: Fusion cuisine in Asian America. In S. Davé, L. Nishime & T. G. Oren (Eds.), *East Main Street: Asian American popular culture* (pp. 72–94). New York, NY: New York University Press.

***Mannur's (2005) chapter explores how Ming Tsai and Padma Lakshmi's "racialized [and] gendered national identit[ies] map onto the public performance of culinarity" (p. 74). Mannur (2005) writes, "Selling Ming Tsai as a model minority is a crucial ingredient in making Tsai successful" (p.

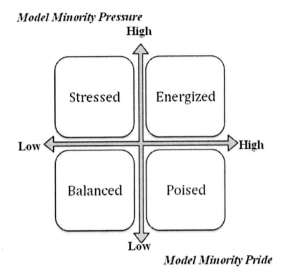

Model Minority Pressure
High

Stressed

Energized

Low

High

Balanced

Poised

Low

Model Minority Pride

FIGURE 5.1.   Resilience model For Asian Americans as model minorities

77). Not coincidentally, Tsai was schooled at Yale University and trained at the prestigious Le Cordon Bleu School, thus embodying the model minority stereotype through-and-through. In terms of the chapter's discussion of Asian fusion cooking, Mannur (2005) explicates how Tsai's cooking shows *East Meets West* and *Ming's Quest* both portray Tsai as an assimilated model minority with great sex appeal. Mannur (2005) comments, "In this way, Ming Tsai emerges as the model minority chef who inhabits a newer stereotype—that of the hyperassimilated, attractive, and yuppified Asian American who seamlessly integrates into American cultural life" (p. 78). Mannur (2005) also analyzes South Asian Padma Lakshmi's Asian fusion cooking show *Padma's Passport*. Mannur (2005) declares the show guilty of commodifying, exotifying, and sexualizing Lakshmi. Mannur (2005) concludes her chapter with the following statement: "The 'arrival' of Asian fusion restaurants and the popularity of cooking shows such as *East Meets West*, and *Padma's Passport* have been read as signs Asian Americans have 'made' it" (Mannur, 2005, p. 89). This chapter is interdisciplinary given that its analyses extend the model minority stereotype into cooking and culinary spaces.

Martinelli, P. C. & Nagasawa, R. (1987). A further test of the model minority thesis: Japanese Americans in a sunbelt state. *Sociological Perspectives, 30*(3), 266–288.

***This study, using the 5% Public Use Microdata Samples (PUMS) of the 1980 United States Population Census, studied the economical, educational, and occupational positions of Japanese Americans in Arizona. According to Martinelli and Nagasawa (1987), "The Japanese Americans in Arizona are not as successful as the *national data* suggest, and bring into question this utility of the model minority success image" (pp. 281–282, italics added). The researchers found that Japanese American men earn less than White males with the same educational levels. One weakness of this study was that it exclusively examined Japanese Americans; the PUMS dataset contained six ethnic categories: Japanese, Chinese, Filipinos, Korean, Indian, and Vietnamese. The study would have been more robust if it had comparatively examined Japanese versus other Asian American subgroups. Nevertheless, the unique contribution this study makes to the literature on the model minority myth lies in its notification that national data has the potential to distort study findings. Martinelli and Nagasawa (1987) explicate:

> Our data suggests that in Arizona the highly educated Japanese Americans systematically receive less income (and prestigious occupations) than similarly qualified whites. The model minority has no basis when examined on a *regional* basis that eliminates the *distortion* caused by *national* comparisons. (pp. 282–283, italics added)

Mayeda, D. T. (1999). From model minority to economic threat: Media portrayals of Major League Baseball pitchers Hideo Nomo and Hideki Irabu. *Journal of Sport and Social Issues, 23*(2), 203–217.

***Mayeda's (1999) article is very interesting and thought-provoking. Moving the model minority discourse from academics to athletics, Mayeda (1999) argues "that American media portrayals of [Hideo Nomo and Hideki Irabu]…two Japanese pitchers have mirrored stereotypical images of Asian Americans and Asian nationals, thereby perpetuating a national culture that already unfairly categorizes Asian Americans and Asian nationals as model minorities and economic threats" (p. 204). Mayeda (1999) writes that "the model minority myth is a conservative tool that falsely debunks any notions of systematic discrimination" (p. 205). This article gives examples of how Asian athletes have been damaged by the media's depictions of them as physically weak and slow. In the words of Mayeda (1999), "Asians and Asian Americans are stereotyped as less athletic but hard working and more intelligent (hence, they are the model minority)" (p. 208). Mayeda (1999) shares his methodology—a content analysis of articles from the sports sections from the *Los Angeles Times* and *The New York Times*—that examines two Japanese Major League Baseball (MLB) pitchers. Results indicated that Hideo Nomo was Orientalized and cast as an athletic model minority. "Hard working, self-sacrificing, and quiet as (he was rarely quoted in newspapers), Nomo reaffirmed to readers that Asian nationals and Asian Americans were model minorities" (p. 211). Hideki Irabu, however, found himself cast as an economic threat when he began to pitch poorly. Given that Irabu negotiated for a contract that was the highest for a player never to have pitched in the American major leagues, his performance made him the target for much media criticism, namely that he was an overpaid pitcher. Mayeda (1999) connects Nomo and Irabu's racialized positions of model minority and economic threat, respectively, well. Mayeda (1999) discusses the treatment of Asian and African Americans in athletics, pointing out how African Americans have been coached out of "thinking positions" such as quarterback in football and pitcher in baseball. Consequently, according to Mayeda (1999), "It should not go unnoticed that all of a sudden Asian nationals (stereotypically viewed as less athletic but more intelligent) are specifically recruited to play in the 'thinking position' of pitcher. If this positional racialization goes without scrutiny, unproven and false images of both Asian and African Americans will be further essentialized in American minds" (p. 214). This article makes a significant contribution to the literature on Asian Americans as athletic model minorities. Scholars of all types will find this an important and worthwhile read. This article can be made a required reading in undergraduate as well as graduate level Asian American studies and educational foundation courses.

Michaels, W. B. (2011). Model minorities and the minority model–The neoliberal novel. In L. Cassuto, C. V. Eby, & B. Reiss (Eds.), *The Cambridge history of the American novel* (pp. 1016–1030). Cambridge, MA: Cambridge University Press.

***Michaels's (2011) book chapter is wonderfully written and structured. In the chapter's beginning, Michaels (2011) writes that "the [model minority] 'myth' persists and, when you examine the most recent census data or the most recent figures on enrollment in elite universities, it's not hard to see why" (p. 1018). Michaels (2011) later indicates that the model minority stereotype serves to compare and contrast Asian and African Americans, "questioning" (actually blaming) why Africans are not succeeding at the level that Asians are. However, this blame game is problematic, and relevant to the way in which race and ethnicity are used in maintaining the *modus vivendi*. Consequently, Michaels (2011) points out that "the American racial system—what is sometimes called the black/white binary—is, in this view a machine that takes people (Slavs, Jews, Asians, whoever) and makes them white. And the most part of this machine is black people—because it's by not being black that you get to be white" (p. 1019). Michaels (2011) contends that the model minority stereotype is a function of *neoliberalism*, which, in of itself, is a function of both racism and capitalism. Michaels (2011) writes that "what makes the Koreans like the Jews is *not* their shared victimization but their *success*, above all their *economic success*" (p. 1025, italics added). In a similar vein, Michaels (2011) notes that "the experience of Asian Americans has in fact been much more like the experience of

Jews than it has been like that of African Americans" (p. 1025). This chapter is deftly written and, thus, very useful for citing in literature reviews. It should be read by undergraduate students in all different types of major fields of study since it illuminates the historical relatedness of Asian American model minority status occupancy and Jewish American model minority status occupancy. This book chapter can also be used in tandem with other literature to help situate the model minority stereotype within the context of racism, capitalism, immigration, and nativistic/nationalistic aggression.

Museus, S. D. (2008). The model minority and the inferior minority myths: Understanding stereotypes and their implications for student learning. *About Campus, 13*(3), 2–8.

***Museus' (2008) article examines the model minority stereotype and the stereotype of the "inferior minority." Museus conducted individual face-to-face interviews with one racial and one ethnic minority student at a predominantly White rural public research university. The article shares the experiences of one female second year Korean American ("model minority") student and one female fourth year African American ("inferior minority") student. Results based on the interview data found that the "model minority" student internalized the model minority myth, which then influenced her classroom experiences and behavior. The intense pressure to meet the standard of the model minority stereotype caused incredible stress for this Asian/Korean American college undergraduate. The "inferior minority" student felt devalued and a need to disprove the inferiority myth by asserting herself as knowledgeable and capable in her college course(s). This undergraduate student felt as if she stood out due to the fact that she was the only African American student in her course(s). The biggest take-away from this study is that *stereotypes*—positive or negative—have the ability to cause college students to behave in ways that can *verify* (internalizing the model minority stereotype) or *disconfirm/disprove* (fighting against the inferior minority stereotype) them. This article makes a unique contribution to model minority research and ends by discussing the potential implications of what is needed to stop the spread and practice of stereotyping students of color. Notwithstanding, the article clearly points out that institutional, educational, and cultural change will continue to be slow-coming if one-day seminars and half-hearted efforts to diversify the professoriate continue to be the norm, rather than the exception. This article is especially valuable for teachers in K–12 and higher education settings who are dedicated to anti-bias education, and is an extremely important read for current and prospective model minority scholars to consider when conducting their future work. Museus (2008) gives us a compelling justification for the importance of this work when he writes the following: "The frequent absence of Asian Americans from discussions about race in higher education is, in part, a function of the persisting systemic disregard of concerns relevant to Asian American college students, which itself is derived from the assumption that all Asian Americans achieve success in education" (p. 6).

Paek, H. J. & Shah, H. (2003). Racial ideology, model minorities, and the "not-so-silent partner": Stereotyping of Asian Americans in U.S. magazine advertising. *Howard Journal of Communications, 14*(4), 225–243.

***Paek and Shah (2003) write "that the model minority stereotype inaccurately [portrays] that all Asian Americans conform to the norms of society, do well in school and at work, and attain self-sufficiency through hard work" (p. 226). Therefore, the purpose of their study was to investigate how Asian Americans are portrayed in U.S. magazine advertising. They were interested in the "images" and "ideological meanings" that the model minority stereotype carries. Paek and Shah (2003) were specifically interested in advertising, which has been considered by some to be "the not-so-silent partner" (p. 227). Paek and Shah's (2003) study used both quantitative and qualitative methods in order to study how Asian Americans are represented in magazine advertising. They analyzed ten randomly selected months from the calendar year 2000, a total of ten issues from the following four mainstream news magazines: *Advertising Age, Time, Newsweek,* and *U.S. News & World Report.* Their analyses included quantitative coding and qualitative textual analysis. Among many findings, Asian Americans were found to be portrayed primarily in business, computer, and Internet advertisements, providing "some evidence that Asian Americans are stereotyped as a 'model minority'" (p. 233). Some of the most salient stereotypes in advertisements were the following: (1) the technologically savvy Asian American, (2) the academically successful Asian American, and (3) the beautiful and/or exotic female Asian American.

Furthermore, advertisements represented Asian Americans as being closer to Whites than other non-White minorities. East Asians, especially, were predominant in advertisements, whereas South Asians and Southeast Asians—for example, Afghanis, Bangladeshis, Pakistanis, Sri Lankans, Malaysians, and Indonesians—were largely absent. The authors discuss several implications caused by advertising that reinforces and reproduces the "hegemonic mode of Asian American stereotyping" (p. 237), namely, what the model minority image fails to reveal: (1) the diversity of this heterogeneous population, (2) the glass ceilings that Asian Americans encounter, (3) the variance of socioeconomic stability, and (4) the ways in which the stereotype exacerbates social conflicts in race relations. Paek and Shah (2003) conclude with the following summary:

> The racial ideology framework…may help us to better understand how the advertising industry, mass media's "not-so-silent" partner, participates in per-

196 • *The Model Minority Stereotype: Demystifying Asian American Success*

petuating stereotypes and social organization infused by racial hierarchy. (p. 240)

Park, G. (2011). Becoming a "model minority": Acquisition, construction and enactment of American identity for Korean immigrant students. *Urban Review*, *43*(5), 620–635.

***Park's (2011) article found, among other things, that "becoming a 'model minority' was a coping strategy for the recent Korean immigrant youth who are facing status marginalization and social isolation in the high school's [City High's] racial hierarchy" (p. 621). This article is significant because "relatively little attention has been paid to how Asian immigrant students *acquire, construct, and enact* the [model minority] stereotype in a school setting" (Park, 2011, p. 622, italics added). Data for this study originate from a previously conducted one and a half year ethnographic study at City High (a pseudonym), an inner city high school in a Midwestern city. Specifically, this article focused on the school experiences of 22 Korean immigrant students (nine female and 13 male). Interviews and participant observations formed the rich data that was analyzed using a critical race theoretical (CRT) framework. The study's CRT framework was enhanced due to the fact that Park (2011) identifies as being a bicultural Korean American. The two most salient findings were as follows: (1) embracing the model minority stereotype was a coping strategy for the Korean immigrant high school students in order to avoid status marginalization; and (2) Korean immigrant high school students "learned that playing the role of quiet and hardworking Asian is rewarded in the classroom" (Park, 2011, p. 629). This *Urban Review* article is valuable for urban high school administrators and counselors to read, considering that the high school context shapes the identities that Asian American (Korean immigrant) students will acquire, construct, and enact.

Poon-McBrayer, K. F. (2011). Model minority and learning disabilities: Double jeopardy for Asian immigrant children in the USA. *Global Studies of Childhood*, *1*(2), 152–158.

***Poon-McBrayer's (2011) essay argues that Asian Americans are placed in a double jeopardy. This colloquium paper sheds light on the social and political consequences of the model minority stereotype for Asian Americans, especially the post-1965 Asian immigrants. According to the author (Poon-McBrayer, 2011), the model minority stereotype is problematic since it homogenizes, demonizes, discriminates, and views Asians in unpatriotic ways. Moreover, Poon-McBrayer (2011) indicates that the model minority trope is a "*social* construction serving a *political* purpose" (p. 154, italics added). Poon-McBrayer (2011) argues "that Asian immigrant students are... disadvantaged and marginalized under the *double jeopardy* of being labelled the model minority, together with difficulties resulting from learning disabilities or learning English as a second language" (p. 155, italics added). This colloquium paper, albeit short at only five pages in length, will be of great professional interest for special education teachers and teacher educators, as well as special educational and parental advocates. Poon-McBrayer (2011) points out the incredible need for scholars to study the under-representation of Asian Americans in special education classes, noting that this phenomenon is understudied. Poon-McBrayer (2011) makes the following valuable observation: "The conflation of the more naturalised and well-off Asian Americans and the less well-to-do recent wave of Asian immigrants into one 'model minority' group has placed Asian immigrants in the USA in a situation of *double jeopardy* and consequent marginalization" (p. 156, italics added).

Poon, O. A. & Hune, S. (2009). Countering master narratives of the "perpetual foreigner" and "model minority": The hidden injuries of race and Asian American doctoral students. In M. F. Howard-Hamilton, C. L. Morelon-Quainoo, S. D. Johnson, R. Winkle-Wagner, & L. Santiague (Eds.), *Standing on the outside looking in: Underrepresented students' experiences in advanced-degree programs* (pp. 82–102). Sterling, VA: Stylus.

***Poon and Hune's (2009) chapter is a study in which they surveyed 114 Asian Americans about their experiences in doctoral programs. Poon and Hune (2009) found that Asian American doctoral students experienced four types of micro-aggressions, which they refer to as "hidden injuries": (1) being the only Asian American, (2) being treated or mistaken as a foreigner, (3) being lumped with other Asian Americans, and (4) being racialized as a model minority. Poon and Hune's (2009) "findings contradict assumptions of success among Asian American doctoral students and show that there are many ways in which they experience the persistence of racism" (p. 99). They go on to state

> The master narratives of Asian Americans as 'model minority' and 'perpetual foreigner' bring a certain level of visibility to them, but in the end these narratives also render Asian Americans invisible and silent in academia, marginalizing their perspectives and the issues they deem important. (Poon & Hune, 2009, p. 100)

Poon and Hune's (2009) chapter will be useful for those who are engaged in educational policy work aimed to increase the visibility of Asian Americans, as well as for those whose work targets Asian Americans as being under-represented in higher education. Poon and Hune's (2009) comment is worth repeating:

> There is a [model minority] stereotype of Asian Americans as engineering of life/physical sciences majors. Our respondents, however, showed a diver-

sity of academic disciplines: social sciences (30.7%), life/physical sciences (23.7%), education (18.4%), arts/humanities (14.9%), engineering (7.9%), and ethnic studies/interdisciplinary field (4.4%). (p. 92)

This chapter can and should be cited in reviews of literature.

Riess, J. (2011, October 4). A "model minority" blends in: Normal Mormons. *Christian Century, 128*(20), 22–25.

Riess (2011) states, "Mormons now find themselves in the familiar situation of being on the defense theologically and politically, but at the same time they are in terra incognita: they are not only a tolerated sect but are viewed as a *model minority* leading the way in preserving family values" (p. 25, italics added). The most important idea presented in this article is the following: "When a group is held up as a *model minority* it tells us as much about what the host culture needs as about the minority itself" (p. 25, italics added). Riess' (2011) article can be used to show how the model minority myth functions as a rhetorical and political device. Rhetorical scholars and students who are interested in history and/or political science will find this article engaging and educative.

Rim, K. H. (2007). Model victim, or problem minority? Examining the socially constructed identities of Asian-origin ethnic groups in California's media. *Asian American Policy Review, 16,* 37–60.

***Rim's (2007) article, through the use of content analysis of articles published in the *Los Angeles Times* and *San Francisco Chronicle* newspapers, evaluates the media's construction of Asian Americans as "model minorities," "victim minorities," and "problem minorities." Rim's (2007) study is important because it traces the construction and evolution of Asian Americans over time (1960s–2000s), especially in the context of affirmative action (1964–1965; 1977–1978; 1984–1985; 1995–1996; and 2002–2003). Rim (2007) found that during 1965–1966 and 1995–1996 Asian Americans were most likely to be categorized as model minorities. During the 1970s and 1980s Asian Americans were constructed as being socioeconomically successful, while during the 1980s and 1990s this construction shifted toward academic excellence. In terms of being constructed as "victims," the 2000s repeat what was being constructed during the 1960s. While Cambodian and Laotian Americans have been constructed as being "victims," they have never been constructed as being "models." During the 1970s Asian Americans were most likely to be portrayed as "problems." Whereas the Chinese and Japanese were found to be frequently portrayed as "models," Rim's (2007) content analysis also found that the Vietnamese and Chinese have been the most consistently branded as "problem minorities." The "problem minority" construction reached its zenith in the 1970s. Rim (2007) notes the following:

In sum, the data suggest that the construction of Asian Americans as a model minority is consistently changing in California's media and that the only stable construction of Asian Americans throughout the last half century has been the victim minority construction. However, the stability of the victim minority construction does not eliminate or weaken the influence of the popular model minority image. Using both images, Asian Americans are often depicted as a successful model group that overcomes its victim experiences. In this respect, the victim construction not only works in preserving the model image, it strengthens it. (p. 56)

Rim's (2007) article contains an epigraph quoting Frank Wu, who mentions the following: "It would be bad enough if the model minority myth were true. Everyone else would resent Asian Americans for what Asian Americans possess. It is worse that the model minority myth is false. Everyone else resents Asian Americans for what they believe Asian Americans possess" (as cited in Rim, 2007, p. 38). The implication of the previous thought is great, and this article is important, especially when it comes to public and educational policy legislation. If Asian Americans are deputized as being model minorities, what does it say about society's supposed belief in colorblindness and meritocracy? Since this article looked solely at two California newspapers, it would be helpful if model minority scholars conduct similar studies in contexts that extend outside of California.

Sakamoto, A., Takei, I., & Woo, H. (2012). The myth of the model minority myth. *Sociological Spectrum, 32*(4), 309–321.

***Sakamoto, Takei, and Woo's (2012) article is one of the best argued on the model minority. Indeed, Sakamoto, Takei, and Woo's (2012) two premises are that the model minority stereotype is based on faulty statistical reasoning and that it "persists because it promotes the socioeconomic self-interests of the professors who currently control the Asian American Studies establishment that in turn provides political legitimacy for the universities that employ them" (p. 309). Sakamoto, Takei, and Woo (2012) spend a good deal of time demonstrating that the "over-education" argument is methodologically false in a sense because it is elitist. In their analysis of the model minority stereotype and the over-education argument (Asian Americans' unequal returns on education compared to non-Hispanic Whites), Sakamoto, Takei, and Woo (2012) write the following:

the over-education view contends that more highly educated Asian Americans are underpaid in that their educational attainment is not rewarded at the same rate as that for non-Hispanic whites. The implication of this view is that Asian Americans with less education are less underpaid. Persons with the lowest level of educational attainment (i.e., high-school dropouts) face little or no disadvantage in the labor market at all. Thus, the over-education view is implicitly most concerned with the highly educated—those who actually tend to be most advantaged in the labor market—because it does not specify (or even mention) any mechanisms of economic disadvantage for the less educated. (p. 316)

They go on to add the following conclusion:

The MMM is not only oblivious to the fact of growing economic exploitation but ironically implies that the current problem with the distribution of income is that it is not unequal enough. The over-education view contends that we need even more inequality so that highly educated Asian American workers can earn even higher salaries (purportedly to put them on par with comparable white workers), thus increasing the wage gap between the richer and poorer even further. However, arguing for more income inequality that would be primarily for the benefit of privileged educated workers is elitist and inequitable. (p. 317)

This article is rife with possibilities for future research and must be considered an instant "touchstone" for model minority scholarship.

Shida, N. (2007, August). *Becoming a model Minority: The portrayal of Japanese Canadians from 1946–2000.* Paper presented at the American Sociological Association Annual Meeting, New York, NY.

***Shida's (2007) ASA conference paper was the early stages of her final publication, [Hawkins, N. (2009). Becoming a model minority: The depiction of Japanese Canadians in the Globe and Mail, 1946–2000. *Canadian Ethnic Studies, 41*(1–2), 137–154.]. Naoko Hawkins née Shida are one and the same person.

Shim, D. (1998). From yellow peril through model minority to renewed yellow peril. *Journal of Communication Inquiry, 22*(4), 385–409.

***Shim's (1998) article examines the history of Asian stereotypes, beginning from the mid-19th century through the Reagan-Bush era. His article reviews U.S. entertainment media (mainly films) using semiotic and ideological analyses, marking historical stages in the transition from yellow peril to model minority back to yellow peril. The first stage in this cycle is that of the villainous Dr. Fu Manchu (a Chinese yellow peril), who was serialized in many movies during the early 1930s. Ten years later, during the 1940s, Charlie Chan movies portrayed Asian males in asexual and effeminate ways, during what Shim labels the "sexually distorted" period. During this sexually distorted period Asian females were portrayed as sexual slaves who were bound to fall in love with white men. Movies such as *The World of Suzie Wong* (Chinese), *Miss Saigon* (Vietnamese), *Sayonara* (Japanese), and *Madame Butterfly* (Chinese) are representative of such racist and sexist ideology. Meanwhile, Asian men were mostly shown to be bachelors during this period of movie production. The next period is associated with post-World War

II and the Korean War, during the 1950s. During WWII, Japanese took the Chinese's place as the "enemy." This changed during the Korean War, when the Chinese returned to the American imagination as being the "enemy." Then, during the 1960s, Asians were painted as "model minorities" in order to divide African Americans who were attempting to assert their civil rights. This civil rights period relied heavily on the media's use of "Asian success stories." The key underpinning of these success stories was their contrasting of African American failure and hardship with that of Asian American success and happiness. The Charlie Chan movies of an earlier period were eerily similar to the divide and conquer ideology used to disenfranchise Asians and Blacks in the 1960s. Sadly, things did not *really* improve during the civil rights period, as Shim (1998) writes that "Asians were still portrayed in negative and misleading ways throughout the 1960s and 1970s in films and TV programs" (p. 395). In the next period, what Shim (1998) labels the "Reagan-Bush Era," Shim (1998) points out that "Asian Americans [once again] became embroiled in a racial 'divide and conquer' policy" (p. 396). During this time the African American community was enduring economic and political hardships due to Republican-controlled and directed socio-political policies. Republican politicians attributed success and failure to issues of family values, demonizing African Americans, while applauding Asian Americans' putative triumphal achievements. What ensued, however, is paradoxical: anti-Asian sentiment did not go away, as feelings of anti-Japanese resentment were perceptible (e.g., Japanese automobile manufacturing as a symbol of yellow perilism once again). The next period, Shim points out, is that of "yellowfacing" and the Asian "other." This period is marked by films that include Asians as either background scenery (secondary acting roles) or that have White actors playing Asian roles. Accordingly, Shim (1998) writes, "In Hollywood, there has been a longstanding practice of 'yellowfacing'—casting whites as Asians by the application of tape to the temples and cheekbones" (p. 401). Shim (1998) ends his article by quoting from Edward Hallett Carr's *What is History?* (1961), "Understanding the society of the past is the prerequisite to the mastery over the society of the present" (p. 405). Any study of the model minority is incomplete without a thorough analysis of its nexus with other stereotypes, such as the yellow peril. This article does this with inimitable ease and should be read by college students and cited by model minority scholars. Shim's (1998) article also appears as the following chapter: [Shim, D. B. (2000). From yellow peril through model minority to renewed yellow peril. In B. Mori (Ed.), *Stand! Contesting ideas and opinions: Race and ethnicity* (pp. 98–106). Madison, WI: Coursewise.]

Sun, C., Miezan, E., & Liberman, R. (2009). Model minority/honorable eunuch: The dual image of Asian American men in the media and everyday perception. In R. Hammer & D. Kellner (Eds.), *Media/cultural studies: Critical approaches (pp. 516–536)*. New York, NY: Peter Lang Publishing Group.

***Sun, Miezan, and Liberman's (2009) chapter is brilliantly conceived. It addresses the duality of emasculated Asian American men and the model minority stereotype. Sun, Miezan, and Liberman (2009) write, "Media stereotypes of Asian American men are reflected in both the 'model minority' image depicted in the news and advertising and the 'emasculated men' portrayed in the movies and on television dramas and sitcoms; together...these characterizations form the model minority/honorable eunuch dual image" (p. 521). Using both a quantitative and a qualitative method, their study examined the ways in which Asian Americans were represented in the media as well as the effect of those representations on Asian Americans. Sun, Miezan, and Liberman (2009) relied on survey data ($n = 538$) conducted with multiracial groups of college students at two universities located on the east coast of the United States. The questionnaire collected information on survey respondents' perceptions of Asian Americans generally (in addition to perceptions of Asian Americans compared to other minority groups specifically). In terms of qualitative data, the researchers conducted focus group interviews. Focus group participants (seven Asian American male groups, seven Asian American female groups, two Black male groups, two Black female groups, one White male group, and two White female groups) were recruited from the same two universities at which the questionnaire was disseminated. Questionnaire findings indicated that "Asian American women were considered feminine, and sexy while their male counterparts were considered nerdy and neither masculine nor sexy" (p 524). Moreover, "the more respondents perceived Asian Americans as sexy, the more they were interested in dating them" (p. 526). Focus group results found that Asian American men were more likely to want to interracially date a White woman. The opposite was true for White women wanting to interracially date. In other words, Asian American females were deemed exotic for White men, and Asian American men deemed White as beautiful. Asian American men were not considered attractive to White women due to their asexualized identities as honorable eunuchs and model minorities. Sun, Miezan, and Liberman's (2009) chapter can be used to develop paradigmatic arguments that have not yet been made in the sociology of the model minority stereotype. The chapter includes references to relevant concepts that might be of use to scholars and theoreticians such as the following: (1) Collins' (1990) "controlling images," (2) Althusser's (1971) "ideological state apparatuses," and (3) Chan's (2001) "non-hegemonic masculinity."

Suyemoto, K. L., Kim, G. S., Tanabe, M., Tawa, J., & Day, S. C. (2009). Challenging the model minority myth: Engaging Asian American students in research on Asian American college student experiences. *New Directions for Institutional Research, 142*, 41–55.

***This article details Suyemoto et al.'s (2009) investigation into Asian American students' experiences. The researchers utilized a "students-as-researchers" method in conducting the research. The article shares the findings of two studies: (1) the Asian American Student Needs Assessment Project and (2) the Asian American Studies Project. The Needs Assessment Project was conducted by 11 faculty members, 10 staff members, and 27 Asian American students (graduate and undergraduate), while the Asian American Studies Project was conducted by one male and seven female Asian American students enrolled in their first Asian American studies course at the same public research university where the Needs Assessment Project was conducted. The article's main contribution is its indication that the "students-as-researchers" method to conducting research contributes to Asian American students' own education and empowerment; its closing declaration that more research is needed to "better understand the diverse experiences of Asian American students in higher education" (p. 54) is also noteworthy given that there continues to be a limited quantity of research on Asian American students' experiences in higher education.

Tayag, M. (2011, Spring). Great expectations: The negative consequences and policy implications of the Asian American "model minority" stereotype. *Stanford Journal of Asian American Studies, 4,* 23–31.

***Tayag (2011) writes the following: "The 'model minority' myth has proven detrimental, because it masks the psychosocial and educational needs of many Asian Americans, such that these needs have been systematically neglected at the institutional level" (p. 26). Indeed, Tayag's (2011) article is devoted to addressing the negative consequences and policy implications of the model minority stereotype. While the model minority stereotype appears to be positive, the characterization is not true of most Asians. After thoroughly reviewing the literature on policy recommendations for Asian Americans, Tayag (2011) feels strongly that "by monitoring different ethnic subgroups separately, establishing and expanding culturally appropriate services to address the educational and psychological needs of Asian Americans, and encouraging the development of important non-academic skills, schools can give all Asian Americans a fair chance at educational and socioeconomic success" (p. 30). This article can be used by educational and social service practitioners, and those in higher education who prepare and train them. The article's main strength lies in its synthesis and clarification of the model minority stereotype and the attending policy implications for Asian American people.

Tsunokai, G. T. (2005). Beyond the lenses of the "model" minority myth: A descriptive portrait of Asian gang members. *Journal of Gang Research, 12*(4), 37–58.

***This useful article is also brilliantly written. "Over the years, social scientists—albeit a relatively small number have gradually turned their attention to the topic of Asian gangs—a phenomenon that seemingly flies in the face of the '*model' minority myth*" (Tsunokai, 2005, p. 38, italics added). Tsunokai (2005) paints a descriptive portrait of Asians by examining 60 variables on gang membership and attitudes. Tsunokai (2005) compares the attitudes and beliefs of self-admitted ($n = 128$) gang members to non-gang members ($n = 157$). Asian American participants were sampled from "[five] various sites located throughout the San Gabriel Valley region—an area comprising 33 contiguous cities in Los Angeles County" (p. 39). Data collection occurred from November 2001 to February 2002 in (1) the Los Angeles County Probation Department/Asian Unit, (2) a private high school, (3) a residential treatment facility, (4) a youth community center, and (5) an adult continuation school. Among many useful and interesting findings, Tsunokai (2005) uncovered the following salient facts: (1) most (96%) Asian gang members became affiliated around 16 years of age or younger; (2) the majority of gang members were male, ranging from 13 to 28 years in age; (3) gang members and non-gang members had similar family income distributions, although the majority of gang members who lived in homes that were below the poverty-line identified themselves as being Cambodian, Laotian, and/or Vietnamese; and (4) gang members tended to feel that society treated them unfairly, getting at the idea of blocked opportunities. Overall, Tsunokai (2005) notes that his study's "results showed that a significant number of gang members were college students whose family earned over $60,000 per year" (p. 54). He goes on to state, "Future research should examine if the 'model' minority myth discourse has any impact on gang involvement" (p. 54). This article can be used to assist in future Asian gang research, and can be used to argue against the idea that Asians are models who do not engage in deviance, crime, and illicit behavior. This is a must-read for model minority researchers.

Tang, J. (1997). The model minority thesis revisited: (Counter)evidence from the science and engineering fields. *Journal of Applied Behavioral Science, 33*(3), 291–315.

***Tang (1997), using panel data from the 1989 Survey of Natural and Social Scientists and Engineers compiled by the U.S. Bureau of Census for the National Science Foundation (NSF), examines the likelihood of Whites, Blacks, and Asians moving into management across occupational fields and organizations. According to Tang, using NSF longitudinal data is better than cross-sectional data that previous studies use. The literature review attends to the problems of aggregate data and how it contributes to the model minority thesis. It also covers topics such as the glass ceiling and the "tokenism" of Asians in occupations. This study finds that there is no empirical support for the model minority thesis: Asian American males lag behind their White peers in business, industry, and other organizations.

According to Tang (1997), "One of the most important findings is that, compared to white males, Asian American males have a lower tendency to enter management in business and industry" (p. 306). Tang (1997) poses a profoundly important question: "How can we reconcile the fact that Asian Americans are well represented in these high-paying professions but lag significantly behind their white peers in getting ahead in major fields and organizations" (p. 310)? Thus, writes Tang (1997), "the racial patterns of the career mobility of scientists and engineers provide mixed evidence for the thesis that Asian Americans are a successful Model Minority in professional occupations" (p. 291). This study is valuable, especially for Asian critical race (AsianCrit) theoreticians, in that it provides counter-evidence that can be used to immediately challenge and re-narrate the professional realities of being a non-White (yellow-bodied) minority.

Trytten, D. A., Lowe, A. W., & Walden, S. E. (2012). "Asians are good at math. What an awful stereotype": The model minority stereotype's impact on Asian American engineering students. *Journal of Engineering Education, 101*(3), 439–468.

***Trytten, Lowe, and Walden (2012), using a mixed-method design, analyzed semi-structured interviews and academic transcript data, as well as administered a survey to engineering students. Trytten, Lowe, and Walden (2012) found five facets of the model minority stereotype, facets implying that Asian Americans are: (1) extremely intelligent, (2) hardworking, (3) have high socioeconomic attainment and goals, (4) seek educational prestige, and (5) show an uncomplaining attitude about racial issues and problems. Trytten, Lowe, and Walden (2012) used critical race theory to inform the design and implementation of their study. From these findings they conclude, "The harm of complimentary stereotypes is potentially as detrimental as negative stereotypes" (Trytten, Lowe, & Walden, 2012, p. 440) and that "the MMS has been used to separate AsAms from solidarity with other racial and ethnic minority groups" (p. 442). This study asked four questions: (1) To what degree does academic data support the assertion that Asian American engineering students conform to the model minority stereotype? (2) How do Asian American engineering students express the impact of the facets of the model minority stereotype on their lived experiences? (3) What, if any, facets of the model minority stereotype are more often reported than others among Asian American engineering students? and (4) How do Asian American engineering students perceive their fellow racial/ethnic peers fitting within the model minority stereotype?

The Asian American engineering students were found to refute the validity of the model minority stereotype while simultaneously casting the label on fellow Asian Americans. Thus, the biggest contribution that this article makes to the model minority stereotype literature is its introduction of "lateral oppression" (p. 460). Consequently, Trytten, Lowe, and Walden

206 • *The Model Minority Stereotype: Demystifying Asian American Success*

(2012) write the following: "Since the MMS is an oppressive device, those within the group that project the MMS on their co-racial peers are engaged in *lateral oppression*, where members of the same minority group oppress each other" (p. 460, italics added). This article can be used in psychology courses and for discussions on "stereotype threat" (e.g., see Steele, 2010; Steele & Aronson, 1995).

Van Ziegart, S. (2006). Re-appropriating the model minority stereotype: Reflections on the 2000 Organization of Chinese Americans Convention. In S. Van Ziegart, *Global spaces of Chinese culture: Diasporic Chinese communities in the United States and Germany* (pp. 21–58). New York, NY: Routledge.

***Van Ziegart's (2006) chapter is the second in her book *Global Spaces of Chinese Culture: Diasporic Chinese Communities in the United States and Germany*. Van Ziegart (2006) reflects on the 2000 Organization of Chinese Americans (OCA) Convention held in Atlanta, Georgia, in the Buckhead district. Van Ziegart (2006) makes the distinction between supplementary narratives and counter narratives. She believes that much of what was done by the OCA at its 2000 convention was supplementary in nature rather than counter to the model minority stereotype. Van Ziegart (2006) shares her belief that the model minority stereotype may be effectively re-appropriated. She cites examples of marginalized and oppressed groups who re-appropriated titular shibboleths, such as "Queer Nation" and "Niggers with Attitude." Van Ziegart (2006) teases apart the differences/intersectionalities of "interpolation," which she defines as "appropriating dominant discourses in the attempt to write oneself into the mainstream narrative," (Van Ziegart, 2006, p. 32) and "interpellation," which she defines as "the act of being appropriated by hegemonic forces" (Van Ziegart, 2006, p. 32). Thus, many of the OCA's approaches to pushing back against the model minority stereotype at the convention relied on "interpolation"—arguing that Asian "Chinese" Americans have made significant contributions to dominant U.S. society. Van Ziegart's (2006) use of Louis Althusser's interpellation theory, as well as examination of the trial of Wen Ho Lee and the murder of Vincent Chin in model minority scholarship, is compelling and methodologically forward-thinking. This book chapter can be used as a reference point for unique ways that Asian Americans can battle the shibboleth that the model minority stereotype represents—in this case—re-appropriating its titular discourse.

Wang, L. (Ed.). (2007). Demystifying model minority's academic achievement: An interdisciplinary approach to studying Asian Americans' educational experiences. *New Waves: Educational Research and Development, 11*(1), 4–28.

***This special issue is devoted to interdisciplinary approached research that studyies the model minority stereotype. Bringing together five short articles, this special issue examines the model minority stereotype using the following five perspectives: (1) ecological, (2) psychological, (3) qualitative (ethnographic) method, (4) quantitative (cross-cultural) method, and (5) summative. *New Waves* is a peer-reviewed online journal published by the Chinese American Educational Research & Development Association (CAERDA). Interested teachers, researchers, and scholars can find CAER-DA's website here: www.caerda.org, where they can access these five open-source journal articles.

Watanabe, Y. (1996). The Nisei as model minority: Self-concept and definition of the American dream. *MultiCultural Review, 4*(2), 46–48, 50–53.

***Watanabe's (1996) article looks at the various ways in which Japanese Americans (mainly Issei and Nisei) define success and the American dream. Watanabe (1996) relies on "a variety of sources, including historical narratives, interviews, essays, autobiographical works, and works of fiction" (p. 47) for material. The article is interesting because it illustrates Japanese Americans' ambivalence and changing attitudes toward assimilation, acquiescence, and how they view "success." Watanabe (1996) writes, "It is ironic that the Nisei, who are thought to stand out on nearly all levels of conventional success, have anxieties about themselves. They have started to reflect on themselves, to realize the Japanese in themselves, and to re-assess their real achievement of their own will" (p. 47). As a result, this article can be used to argue how the narrow model minority stereotype limits Asian Americans in terms of identity and self-empowerment.

Wong, P., Lai, C. F., Nagasawa, R., & Lin, T. (1998). Asian Americans as a model minority: Self-perceptions and perceptions by other racial groups. *Sociological Perspectives, 41*(1), 95–118.

***Wong, Lai, Nagasawa, and Lin's (1998) article was based on a sample survey administered to 1,257 students who enrolled at the four Washington State University (WSU) campuses. Although their study employed a stratified random sample "in order to give adequate representation to five different racial and ethnic groups—Asian, African American, Native American, Hispanic, and white" (Wong, Lai, Nagasawa, & Lin, 1998, p. 101), readers are neither told when the data was collected, nor the students' ages and the year they were in college when the data was procured. The four authors treated White students as the study's comparison group and performed regression analyses and analysis of variance (ANOVA) analyses. Study findings indicated that Asian American students perceived themselves as more prepared, motivated, and more likely to have greater career success than White students. Furthermore, African American students, Hispanic students, and Native American students each perceived Asian American students as being superior to White students. Interestingly, though, these very same students (African American, Hispanic, and Native American) saw themselves being inferior to White students. Wong, Lai, Nagaswa, and Lin's *Sociological Perspectives* article was reprinted by the Gale Group (interested readers can access it online for free here: http://maxweber.hunter.cuny.edu/pub/eres/ SOC217_PIMENTEL/asians3.pdf). This article can be used in concert with racial triangulation theorists, such as Claire Jean Kim (see Kim, 1999).

Wong, E. F. (1985). Asian American middleman minority theory: The framework of an American myth. *Journal of Ethnic Studies, 13*(1), 51–88.

***Wong's (1985) article is incisive. He argues that the notion that Asian Americans are middleman minorities is suspect and unsupportable, especially when taking into consideration anti-Asian racism. Like the model minority stereotype, the idea that Asian Americans are middleman minorities is also a myth. Wong (1985) writes that "rather than blaming the victim, the 'model minority' thesis sets its own unique structural trait, namely, *praising the victim*" (p. 63, italics in original). Wong (1985) describes why Asians fall outside of the White-Black dyad, thus illustrating that Asians are not between Whiteness and Blackness, but rather, outside of it. The most insidious element of the middleman minority theory is its unwillingness to engage with issues of racism, social exclusion, and racial and ethnic injustice. This article should be read by graduate students in Asian studies programs, as well as by model minority stereotype academics. The reason this article is so compelling is that the idea that Asians are racial middlemen is ubiquitous and oft-used within model minority scholarship. Published in 1985, this article is foundational in the way scholars situate Asian Americans within a Black/White binary. In many ways, this article should be read in conjunction with Claire Jean Kim's (1999) *The Racial Triangulation of Asian Americans,* which is also examined in this book.

Wong, W. (1994). Covering the invisible "model minority." *Media Studies Journal, 8*(3), 49–59.

***Wong's (1994) article pertains to the need for responsible journalism when covering Asian Americans. Wong (1994) addresses problematic ways in which Asian Americans are covered by news print media and/or journalists. By and large, Asian Americans are made invisible, and when present, portrayed in stereotypical ways. The language that journalists use in their stories needs to be more balanced, as oftentimes headlines and stories rely on "tiresome clichés or rhyming phrases when they talk about Asians and Asian American subjects" (Wong, 1994, p. 55). This use of "cutesy phrases"—such as the "Asian invasion"— is problematic according to Wong (1994) because they reify and reinforce sociopolitical as well as ethno-cultural misunderstandings. Written in very accessible language, this short article is very useful for model minority scholarship given its documentation of journalistic bias when reporting on Asian Americans. Journalism students in college ought to read this article. It can also be used in literature reviews, as well as for evidence of sensationalizing Asian Americans. Wong's (1994) article also appears as a book chapter [see Wong, W. (1997). Covering the invisible "model minority." In S. Biagi & M. Kern-Foxworth (Eds.), *Facing difference: Race, gender, and mass media* (pp. 97–102). Thousand Oaks, CA: Sage Publications.].

Wortham, S., Mortimer, K., & Allard, E. (2009). Mexicans as model minorities in the new Latino diaspora. *Anthropology & Education Quarterly, 40*(4), 388–404.

***Wortham, Mortimer, and Allard (2009) studied Marshall (a pseudonym), "a suburb of 30,000 in the Northeastern United States" (p. 388). They found that "in Marshall, Mexican immigrants are often identified as 'model minorities'—as hardworking contributors to the community who do not expect special treatment and do not complain" (Wortham, Mortimer, & Allard, 2009, p. 388). They point out four reasons Mexicans are perceived to be model minorities in Marshall. First, the group is different from African Americans. Second, they work hard and succeed. Third, they refuse public and social "handouts." And fourth, they do not complain. Comparing African Americans to Mexicans serves to cast Mexicans as victims and African Americans as criminals who exploit the system. This article can be cited in literature reviews and used to change the ways in which we conceptualize model minority status and which groups are successful academically. This article has many implications for Mexicans in Marshall, especially the Mexican students who may not be high-performing or high-achieving.

Yamanaka, K. & McClelland, K. (1994). Earning the model-minority image: Diverse strategies of economic adaptation by Asian-American women. *Ethnic and Racial Studies, 17*(1), 79–114.

***Using data from a sub-file of the five per cent Public Use Microdata Samples (PUMS) of the 1980 U.S. Population Census, Yamanaka and McClelland's (1994) article examines four different theories of the census data—assimilation, dual economy, ethnic-enclave economy, and middleman minority—to determine the strategies of economic adaptation that working-age immigrant Asian American women endorse. Yamanaka and McClelland's (1994) study is important for model minority research because, as they note, "Past studies tend simplistically to depict Asian women as economically successful women" (p. 83). The study included the analyses of numerous Asian American subgroups (39,701 total): "10,869 Japanese, 8,983 Chinese, 8,930 Filipino, 4,741 Korean, 4,147 Indian, and 2,031 Vietnamese" (Yamanaka & McClelland, 1994, p. 88) compared to 41,557 non-Hispanic White women. The study found that Asian-American women tend to work more hours per year and receive lower economic returns than Whites on their education. Yamanaka and McClelland (1994) conclude the following: "In summary, the generalization that Asian-American women are a successful minority group becomes less tenable the more closely the group is examined" (p. 109). In other words, the Asian American population defies such characterization. This article can be used in a sociology course whose syllabus covers theories of immigrant economic adaptation (e.g., assimilation, dual-economy, ethnic enclave, and middleman minority, etc.).

Yee, G. A. (2009). She stood in tears amid the alien corn: Ruth, the perpetual foreigner and model minority. In R. C. Bailey (Ed.), *They were all together in one place? Toward minority Biblical criticism* (pp. 119–140). Atlanta, GA: Society of Biblical Literature.

***Yee's (2009) book chapter views the Biblical book of Ruth through the lenses of the model minority stereotype and perpetual foreigner stereotype. According to Yee (2009), the model minority stereotype is more of a denigration of other non-White and non-Asian groups than a compliment to Asian Americans. Yee's (2009) chapter is helpful in that it is written from the standpoint of both the perpetual foreigner position and the model minority stereotype: both of which obscure and collude what is real. Indeed, Yee (2009) writes that by "refracting the story of Ruth through the prism of the Asian American experience, I argue that, in its own way, the ideology of the text constructs Ruth the Moabite as a *model minority* and *perpetual foreigner*" (p. 127, italics added).

Yoo, H. C., Burrola, K. S., & Steger, M. F. (2010). A preliminary report on a new measure: Internalization of the model minority myth measure (IM-4) and its psychological correlates among Asian American college students. *Journal of Counseling Psychology, 57*(1), 114–127.

***Yoo, Burrola, and Steger (2010) developed a measure that is important for model minority stereotype research, the "Internalization of the Model Minority Myth Measure," which they shorten to IM-4. The authors "define *internalization of the model minority myth* as the extent to which individuals believe Asian Americans are more successful than other racial minority groups based on their values emphasizing achievement and hard work and belief in unrestricted mobility toward progress" (Yoo, Burrola, & Steger, 2010, p. 117). Their research builds on the dissertation research of Chen (1995) and Chu (2002). The implications are great because as Yoo, Burrola, and Steger (2010) state:

> The IM-4 has a wide range of research and clinical applications. For instance, studies can now identify the extent to which internalization of the model minority myth and its subtypes affect academic outcomes. (p. 124)

This article can be used when conducting future model minority internalization research. It can also be cited in reviews of the literature.

Yokohama, K. & Lee, D. (2005). Managing the model minority myth and other misconceptions: The struggles and strengths of Asian American gifted girls.

In S. Kurpius, B. Kerr, & A. Harkins (Eds.), *Handbook for counseling girls and women: Ten years of gender equity research at Arizona State University* (pp. 123–156). Mesa, AZ: Nueva Science Press. Retrieved from http://www.stemwomen.net/handbook/Chapter%205.pdf

***Yokohama and Lee's (2005) chapter attempts "to synthesize the available literature [on Asian American giftedness] and to introduce re-conceptualizations of giftedness within the community of bright Asian American girls who are also at risk" (p. 124). Their chapter remains timely despite being several years old, given that research on Asian American female giftedness remains sparse. Yokohama and Lee (2005) indicate that Asian American females have been sexually objectified, exoticized, and fetishized, thereby impacting their self-concept and personal/academic identity. For this reason, Yokohama and Lee (2005) note the following: "Teachers must work with parents of gifted Asian American girls to establish together how to best provide challenges for the child" (p. 147). This chapter mentions that it is important to provide career counseling, stress management strategies, and wellbeing services to Asian American females since many times these individuals may feel voiceless and/or powerless. Given that "gifted Asian American girls face a variety of pressures to achieve according to social (model minority myth) and cultural (Asian and Confucian value of achievement) expectations" (Yokohama & Lee, 2005, p. 143), this chapter is a necessary read for parents, school administrators, counselors, educators, and educational policymakers. Furthermore, scholars engaged with research on the model minority stereotype will find this chapter to be a critically-important read, due to the fact that female Asian American giftedness remains under theorized and explored.

CHAPTER 6

ENCYCLOPEDIC AND BIBLIOGRAPHIC RESEARCH ON THE MODEL MINORITY STEREOTYPE

The writings that are annotated in this chapter come from encyclopedias and/or other bibliographic research that address the model minority stereotype. As the reader will quickly ascertain, the model minority stereotype is a fundamental part of Asian American history. Meanwhile, not every editor/author feels the same way as I do. Some encyclopedias have failed to include an entry on the model minority stereotype (e.g., see Lee & Nadeau, 2010). Nevertheless, the entries and citations that are provided here will help researchers, teachers, and practitioners locate materials for their work.

Aoki, A. L. (2000). Model minority. In J. D. Schultz, K. L. Haynie, A. M. McCulloch, & A. L. Aoki (Eds.), *Encyclopedia of minorities in American politics: African Americans and Asian Americans* (pp. 309–310). Phoenix, AZ: Oryx Press.

***Aoki's (2000) entry is short and sweet. Aoki (2000) addresses Hmong Americans in his entry. According to Aoki (2000) Hmong Americans have

The Model Minority Stereotype: Demystifying Asian American Success, pages 213–220.
Copyright © 2013 by Information Age Publishing

struggled, highlighting the diversity of the Asian American population. Aoki (2000) writes that "Asian American success has been deliberately exaggerated to undermine the claims of racial minorities when they call for race-based compensatory policies" (p. 309). This encyclopedia contains references to important model minority stereotype articles and thus can be used when hunting down references to build a literature review and/or aid in classroom instruction.

Bascara, V. (2008). Model minority. In R. T. Schaefer (Ed.), *Encyclopedia of race, ethnicity, and society* (pp. 910–912). Thousand Oaks, CA: Sage Publications.

***Bascara's (2008) entry on the model minority presents an extremely limited understanding of the model minority stereotype. Bascara provides a quick history of the stereotype, why and how the model minority serves as supposed evidence that America is truly meritocratic, and ends by providing the reader with three further readings. This encyclopedia entry is a great beginning reference for researchers interested in conducting investigations on how the model minority stereotype is used to disavow Asian Americans' need for racial affirmative action in order to maintain the *status quo*.

Cheryan, S. & Bodenhausen, G. V. (2011). Model minority. In S. M. Caliendo & C. D. McIlwain (Eds.), *Routledge companion to race & ethnicity* (pp. 173–176). New York, NY: Routledge.

***Cheryan and Bodenhausen's (2011) encyclopedia entry discusses commonly written-about issues related to the model minority stereotype, such as the importance of disaggregating data, the "glass ceiling" that Asian Americans face in the employment sector, and Asian Americans' disproportionately high rates of poverty. According to Cheryan and Bodenhausen (2011) the "model minority stereotype is problematic because it masks many of the struggles faced by Asian Americans" (p. 174). They add that "focusing on the Asian Americans who have 'made it' renders invisible those in the community who continue to struggle" (p. 174). The entry provides seven key readings, most of which center on stereotyping and "stereotype threat" (e.g., see Steele, 2010; Steele & Aronson, 1995).

Fong, C. (1995). The model minority. In F. Ng (Ed.), *Asian American encyclopedia* (pp. 1072–1086). New York, NY: Marshall Cavendish.

***Fong's (1995) entry provides a "discussion of the debate over the Model Minority thesis, its origins, historical context, proliferation and development, and impact on Asian American women; criticisms of the Model Minority thesis and how proponents have responded; and some of the effects of the stereotype" (p. 1072). Fong (1995) concludes his entry by providing several suggested readings. This encyclopedia entry can be cited in literature reviews, but it is probably most helpful for individuals who wish to read a brief but nevertheless information-rich document on the model minority stereotype. Several pictures, graphs, and tables accompany the text, thereby enriching the reader's comprehension and understanding.

Hartlep, N. D. (in press). The model minority as a rhetorical device. In S. Thompson (Ed.), *The encyclopedia of diversity and social justice*. Lanham, MD: Rowman and Littlefield.

***Hartlep (in press) indicates that the model minority stereotype is a rhetorical device given that it is based on exaggerated claims. The model minority myth is a racialized exaggeration that serves as a rhetorical device since it exaggerates success by portraying Asian Americans as problem free and well integrated. Provided that the myth originated during the 1960s, at the height of the African American civil rights movement, it is little wonder that pointing out Asian American success and African American failure causes interracial strife and conflict. Hartlep's (in press) entry can be used in literature reviews as well as by authors who are searching for material to reference when building conceptual arguments regarding the model minority stereotype.

Helweg, A. (2005). Model minority. In C. Skutsch (Ed.), *Encyclopedia of the world's minorities* (Vol. 2, pp. 832–834). New York, NY: Routledge.

***Helweg's (2005) encyclopedic entry contains many errors (incorrect citations and spellings) and unspecified claims. For instance, according to Helweg (2005), the model minority stereotype was first introduced in 1965. Helweg (2005) also incorrectly cites William Petersen's (in)famous *New York Times Magazine* story "Success Story: Japanese American Style" as being published in 1996, not 1966.

Junn, E. N. (2006). The model minority myth. In Y. Jackson (Ed.), *Encyclopedia of multicultural psychology* (p. 308). Thousand Oaks, CA: Sage Publications, Inc.

***Junn's (2006) encyclopedic entry indicates that the model minority stereotype has been discredited by many social scientists, yet still persists. Junn (2006) writes that "invoking the Asian model minority has been a new political tool for showing that racism does not exist—that America is indeed a color-blind meritocracy" (p. 308). She also mentions that the stereotype "has been used as an argument for eliminating affirmative action altogether" (p. 308). The further readings that Junn (2006) provides are helpful, but could have been selected more cautiously/judiciously. In other words, there are many better articles/reports on the model minority stereotype that could have better aided encyclopedia readers.

Kim, H. (1986). Model minority. In H. Kim (Ed.), *Dictionary of Asian American history* (p. 411). Westport, CT: Greenwood Press.

***Kim's (1986) dictionary entry defines model minority as a "concept that implies that other minorities should emulate Asian Americans in their thought and behavior" (p. 411). Kim (1986) goes on to state, "Asian Americans are considered more successful because their values are similar to those of whites, whereas the values of less successful minorities are remote from those of whites" (p. 411). Kim's (1986) dictionary definition can be used for teaching/learning, as well as in scholarly research on the model minority stereotype.

Kitayama, G. (2001). Model minority. In B. Niiya (Ed.), *Japanese American history: An A-to-Z reference from 1868 to the present* (p. 282). New York, NY: Checkmark Books.

***Kitayama's (2001) entry is one page but packs a strong punch. Many of the classical pro-model minority articles/writings are referenced. In fact, this encyclopedia entry includes many important "further" readings that model minority researchers might consider reviewing. This entry, though basic, is nevertheless important for model minority scholarship and teaching. This reading might be used in a classroom to introduce the concept of the model minority stereotype.

Kwon, H. & Au, W. (2010). Model minority myth. In E. W. Chen & G. J. Yoo (Eds.), *Encyclopedia of Asian American issues today* (Vol. 1, pp. 221–230). Santa Barbara, CA: Greenwood Press.

***Kwon and Au's (2010) encyclopedia entry suggests that the model minority stereotype is inaccurate due to the fact that it "obscures the importance of structural barriers and disparities among Asian American populations while also encouraging an inaccurate depiction of the American opportunity structure" (p. 228). In other words, the model minority stereotype supports the notion that America is a meritocracy and a country where anyone can succeed. Kwon and Au's (2010) conclusion is worth quoting: "The model minority myth continues to have an undeniable impact on the way that Asian Americans are perceived in the educational realm and in broader society" (p. 228). It is their concluding statement that is so impactful: the model minority stereotype impacts the lives of Asian Americans. This entry is thoroughly researched and written and contains references to numerous writings that will aid researchers and scholars in the field of model minority stereotype education.

Lee, R. G. (2008). Model minorities. In J. H. Moore (Ed.), *Encyclopedia of race and racism* (pp. 311–312). Detroit, MI: Thompson Gale.

Lee's (2008) *Encyclopedia of Race and Racism* entry contends that the model minority stereotype is an old "political ploy" (p. 311) that White supremacy uses in order to demonize non-Asian minorities, and to divide and conquer Asian Americans and other ethno-racial minorities.

Lew, J. W., Chang, J. C., & Wang, W. W. (2005). UCLA community college review: The overlooked minority: Asian Pacific American students at community colleges. *Community College Review, 33*(2), 64–84.

***This review focuses on Asian Pacific American (APA) community college students. Lew, Chang, and Wang (2005) state that APAs at community colleges have been an "overlooked" population, hence the title of their review. This important review highlights, among other things, the demographics and diversity of APA students, pointing to the need of "disaggregation of groups in order to better understand and address the needs of all students" (p. 66). More specifically, the authors of the review address APA students' *bimodal distribution* by stating the following:

> While there are certainly APA students who live up to the model minority image of academic success, there are also many who are considered "at risk" in higher education due to a combination of individual, family, school, and community factors that put them in danger of not completing a college degree. (p. 70)

The review notes that APA community college students face myriad challenges when it comes to educational attainment and achievement. Consideration must be given to these structural, familial, and sociocultural challenges, especially since the poverty rates for APAs are nearly double those of Whites. Also, the model minority stereotype doesn't help APA students' situation: According to Lew, Chang, and Wang (2005) the model minority stereotype "homogenizes what in reality is an extremely diverse population and ignores the long history of hostility, racism, and discrimination that APA communities have faced in the United States and, in some cases, continue to face" (pp. 74–75). This review rightly observes that APA community college students are an "overlooked" minority group in higher education because two-year college students do not fit the model minority characterization that APA students attend four-year prestigious Ivy League institutions. Lew, Chang, and Wang (2005) advocate for more academic research on the APA community college population in order that "no segment of the population will be an overlooked minority" (p. 78). Their review concludes with several implications for practice and recommendations for future research.

Liu, A. (2007). Asian Americans in community colleges: UCLA community college bibliography. *Community College Journal of Research and Practice, 31*(7), 607–614.

***This article is an annotated bibliography of scholarship on Asian Americans in community colleges. The references include educational reports, case studies, literature reviews, and other germane analyses. According to Liu (2007), "It is important to recognize the need to disaggregate amongst the diverse group of ethnicities and cultures that comprise the Asian American and Pacific Islander (AAPI) community and to dispel the 'model minority' myth" (p. 607).

Macaranas, F. M. (1980, April). *Social indicators of education and the model minority thesis.* Paper presented at the National Conference of the National Association for Asian and Pacific American Education, Honolulu, Hawai'i.

***Macaranas' (1980) conference paper focuses on social indicators of education while attempting to empirically test the model minority stereotype construction. Macaranas (1980) argues that high educational levels do not necessarily imply that Asian Americans have healthy wellbeings. This conference paper shares an *interdisciplinary* model focusing on educational and income variables to empirically isolate the negative factors inhibiting the full and equal participation of Asian Americans in the United States economy. Current researchers may consider revisiting some of the variables and constructs identified in Macaranas's (1980) model(s).

Pang, V. O. & Palmer, J. D. (2012). Model minorities and the model minorities myth. In J. A. Banks (Ed.), *Encyclopedia of diversity in education* (p. 1518). Thousand Oaks, CA: Sage Publications.

***Pang and Palmer's (2012) encyclopedia entry cites the two major seminal writings that spawned the creation of the model minority myth. One-page in length, this encyclopedia entry is concise and critical of the stereotype. Pang and Palmer (2012) write, "The model minority myth reinforces the belief that the United States is a country with color-blind meritocracy, and where hard work and educational achievements can earn individuals well-paying careers and higher social status" (p. 1518). According to the authors of this entry, the model minority stereotype is divisive. Pang and Palmer's (2012) entry concludes by providing its readers with three relevant further readings.

Tan, E. (2010). Asian boys and the model minority label. In S. R. Steinberg, M. Krehler, & L. Cornish (Eds.), *Boy culture: An encyclopedia* (pp. 54–57). Santa Barbara, CA: Greenwood.

***This encyclopedia entry indicates that articles published in the 1960s, especially William Petersen's (1966) "Success Story: Japanese American Style" fed the public's imagination that Asians were "model minorities" worthy of emulation. Tan's (2010) entry has many quotable thoughts; a few are as follows:

- "What these articles were contributing to was *the racializing of success.* Academic and educational success became outcomes solely associated with whiteness. Indeed the work ethic that the media praised Japanese and Chinese immigrants for was strangely similar to the Protestant work ethic" (Tan, 2010, p. 55, italics added).

- "As much as stereotypes limit they also mask and hide" (p. 56).
- "Educators might not be aware of how their acceptance of the model minority myth influences their interactions with students" (p. 56).
- "The words model minority do not only imply that Asian boys are smart, they also assume that Asian boys are lacking in creativity, independent thought, athletic ability, and social ease" (p. 57).
- "When we stop questioning stereotypes we begin to turn away from problems and consequently from the Asian youth who are dealing with the pressures of the model minority" (p. 57).

The largest contribution this entry makes is its clarity in showing that the model minority stereotype *racializes success*. This encyclopedia citation can be used by scholars who need references pertaining to the model minority stereotype's impact on Asian American males.

Tu, D. L. (2011). Model minority. In J. H. X. Lee & K. M. Nadeau (Eds.), *Encyclopedia of Asian American folklore and folklife* (pp. 69–71). Santa Barbara, CA: Greenwood Publishing.

***Tu's (2011) encyclopedia entry is three pages in length and talks about how the model minority stereotype is a form of folklore. The entry addresses the stereotype's shifts in racialization—in the 1960s it referred to the Japanese and Chinese and in the 1980s included most subgroups. The biggest contribution this encyclopedia entry makes, which other encyclopedia entries do not, is that it analyzes the functions of the model minority stereotype. For instance, according to Tu (2011) the model minority stereotype disciplines dissenting African Americans, provides evidence and support that America is not a racist country, and creates a racial hierarchy. Tu's (2011) entry concludes by providing four additional readings on the model minority stereotype—all of which are annotated in this book.

Yates, L. S. (2009). Model minorities. In H. T. Greene & S. L. Gabbidon (Eds.), *Encyclopedia of race and crime* (pp. 529–531). Thousand Oaks, CA: Sage Publications, Inc.

***Yates' (2009) entry links the model minority stereotype to invisible issues of violence and criminal activity that lurk within the supposed harmonious law-abiding Asian American population. Partially because, as Yates (2009) points out, "the model minority stereotype has resulted in the creation of unrealistic standards and social and psychological pressures among the Asian American population" (p. 529), Asian Americans experience myriad stigmatization and inequities, sometimes which drive them to commit criminal acts. The model minority stereotype is misleading, and according to Yates (2009), "related to the recent growing number of Asian American youth gangs and criminal activities in large cities and Chinatowns" (p. 530).

Wang, Y. & Shen, F. C. (2008). Model minority myth. In F. T. Leong (Ed.), *Encyclopedia of counseling* (Vol. 3, pp. 1211–1214). Thousand Oaks, CA: Sage Publications. Retrieved on March 28, 2012, from http://www.sagepub.com/healey-regc6e/study/chapter/encycarticles/ch09/WANGYU~1.PDF

***Wang and Shen's (2008) encyclopedia entry does a nice job at explaining how and why the model minority stereotype is actually part of a "set" of stereotypes that are supposedly uniquely Asian American. Their entry contains a concise and cogent summary of the otherwise imprecise and messy model minority myth.

REFERENCE

Takaki, R. T. (1998). *Strangers from a different shore: A history of Asian Americans.* Boston, MA: Little, Brown.

CHAPTER 7

MODEL MINORITY MOVIES AND MEDIA

This chapter looks at the ways in which Asian Americans are cast as model minorities in movies, audio, and visual media. Although initially I thought that there was not enough material to warrant a chapter, I decided to make an exception since there has not been a similar chapter or book on this topic. Suffice to say, this chapter illustrates an underexplored area of model minority stereotype research. In other words, with the exception of Darrel Hamamoto's (1994) *Monitored Peril: Asian Americans and the Politics of TV Representation,* scholars have not thoroughly analyzed the ways in which television and movies construct and promote the idea that Asian Americans are model minorities. Also keep in mind that the construction of Asian Americans as model minorities is related to their construction as "aliens" and "yellow perils."

Lin, J. (Director). (2002). *Better Luck Tomorrow* [Motion picture]. United States: MTV Films & Paramount Pictures.

***Better Luck* Tomorrow (2002) is a movie about over-achieving Asian-American high school students who engage in extra-curricular criminal activities. The movie problematizes many assumed model minority stereo-

The Model Minority Stereotype: Demystifying Asian American Success, pages 221–229.

typic characteristics of Asian Americans, mostly that Asian Americans do not engage in criminal activity.

The Center for Asian American Media (CAAM). [Non-profit organization]. http:// caamedia.org/

***The Center for Asian American Media (CAAM), according to its website, describes itself as follows:

> The Center for Asian American Media (CAAM) is a non-profit organization dedicated to presenting stories that convey the richness and diversity of Asian American experiences to the broadest audience possible. We do this by funding, producing, distributing and exhibiting works in film, television and digital media.

The work that CAAM does is extraordinarily important for the Asian American community; however, the organization has not fully examined the model minority stereotype in detail. This would be a great undertaking for the CAAM, especially given the hostility directed at Asian Americans (e.g., the Pete Hoekstra, U.S. Senate candidate political ad that was aired on the television during the Super Bowl; see Mak, 2012).

Schott, W. (Producer) & Tykwer, T., Wachowski, A., & Wachowski, L. (Directors). (2012). *Cloud Atlas* [Motion picture]. United States: Warner Brothers Pictures.

***Cloud Atlas* has been critiqued heavily for its use of "yellowface"—casting White actors as Asians (e.g., see Allen, 2012; Brooks, 2012; Habacon, 2012; Rosen, 2012).

Berman, B., Kahn, J., Moore, T., & Richman, A. (Producers) & Eastwood, C. (Director). (2008). *Gran Torino* [Motion picture]. United States: Warner Brothers Pictures.

***Gran Torino* portrays the Hmong as gangsters. Directed by Clint Eastwood, this movie has been critiqued to be racist and sexist in its portrayal of Hmong as the "other" (e.g., see Ward, 2011). Bee Vang, the lead Hmong actor from the movie said this about the film in an interview; "The thing is, the story can't take place without those Hmong characters, especially mine. But in the end, it's Walt [Clint Eastwood] that gets glorified. We fade out in favor of his heroism. I felt negated by the script and by extension in my assuming the role. It's almost like a non-role. Strange for a lead..." (Vang & Schein, 2010, p. 3).

Nakasako, S. (Producer & Director). (1998). *Kelly Loves Tony* [Motion picture]. United States: Public Broadcasting Service (PBS).

***Kelly Loves Tony* is a documentary directed by Spencer Nakasako about two Asian Americans who struggle to overcome obstacles, such as parenthood, in order to actualize their educations. The struggles they face are ones that proponents of the model minority stereotype often do not seem to believe exist.

Media Action Network for Asian Americans (MANAA). [Non-profit organization]. http://www.manaa.org

***MANAA is dedicated to monitoring the media and advocating balanced, sensitive, and positive coverage and portrayals of Asian Americans. They have an excellent website that contains many helpful resources.

Huens, M., James, B., Mariye, M., & Spence, W. (Producers) & Mariye, M. (Director). (2012). *Model Minority* [Motion picture]. United States: Nice Girls Films.

***L.A. teenagers survive the treacherous world of peer pressure, drug dealers, juvenile hall, and dysfunctional families. Kayla, an underprivileged Japanese American 16-year-old, endangers her promising future as an aspiring artist when she becomes involved with a drug dealer. *Model Minority* (2012) had its world premiere May 11 and May 15 at the 28th Annual Los Angeles Asian Pacific Film Festival. The movie's website is http://www.modelminoritymovie.com/.

Arboleda, T. & Price, D. L. P. (Producers). (2011). *Model Minority: Do the Math* [Documentary]. Available at https://www.youtube.com/watch?v=FxLVKROww7s

***Model Minority: Do the Math* reveals the impact of the model minority myth on the experiences and perspectives of Asian American (AA) college students. The myth is a complex and contradictory stereotype of Asian Americans as academic over-achievers. While many believe the stereotype is positive, it causes many problems. Asian Americans are overlooked for affirmative action and academic assistance. Tracked by parents, counselors, and social expectations to excel in math-intensive fields, despite their preferences, they struggle to balance personal goals and mental health. The myth diverts attention from systematic structural racism by emphasizing individualism and pitting AAs against other groups. Viewed as too competitive and taking over colleges, AAs face racial resentment, discrimination, and hate crimes. *Model Minority: Do the Math* overcomes misconceptions of AA students.

Hartlep, N. (2012). *Model Minority Myth Interview* [Interview]. WORT 89.9FM, August 7, 2012.

***This interview (http://www.wortfm.org/tag/nicholas-hartlep/) can be live-streamed or downloaded as a Podcast (http://redroom.com/member/nicholas-hartlep/media/audio/model-minority-stereotype-interview-wort-899-fm). On Tuesday, August 7, 2012, Cynthia Lin interviewed Dr. Nicholas Hartlep, a critical race theory scholar from the Illinois State University. Professor Hartlep discussed a critique he wrote regarding Rosalind S. Chou and Joe R. Feagin's book *The Myth of the Model Minority,* as well as this present book *The Model Minority Stereotype: Demystifying Asian American Success.* This interview can be used in a "flipped" high school or college classroom as an instructional approach: A reversed teaching model that delivers instruction at home through interactive, teacher-created videos and moves "homework" to the classroom.

Park, R. (Producer & Director). (2007). *Neverperfect* [Documentary]. United States: Single Drop Films.

***This incisive and provocative 65-minute documentary details *blepharoplasty* surgery and Asian Americans' quest for beauty. The movie follows the personal journey of Mai-Anh, a 27-year-old Californian Vietnamese American who ends up having double eyelid surgery. Several model minority scholars are interviewed on their thoughts about this cosmetic phenomenon. This documentary (distributed on DVD by The Cinema Guild) could be used in a gender studies course, as well as a critical media studies course. Anthropologists may find the documentary beneficial for their scholarly work too. The documentary does show Mai-Anh's surgery, so caution should be given in terms of the graphic nature of clips of this film. *Neverperfect* (2007) was awarded the following prizes in 2007: Silver Award at the Houston WorldFest International Film Festival; Official Selection at the American Psychological Association's Annual National Convention; Official Selection at the Asian Film Festival in Dallas, Texas; and Official Selection at the DC Asian Pacific American Film Festival.

Lal, P. (2012). *TEDTalk—Redefining "Model Minority"*

*** Prerna Lal is a law student at The George Washington University Law School. She was born in the Fiji Islands and came to the U.S. with her parents when she was 14. In 2011, on the tenth anniversary of 9/11, Prerna was awarded the Changemaker of the Year award from South Asian Americans Leading Together (SAALT). Lal's TEDTalk on the "model minority" is a useful media source for teaching about the model minority stereotype. Access the video here: http://www.youtube.com/watch?v=Q1RLnS2atsA&list=UUsT0YIqwnpJCM-mx7-gSA4Q&index=8.

California Newsreel (Producer). (2001). *Unnatural Causes...Is Inequality Making Us Sick?* [Documentary series]. United States: Public Broadcasting Service (PBS).

***Unnatural Causes* (2001) is a documentary series that explores racial and social inequalities in health. The documentary is chronicled in seven different episodes. Episode five, "Place Matters" tells of the health needs of Southeast Asian American immigrants and may be of interest to model minority scholars and academicians. In particular, Gwai Boonkeut, a refugee from Laos living in Richmond (a city in the San Francisco Bay Area) knows first-hand how living in a neglected neighborhood is bad for one's health.

This particular video clip is 29 minutes and is also available in an Asian Languages Edition (Cantonese, Mandarin, Hmong, Lao, and Vietnamese). The 29-minute segment can be used in K–12 and/or college level classrooms to facilitate a discussion about how the model minority stereotype implies that Asian Americans do not experience inequitable health outcomes, which impedes advocacy and healthcare for this population of people. The Asian Languages Edition could also be used in community classrooms or adult education courses for individuals who may not understand/speak English. The *Unnatural Causes* (2001) documentary DVD has a companion website that can be accessed here: http://www.unnaturalcauses.org/

Lee, A. (Director) & Hope, T., Lee, A., & Schamus, J. (Producers). (1993). *The Wedding Banquet* [Motion picture]. United States: MGM.

***The Wedding Banquet* showcases many racist stereotypes of Asian (Chinese) Americans. The film is about a gay Taiwanese immigrant man who marries a mainland Chinese woman to placate his parents and help her obtain a green card. His plan backfires when his parents arrive in the United States to plan his wedding banquet.

BUT VISUAL MEDIA IS NOT ALL THAT THERE IS: ASIAN AMERICANS IN PRINTED MEDIA

Visual media such as movies and television are important to examine, especially when they reinforce the widely accepted stereotype of Asians as model minorities. However, equally vexing is how printed media—such as cartoons and popular press covers—promote the idea that Asian Americans are universally successful. The following images capture the insidious ways that the model minority stereotype influences not only people, but policy, such as affirmative action.

In a collaboration between the National Portrait Gallery and the Smithsonian Asian Pacific American Program, "Portraiture Now: Asian American Portraits of Encounter" is an exhibition that attempts to break down the stereotypes of Asian Americans in contemporary as well as historical times. This exhibit was housed in the National Portrait Gallery, Smithsonian Institution and was held August 12, 2011 through October 14, 2012 (http://www.npg.si.edu/exhibit/encounter/). Attempts like this are important; artistic methodologies and artistic counterstories are important to debunk the model minority stereotype.

IMAGE 7.1.   Cartoon illustrating model minority stereotype.

IMAGE 7.2.   Cartoon illustrating Asian (Chinese) tiger parenting stereotype.

IMAGE 7.3.   Cartoon illustrating Asian American stereotype.
Secret Asian Man © 2005 Tak Toyoshima. Reprinted with permission of Tak Yoyoshima. Retrieved from:
http://webpages.scu.edu/ftp/mawong/modelminority/Images/foodcomic.gif

IMAGE 7.4.   Cartoon illustrating Asian American model minority stereotype.
Secret Asian Man © 2012 Gene Luen Yang. Reprinted with permission of Gene Luen Yang. Retrieved from:
http://geneyangabc.files.wordpress.com/2011/11/modelminority.jpg

IMAGE 7.5. Magazine cover illustrating model minority stereotype.
Retrieved from: http://abagond.files.wordpress.com/2008/05/time-asianamwhizkids.jpg

IMAGE 7.6. Magazine cover illustrating model minority stereotype.
Retrieved from: http://nakasec.org/blog/wp-content/files/2012/06/Doo-Yong-1.jpe

IMAGE 7.7.   Pictures illustrating athletic model minority stereotype of Jeremy Lin.
Retrieved from: http://colorlines.com/assets_c/2012/02/lin-sanity-ben-jerrys-thumb-640xauto-5416.jpg

CHAPTER 8

MODEL MINORITY NEWSPAPER ARTICLES

Chen, C. (2012, December 19). Asians: Too smart for their own good? *The New York Times* [op-ed]. Retrieved from http://www.nytimes.com/2012/12/20/opinion/asians-too-smart-for-their-own-good.html?_r=0

***Chen's (2012) op-ed discusses her thoughts about Asian Americans' prospects of gaining admission into the nation's top colleges and universities. She focuses on how Asian Americans are disadvantaged compared to White applicants when it comes to meritocratic college admissions. Although unintentional, Chen's (2012) writing reinforces the model minority myth, despite her precautionary statement:

> To be clear, I do not seek to perpetuate the "model minority" myth—Asian-Americans are a diverse group, including undocumented restaurant workers and resettled refugees as well as the more familiar doctors and engineers. Nor do I endorse the law professor Amy Chua's pernicious "tiger mother" stereotype, which has set back Asian kids by attributing their successes to overzealous (and even pathological) parenting rather than individual effort. (para 10)

It is unfortunate that Chen's writing reinforces the hegemonic understanding of Asian Americans as model minorities. I think that she, as an associate professor of sociology and director of the Asian American Studies Program at Northwestern should understand the consequences of her highlighting and the implications it holds for the stereotyping of Asian Americans.[1] This op-ed was published in print form in the following citation: [Chen, C. (2012, December 20). Asians: Too smart for their own good? *The New York Times*, p. A43.].

What "model minority" doesn't tell. (1998, January 3). *Chicago Tribune*. p. 18.

***This newspaper article points out that "as convenient as it may be to… stereotype…Asian-Americans as an overachieving, super-successful ethnic group…the truth is far more complex and disturbing" (*Chicago Tribune*, 1998, p. 18). It underscores this thesis by raising issues of Asian American poverty, differences in academic achievement, and disparate college aspirations among Asians of different subgroups. This is a reference that can be used in literature reviews for various scholarly writing and advocacy needs.

Cobb, K. (1991, November 27). Asian Americans reveal dark side of "model minority" stereotype. *The Houston Chronicle*, p. A27.

***Cobb's (1991) newspaper article discusses the "dark side" of the model minority stereotype. This includes using the model minority stereotype to argue that Asian Americans do not deserve affirmative action protection. It also includes mental illness, which often becomes an invisible issue for Asian Americans since they are believed to be model minorities. Lastly, according to Cobb (1991), "the delivery of medical and social services to Asian Americans based on the 'model minority' stereotype" (p. A27) becomes impacted as well. This newspaper article can be used in literature reviews.

Graham, J. (2009, April 2). Asian American suicides spark concern. *Chicago Tribune* [online]. Retrieved from http://newsblogs.chicagotribune.com/tri-age/2009/04/asian-american-suicides-spark-concern.html

***Graham (2009) writes about the high levels of suicide within the Asian American community. She also shares about how "many Asian American students feel compelled to live up their image as the 'model minority'—a stereotype that assumes Asian Americans are hard-working, academically and financially successful, and well-adjusted" (para. 15). Graham (2009) also cites Chicago's Asian American Suicide Prevention Initiative (AASPI) (Link to their website: http://aaspi.blogspot.com). This newspaper entry builds individuals' background knowledge about how the model minority

---

[1] For a more detailed examination of how Asian Americans are at times complicit, and perpetuate the model minority stereotype themselves, see Sakamoto, Takei, and Woo (2012) as well as Hartlep and Porfilio (2012).

stereotype may be connected with high levels of pressure, which sometimes may result in Asian Americans taking their own lives.

Kim, I. (2004, May 12). Shattering the myth: Asian youth face a harsh reality: The image of being a "model minority" masks the struggles of those who fail to fit the mold. *Newsday*, p. A49.

***Kim's (2004) short op-ed states that if you look at the model minority stereotype closely, you will quickly see that it's incorrect. There are many Asian American students who are suffering from absent parents, language barriers, acculturative stress, abuse, and drug addiction. This op-ed is brief and highlights the generational and cultural challenges that many Asian (refugees) Americans are facing in the United States.

Korn, P. (2012, September 27). Struggles of a model minority. *Portland Tribune*, pp. A1, A2. Retrieved from http://portlandtribune.com/pt/9-news/115868-struggles-of-a-model-minority%20%20

***Korn's (2012) newspaper article begins by noting the U.S. Congressional resolution to apologize for the 1882 Chinese Exclusion Act. Korn (2012) mostly discusses Asian Americans in the Portland, Oregon area. The article relates the stories and insights of one Asian American mother in Portland who fights the tiger mom image on a daily basis. It also suggests that the model minority is a narrow perception and that the Pew's survey *The Rise of Asian Americans* does not help the Asian American community. This newspaper article is a nice piece of model minority writing and raises many relevant and timely issues related to the myth. It can be used to supplement a literature review as well as to teach people that using Asian Americans as paragons of success is problematic.

Lewin, T. (2008, June 10). Report takes aim at "model minority" stereotype of Asian-American students. *The New York Times*, p. A18. Retrieved from http://www.nytimes.com/2008/06/10/education/10asians.html?_r=0

***Lewin's (2008) newspaper story reports on Robert Teranishi's report "Facts Not Fiction: Setting the Record Straight," which was published in 2008. Much of Lewin's (2008) *New York Times* article addresses issues of homogeneity, diversity, and the fact that the model minority stereotype is an incorrect characterization of the Asian American population. For complete access to the report, visit here: http://professionals.collegeboard.com/profdownload/08-0608-AAPI.pdf

Lewis, C. (1991, August 15). Asian-Americans and the "model minority" trap. *Chicago Tribune*, Section 1, p. 25. Retrieved from http://articles.chicagotribune.com/1991-08-15/news/9103280829_1_asian-american-chinese-americans-suicide-rate

***Lewis's (1991) newspaper story addresses the negative effect that the model minority stereotype has on Asian Americans. Says Lewis (1991), "Many live lives of quiet desperation" (p. 25). Lewis (1991) is referring to higher than average suicide rates among Asian American subgroups. He shares a story about Kio T. Konno, an excellent student who hung herself due to unusually high pressure to succeed. Lewis's (1991) newspaper article can be cited in literature reviews and can also be used in the classroom to begin conversations around the mental health needs of Asian Americans generally, and Asian American students specifically.

Muratsuchi, A. Y. (1989, May 3). Affirmative action and the "model minority." [op-ed]. *The Washington Post,* p. A26.

***Muratsuchi's (1989) op-ed feature responds to an op-ed written by George Will on April 16, 1989. Muratsuchi (1989) writes that Mr. Will perpetuates the idea that Asian Americans are model minorities. Writes Muratsuchi (1989), "Mr. Will only perpetuates such stereotypes by declaring Asian Americans to be 'the nation's model minority.' Respectable columnists such as Will should be informed that while Asian American students may seem to be 'storming the citadels of status,' they are also three times as likely as white students to not even complete elementary school" (p. A26). Muratsuchi (1989) goes on to write that "thirteen percent of the highest SAT scores were achieved by Asians in 1985, but 14 percent of the worst scores also went to Asians" (p. A26). This op-ed column documents that in the 1980s there were individuals who saw and understood how wrong-headed the model minority stereotype was, actively speaking out against its veracity. This document can be used in the secondary and post-secondary classroom in order to show that fact.

Navarette, R. (1989, May 28). Only "model minorities" need apply. *San Francisco Examiner,* p. 20/Z1.

***Navarette's (1989) newspaper article shares his experience applying to Harvard University in spring of 1985. Mr. Rubin Navarette was a senior at Harvard when this story was published. Although he never mentions Asians, he finishes his story by saying the following: "I can no longer turn my back on the hundreds of thousands of other Hispanic students who have been pushed aside by colleges intent on finding the 'model minority'" (p. 20), leaving readers to suspect that Hispanics are not the racial model minority, but that Asian Americans might well be.

Page, C. (1987, November 18). Prejudice follows prominence for a "model minority." *Chicago Tribune,* Section 1, p. 21.

***Page's (1987) newspaper article addresses the impact the model minority stereotype has on Asian Americans in the context of college admissions. Since Asian Americans are believed to be model minorities, they are also perceived to be taking over college campuses. This has resulted in discriminatory admission policies, ceilings, and quotas. Page (1987) introduces what he labels the Page Principal of Prejudice, which "holds that prejudice is 90 percent presence. The most prominent minority group in a community or region tends to bear the brunt of negative stereotypes, social rejection, and half-wit humor no matter who they may be" (p. 21.) Page's (1987) article can be used in concert with Nakanishi's (1989) "Quota on Excellence" *Change* article.

Page, C. (1986, July 30). Asian Americans: Our "model minority"? *Chicago Tribune*, p. 11.

***Page's (1986) newspaper article indicates that the model minority stereotype label is used by people who do not want to help minorities. According to Page (1986), "Asian Americans have a problem. Most minorities get discriminated against because they are not successful enough. Asian Americans get discriminated against because they are more successful than anyone else" (p. 11). Page (1986) shares a story about Kim Suyehiro, a freshman at the University of California at Berkeley who was a finalist in the Japanese American Citizens League oratorical contest. Page (1986) describes how Suyehiro discussed "Asian Americans: A Model Minority?" for which she won a prize. This newspaper article contains many useful and quotable statements. Page (1986) indicates that "Asian Americans can take great pride in their achievements. But labels like *'model minority'* are a dubious honor" (p. 11, italics added).

Pimental, B. (2001, August 5). Model minority image is a hurdle. *San Francisco Chronicle*, p. A25.

***Pimental, a *Chronicle* staff writer, documents several hurdles that stand in the way of Asian Americans fighting to be recognized as part of the mainstream. This short newspaper story discusses obstacles such as invisibility, being perceived as foreigners and/or spies, and homogenization. This newspaper article can be used in scholarly literature reviews since it is important to include not only peer-reviewed literature, but also mainstream media (this includes newspapers). It can also be used by scholars new to the field for locating other relevant literature (*viz.* looking up scholars cited in the article that do work on Asian American issues).

Rich, S. (1985, October 10). Asian Americans outperform others in school and work: Census data outlines "model minority." *Washington Post*, pp. A1 & A19.

***Rich's (1985) newspaper article discusses Asian Americans' supposed success based upon analysis of 1980 U.S. Census data. Representative of a classical writing on the model minority stereotype, Rich's (1985) story supports the validity of the model minority myth. For example, Rich (1989) writes that "Chinese Americans led the way in college attendance, with 60 percent of those between the ages of 20 and 24 enrolled in school" (p. A19). This newspaper article, like all model minority stereotype articles, is helpful in establishing a historical understanding of how Asian Americans were slowly re-cast from inassimilable aliens to model minorities.

Toth, R. C. (1977, October 17). Japanese in U.S. outdo Horatio Alger. *Los Angeles Times, 96,* pp. 10–11.

***This *Los Angeles Times* story reports on the supposed success that Japanese Americans were experiencing. Toth (1977) begins with this dubious observation: "Despite great odds, Japanese Americans have become the most successful racial minority in U.S. history" (p. 10). This comment sets the tone for the entire story. The argument Toth (1977) makes is that there is something distinct about being Japanese. He notes that the Japanese are becoming more-or-less fully assimilated. However, assimilation has its costs, since as Japanese become more Americanized or Westernized they experience more lifestyle problems. Thus, Toth (1977) extends the argument that Japanese cannot be assimilated *and* retain the Japanese traits that allow for their unheralded success. This *Los Angeles Times* article captures what was being reported in the late 1970s.

CHAPTER 9

CLASSICAL MODEL MINORITY ARTICLES

The citations provided in this chapter represent what I am classifying as "classical model minority" articles. It is important to understand that an overwhelming number of classical pieces rely on cultural explanations for Asian Americans' success. In fact, sometimes Asian Americans are thought to possess genetic differences that predispose them to academic success. As recently as the mid-1990s, authors have proposed that Asian Americans are genetically or biologically predisposed to be successful in academics. However, genetic and cultural explanations are dangerous.

Rushton (1995, pp. 166–168) asserted that Asian Americans are smart due to genetic and bodily characteristics. While African American men had small brain sizes, Asian American men had larger brain sizes. Brain size and penis size were inversely related: small and large, respectively for African Americans and large and small, respectively, for Asian Americans. Critics of Rushton will quickly point out that what he is espousing as "science" is actually "pseudo-science," otherwise known as eugenics. Thus, it is important to document classical pieces of writings that showcase what the proponents of the model minority stereotype believe. By reading what proponents write,

The Model Minority Stereotype: Demystifying Asian American Success, pages 237–253.
Copyright © 2013 by Information Age Publishing
All rights of reproduction in any form reserved.

opponents of the model minority stereotype will be better able to defuse such ludicrous and unfounded thoughts.

Allis, S. (1991, March 25). Kicking the nerd syndrome. *Time, 137*(12), 64–65.

***Allis' (1991) *Time* article, published in the "Education" section, points out that "four out of every five [Asian American] students are in public two- or four-year institutions rather than elite universities" (p. 64). Despite its intentions of refuting the model minority stereotype, "Kicking the Nerd Syndrome" reinforces it. It reinforces the construction because the counter-narratives it shares are ineffective. Writing that Asian Americans are pushing back against the stereotype is great, but in the process, Allis (1991), in effect, supports the notion that Asian Americans are in fact stereotypically smart. For instance, Allis (1991) shares that a senior at Harvard University made a conscious decision not to study science. But in the process, Allis (1991) also shares two facts that reinforce the model minority myth: (1) the student scored 1580/1600 on the SAT, and (2) he did not go to MIT, but rather attends Harvard now. Stories like Allis's (1991) are classical given that they—in effect (not intent)—support the model minority stereotype. This *Time* article also illustrates that the classical period of the model minority stereotype (read: when narratives supported the model minority stereotype) is not merely during the mid-to-late-1960s, but also continued on into the 1990s.

Bell, D. A. (1985, July 15 & 22). America's greatest success story: The triumph of Asian-Americans. *The New Republic, 193,* 24, 26, 28–31.

***Bell's (1985) article is written from a conservative point of view. At the time of publication, Bell was a graduate student in history at Princeton University. He addresses reasons why Asian Americans are faring well. His examples and assertions largely rely on "self-sufficiency" rationales that draw from cultural and familiar solidarity. In other words, Asians' values and culture promote hard work and achievement. The article points to indicators such as Ivy League school representation for support of the claim that Asian Americans are becoming more American and less minority. This article can be used in literature reviews, documenting classical views of Asian American success. Moreover, scholars whose work includes affirmative action and Asian Americans will find this article worthwhile to read. Bell's (1985) article also appears in *Current* [Bell, D. A. (1985, November). An Asian American success story: The triumph of Asian-Americans. *Current, 277,* 33–39.].

Brand, D. (1987, August 31). The new whiz kids. *Time, 130*(9), 3, 42–46, 49, 51.

***Brand's (1987) education article is the cover story. The story is briefly highlighted in the beginning of the periodical. It says this:

Just 2% of the population, they will be 14% of the new Harvard freshman class, 25% of Berkeley's. But the sky-high marks and superlatives are exacting a price: stress, a drop-out problem among the poorer and less gifted, even the specter of anti-Asian quotas at the best universities. Still, this is the most impressive generation of immigrants' children in decades. (p. 3)

Brand's (1987) story is much like Quindlen's (1987, see below) in that although it does cover struggles and reasons why the model minority stereotype is problematic, it nevertheless reinforces the model minority stereotypical argument. The story's title, "The New Whiz Kids" and its subtitle "Why Asian Americans are Doing So Well, and What it Costs Them" foists the fable that Asian American students succeed despite the odds. For example, the article includes seven stories of Asian Americans—*Satia Tor*, a Cambodian 19-year-old admitted to Stanford; *Lucia and Maria Ahn*, 18-year-old South Korean sisters who participate in Julliard's pre-college musical program; *Angie Tang*, an 18-year-old undocumented student from Hong Kong who was admitted to Phillips Exeter Academy in New Hampshire; *Hoang Nhu Tran*, a 22-year-old Vietnamese Rhodes Scholar who aspires to attend Harvard Medical College; *Michael Rendore De Guzman*, a 14-year-old Filipino who was admitted to Chicago's highly competitive Lane Technical High School; and *Chua Pham*, a 17-year-old Vietnam escapee who was valedictorian of Abramson High School, received multiple scholarships, and begins pre-med studies at Vanderbilt University—that all serve as paragon reinforcement for the model minority stereotype. Brand's (1987) story also quotes some of the same material that Quindlen's (1987) article did, like the success of the Kuo family. Many useable quotes and ideas are contained in this *Time* story (e.g., references made to the notion of segmented assimilation, Asian American affirmative action cases, and biological/genetic and/or cultural explanations for academic success, etc.). This story should be cited in scholarly literature reviews given that it represents a classical 1980s narration of the model minority stereotype.

Butterfield, F. (1986, August 3). Why Asians are going to the head of the class. *The New York Times*, p. EDUC18.

***Butterfield's (1986) story appears in *The New York Times* and addresses Asian American academic success. This should be considered a "classical" piece of model minority literature given that it highlights Asian American success through popularly used indicators of academic achievement (e.g., number of recipients of the Westinghouse Talent Search Award, number of Harvard admissions, grade point averages, etc.). According to this story, culture (Confucian) and family values (filial piety) are largely the forces that help explain why Asian Americans tend to be more academically successful than Whites and other non-White minorities. Says Butterfield (1986), "Whites have withdrawn from courses that have a large number of

Asians because they feared their standings on the grading curve would suffer" (p. 18). This article should be cited whenever writing about the model minority stereotype, especially when referencing the 1980s period during the myth's evolution and transformation.

Dillin, J. (1985, October 10). Asian-Americans: Soaring minority. *The Christian Science Monitor*. Retrieved from http://www.csmonitor.com/1985/1010/apop. html

***Dillin's (1985) *Christian Science Monitor* article begins by claiming that Asian Americans are America's model minorities. It also implies that Asian immigrants are "good" minorities, since they are "legal," leaving the reader to infer that "illegal" immigration is problematic. For instance, Dillin (1985) writes that since 1980, nearly half of all legal immigrants have come from Asia. The article states that family is responsible for the success that Asian Americans, a "soaring minority," have experienced. According to the reporting of Dillin (1985), success is indexed in terms of SAT scores, socioeconomic indicators (i.e. family income), and educational attainment and achievement. This *Christian Science Monitor* article is a textbook example of how Asian Americans were covered in the popular press during the 1980s and thus should be cited in scholarship on the model minority stereotype.

Givens, R. (1984, April 15). The drive to excel: Strong families and hard work propel Asian-Americans to the top of the class. *Newsweek On Campus*, 4–13.

***Givens' (1984) "The Drive to Excel" describes Asian Americans from a classically model minority perspective. Writes Givens (1984), "In the end, most authorities conclude, the success of Asian-Americans can be traced to one major factor: hard work" (p. 13). This story, which appeared in *Newsweek on Campus,* shares images that are stereotypically associated with Asian Americans, such as the piano, violin, and pictures of graduates donning their regalia and mortarboards. Another quote that illustrate the writer's beliefs is as follows:

> On one issue, no one disagrees—the willingness of Asian-American students to pay almost any price to get ahead. With Asian-Americans in a class, "you've got some competition," says Georgetown physics Prof. Joseph McClure. "They'll work you into the ground. They aren't out on Saturday night getting drunk—they're hitting the books." Even when they lay down the books, Asian-Americans seem not to overlook the academic. (pp. 7–8)

Givens' (1984) article may have inspired Quindlen's (1987) *New York Times Magazine* article by the same title. This *Newsweek On Campus* story should be cited as an example of 1980s classical model minority stereotypic journalism.

Graubard, S. G. (1988, January 29). Why do Asian pupils win those prizes? *The New York Times,* p. A35.

***Graubard's (1988) *New York Times* story discusses the success that Asians in New York have had in winning the prestigious Westinghouse Science Award. According to Graubard (1988), when considering Asian success, one must look at economic and familial factors. Graubard (1988) cites examples of more affluent Asians families capitalizing on their own sociocultural and socioeconomic capital in order to best position their student, such as calling a Massachusetts Institute of Technology professor for assistance on a science project. Cited in much model minority stereotype work, Graubard's "Why Do Asian Pupils Win Those Prizes" illustrates the discourse of the model minority stereotype during the late 1980s.

Hadar, L. (2012, April 3). Latest example of a success story—Korea-born doctor's nomination as World Bank Chief highlights Asian-Americans' contributions in various fields in the US. *The Business Times.*

***This op-ed appears in the "views and opinions" section of *The Business Times* and highlights Dr. Jim Yong Kim, who was named the president of the World Bank. Two quotations from Hadar (2012) are sufficient to indicate why this article is classical model minority:

> Dr. Kim, who was born in Seoul in 1959 and moved with his family to the United States when he was a child, who was *educated at Harvard* and who has *served as president of Dartmouth College* in New Hampshire for several years, is also the most recent example of the *success story of the rising Asian-American community.* (para. 2, italics added)

And

> It may be considered a stereotype, but based on overwhelming evidence of their high household income (and low incarceration rate) and educational and professional achievements by comparison to other minorities and the declining white majority, it is difficult not to come to the conclusion that *Asian-Americans are, indeed, a 'model minority.'* (para. 6, italics added)

Hadar's (2012) writing also includes positive references to Amy Chua's (2011) book *Battle Hymn of the Tiger Mother.* This op-ed should be evidence that, despite it being false, many individuals still buy into the model minority stereotype.

Hirschman, C. & Wong, M. G. (1986). The extraordinary educational attainment of Asian-Americans: A search for historical evidence and explanations. *Social Forces, 65*(1), 1–27.l

***Hirschman and Wong (1986) sought to examine Asian Americans' extraordinary educational attainment through an analysis of historical evidence using structural explanations. Based largely on longitudinal analyses of cohorts contained in U.S. decennial census data, Hirschman and Wong (1986) point out that interpretation is a complex task. The authors first note that the Chinese were the first to come to the United States, where they initially worked in gold mines in California. The Japanese were the second major Asian American group to enter the United States. Filipinos were the third group to come to the United States; many worked on sugar plantations in Hawaii. Hirschman and Wong (1986) provide charts and historical trends in educational attainment of native-born Asian Americans. According to their analyses, changes in occupational structures provided incentives for continued schooling, which may explain Asian Americans' high levels of educational attainment. Hirschman and Wong (1986) point out how restrictive immigration also influenced Asian American educational attainment: "Ironically, the racist character of U.S. immigration policy toward Asia, prior to 1965, may have strengthened the resources of the Asian communities in the U.S. for educational and economic advancement." (p. 10). Hirschman and Wong (1986) later state that "the selective character of the immigrant stream strengthened the Asian-American community in a way that probably led to higher educational expectations for their children" (p. 10). The historical picture painted through Hirschman and Wong's (1986) analysis is that the educational attainment of the Chinese continued to increase during the postwar era, while that of Filipinos lost ground. This article is an important contribution to the model minority literature since it provides evidence that contemporary Asian American educational attainment can be linked to historical factors such as the restrictive immigration policies of the United States and a "middleman thesis" of upward social mobility through the prioritization on education.

Kasindorf, M. (1982, December 6). Asian-Americans: A "model minority." *Newsweek,* 39, 41–42, 51.

***Kasindorf's (1982) *Newsweek* article represents a significant look at how the press views Asian Americans given that 1982 represented the centennial year of the Chinese Exclusion Act of 1882. Despite giving facts or statistics that can be used to falsify the fable of Asian American success (e.g., Connie Chung, the CBS TV newscaster, comes from a family background that is socially privileged; there are poor refugee Asians who are suffering, facing continuing problems, and socially dependent on welfare programs), Kasindorf's (1982) article largely reinforces the model minority stereotype. The article relies on "cultural" explanations for Asian Americans' prowess and performance in school, on string instruments such as the violin, and within the larger society. The narrative this article tells is one of Asian triumph over obstacles. This article is conservatively written and supports the model minority thesis. For these reasons, it is important for model minority scholars to read and cite in their scholarly work. Undergraduate students could read this in educational seminars centered on the topic of the model minority stereotype.

Kim, R. Y. (2006). *God's new whiz kids?: Korean American evangelicals on campus.* New York, NY: New York University Press.

***Kim's (2006) book, according to NYU Press's website (http://nyupress. org/books/book-details.aspx?bookid=10096):

> In the past twenty years, many traditionally white campus religious groups have become Asian American. Today there are more than fifty evangelical Christian groups at UC Berkeley and UCLA alone, and 80% of their members are Asian American. At Harvard, Asian Americans constitute 70% of the Harvard Radcliffe Christian Fellowship, while at Yale, Campus Crusade for Christ is now 90% Asian. Stanford's Intervarsity Christian Fellowship has become almost entirely Asian. *God's New Whiz Kids?* focuses on second-generation Korean Americans, who make up the majority of Asian American evangelicals, and explores the factors that lead college-bound Korean American evangelicals—from integrated, mixed race neighborhoods—to create racially segregated religious communities on campus. Kim illuminates an emergent "made in the U.S.A." ethnicity to help explain this trend, and to shed light on a group that may be changing the face of American evangelicalism.

The book's table of contents can be found here: http://www.nyupress. org/webchapters/0814747906toc.pdf. Kim's (2006) book can be used in concert with the writings of Busto (1996), Ecklund (2005), and Muse (2005) in order to see intersections between Christianity and the construction of a religious model minority stereotype.

Kristof, N. D. (2006, May 14). The model students. *The New York Times.* [op-ed], p. WK13. Retrieved from http://www.nytimes.com/2006/05/14/ opinion/14kristof.html?_r=0

***In this opinion piece, Kristof (2006) writes, "Increasingly in America, stellar academic achievement has an Asian face" (p. WK13). He attributes the academic success of Asian Americans to filial piety and Confucianism. Says Kristof (2006), "If I'm right, the success of Asian-Americans is mostly about *culture*, and there's no way to transplant culture" (p. WK13, italics added). This op-ed is verifiably a classical model minority piece of writing.

Lord, L. & Linnon, N. (1988, March 14). What puts the whiz in whiz kids. *U.S. News & World Report, 104*(1), 48–58.

***Lord and Linnon's (1988) article is a classic in that it highlights the pursuit and attainment of the Westinghouse Science Talent Search Award. Are Asian Americans predisposed to winning the prestigious prize? According to Lord and Linnnon (1988), it is not heredity but rather hard work that is necessary to win first place. Lord and Linnon's (1988) article provides tables and profiles of the schools and students who have won the prize present and past. Lord and Linnon (1988) write, "The two schools that do best in the Westinghouse Science Talent Search—Bronx High School of Science and Stuyvesant High in Manhattan—don't have the problems that plague the average school. For starters, their student are motivated—*40 percent are of Asian descent*—and feel lucky to be there" (p. 57, italics added). This *U.S. News & World Report* article implies that hard work leads to Asian American success, further implying that Asians feel lucky to be able to attend good schools. This is a necessary citation in literature reviews.

Matthews, J. (1988, June 15). Asians make "average" school academic giant. *Montreal Gazette*, pp. A1, A7.

***Matthews' (1988) newspaper article appears in the *Montreal Gazette* and highlights Alhambra High School, a small school located in Alhambra, a small suburb of Los Angeles. Matthews (1988) highlights the many awards and competitions that Alhrambra High School students have won, pointing out that Asians are contributing to the school's overall success. The story's headline, coupled with a photograph of "Eastern" looking Asians atop a caption that reads "Calculus class at Alhambra High School, where advanced-math classes are common" reinforces the imagery that Asians are somehow academically superior to other students (namely Whites and Blacks). This newspaper article points out that "in the new wave of immigration now flooding the United States' western cities, Alhambra High— through an accident of geography and real-estate promotion—has found itself serving the largest suburban Asian community in the United States. Its student body is 54 per cent Asian, one of the highest concentrations in the U.S. anywhere outside Hawaii" (Matthews, 1988, p. A1). This newspaper article is a textbook example of classical 1980s reporting on Asian Americans and the model minority stereotype. This newspaper article is a source to cite classical writings on Asian Americans.

McGurn, W. (1991, June 24). The silent minority. *National Review, 43*, 19–20.

***McGurn's (1991) *National Review* article showcases the Republican party's attempt to recruit Asian Americans into its ranks. The argument is made that Asian Americans, who are successful, ought to align with the Republican Party. According to the article, a "Filipino high-school senior ranked at the top of her class with a better-than-perfect 4.5 grade-point average was not accepted to Berkeley, while others in her class with lower test scores and GPAs were admitted" (pp. 19–20). The gist of McGurn's editorial is that Asian Americans are portrayed as silent minorities insofar as they are quiet and diligent workers. This makes them patriotic and their success heroic. Stories such as "The Silent Minority" document the mainstream's perception of Asian Americans and their attendant successes.

Michaels, M. (1985, June 2). Where the family comes first. *Parade Magazine,* 4–6.

***Michaels' (1985) story is published in *Parade Magazine,* a weekly magazine given out in various newspapers through out the country. Michaels (1985) reports on Koreans in America who have "succeeded." Michaels (1985, p. 4) says,
Some measures of the immigrant parents' success:

- According to the 1980 census, the median income for White families was $20,835; for Asian American families, $22,713.
- Among Asian-American families, 8.5 percent earned $50,000 or more, vs. 6.2 percent among White families.
- Asian-Americans (both sexes) had lower unemployment rates than Whites.
- Asian-Americans are also better educated. Among those 25 or older, 32.5 percent completed at least four years of college; the comparable figure for White Americans is 17.2 percent. And 75 percent of Asian-Americans are high school graduates, compared with 69 percent of Whites.

Michaels (1985) goes on to make the following appraisal: "To appreciate the astounding success of Asian immigrants in this country is to remember that as recently as World War II, thousands of Japanese-Americans were interned in prison camps in California" (p. 5). "Where the Family Comes First" highlights Asian American (notably Korean) success, which makes it representative of classical "model minority" journalism. Further evidence can be seen in Michaels' (1985) gloss of Asians' achievements:

Seven of the 40 finalists for the 1985 Westinghouse Science Talent Search were Asian. At Julliard, New York's noted school for the arts, 10 percent of the enrollment is Asian. At major graduate schools of business, such as Harvard and Stanford, there has been a disproportionate representation of Asians for almost a decade. At Stuyvesant High School in New York—one of the most selective in the country, where nearly 10,000 applicants competed last year for 750 seats in the freshman class—about 31 percent of the students are Asian, although Asians represent less than 2 percent of the population. (p. 5)

This piece of classical model minority scholarship ought to be cited in reviews of literature for scholarly writing, teaching, and learning. The story indicates that "after only one generation in this country, Asian-Americans are now a 'model minority'" (Michaels, 1985, p. 5).

Neimark, E. D. (1988, February 12). The new Protestant ethic is the Asian ethic. *The New York Times* [Letter to the editor], p. A34.

***In Neimark's (1988) op-ed she proposes that a likely explanation for Asian Americans' success is their work ethic. A professor of psychology at Rutgers University, Neimark cites Asian American students' high mathematics achievement to support the scholarly work of University of Michigan professor Harold Stevenson. Neimark (1988) posits that, instead of a *Protestant ethic*, people consider an *Asian ethic*. Demonstrably false in its premise, this op-ed shows the major line of reasoning in the 1980s toward Asian American success. Neimark's (1988) writing can be used in concert with the writings of Gerald W. Bracey in the late 1990s and 2000s, which remain largely the same (e.g., see Bracey, 1999, 2005).

Oxnam, R. B. (1986). Why Asians succeed here. *The New York Times Magazine*, 89–92.

***Author Robert B. Oxnam at the time of this publication was president of the Asia Society, a non-profit cultural and educational organization based in New York. While not entirely "classical"—the article is not entirely one-sided—the article does focus on why Asians succeed in America. Oxnam (1986) discusses how Asian Americans (and Asian immigrants) have gained middle-class status largely due to their modesty, hard work, discipline, and devotion to work. This article does not go anywhere per se; rather, the article addresses many large issues without clarifying much of anything. This results in readers simply leaving with the general impression that Asian Americans are successful.

Page, C. (2007). Defining a new "model minority." *Oakland Tribune*. [op-ed].

***Page's (2007) piece appears in the opinion section of the *Oakland Tribune*. Page (2007) offers commentary on the fact that African immigrants appear to be successfully gaining admission into Harvard University. As a result, Page (2007) says "that [fact] defies the usual stereotypes of Asian Americans as the only 'model minority'" (para 3). Page's (2007) newspaper article can be used with the scholarship of others, like Diouf-Kamara (1997), Kaba (2008), and Fuller (2012) in order to build arguments that Asian Americans are not alone. In other words, Asian Americans are not the only ones who can be racialized as a model minority.

Petersen, W. (1966, January 6). Success story: Japanese American style. *The New York Times Magazine*, 20–21, 33, 36, 38, 40.

***Petersen's (1966) article—also published as [Petersen, W. (1970). Success story: Japanese style. In M. Kurokawa (Ed.), *Minority responses* (pp. 169–178). New York, NY: Random House.]—describes how the Japanese in America are doing well, despite being discriminated against. The article compares and contrasts the success and failures of Japanese and African Americans, respectively, pointing out the supposed differences between the two:

But a Negro who knows no other homeland, who is as thoroughly American as any Daughter of the American Revolution, has no refuge when the United States rejects him. Placed at the bottom of this country's scale, he finds it difficult to salvage his ego by measuring his worth in another currency. The Japanese, on the contrary, could climb over the highest barriers our racists were able to fashion in part because of their meaningful links with an alien culture. (Petersen, 1966, p. 40)

The most commonly cited quotation from this article is the following: "By any criterion of good citizenship that we choose, the Japanese Americans are better than any other group in our society, including native-born whites" (Petersen, 1966, p. 21). However, readers of this *New York Times Magazine* article should also read "Chapter 3: War Against Japanese America" (pp. 64–96) in Darrel Hamamoto's (1994) *Monitored Peril: Asian Americans and the Politics of TV Representation* since it does a nice job at clarifying Petersen's intentions, which—to be frank—were to demonize African Americans and make it appear as if America was truly a meritocratic and open society, not racist and bigoted.

Quindlen, A. (1987, February 22). The drive to excel. *The New York Times Magazine,* 32–40. Retrieved from http://www.nytimes.com/1987/02/22/magazine/ the-drive-to-excel.html?pagewanted=all&src=pm

***Quindlen's (1987) *New York Times Magazine* story "The Drive to Excel" shadows the life and educational success of David Kuo, a 16-year-old Bronx High School of Science student who at the time this story was published, "had been selected one of the top 40 young scientists in America" (Quindlen, 1987, p. 32). Quindlen's (1987) story documents Kuo's already successful family—pointing out that "the Kuos had become the first family in the history of the [Westinghouse Science Talent Search] competition to have a child in the Westinghouse finals for three consecutive years" (p. 32). Kuo's father was a surgeon in Kaohsiung, Taiwan; his mother was a nurse. This article is a textbook example of classical reporting on Asian Americans and the model minority stereotype: although it presents a cursory view of Asian American success (i.e., due to structural relativism, cultural and familial values, and being children of "brain-drain" immigrants, etc.), it nevertheless focuses on arguments that reinforce the model minority myth. By narrowly defining academic success, Quindlen reinforces Asian American students as model minorities. For instance, Quindlen (1987) writes the following (which is true), but which inevitably reduces Kuo to being academically extraordinary:

Each morning, David takes the express bus for the 45-minute ride from Queens to the Bronx. Most nights, he does not finish studying until after midnight; two days a week he does not even return home until after 8 P.M., because he is taking graduate courses in combinatorial math and introduction to math analysis at New York University's Courant Institute. (p. 36)

Quindlen's (1987) story classically reifies the notion that Asian American students are all mathematical and scientific giants. This *New York Times Magazine* article can be cited in literature reviews as well as be assigned in high school or college classrooms in order to compare and contrast contemporary perceptions of Asian American students with those perceptions of the past.

Ramirez, A. (1986, November 24). America's super minority. *Fortune, 104*, 148–149, 152, 156, 160, 161.

***Ramirez's (1986) piece presents Asian Americans as a "super" minority. His opening paragraph says this: "Asian Americans have wasted no time laying claim to the American dream. They are smarter and better educated and make more money than everyone else. Now they are vaulting the last obstacles that stand between them and this country's corner offices" (Ramirez, 1986, p. 148). The imagery that is conjured up when reading Ramirez's (1986) journalism is one of hyperbole. Asian Americans are presented passively and as if almost all are successful. Much energy is spent on highlighting why Asian Americans are successful, such as assimilating into dominant White America. For instance, Ramirez (1986), when addressing what Indochinese refugees could do to become more successful, writes, "Indochinese refugees may eventually solve their problem themselves by becoming assimilated" (p. 156). Ramirez's (1986) journalism serves to blame Asian Americans for being the victims of glass ceilings. Writes Ramirez (1986), "Asian Americans sabotage themselves because they are culturally conditioned to be humble" (p. 161) and "to get promotions Asian Americans have to learn more about promoting themselves" (p. 161). All in all, this article serves as an example of how the model minority stereotype has evolved. Ramirez's (1986) *Fortune* story represents the 1980s quite well. This is an important document to know about and read, since it should be included in literature reviews whenever discussions of the model minority stereotype come about.

Reglin, G. L. & Adams, D. R. (1990). Why Asian-American high school students have higher grade point averages and SAT scores than other high school students. *High School Journal, 73*, 143–149.

***Reglin and Adams' (1990) article examined whether or not there were cultural differences that could explain Asian American high school students' higher grade point averages and SAT scores. Results of their survey study are classical model minority stereotypic insofar as it is suggested that Asian American parents and Asian culture contribute to higher Asian American high school student achievement. The study participants (29

Asian Americans and 70 non-Asian Americans) were drawn from a high school in Mecklenberg County in North Carolina. Reglin and Adams' (1990) article includes their questionnaire, which other researchers can use in order to invalidate their findings that Asian Americans are uniquely destined to achieve academically compared to non-Asian Americans. Their article does not include much information regarding its sample. Neither are statistics shared in tabular format, making it difficult to follow their statistical analyses.

Roberts, S. (1985, December 19). Amazing Asians: The secret of their academic success. *The Columbia Flier, 18*(28), 38–41.

***Roberts' (1985) article shares several examples of Asian American high school and college students who are succeeding academically. The article is a classic example of 1980s model minority reporting in that it highlights supposedly "cultural" attributes, like Confucianism and patience, as the reasons Asian Americans are successful in the classroom. The story shares the grisly journey that Vietnamese refugees have made in order to live in the United States. Roberts' (1985) four-page article includes several photographs of Asian American students in stereotypical poses: a young Chinese girl writing Chinese characters with black ink and paintbrush (under which the headline reads "Amazing Asians: The Secret of Their Academic Success") and another girl poised with her violin (Katherine Wu, a 1985 U.S. Presidential Scholar). Despite highlighting the struggles that Asian American students face, stories like Roberts' (1985) solidify the stereotypical image of Asian academic success in readers' minds.

Seligman, D. (1991, April 15). Is America smart enough? *National Review, 43*(6), 24–31.

***Seligman's (1991) "Is America Smart Enough?" is the cover story of this *National Review* edition. On the cover, below *National Review*, the magazine reads as follows: "If You're So Smart…How Come You're Not Japanese?" This *National Review* article is a classical representation of the Asian model minority stereotype since it advances an extremely nationalistic perspective of intelligence (IQ), namely the argument that Japanese are more intelligent than White Americans. The article is nationalistic insofar as it emphasizes the East-West IQ gap. Seligman (1991) concludes by writing that there is no "reason to believe American IQs are gaining on those of the East Asians" (p. 31). This article was published in the early 1990s and can be used along with 1980s writing when discussing how the ascendancy of the Japanese led to issues such as Jap-bashing and the death of individuals like Vincent Chin, who was thought to be Japanese by his murderers (Wu, 2012).

Sheppard, R. (1992, February 3). Kitchen table the key to success. *The Globe and Mail,* p. A11.

***Sheppard's (1992) commentary is published in the (Toronto based) Canadian newspaper *The Globe and Mail* and addresses how Indochinese immigrant children are succeeding in school. Citing a scholarly study, Sheppard (1992) discusses how these Asian American children are resisting assimilating, opting for maintaining their cultural and heritage practices. This newspaper article can be used with other scholarly writing on segmented assimilation, as well as "immigrant optimism."

Still, T. (1998, March/April). Whiz kid. *Brown Alumni Magazine,* p. 17

***This article found in the *Brown Alumni Magazine* highlights Bobby Jindal, at the time a Rhodes Scholarship recipient and Brown alumna. Still (1998) discusses Jindal's experience being an Asian Indian and being confronted about why all Asians are so smart. The story highlights the success Jindal had as a young politician at the tender age of 27. This story is interesting since it highlights Jindal, a well-known Asian Indian, who is, as of this writing, the Republican Governor of Louisiana.

Ueda, R. (1989). False modesty: The curse of Asian American success. *The New Republic, 201*(1), 16–17.

***Ueda's (1989) article appears in the July 3, 1989 edition of *The New Republic* and can only be interpreted as a pro-model minority article. Although Ueda (1989) devotes considerable attention to why the model minority stereotype may in fact be empirically invalid, he concludes his article with two untenable statements that demonstrate his personal and professional ideology. The first statement is, "Many ordinary Asian Americans have embraced the model image not out of any desire to placate whites, but because they believe it" (Ueda, 1989, p. 17), while the second is, "The model minority image may be imperfect, but many Asian Americans feel that it's not a bad place to start" (Ueda, 1989, p. 17). Both of those dubious remarks serve to invalidate other issues that Ueda (1989) addressed, such as the following: (1) "The affluence attained by Asian American households tells the wrong part of the story" (Ueda, 1989, p. 16); (2) "Today Asian American advocacy groups, far from taking pride in group success, criticize it [the model minority stereotype] as a form of racial subordination" (Ueda, 1989, p. 16); and (3) "Liberal and radical Asians thus hastened to defy the image of successful Asian assimilation and expose it as just another form of majority oppression" (Ueda, 1989, p. 17). This article is an important document to include in literature reviews in that it documents the prevailing attitude toward the model minority stereotype in the late 1980s.

U.S. News & World Report. (1966, December 26). Success story of one minority group in the U.S., 73–76.

***This particular *U.S. News & World Report* article embodies many of the classical mental images associated with Asian Americans that are, alas, contemporarily alive and well: (1) their low rates of committing crimes; (2) their strict parental discipline; and (3) their seemingly natural disposition to work hard and to be obedient to family, elders, and their superiors. This article affirms the model minority myth that Asian Americans are industrious and law-abiding citizens who work diligently to overcome their own individual and collective trials and tribulations in order to get ahead in American society. A signature and defining characteristic of the myth is its demonization of Black and Brown minorities by vilifying their use of social and welfare services. This discursive and rhetorical opposition to "welfare queens" begins immediately: "At a time when it is being proposed that hundreds of billions be spent to uplift Negroes and other minorities, the nation's 300,000 Chinese-Americans are moving ahead on their own—with no help from anyone else" (p. 73). It is clear that this article and the discourse it promulgates serve to divide Asian Americans and Whites from other minioritized groups. It is also clear, given the article's usage of the terms "Negroes" and "Orientals," that this article is written from an extremely important evolutionary/historical time period (the 1960s). Since this piece is written from a classical and/or pro-model minority stereotype point of view, many quotes can be extracted for use in scholarly writing. A few of the most salient and significant examples are as follows:

> Few Chinese-Americans are getting welfare handouts—or even want them. (p. 73)

> What you find, back of this remarkable group of Americans, is a story of adversity and prejudice that would shock those now complaining about the hardships endured by today's Negroes. (p. 73)

> But the large majority [of Chinese Americans] are moving ahead by applying the traditional virtues of hard work, thrift and morality. (p. 74)

> The Chinese people here will work at anything. I know of some who were scholars in China and now are working as waiters in restaurants. That's the stopgap for them, of course, but the point is that they're willing to do something—they don't sit around moaning. (p. 74)

And

> It must be recognized that the Chinese and other Orientals in California were faced with even more prejudice than faces the Negro today. We haven't stuck Negroes in concentration camps, for instance,...as we did the Japanese in World War II. (p. 76)

This classic article can and should be read by undergraduates and graduates in foundations and/or sociology of education courses. Many of the quotes above can be used in scholarly writing that attempts to illustrate how the model minority stereotype is used as a wedge to separate the mainstream (Whites) from the margins (non-Whites).

Walsh, J. (1993, Fall). The perils of success: Asians have become exemplary immigrants, but at a price. *Time*, 55–56.

***Walsh's (1993) special issue in *Time* focuses on the image that Asians in America have become successful. Despite the title, readers are left thinking that Asian Americans are in fact successful and doing well. The story begins and ends with an attitude that supports the idea that Asian Americans are model minorities. It is only in the middle that readers are exposed to the notion that the model minority stereotype has negative implications. For instance, with remarks like the one that follows, it is little wonder why the general public continues to believe in the existence of an Asian American model minority: "As a rule, Asians in America have reflected extremely well, especially those who have drawn from the wellsprings of the older civilizations of India, China, Japan, and Korea" (Walsh, 1993, p. 55).

Williams, D. A. (1984, April 23). A formula for success. *Newsweek*, 77–78.

***Williams's (1984) *Newsweek* article is a classical piece. Although he notes that the stereotype that Asian Americans are successful—the model minority myth—has negative social and mental health consequences for Asian Americans, he ends his story by writing the following: "To the extent that 'minority' means 'educationally disadvantaged minority,' many Asians, in fact, no longer qualify. That might be the sort of disadvantage that any group striving for recognition and equality would welcome" (p. 78). This serves to delegitimize the concern that Asian Americans remain disadvantaged. By highlighting so many examples of extraordinary Asian American student success stories, coupled with the title "A Formula for Success," Williams (1984) effectively paints Asian Americans as model minorities. Meanwhile, by relying on cultural explanations for Asian American student success, Williams (1984) reinforces the commonly held cultural argument for Asian American student exceptionalism. Writes Williams (1984), "The success of Asian-Americans is rooted in a traditional reverence for learning in Asian culture, the fierce support of family and, in some cases, a head start at home" (p. 77). Therefore, this *Newsweek* article serves as a historical marker for the cultural thesis that is a model minority stereotype antecedent. This article can be used in literature reviews as well as for teaching/learning the sociology of the model minority stereotype.

Yin, X. (2000, May 7). The two sides of America's "model minority." *The Los Angeles Times*, pp. M1 & M6.

***Yin's (2000) news story addresses the model minority stereotype through the frame of "uptown" Asian Americans and "downtown" Asian Americans. The uptown Asian Americans are wealthier and more concerned with the glass ceiling, while the downtown Asian Americans struggle in silence in the inner city. Yin (2000) highlights the bipolar characteristic of the Asian American community, pointing out that the Immigration Act of 1965 radically impacted Asians who entered the United States (e.g., more educated and skilled individuals and individuals with family members already in the U.S.). Yin (2000) writes that "the stereotypical image of Asian   Americans as the model minority makes it difficult for these [downtown] Asians to seek support from the larger society, and their misery is often ignored by the media" (p. M6). Yin's (2000) notion of there being "two sides of the model minority" is contained visually in this newspaper article, encapsulated by an image of a reflection of an Asian American man in a mirror. One side shows a man sewing what looks to be a garment of some sort, while the other side shows the same man behind a computer, at what looks like a professional, white-collar job. This newspaper article can be used in middle and high school classes since it is written in accessible language. Students can debate both sides of the stereotype, teasing out its causes and its consequences.

CHAPTER 10

DISSERTATIONS AND THESES ON THE MODEL MINORITY STEREOTYPE

This chapter catalogues dissertations and theses conducted on the topic of Asian Americans and the model minority stereotype. The sheer number of theses and dissertations on the topic of the model minority stereotype indicates the subject's popularity (see Table 10.1 below; also see Hartlep, 2012).

TABLE 10.1.   Model Minority Dissertations and Theses by Decade

Decade	Theses	Dissertations
1960s	0	0
1970s	0	1
1980s	1	2
1990s	10	5
2000s	26	23
Total:	n = 37	n = 31

The Model Minority Stereotype: Demystifying Asian American Success, pages 255–260.
Copyright © 2013 by Information Age Publishing
All rights of reproduction in any form reserved.

Summaries and/or annotations are not provided, but the cataloging of them should help those individuals who may wish to locate and read them.

DISSERTATIONS AND THESES

Andrews, J. L. (2009). *From internment to "model minority": The reintegration of Japanese Americans in United States society after World War Two.* Dissertation, George Washington University, Washington, DC.

Balan, S. (2009). *Being Asians, good "moms," and great workers: Investigating the psychological contours of Asian Indian immigrant women's "model minority" experience.* Doctoral dissertation, The University of Michigan, Ann Arbor, MI.

Bowman, E. (2008). *Asian students' perceptions of the model minority label.* Master's thesis, College of St. Catherine, University of St. Thomas, Saint Paul, MN.

Chau, C. (1996). *A model minority: A study of selected Chinese Canadians and their strategies for coping with marginal status in Canadian education.* Master's thesis, University of Toronto, Toronto, Canada.

Chen, A. (1998). *The model minority stereotype in the media: A personal perspective.* Bachelor's thesis, Pennsylvania State University, University Park, PA.

Chen, C. H. (2000). *From pariah to paragon: Mormon and Asian American model minority discourse in news and popular magazines.* Doctoral thesis, University of Iowa, Iowa City, IA.

Chen, J. L. (1995). *The internalization of the model minority stereotype as a predictor of depression among Chinese Americans.* Doctoral thesis, California School of Professional Psychology, Alliant University, Fresno, CA.

Cheung, E. M. -W. (2003). *The model minority myth: Voices of Chinese-American mathematics students and their approach to mathematics.* Master's thesis, University of Illinois at Urbana-Champaign, Urbana, IL.

Chi, J. S. (2011). *Teaching Korea: Modernization, model minorities, and American internationalism in the cold war era.* Doctoral thesis, University of California, Berkeley, Berkeley, CA.

Cho, H. (2011). *The relationship of model minority stereotype, Asian cultural values, and acculturation to goal orientation, academic self-efficacy, and academic achievement in Asian American college students.* Doctoral dissertation, University of Southern California, Los Angeles, CA. Retrieved on March 29, 2012 from http://gradworks.umi.com/3465964.pdf

Chou, R. S. (2007). *Malady of the "model minority": White racism's assault on the Asian American psyche.* Thesis, Texas A & M University, College Station, TX.

Dailsay, F. S. (2006). *The implications of the Asian American "model minority" stereotype on perceptions of African Americans.* Master's thesis, Washington State University, Pullman, WA.

Diamond, R. H. (2008). *One size does not fit all: The effect of the model minority stereotype on the academic journeys of ten Chinese American and Korean American women.* Thesis, Rutgers University, New Brunswick, NJ.

Fong, C. (1989). *Tracing the origins of a "model minority": A study of the depictions of Chinese-Americans in popular magazines.* Doctoral thesis, University of Oregon, Eugene, OR.

Gu, L. (1999). *Model minority?: An analysis of Asian women in the U.S. labor force.* Master's thesis, University of Washington, Seattle, WA.

Gupta, A. (2010). *Acculturation and Asian values as moderators of the relationship between endorsement of positive stereotypes and Asian's subjective overachievement, psychological distress, well-being, and attitudes toward help seeking: An analysis of the "model minority myth."* Doctoral thesis, University of Tennessee, Knoxville, TN.

Hardiman, M. J. (1989). *The myth of the model minority: Depression and low self esteem in Chinese Americans.* Doctoral thesis, Pace University, Pleasantville, NY.

Hartlep, N. D. (2012). *A segmented assimilation theoretical study of the 2002 Asian American student population.* Doctoral thesis, University of Wisconsin-Milwaukee, Milwaukee, WI.

Hirata, T. M. (1999). *Valuing Asian Americans: The "model minority" thesis and impoverished conceptions of equality in racial politics.* Doctoral thesis, University of Southern California, Los Angeles, CA.

Hogan, C. M. (2010). *The self-protective function of the model minority myth for White Americans.* Doctoral thesis, Stanford University, Stanford, CA.

Hutchinson, P. A. (2009). *From "aliens ineligible for citizenship" to the "model minority": Asian Americans and the state in the (post-) civil rights era.* Master's thesis, University of California, Los Angeles, Los Angeles, CA.

Inkelas, K. K. (2000). *Demystifying the model minority: The influences of identity and the college experience on Asian Pacific American undergraduates' racial attitudes.* Doctoral thesis, University of Michigan, Ann Arbor, MI.

Jang, D. (2012). *Social bonding theory, model minority stereotype, and differences in drug use between Whites and Asians.* Honors thesis, Baylor University, Waco, TX.

Jo, L. (2012). *Asian American college students' mathematics success and the model minority stereotype.* Dissertation, Columbia University, New York, NY.

Kakimi, S. M. (2012). *The effect of the model minority myth on social work students' judgment and decision making.* Master's thesis, California State University, Los Angeles, CA.

Kaneshiro, E. N. (1996). *Multiculturalism and the model minority: Japanese Americans' ethnic identity and psychosocial adjustment.* Doctoral thesis, Claremont Graduate School, Claremont, CA.

Kanukollu, S. (2010). *Model minority myth and perceptions of child sexual abuse among South Asian immigrants.* [Dissertation].

Kim, H. (1994). *Reexamination of the model minority stereotype through the analysis of factors affecting higher education aspirations of Asian American students.* Doctoral thesis, North Carolina State University, Raleigh, NC.

Kim, P. H. (2004). *A Korean American educational experience: An analysis through the lens of the model minority thesis.* Doctoral thesis, University of California at Los Angeles, Los Angeles, CA.

Kim, S. (2007). *"Cause you're Asian": Influence of the model minority stereotype as a source of social comparison affecting the relationship between academic achievement and psychological adjustment among East Asian American high school students.* Doctoral thesis, University of California at Los Angeles, Los Angeles, CA.

Kim, S. C. (2009). *A model minority in distress: Threats to Korean American undergraduates' identity and well-being.* Doctoral thesis, University of Wisconsin-Madison, Madison, WI.

Kong, I. S. (2001). *Family conflict and the evaluation of model minority stereotype as predictors of Asian American delinquency.* Bachelor's thesis, University of Illinois at Urbana-Champaign, Urbana, IL.

Kwon, M. L. (2009). *The impact of the model minority stereotype on Asian American college student leadership involvement.* Doctoral thesis, University of California, Santa Barbara, Santa Barbara, CA.

Lam, D., & Vang, P. N. (2012). *Distorted views and perceptions of Asian American college students under the model minority stereotype.* Master's project, California State University, Sacramento, CA. Retrieved from http://csus-dspace.calstate.edu/bitstream/handle/10211.9/1765/Lam%20Vang%20MSW%20Project.pdf?sequence=5

Le, J. A. (2003). *Model minority deviance: Asian Americans in juvenile hall.* Master's thesis, San Jose State University, San Jose, CA.

Lee, K. (2012). *The tiger mother and model minority: How the Asian American parent-adolescent relationship affects mental health and education.* Senior thesis, Claremont McKenna College, Claremont, CA.

Lee, N. (2011). *The internalization of the model minority stereotype in Asian American adolescents and its psychological implications.* Doctoral thesis, California School of Professional Psychology, Alliant International University, Los Angeles, CA.

Leung, B. (1997). *Not your model minority: Asian/Asian-American crime and gangs.* Thesis, Hampshire College, Amherst, MA.

Li, M. A. (1993). *Vietnamese Americans and the myth of the model minority.* Honors thesis, University of Oregon, Eugene, OR.

Lieu, A. (2010). *The effects of the model minority theory on Chinese-Americans and Southeast Asians.* Master's thesis, San Francisco State University, San Francisco, CA.

Liu, M. (2004). *The realities of the model minority myth.* Master's thesis, Bank Street College of Education, New York, NY.

Man, B. D. (1978). *Chinese occupational achievement patterns: the case of a "model minority."* Thesis, University of California, Los Angeles, Los Angeles, CA.

Metzger, K. T. (1997). *Ideological aspects of stereotyping Asian Americans as a "model minority" in mass media.* Master's thesis, University of Colorado, Boulder, CO.

Navaratnam, S. (2011). *Guilt, shame and model minorities: How South Asian youth in Toronto navigate the Canadian educational system.* Master's thesis, University of Toronto, Toronto, Canada.

Nguyen, D. N. (2006). *Model minority: A study on the background, the myth, and a reexamination.* Master's thesis, Bethel University, St. Paul, MN.

Oh-Willeke, S. J. (1996). *Moving beyond the model minority myth: First and second generation Korean women in Buffalo and the culture of succeeding oneself.* Master's thesis, University of New York at Buffalo, Buffalo, NY.

Park, C. (2011). *Between a myth and a dream: The model minority myth, the American dream, and Asian Americans in consumer culture.* Dissertation, Purdue University, West Lafayette, IN.

Patel, N. (2003). *The relationship between acculturation and internalization of the model minority stereotype in a sample of Asian American undergraduate students.* Master's thesis, Southern Illinois University, Carbondale, Carbondale, IL.

Pope, J. J. (2005). *Exploring the origins of the model minority myth: A visual and cultural analysis of Idaho's Japanese American detainment camp.* Master's thesis, Idaho State University, Pocatello, ID.

Poy, K. (2000). *The model minority stereotype: The cost of the American dream for Asian Americans.* Senior honors thesis, Brandeis University, Waltham, MA.

Rimando, R. H. (2011). *Not overrepresented: The model minority stereotype at an Asian American Native American Pacific Islander serving institution.* Doctoral thesis, Washington State University, Pullman, WA.

Sandosharaj, A. (2008). *Ghetto proclivities: Race and class in a model minority memoir.* Doctoral thesis, University of Maryland, College Park, MD.

Shim, H. (1997). *The invisible "model minority": Images of Koreans on American TV.* Master's thesis, Iowa State University, Ames, IA.

Soodjinda, D. (2009). *A response to the model minority thesis: Intragroup differences among Asian American college students in the Los Angeles community college district.* Doctoral thesis, University of Southern California, Irvine, CA.

Suk, J. L. (1995). *Asian-American college undergraduates' perceptions of the "model minority" stereotype: A descriptive study: A project based upon an independent investigation.* Master's thesis, Smith College School for Social Work, Northampton, MA.

Sun, J. (1999). *Assessing the "model minority" and the "yellow peril" images of Asian Americans: A content analysis of major newspapers' coverage of Asian Americans, 1990 throughout 1997.* Doctoral thesis, State University of New York at Buffalo, Buffalo, NY.

Sun, W. (2002). *Perceptions of minority invisibility and model minority status among selected Asian American professionals.* Doctoral thesis, Howard University, Washington, DC.

Sun, Y. (2011). *National hero and model minority: Media representations of Chien-Ming Wang in Taiwan and in the US, 2005 to 2009.* Thesis, University of Iowa, Iowa City, IA.

Tak, Y. S. (1992). *Asian Americans as the model minority: The stereotype.* Master's thesis, Baylor University, Waco, TX.

Tandana, C. (2012). *The Asian American dream?: Perspectives from the "model minority" in Flushing, Queens.* Honors college thesis, Dyson College of Arts and Sciences, Pace University, New York, NY.

Taniguchi, C. A. (2000). *Perceptions of achievement in "model minority" undergraduates.* Doctoral thesis, Harvard Graduate School of Education, Cambridge, MA.

Thompson, T. L. (2009). *Portrait of a stereotype: Asian Americans' experiences with the model minority stereotype during adolescence.* Master's thesis, Wake Forest University, Winston Salem, NC.

Tsuru, W. A. (2001). *Social identity salience and the effects of stereotype consensus in Asian Americans: Revisiting the model minority myth.* Master's thesis, Western Washington University, Bellingham, WA.

Wiltshire, A. (2012). *Exploring the model minority: Views of Asian American students on school climate with implications for school professionals.* Doctoral thesis, Rutgers University, New Brunswick, NJ.

Wu, Y. (2010). *Model minority stereotypes of Asian American women in the media: Perceptions and influences among women of diverse racial-ethnic backgrounds.* Master's thesis, Kansas State University, Manhattan, KS.

Yi, H. (2000). *From "yellow peril" to "model minority": The educational history of Chinese Americans, 1850–1990.* Doctoral thesis, Columbia University, New York, NY.

Yim, J. Y. (1988). *"Being an Asian American male is really hard actually": Cultural psychology of Asian American masculinities and psychological well-being.* Doctoral dissertation, The University of Michigan, Ann Arbor, MI.

Yum, M. R. (2000). *Korean American women in Boston: A new model minority.* Bachelor's thesis, Harvard University, Cambridge, MA.

CHAPTER 11

METHODOLOGY

The focus of this book was the model minority myth generally, but research that attempted to disprove the myth's veracity specifically. To begin, I searched the library catalogs and electronic databases such as Education Resources Information Center (ERIC), Education Full Text, and Social Sciences Abstracts using the following search terms and Boolean operators: Asian American, Chinese, Filipino, Japanese, Korean, Lao, Hmong, Vietnamese, Cambodian, Indochinese, Southeast Asian, South Asian, model minority myth, model minority stereotype, model minority, Khmer (another name for Cambodian), and Asian American education. I also examined the reference lists of articles, dissertations, theses, monographs, reports, books, and book chapters. I narrowed the scope of the literature that I read by first reading the abstract, executive summary, or the book's foreword, table of contents, back matter, or description. This was necessary due to the immense wealth of literature on the model minority stereotype. For example, as of November 30, 2012, a search of the term "model minority" in the Education Resources Information Center (ERIC, www.eric.ed.gov) database resulted in over 2,732 sources. Dates of these publications ranged from 1965 to 2012. Moreover, searching for the term "model minority" in Google Scholar produced 1,550,000 articles. In addition to ERIC, I also

The Model Minority Stereotype: Demystifying Asian American Success, pages 261–264.
Copyright © 2013 by Information Age Publishing

searched using the same search terms in WorldCat (www.worldcat.org). What makes WorldCat an effective search tool to locate sources on the model minority is that it is the "World's Largest Library Catalog." According to its website, "WorldCat is the world's largest network of library content and services. WorldCat libraries are dedicated to providing access to their resources on the Web, where most people start their search for information." Important to mention is the fact that journalistic, as well as scholastic and academic articles, were included in this book.

I also set up Google Alerts. According to Google, Google Alerts are email updates of the latest relevant Google results (web, news, etc.) based on your queries. My queries were as follows: (1) Asian American AND the model minority myth, (2) Asian American AND the model minority stereotype, (3) model minority myth, (4) model minority stereotype, (5) Asian American success, (6) tiger mothering, (7) tiger parenting, (8) homogenization AND Asian American, (9) Asian American intelligence, and (10) ethnic gloss. In addition to Google Alerts, I posted and emailed numerous queries on list-serves, Facebook pages, and websites. These queries asked questions regarding ecological fallacies and whether people had read or were familiar with the possibility of ecological fallacious generalized research, and if they knew of any model minority research I excluded.

The Library of Congress was also consulted (www.loc.gov). For instance, the same terms used previously were also entered into the LOC website. Books' tables of contents were reviewed for relevant material. Moreover, in order to ensure that this book's methodology was rigorous, current, and reviewed germinal and seminal works, I assembled a group of peer reviewers. Each editorial board member read and gave critical feedback, such as missing literature that ought to be included, and other insights that they wanted to share with me.

THE MODEL MINORITY STEREOTYPE GAINS POPULARITY

The "model minority" stereotype is a sexy academic buzzword that has been increasingly used, but with decreasing specificity. Much of the scholarship on the model minority stereotype is repetitive and duplicative: both do not help. Unless scholars move away from this framework of heterogeneity and bimodal distribution, we will continue to be theoretically confined. The annotations and synthesis of literature in this book are intended to provide insight and foresight that will inspire scholars to develop cutting edge scholarship. This inspiration is a means to an end, not an end in itself—to fight the perception that Asian Americans constitute a model minority. Innovative paradigms as well as cadres of critical scholars are needed to champion counter-stories to the stock stories of universal Asian success. Four winnable strategies may include the following:

1. *Using Finite Mixture Modeling to Demystify the Model Minority Stereotype.*
    Finite mixture modeling (FMM) refers to a family of procedures
    that are used when a set of data are hypothesized to be comprised
    of multiple subpopulations of unknown form and frequency *a pri-
    ori.* The form of the subpopulation refers to group-specific means,
    variances, and co-variances, and the frequency refers to the num-
    ber of underlying groups. FMM treats the underlying class as a cat-
    egorical, latent variable. When used for the purposes of classifi-
    cation, FMM offers significant improvement over the traditional,
    distance-based clustering procedures (i.e., cluster analysis, multidi-
    mensional scaling) without significant limitation. As a model-based
    approach, FMM allows researchers to estimate specific parameters
    of interest (i.e., free) or to restrict (i.e., fix) parameters that are not
    of interest. Model parameters may be fixed or freed to correspond
    with theory, assumptions, model characteristics, or relationships
    among variables. Another advantage of FMM over other clustering
    procedures is the inclusion of a variety of fit indices and measures
    of classification certainty that can aid in model selection. Over-
    all, FMM offers a more flexible approach that recognizes and ac-
    counts for subgroup membership when analyzing data that reflects
    multiple underlying subgroups. Consequently, FMM will allow for
    analyses that better examine subpopulations and bi-modality of the
    Asian American student population.

2. *Problematizing the Model Minority Stereotype's Foundational Arguments.*
    Sakamoto, Takei, and Woo's (2012) article "The Myth of the Model
    Minority Myth" does an excellent job at problematizing the moor-
    ings of the model minority stereotype. The myth is, indeed, elitist,
    and thus ought to be further theorized. The foundational argu-
    ment, that Asians do not reach parity with Whites, is untenable
    since it fails to consider Asian Americans' position compared to
    other non-White minorities, within a contextually White suprema-
    cist society.

3. *Utilizing Ethnomethodological Approaches in Order to Debunk the Model
    Minority Stereotype.* None of the documents that were reviewed in
    this book used an ethnomethodological perspective. According to
    Harold Garfinkel (1967), ethnomethodology documents the meth-
    ods and practices through which society's members make sense of
    their world. Consequently, ethnomethodologists might consider
    engaging in research that examines: Who decides that Asian Amer-
    icans are model minorities? How does society—Asian Americans
    and non-Asian Americans—make sense of the racial positioning
    of Asian Americans as model minorities? Moreover, if Asians are
    "commonly" thought to be model minorities, then ethnomethod-

ologists might consider using the "common sense" analytical lenses that it has already created (e.g., see Leiter, 1980) in approaches to debunk the model minority myth. Additional scholarship might also capitalize on previously published ethnomethodological research conducted on how teachers categorize students into "social types" (Berg, 1983, p. 342).

4. *Focusing on the Practical Negative Consequences of the Model Minority Stereotype Rather Than on Conceptual Facets of the Model Minority Stereotype.* The central argument that research should make is that the "model minority" stereotype affects Asian Americans in very particular ways that need to be distinguished from research purely on the concept of model minorities. This requires scholars to focus on the practical consequences of the model minority stereotype rather than rehashing conceptual facets of the stereotype itself. Model minority research should not only problematize the racism that is contained in the stereotype, but the impact the "halo" has on Asian Americans in realpolitiks. Unz's (2012) scholarship embodies this focus. Unz (2012) shares the impact that "meritocracy" has had on Jews, and the "new Jews" (Asian Americans) in his article "The Myth of American Meritocracy: How Corrupt Are Ivy League Admissions?" published in *The American Conservative*. Work like this (including historical analyses and longitudinal data) is important for future model minority research. Arguments need to be made about the practical consequences of the model minority stereotype—such as being denied admission to college or not being granted affirmative action protection—rather than regurgitating previously written material on the myth. Much of this work should also examine the role the mainstream media, including the Internet, has on perpetuating false beliefs about Asian Americans (e.g., see Kurylo, 2012).

AFTERWORD

Robert Teranishi, PhD

This sourcebook consists of a rich body of resources that address the Asian American community. The material spans topics ranging from the demography of the Asian American population and factors that impact their educational and occupational trajectories, to historical and contemporary perspectives on the stubbornly persistent model minority myth. The material covered in this body of work is critical for understanding the extent to which Asian Americans have been excluded from broader discourse on equity and social justice, raising awareness about their unique needs, challenges, and experiences relative to the social and political climate relative to race and social stratification. Addressing these challenges is critical at the dawn of the 21st century, where Asian Americans continue to find themselves mostly invisible in mainstream media, academic research, and policy considerations at the federal, state, and local levels (U.S. Government Accountability Office, 2007; Lee & Kumashiro, 2005).

While the material in this sourcebook is a useful resource as a body of work, Professor Hartlep should also be commended for the emphasis on being forward thinking, as opposed to reactionary, in his effort to transcend the model minority myth. I often see the importance of such a stance when it comes to my own work on Asian Americans in the context of education.

The Model Minority Stereotype: Demystifying Asian American Success, pages 265–269.

We must find ways to emphasize the relevance of Asian Americans when it comes to broader national discussions about the potential of a more accessible and equitable system of education. We need to think about the consequences of a system of education that is unresponsive to the changing demography of our nation.

Indeed, the nation is at the crossroads of tremendous demographic changes to which American higher education must respond. The future of American higher education and the nation as a whole cannot be told without regard to its changing demographic landscape. The release of the 2010 Census data, for example, shows that Asian Americans are a significant contributor to the growth of the U.S. as a whole. While the Asian American and Pacific Island (AAPI) population was, indeed, relatively small up to 1960 when the AAPI population was less than one million persons, it has been doubling in size nearly every decade since then. Between 2000 and 2010, Asian Americans grew faster than any other major racial group. Contributing to the changing demography of the nation as a whole, the growth in the population is projected to continue at a significant pace based on projections to 2050, when they are estimated to reach nearly 40 million persons. Therefore, while the historical trends in the demography of the nation has been a remarkable story in itself, the reshaping of the nation is projected to continue at a fast pace for decades to come and will be a fundamentally different story than in the past.

In addition to the remarkable growth of the Asian American population, it is important to recognize the shifting demographic makeup of the nation, which is revealing a younger population that differs a great deal from the older population. William Frey at the Brooking Institution recently said of this phenomenon, "The white population is older and very much centered around the aging baby boomers... [and] the future of America is epitomized by the young people today" (Ohlemacher, 2008, para. 4). He says of America's youth, "They are basically the melting pot we are going to see in the future" (Ohlemacher, 2008, para. 4). Therefore, the older age cohorts are representative of the face of America from the past (e.g., White) while the younger age cohorts look a lot more like the future of the nation (e.g., people of color).

The growth in minority groups can be attributed largely to increases among two populations: Hispanics and Asian Americans. In California, for example, nearly all of the growth in the population between 2000 and 2010 could be attributed solely to Latinos and Asian Americans (Morello & Keating, 2011). These trends are being fueled largely by high rates of immigration. By 2007, for example, the foreign-born population had doubled over the past two decades to over 38 million residents, with the foreign-born population now representing 13% of the total U.S. population (U.S. Bureau of the Census, 2007). This trend in rapid growth among immigrants is projected to increase in coming decades. While the U.S. population is projected to expand by 50% between 2010 and 2050, immigrants are estimated to represent 82% of that growth (Passel, 2011). At this rate, by 2050 it is estimated that one in five U.S. residents will be foreign born, making them an increasingly formidable sector of American society by any measure.

Data that reveals the rise of immigrant populations that are fueling tremendous demographic changes in the nation as a whole also points to the extent to which the Asian American population is remarkably diverse. Disaggregated data on the Asian American population reveal a wide range of demographic characteristics that are unlike any other racial group in America with regard to their heterogeneity, consisting of ethnic groups that occupy positions along the full range of the socioeconomic spectrum, from the poor and under-privileged, to the affluent and highly-skilled. Asian Americans also vary demographically with regard to language background, immigration history, culture, and religion. Therefore, while a significant proportion of immigrants from Asia come to the U.S. already highly educated, others enter the U.S. from countries that have provided only limited opportunities for educational and social mobility. Thus, while the Asian American population represents a single entity in certain contexts, such as for interracial group comparisons, it is equally important to understand the ways in which the demography of the population is comprised by a complex set of social realities for individuals and communities that fall within this category.

In the context of my own work in education, we must consider how changing trends in the demography of the U.S., and especially among young Americans, has profound implications for our education system. Among the most significant trends in public K–12 enrollment is that student populations are increasingly diverse and non-White. Between 1989 and 2009, for example, the share of the K–12 enrolment that was White decreased from 68% to 55% (Aud et al., 2011). These shifting demographics can be attributed to significant increases among Asian Americans and Latinos, who are also largely immigrants and English Language Learners.

While on a national level, these trends are quite remarkable, it is also important to note how they impact different states and local communities. In 12 states (Arizona, California, Florida, Georgia, Hawaii, Louisiana, Maryland, Mississippi, Nevada, New Mexico, New York, and Texas) and the District of Columbia, a minority-majority enrollment has already occurred. For many of these states, it is the large concentrations of immigrant students of color, who are predominately Hispanic and Asian American, that has driven this trend. In the state of Washington, for example, 40% of all Asian American students are non-native English speakers (Hune & Takeuchi, 2008). In other states, these changes are occurring now at a rapid pace. In Georgia, there was a 76% increase in Asian American K–12 students over the past decade, from 32,584 to 57,339 (Georgia Department of Education, n.d.).

These national and local trends are representative of a changing demography of our schools that is projected to continue in the future. Public K–12 enrollment projections, for example, are showing that this trend will continue through 2019, with the proportional representation of Whites and Blacks decreasing by 4% each, while Hispanics are projected to increase by 36%, Asian Americans by 31%, and Native Americans by 13% (NCES, 2011).

As we discuss and construct a national education policy agenda that is increasingly concerned with global competition, we need to think about how the Asian American community is a factor in how we think about diversity relative to our ability to be competitive in an increasingly global society. The extent to which the U.S. can continue to be a world leader will depend on how we conceptualize and utilize our nation's diversity as an asset. I am hopeful that this sourcebook will be a major contribution to the broader effort to disrupt the *status quo* that has maintained the model minority myth as a mainstream narrative about the Asian American experience. It offers a vision for a national agenda inclusive of Asian Americans, who are too often overlooked and underserved. This is precisely the kind of forward-thinking work that is needed to critically examine and ultimately challenge the model minority myth.

Robert Teranishi, PhD
Associate Professor of Higher Education
Co-Director for the Institute for Globalization and
Education in Metropolitan Settings
New York University
Spring 2013

REFERENCES

Aud, S., Hussar, W., Kena, G., Bianco, K., Frohlich, L., Kemp, J., & Tahan, K. (2011). *The condition of education 2011* (NCES 2011-033). Washington, DC: U.S. Department of Education, National Center for Education Statistics.

Georgia Department of Education. (n.d.). Retrieved June 2, 2011 from http://app3.doe.k12.ga.us/ows-bin/owa/fte_pack_ethnicsex.entry_form

Hune, S. & Takeuchi, D. (2008). *Asian Americans in Washington State: Closing their hidden achievement gaps.* Olympia, WA: The Washington State Commission on Asian Pacific American Affairs.

Lee, S. & Kumashiro, K. (2005). *A report on the status of Asian Americans and Pacific Islanders in education: Beyond the "model minority" stereotype.* Washington, DC: National Education Association.

Morello, C. & Keating, D. (2011, March 24). Census offers new proof that Hispanic, Asian growth skyrocketed in past decade. *The Washington Post.* Retrieved from http://www.washingtonpost.com/local/new-census-portrait-hispanics-and-asians-skyrocketed-over-past-decade/2011/03/23/ABpKDQOB_story.html

National Center for Education Statistics (NCES). (2011). *NCES, projections of education statistics to 2019: Thirty-eighth edition.* Washington, DC: Author.

Ohlemacher, S. (2008, August 14). White Americans no longer a majority by 2042. *USA Today.* Retrieved from http://usatoday30.usatoday.com/news/topstories/2008-08-13-1800156177_x.htm

Passel, J. S. (2011). Demography of immigrant youth: Past, present, and future. *The Future of Children, 21*(1). Retrieved from http://futureofchildren.org/futureofchildren/publications/journals/article/index.xml?journalid=74&articleid=539

U.S. Census Bureau, 2006-2010 American Community Survey. (2007). *Selected characteristics of the native and foreign-born populations.* Washington, DC: Author.

U.S. Government Accountability Office. (2007). *Information sharing could help institutions identify and address challenges that some Asian Americans and Pacific Islander Students face.* Washington, DC: Author.

PERMISSIONS

INTRODUCTION

Image Credit: Gene Kim, Congressional Asian Pacific American Caucus. "Breaking the Model Minority Myth." May 2012. http://capac-chu.house.gov/media-center/model-minority-myth

CHAPTER 7

Doonesbury © 1988 G.B. Trudeau. Reprinted with permission of Universal Press Syndicate. All rights reserved.

Retrieved from: http://abagond.files.wordpress.com/2008/05/time-asianamwhiz-kids.jpg

Retrieved from: http://nakasec.org/blog/wp-content/files/2012/06/Doo-Yong-1.jpe

Retrieved from: http://colorlines.com/assets_c/2012/02/lin-sanity-ben-jerrys-thumb-640xauto-5416.jpg

ABOUT THE AUTHOR

Nicholas D. Hartlep (Koh Moil) earned his PhD from the University of Wisconsin-Milwaukee in urban education (social foundations of education) with a minor area of study in sociology. He previously taught in Minnesota and Wisconsin. He has published book chapters, book reviews, and journal articles on Asian Americans, the model minority stereotype, and affirmative action. These works appear in *Critical Questions in Education, International Journal of Peace and Developmental Studies, Radical Teacher, Journal of Identity and Education, Journal of At-Risk Issues, Berkeley Review of Education, Journal of Educational Administration, Comparative Education Review, Journal of American Culture, Education Review, Teachers College Record,* and *Academic Exchange Extra.* He is currently completing two other book projects: *The Model Minority Stereotype Reader: Critical and Challenging Readings For the 21st Century* (Cognella) and *Unhooking From Whiteness: The Key To Dismantling Racism in the United States* (Sense Publishers, co-edited with Cleveland Hayes). He is an assistant professor of educational foundations at Illinois State, where he is also a part-time school psychology PhD student. He is married to Stacey Elise Hartlep and is the father of three Amerasian daughters—Chloe Haejin, Avery Hana, and Olivia Eunhae. He lives in Bloomington, IL.

SUBJECT INDEX

An *f* following a page number indicates a figure. A *t* following a page number indicates a table. An *i* following a page number indicates an image.

A

A Community of Contrasts (Asian American Center for Advancing Justice), 55–56

"A Little Girl of Hester Street" (Epstein), 178

AACF (Asian American Christian Fellowship), 168

AANAPISIs (Asian American and Native American Pacific Islander-Serving Institutions), 38

AANHPI (Asian Americans, Native Hawaiians, and Pacific Islanders), 73

AAP (Affirmative Action Programs), 5–6

AAPCHO (Association of Asian Pacific Community Health Organizations), 73

AAPI. *See* Asian Americans and Pacific Islanders

AASPI (Asian American Suicide Prevention Initiative), 232

ABCD (American Born Confused Desi), 117

academic achievement
    adolescents' attitudes toward, 30–31
    demystifying myth of, 206–207
    new whiz kids, 238–239, 243–244
    rags-to-riches story, 1–2

academic performance research, 44, 134–135

acculturation, 26, 156

achievement gap, 32, 38–39

acquiescing with White society, 13–14

activism among Asian immigrants, x–xi

The Model Minority Stereotype: Demystifying Asian American Success, pages 275–290.

NAME INDEX

A

Abe-Kim, J., 145–146
Abraham, M., 140
Adams, D. R., 248–249
Adams, G. R., 81
Adler, S. M., 53–54
Agbayani, A., 3–4
Aguilar-San Juan, K., 132
Ahn, Lucia, 239
Ahn, Maria, 239
Alaniz, Y., 22
Allared, E., 209
Allis, S., 238
Allred, N. C., 4
Althusser, Louis, 202, 206
Alumkal, A. W., 166
Alvarado, D., 41–42
Alvarez, A. N., 79–80, 105, 166–167
Ancheta, A., ix
Andrews, J. L., 256

Ang. S. W., 54
Anyon, Jean, 32
Aoki, A. L., 213–214
Appiah. O., 54–55
Arboleda, T., 223
Arguelles, D., 92, 136
Arsenault, L., 110
Asher, N., 55
Askounis, A. C., 20–21
Au, W., 11, 216
Aud, S., 267, 268

B

Bailey, R. C., 210
Baker, B. D., 5
Baker, L. D., 28
Balan, S., 256
Bang, H., 108–109
Banks, J. A., 218
Barnard, Fred R., 170

The Model Minority Stereotype: Demystifying Asian American Success, pages 291–300.